# Ravana's Kingdom

# Ravana's Kingdom

## *The Ramayana and Sri Lankan History from Below*

JUSTIN W. HENRY

OXFORD
UNIVERSITY PRESS

OXFORD
UNIVERSITY PRESS

Oxford University Press is a department of the University of Oxford. It furthers the University's objective of excellence in research, scholarship, and education by publishing worldwide. Oxford is a registered trade mark of Oxford University Press in the UK and certain other countries.

Published in the United States of America by Oxford University Press
198 Madison Avenue, New York, NY 10016, United States of America.



CIP data is on file at the Library of Congress
ISBN 978–0–19–763630–5

DOI: 10.1093/oso/9780197636305.001.0001

Printed by Integrated Books International, United States of America

*This book is dedicated to my parents, Donald and Donna Henry.*

# Contents

# Figures

# Acknowledgments

This book was made possible through the input, guidance, and generous assistance of a great many people. The impetus for this research project must be credited to Larry McCrea, who some fourteen years ago when I was a master's student at Cornell University asked me if there was a Sinhala *Ramayana*. This monograph is a long answer to that question. The academic preceptors who have from that time provided me with invaluable council deserve special mention here. The influence of Steven Collins, my late doctoral supervisor, will no doubt be apparent in the pages which follow, as his ideas on historiography and the sociology of religion were formative to my own intellectual development. I extend extraordinary gratitude also to Anne Blackburn and to Charles Hallisey for devoting much time and patience in supporting me to this point in my career.

Several *kalyāṇa-mitrāḥ* enriched this book considerably with notes on chapter drafts: Eva Ambos, Sam Fox, Carter Higgins, Dennis McGilvray, Ravi Ratnasabapathy, and Ben Schonthal. I am grateful to a number of people at the University of Chicago, where many ideas central to this book gestated during the course of my doctoral degree. I thank especially Whitney Cox for his careful feedback on my dissertation, E. Annamalai for his sustained interest in my work, and Wendy Doniger for her continued support. I fondly thank those fellow students and colleagues who indulged early versions of portions of this book through conference panels and informal conversation: Stephen Berkwitz, Jetsun Deleplanque, Dominick Esler, Philip Friedrich, Deborah de Koning, Eric Gurevitch, Neena Mahadev, Nabajan Maitra, Alexander McKinley, Adam Miller, Justin Smolin, Charles Preston, Paride Stortini, Sarah Pierce Taylor, Margherita Trento, Mark Whitaker, Bruce Winkelman, Jonathan Young, and of course many others.

The American Institute for Sri Lankan Studies has been steady source of support to me for many years, for which reason I must thank John Rogers along with the organization's Colombo Centre staff: Vagisha Gunasekara, Ramla Wahab-Salman, Crystal Baines, Sharmini Nagendran, and Deepthi Guneratne. A July 2016 AISLS sponsored workshop on the *Ramayana* in Sri Lanka allowed me to exchange ideas with fellow scholars crucial to my understanding of the subject, with participants including Sandagomi Coperahewa, K.N.O. Dharmadasa, Tissa Jayatilake, S. Jeyasankar, Sree Padma, Pathmanesan Sanmugeswaran, N. Shanmugalingam, Kevin Trainor, and Dileepa Witharana. I thank others who at various points shared their extensive knowledge of Sri Lankan literature and history with me in service of this project: Gananath Obeyesekere, S. Pathmanathan, Sudarshan Seneviratne, and Udaya Meddegama.

Special thanks are owed to Krishantha Fedricks, Bandara Herath, and Chinthaka Ranasinha, who took the time to assist with some of the thornier portions of the Sinhala materials that I worked with. S. Suseendirarajah graciously aided in reading several Sri Lankan Tamil historical texts. Nayomi Madhupani Konara produced detailed and extremely helpful summaries of a number of the modern Sinhala works to which I refer. I thank Sudesh Mantillake for alerting me to current theatrical work reinterpreting the *Ramayana*, and for sharing his recording of *In Search of Ravana* with me. Garrett Field pointed out several twentieth-century Sinhala musical and dramatic works related to the *Ramayana*, kindly assisting me on several occasions. I thank Sanjana Hattotuwa for his analysis of the frequency with which Ravana is mentioned on various social media platforms. Harin Amirthanathan continues to keep me updated by sharing all that he gleans as his finger rests on the pulse of the online Sinhala Ravana movement.

I am immensely grateful to Buddhika Konara for the many hours he volunteered assisting me in the University of Peradeniya Library, and to Rohana Seneviratne for helping me to procure several modern Sanskrit works which were of serendipitous value to this project. Other essential and rare materials I located with assistance from the staff of the National Archives of Sri Lanka, the Colombo Museum Library, the Sri Lankan Department of Hindu Religious and Cultural Affairs, the Library of the Colombo Young Men's Buddhist Association, the Bodleian Library at Oxford University, and The British Library.

Theo Calderara actualized this project by shepherding the manuscript through to publication at Oxford University Press, where I must also thank Zara Cannon-Mohammed for her attentive work in coordinating the book's production. Input from three anonymous reviewers was of immense help in strengthening the manuscript throughout. I remain indebted to Niran Anketell for his *pro bono* legal assistance with the copyrights for several of the images reproduced here. I thank Taylor & Francis for permission to reproduce portions of an article of mine published in *South Asia: Journal of South*

*Asian Studies* (vol. 42, no. 4), which appear here in Chapter 2. Research for this book was underwritten by financial support in the form of fellowships from the Robert H. N. Ho Family Foundation in conjunction with the American Council of Learned Societies, and from the Council of American Overseas Research Centers in conjunction with the National Endowment for the Humanities.

I thank all my faculty colleagues for their general encouragement during the peripatetic phase of my early career, notably Paul Parker at Elmhurst College, Bret Lewis, Hugh Nicholson, and Omer Mozaffar at Loyola University Chicago, and Sunita Manian, Jim Winchester, Juli Gittinger, and Jim McManmon at Georgia College. Those who made Sri Lanka feel like a second home by hosting me over the course of my many visits deserve special mention: Kalyani Karunatillaka and family, R. M. Willson Rajapaksha, Karina and Kayla Kassim, Nethra Samarawickrema and family, Annemarie De Silva, Anu Weerasuriya, Chris Silva, and, most especially, Hema and Sarasi Gunaratne. I am also grateful to Liyanage Amarakeerthi and Sarojini Dassanayaka for their reliable hospitality and friendship over many years. Finally, I must acknowledge the unwavering support of my family, Donald, Donna, and Marshall Henry, without whom this book would not have been possible.

# Note on Translation and Transliteration

Throughout this book I follow the common transliteration system for Sinhala, Pali, and Sanskrit. Vowels marked with a macron are long (ā, ī, ū, ē, ō), and retroflex consonants are indicated with a dot below (ṭ, ḍ, ṇ). The Sinhala umlaut appears in short form as *ä* and long form as *ǟ*. The prenasalized consonants are written as *n̆d*, *n̆ḍ*, *n̆g*, and *m̆b*. I have translated Tamil words following the scheme used by the *Madras Tamil Lexicon* (1924–1936) and the Romanization system of Tamil of the Library of Congress. Plural forms of foreign language terms are rendered by the unitalicized suffix "s." I have rendered proper names, place names, and Sanskrit terms which commonly appear in English without diacritics, except in cases of proper names for which there are few or no published English language references. I refer to the story of the *Ramayana* without diacritics to avoid giving the impression that I use the term in specific reference to the *Vālmīki Rāmāyaṇa* or any other posited ur-text. For the sake of consistency, I render Sanskrit *yakṣa* (which appears with various spellings in Sinhala) simply as "Yaksha," except when referring to or quoting from Pali texts, where I use Pali "Yakkha." Unattributed translations throughout are my own.

# 1

# ECHOES OF THE PAST, PRESSURES OF THE PRESENT

## 1.1 "WE BELONG TO THE YAKSHA CLAN!"

On December 3, 2018, at a packed outdoor rally in Colombo supporting an immediate presidential referendum, actress Anusha Damayanthi was greeted by thunderous applause when she addressed the crowd declaring, "we may have been tamed by the preaching of the Buddha, but we still belong to the Yaksha clan!"[1] *Api yakku bolavu* was evidently a recognizable shibboleth for the audience there to support Mahinda Rajapaksa, Sri Lanka's president from 2005 to 2015 (currently Prime Minister), and his brother Gotabaya, former Defense Secretary and now the nation's elected president. "Yakku" is the Sinhala plural equivalent of Sanskrit *yakṣa*, a ferocious, semi-divine class of mythological beings famous in Indian literature, named in Sri Lanka's Pali chronicles as the original, pre-human inhabitants of the island. Since the conclusion of Sri Lanka's civil war in 2009, the notion that Sinhala Buddhists are themselves descended from the ancient Yakshas has come into ascendency in public consciousness, closely associated with the proposition that Ravana—the demon-king antagonist of the famed Hindu epic, the *Ramayana*—was himself a real historical person, the king of the "Yaksha tribe."

Ravana has emerged as a cultural hero of the victorious Sinhala people in books, newspapers, television programs, and online forums, popularized by a motley assortment of politicians, Buddhist monks, tourism promoters, and amateur and professional historians. References to Ravana's kingdom have found their way into popular Sinhala music, secondary school textbooks, and official government publications. A model of the king's aerial chariot (his "flying mechanical peacock") now hangs in the Sri Lankan Airforce Museum in Ratmalana. Shrines to Ravana have popped up at prominent Buddhist temples. The Sri Lankan Ministry of Tourism now actively promotes its "Ramayana Trail," a circuit of some fifty locations throughout the island

*Ravana's Kingdom*. Justin W. Henry, Oxford University Press. © Oxford University Press 2023.
DOI: 10.1093/oso/9780197636305.003.0001

each with some putative connection to the "historical Ramayana." In June 2019, Sri Lanka launched its first research satellite into low orbit around the earth—the "Ravana One."

This book explores the conditions of possibility for this curious reworking of the mythological origins of the Sinhala Buddhist people, beginning with a study of the transmission of written and oral versions of the *Ramayana* in Sri Lanka from the fourteenth century. I go on to trace impressions of the *Ramayana* in late nineteenth and twentieth century Sri Lankan literary fiction, stage drama, and film, and conclude with an examination of the character of Ravana and the aesthetics of his "Yaksha tribe" as they have evolved on online forums including Facebook, YouTube, and dedicated blog sites. Throughout, I trace historical continuity in representations of Ravana as a symbol of Lankan political sovereignty, in the destruction of Ravana's ancient kingdom as a metaphor for colonial loss and neo-colonial exploitation, and in a uniquely sympathetic view of Ravana's character, which I argue was originally a Sri Lankan Tamil Hindu innovation, adopted by Sinhala Buddhists in the Kandyan period.

There is much to be said regarding the government victory over the Liberation Tigers of Tamil Elam (LTTE) as a catalyst for the twenty-first-century Ravana revival, one which inaugurated a quest for a grander, autochthonous vision of the origins of the Sinhala Buddhist people.[2] Many readers will be sensitive to the irony of the Sinhala appropriation of Ravana as a cultural hero in light of the fact that the Rakshasa king served as an emblem for the Dravidian independence movement of nearly a century ago in South India, a political discourse which influenced the Tamil separatist movement in Sri Lanka. There are today additional aspects of the Sinhala Ravana phenomenon familiar from other national contexts—we find, for example, in both India and Sri Lanka, visions of a prelapsarian distant past, ruled by indisputably Dharmic kings, possessed of fantastic technological innovations, all reconstructed for the modern reader within an aesthetic that foregrounds martial and vitalist imagery. In this capacity, the Sinhala Ravana imaginary reproduces in Sri Lanka what Banu Subramaniam identifies as being at the at the heart of Narendra Modi's brand of contemporary Hindu nationalism, a magnificent past "where science, technology, and philosophy thrived," melding "science and religion, the ancient and the modern" within "a vision of India as an 'archaic modernity.'"[3]

The intention of this book however is not to rehearse Sri Lankan instances of phenomena already documented elsewhere in South Asia, nor to reduce

Sri Lanka to a mere token of a general type. Instead, I seek to explain what is unique to the Sri Lankan case, and what about it is relevant to the current moment of global populism, discourses of sovereignty, and the role of alternative media in nationalist politics. I highlight the island's diversity of local traditions relating to the characters and events of the *Ramayana* to argue that the twenty-first-century Ravana renaissance did not create its topography of the demon-king's domain altogether *ex nihilo*, but rather built upon a preexisting repertoire of lore and textual tradition. The notion that the island of Lanka was Ravana's "Lankapura" was from early on a tradition of common people, an idea preserved in the vernacular, and a proposition (most likely intentionally) excluded by the learned monks who wrote the first histories of the island in Pali. It is on this basis that I refer to Ravana's kingdom as a *populist* vision of history—first in reference to the premodern context wherein legends of Rama, Ravana, and Sita remained the provenance of popular, rather than scholastic history, and second to denote the manner in which the Sinhala Ravana phenomenon has manifested in the twenty-first-century information age. The bricoleurs hard at work constructing this new vision of Sinhala history come from all strata of Sri Lankan society: they include amateur historians, social media "influencers," ambassadors, poets laureate, prominent university professors, and even the current and previous Presidents of Sri Lanka. While I document state-level endorsement of the Sinhala Ravana narrative in several instances, "Yaksha civilization" has in large part been reconstructed informally over the past decade by communities of private enthusiasts—united around interests as varied as pop-art, home gardening, video games, and mixed martial arts—all of whom have found inspiration in the island's putative king of deep antiquity, and who celebrate his legacy.

## 1.2 RAVANA'S KINGDOM AND TWENTY-FIRST-CENTURY POPULISM

In Sri Lankan today, one repeatedly hears that the story of Ravana is "a true account" (*säbǟ caritayak*), that it is "not a mythical fiction" (*mithyā prabandhayak neme*). Historical details found in classical literary works—including Sri Lanka's Buddhist chronicles, canonical Pali Suttas, and Sanskrit epics—are given boilerplate literal readings by Ravana enthusiasts, for whom positivism has become a static interpretative paradigm (Leopold von Ranke is even invoked by name).[4] Beyond such naïve empiricism (to which we are already well accustomed in the context of other South Asian archaic modernities), *physical evidence* is paramount to the reclamation of Ravana's kingdom in Sri Lanka today. Leading voices of the movement have produced allegedly never-before-seen palm-leaf manuscripts, epigraphs, and archaeological discoveries in startling volume. Amateur treasure hunters make headlines trespassing on government property in search of Ravana's buried technological wealth. GoPro-captured video of spelunkers exploring "Ravana's caves" in the island's central highlands have garnered millions of views on YouTube. In July 2020 the Sri Lankan Civil Aviation Authority published a newspaper advert soliciting the general public for any documents which might allow them to further reconstruct the schematics of Ravana's mechanical aircraft (having determined at a massive symposium the year prior that Ravana, not the Wright Brothers, was the world's first aviator). Within a week the agency reported that they had received one hundred responses.

Ravana's kingdom is imagined today as something tangible, something immediately accessible to all, with its reconstruction having taken the form of a participatory public spectacle. The operative word here—a word reiterated again and again amid discussions between Ravana researchers—is *sākṣaya*, the Sinhala word for "evidence," derived from a Sanskrit term meaning "[seen] with the eyes." This dimension of Ravana's kingdom reveals a variety of populist epistemology with significant contrasts to that found in the United States today. The right-wing assault on academics, journalists, and scientists in the post-truth era of America is underwritten by a radically interior theory of knowledge, in which moral uprightness is viewed as necessary for a clear perception of the facts of the world. The conceit that conventional authorities in the realm of knowledge production have been lured and corrupted by monied interests renders it the individual's responsibility to determine for himself the most sensible precautions to take amid a virus outbreak, the suitability of a vaccination regimen for children, and the reality of anthropogenic climate change.[5] Such a perspective, along with its corresponding antagonism on the part of factions of the American right toward journalists and academics, has no real parallel in the twenty-first-century Sinhala Ravana movement. Although a contingent of Sri Lankan academics have repudiated the movement's claims,[6] in general Sinhala Ravana enthusiasts do not give the sense that they are academic outsiders, nor that their views are in some way removed from current scholarly consensus. Indeed, a number of high-profile Sri Lankan academics have come out in support of the Sinhala

Ravana movement, and several leading Ravana promoters with no scholarly credentials style themselves "professor." Leading Colombo newspapers have carried full-page spread interviews with Ravana promoters. In the quest for the lost treasures of Ravana's kingdom, only very rarely do we find appeals to distinguish "native" from "western" forms of scientific knowledge, as is, for example, common among Hindutva promoters of "Vedic" math and science in India.[7] To the contrary, Sinhala Ravana enthusiasts appear convinced of the potential universal value of the lost technology (*tākṣaṇaya*) of the Hela-Yaksha civilization of antiquity. This outlook is illustrated in the words of one Ravana treasure-seeker, a young Sinhala Buddhist woman reporting to have been directed to a cache of ancient technological goods in the vicinity of the remote mountain town of Ella by a cohort of invisible *devas*. After the story of her expedition party appeared in a Colombo newspaper, she explained in a 2016 interview that hidden within the region's caves are:

> powerful things (*prabala vastu*) which Ravana possessed—things which to this very day have enhanced our country, but which in the future may serve to enhance *all* the nations of the world . . . while these are not valuables in the sense of gems, etc., they are great things such as oil (*tel*), medicine, and medicinal knowledge, capable of curing any disease.[8]

Insistence on the immediate accessibility of the treasures of Ravana's kingdom exemplifies a central feature of twenty-first-century populism—a rejection of the institutions of liberal societies designed to mediate between the public at large and regimes of government and knowledge production. Summarizing the work of Eric Santner, William Mazzarella explains that, today:

> Populism puts pressure on the liberal settlement by dreaming of a direct and immediate presencing of the substance of the people and, as such, a reassertion, a mattering forth of the collective flesh—where the matter is at once the sensuous substance of the social, the flesh, and the meaningful ways in which it comes to matter.[9]

Whereas in Trump-era politics of the United States, the "challenge of mediation as such" has meant the rejection of "the media" and the authority of legislative bodies in an often simple sense, in twenty-first-century Sri Lanka the "immediate presencing of the substance of the people" has overflowed the confines of the political rally to manifest as an invitation to the average citizen to fan out, explore, and discover a new "embodied archive" secreted within the (quite literal) archaeological bedrock of Sinhala civilization.

The participatory dimension to the twenty-first-century Sinhala Ravana phenomenon underscores another, in fact consequential, thesis of this book: Ravana is *fun*. Looking for buried treasure is fun. Mixed martial arts said to be passed down by the ancient Yakshas are fun. The fact that Sinhala speakers clearly knew and entertained themselves with *Ramayana* stories centuries ago is central to my argument in Chapter 3, where I work to account for censorious remarks on the part of Buddhist monks toward Hindu epics, as they enjoined lay audiences to occupy themselves instead with stories of the virtues of the Buddha ("stories of Rama and Sita" being frivolous from their point of view—in part, too much fun). The *Rāvaṇa Katāva*, a Kandyan period Sinhala poem translated as an appendix to this book, the closest we have to a "Sinhala Ramayana," is in large part a lighthearted caper starring Hanuman. Today Ravana inspires fantasy-genre visual art, music and theater productions, online discussion forums and "research groups," and, since 2018, a flashy, action-packed Sinhala language television series (Derana TV's *Rāvaṇa*, currently in its seventy-first installment). While the Civil Aviation Authority's call-for-documents relating to the schematics of Ravana's flying craft seems to have been serious and in earnest, the Ravana Aviation Kite Association holds an annual kite flying competition on Colombo's Galle Face Green, inviting participants to use their imagination in designing a model of the ancient king's flying machine (his *dan̆ḍu-monara*).

I should confess that I myself had an immense amount of fun researching this book. My time questing after obscure textual materials in backroom shelves, chatting with monks in remote upcountry temples, and scouting for new statues of Ravana and his mechanical flying peacock became a kind of treasure hunt. Those I met along the way were intensely interested in what I was doing, often going out of their way to be helpful. The wonder provoked upon sharing some of the documents and images that I had scrounged out of library archives made me feel at times as if I was a part of something exciting—it made me feel as if I was a part of the collective public movement of which I am here writing.

There are also deeply disquieting aspects to the Ravana phenomenon. While a careful study of the derivation of Ravana's modern image in Sri Lanka has much to teach us concerning the intersection of linguistic, religious, and cultural traditions on the island historically, this message is, generally speaking, not a part of the public discourse. The twenty-first-century Sinhala

Ravana movement is triumphalist, insular, and monological. With respect to their scope of vision, archaic modernities are in some sense a reversal of the early modern outlook on the world as defined by Sanjay Subrahmanyam in his seminal 1997 essay on "Connected Histories." Redefining "early modernity" as a pan-Eurasian, rather than strictly western European phenomenon, Subrahmanyam remarks on the efforts, beginning in around the mid-fourteenth century and including the Ming and Timurid Empires, "to push back the limits of the world" through nautical exploration and through radically expanded ethnographic and cartographic perspectives on the world abroad.[10] By contrast, both literary and putatively factual reconstructions of Hela-Yaksha civilization today proclaim that, in deep antiquity, "Sri Lanka was the center of the world." Ravana enthusiasts are preoccupied with hyperdiffusionist speculation over Sinhala as the first human language, the Hela (proto-Sinhala) people as the progenitors of world culture, and so on. Within such a view, horizons are prone to collapse, rather than to expand.

Inward-looking nationalism characterized by a retreat from the complexities of globalization is a hallmark of populist movements throughout the world today. In this sense the Sri Lankan case is little different. Where the Sinhala Ravana movement stands out as unique, as for instance in comparison to Trumpism in the United States and Modi-era Hindutva in India, is in the absence of oppositional rhetoric directed toward domestic "elites." We hear that Angampora was "the people's art," that the memory of Hela-Yaksha civilization was preserved "by ordinary people," but not that knowledge of Ravana's kingdom was at any point repressed by Lankan politicians, academics, or journalists. Instead, the narrative focuses on the effacement of traditional Sinhala Buddhist culture under colonial subjugation, and on the continued legacy of intervention in Lankan economic and political affairs by India and the West.[11]

I take this observation as a point of departure to appeal to Ernesto Laclau's semiological anatomy of populist movements to make sense of several unique dimensions of the Sinhala Ravana phenomenon. Working to account for the rise of political leaders throughout the globe whose ideological platforms violate the conventional taxa of left–right binaries, Laclau, in *On Populist Reason* (2005), reconstructs the genesis of populist movements as an assortment of disparate "demands" unified under what he calls an "empty signifier." This can be any word, figure, or slogan ("freedom," "Perón," "Good days are coming") sufficiently underdetermined in meaning and reference to serve as a banner for a maximally diverse set of principles, coalitions, and grievances. This is, for Laclau, the essence of populism, which is better defined through its *form* than its ideological *content*, as populist movements often contain contradictory ideologies and unrelated political demands. Populist movements, he demonstrates, gain unity and coherence in their opposition toward a postulated "dominant ideology" or hypothetical "institutional system" ("the one percent," "the swamp").[12]

Laclau offers a means of theorizing, first, the contours of the Sinhala Ravana movement as a populist phenomenon constituting itself primarily through the image of Lankan sovereignty. The oppositional menace against which the Sinhala Ravana movement defines itself is not a dominant ideology or an institutional system per se, but rather the specter of foreign intervention in Sri Lanka. The two greatest perceived threats to Lankan sovereignty—India and the Western Block—are repeatedly cast as adversaries in popular literature, television programs, informal online discussions, and putative historical research relating to Ravana. In the case of India, the geography of the *Ramayana*'s central conflict (Rama's forces invading the southern land of Lanka) maps conveniently onto grievances and suspicions which have become mainstays of Sri Lankan political memory—Indian military intervention on the island in the 1980s and 1990s, rumored support for the LTTE, and decades of perceived diplomatic strong-arming. The adversarial position of the West (often, metonymically, the United States) in Sinhala Ravana discourse has more complex significance, relating in some instances to perceived threats to Sri Lankan autonomy by way of inquiries into human rights violations (e.g., the 2013 UNHRC resolution against the Sri Lankan government), but also, more interestingly, in other instances relating to memories of colonial loss and perceptions of enduring, neo-colonial forms of exploitation.

Second, Laclau provides a theoretical scaffolding to posit Ravana as kind of a *plenary signifier*, allowing for a maximal synthesis of claims relating to Sri Lanka's political and cultural status historically. Sinhala Ravana enthusiasts today assign a dizzying array of attributes to Ravana and his domain of antiquity, some counterintuitive, some seemingly contradictory. Ravana was a speaker of Hela, the indigenous, "non-Ayran" Sinhala vernacular, while at the same time a master of Sanskrit *śāstra*s. Ravana's ancient kingdom was a monarchy but also a healthy republic, in which ordinary citizens were elected to high office. The Yaksha people were ferocious warriors but also spiritual adepts and advanced yogis—in some accounts, they were Buddhists. Ravana was the embodiment of all kingly virtues while simultaneously a progressive feminist (women occupied leadership positions in Yaksha civil society and trained in weapons and the martial arts, we are told).

Ravana's great civilization (*mahā-śiṣṭācāraya*) is thus at once a retrograde and a futurist political imaginary, the alpha and the omega of Hela cultural genius—both a halcyon society of the distant past and a utopian desideratum to which Sri Lanka may one day potentially restore itself. The twenty-first-century Sinhala Ravana landscape is accordingly saturated with millennial imagery, drawing from an alternate ending to the *Ramayana* story circulating in Sinhala oral tradition from the Kandyan period, in which Ravana lives on after his battle with Rama, in some versions laying down to sleep indefinitely deep within his mountain lair. Ravana, I argue in the coming chapters, is the defining symbol of the post-war palingenesis of the Sinhala Buddhist people—depicted on book covers and online fan art as valiantly soaring above his kingdom on his peacock conveyance, like a phoenix out of the ashes of an intractable conflict with the LTTE, characterized by the Sri Lankan media as "the most potent terrorist organization on earth."[13]

The subtitle of this book, "Sri Lankan History From Below," gestures to the vernacular tradition of the transmission of the *Ramayana* in Sri Lanka, out of which I work to reconstruct late medieval and early modern popular traditions of Sinhala storytelling and poetry, along with their implications for views held by Sri Lankans concerning the island's distant past. (The spatial metaphor also braids well with the modern vision of a massive subterranean extension to Ravana's hoary domain, a centuries-old conceit of Sinhala poetry, see Chapter 3, section 3 and Chapter 5, section 2.) In juxtaposing attitudes between works belonging to the "greater" (*mahā*) and "lesser" (*cūḷa*) traditions of Sinhala literature, methodologically my approach diverges from that of other recent studies in South Asian civilizational history. Sheldon Pollock addresses a potential limitation to his monumental contribution to this class of works, *The Language of the Gods in the World of Men* (2006), acknowledging that his primary literary sources were, overwhelmingly in their original context, produced and consumed at the elite level of society. In rejoinder to this elementary problem—that of a documentary archive which underrepresents the voices of a numerically vast percentage of the population of the civilization under investigation—Pollock reassures us that, "if concentrating on elite representations means we miss the role of 'the people' in history, we do capture something of the ideas that ultimately transformed the people's world."[14] In the absence of written records which might divulge something of the beliefs, impressions, and mental life of the common people, it is true that historians of the premodern often find themselves at pains to arrive at a better answer.[15]

On the other hand, it is precisely the desire to recover the agency of the voiceless (the "sub-proletariat") which motivated the field of Subaltern Studies from its inception. Making use of a broad and, in many cases, underutilized archive of vernacular texts in both Sinhala and Tamil, this study attempts to do precisely this. Putting aside the question of the feasibility of recovering the mental life of common people in past eras for which our evidence base shades away, we may also question the suitability of the academic mandate of "history from above" in the context of the current global populist moment.[16] Murray Rothbard, in a passage from his classic manifesto of the American Libertarian movement, sounds frightfully out of step with the sentiments of the right-libertarian minded today when he declares:

> In all societies, public opinion is determined by the intellectual classes, the opinion molders of society. For most people neither originate nor disseminate ideas and concepts; on the contrary, they tend to adopt those ideas promulgated by the professional intellectual classes, the professional dealers in ideas.[17]

With populist initiatives of all stripes throughout the world today making the rejection of such elitist propositions primary to their cause, historians in search of the genealogies of these movements may realize an imperative to expand upon their archives of first resort. This book represents a case study in a vision of Sri Lanka's history forged and transmitted by "the people" which would ultimately displace that of the (monastic) intellectual classes—a vision with a centuries long career "underground" in oral and vernacular literature, which came to full fruition over the past ten years enabled by the speed of travel of images and ideas in our current digital age.

## 1.3 THE PALI CHRONICLE TRADITION AND HISTORY FROM BELOW

Since Sri Lanka's independence in 1948, the imagery, rites, and vocabulary of the Buddhist monarchy have played a formative role in the island's political discourse. Early nationalist polemics argued that modern democratic government was obligated to fulfill the traditional duties of Buddhist kings: upholding the Buddhist religion (*buddha sāsana*), preserving the institutions of Buddhist monks (the Sangha), and safeguarding the collective interests of the island's Sinhala Buddhist majority. Central to this reanimation of premodern political imagery has been Sri Lanka's Pali chronicles: the *Dīpavaṃsa* (late-third or early-fourth century CE), and the *Mahāvaṃsa*, a history of the island's Buddhist kings, begun in the fifth or sixth century CE and updated six times since.[18] The *Mahāvaṃsa* begins with the three visits of the Buddha Gotama to the island, during each of which respectively he expelled resident demons (*yakkha*s, Sanskrit: *yakṣa*s), preached to the Nagas of Nagadipa, and meditated at the sites of future Buddhist devotional significance across the island.[19] The arrival of the first *human* inhabitants of the island of Lanka corresponds to the exact moment of Buddha's *parinibbāṇa*, that is, his death and final passing into "Nirvana without any karmic remainder," designated as the year 486–487 BCE by Pali Buddhist convention. These settlers—a band of seven hundred castaways from the kingdom of Lāṭa[20], led by one Prince Vijaya—were according to the chronicles the stock from which the "Sīhaḷa" kings of the island are descended, and, on the interpolation of later tradition, the progenitors of the Sinhala people as a race.[21] The *Mahāvaṃsa* goes on to recount the succession of kings of the island, with special attention given to military exploits, defense of the island and Buddhist religion from foreign incursions, and patronage of the Buddhist Sangha.

The proposition that the Sinhala people are descended from the Yakkhas of the Pali chronicles presents a number of difficulties. Ravana in the Indian literary tradition is not a *yakṣa* but rather a *rākṣasa*. To call someone "*yakā*" in Sinhala is a mild curse implying moral reprehensibility, the kind of thing one says to a leering man on the street. In the *Dīpavaṃsa* and *Mahāvaṃsa*, the Yakkhas are phantasmagoric, ghoulish homovores—they are clearly not human beings.[22] Parsing these incongruities requires an understanding of the process by which Yakkhas were domesticated from their Sanskrit equivalents in Sri Lankan Buddhist literary, aesthetic, and ritual culture.

The Yakshas known to us from the Sanskrit literary tradition are a class of generally benevolent spirit beings associated with the natural world, often inhabiting trees, mountains, and bodies of water, akin to the fairies of European mythology. In early Buddhist and Jain sources, Yakshas take on a more sinister character akin to that of Rakshasas, accosting unsuspecting travelers in the wilderness and haunting caches of buried treasure.[23] Yakshas (along with Nagas) are, however, at the same time exemplary converts to the Buddha's Dhamma in early Pali literature,[24] depicted in some of the earliest examples of Buddhist visual art, and with Indian sites of Yaksha worship converted to Buddhist holy places.[25] The motif of Yakshas and Nagas as exemplary Buddhist converts in early Pali literature is recapitulated in the *Dīpavaṃsa* and *Mahāvaṃsa*, with Kristin Scheible observing that, in these chronicles, "the transformation of certain characters, the *nāgas* and *yakkhas*, parallel the transformation of the place, Laṅkā."[26] The collapse of a variety of non-human, prehistoric denizens of the island of Lanka in the *Dīpavaṃsa* (six species are named in total)[27] into *two* in the subsequent *Mahāvaṃsa* (Nagas and Yakkhas only) attests to the dilution of a clear distinction between Rakshasas and Yakshas early on in the Sri Lankan literary imaginary.[28] (Rakshasas in later Sinhala works—notably Ravana and his brother Vibhishana—are frequently referred to simply as Yakshas.[29])

The Buddha's expulsion of the resident non-humans from Lanka in the Pali chronicle account was evidently temporary because , in addition to the fact that some Yakkhas had returned to the island by the time of Vijaya's arrival,[30] Sri Lankans still today associate these demons with possession, various mental and physical illnesses, and custodianship of sacred places. On the traditional Sinhala Buddhist view, Yakkhas (Sin. pl. *yakku* or *yakun*) are beings of depreciated karmic status, inhabiting the lowest of the "three worlds" over which the Buddha presides (the *tunlova* consisting of the worlds of spirit beings, humans, and *devas*).[31] Yakkhas are understood to be a dangerous nuisance, with the capacity to telekinetically inflict physical maladies (*yakṣa doṣa*) or to "possess" individuals, resulting in a lapse of mental and physical function. Mitigation of the influence of Yakkhas is a preoccupation of Sri Lankan Buddhist ritual life,[32] and is the objective of the "Yak Tovil" rite, in which ritual specialists ward off the effects of sorcery or the malevolent influence of Yakkhas.[33]

In the narrative context of the *Mahāvaṃsa*, the Buddha's ejection of the resident demons is central to his effort "to cleanse the island of Lanka" (*laṅkādīpaṃ visodhetuṃ*) in anticipation of the eventual establishment of the Buddhist religion.[34] The significance of the presence of the Yakkha in the Pali chronicle account—the question as to what the Yakkha represented to early Sri Lankans, and as to how their inclusion in the chronicles might be treated allegorically—is an issue of substantial concern for present day Sinhala Ravana enthusiasts. In their quest to reverse negative impressions of the Yakkhas from whom they claim descent, Ravana promoters do in fact approach a genuine ambiguity in the textual tradition regarding the status of these mysterious denizens of Lanka. While according to the *Mahāvaṃsa* the Buddha saw fit to eject the demons from his future preserve of the *buddha sāsana*, the chronicle also indicates that the Yakkha were treated with deference in ancient Sri Lanka, stating that Paṇḍukābhaya (Vijaya's grand-nephew) settled two Yakkhas and a Yakkhinī around his capital of Anuradhapura, establishing annual sacrificial offerings to them and to others of their kind. The *Mahāvaṃsa* also mentions "the banyan tree of Vessavaṇa" at the western gate of Paṇḍukābhaya's city, in an apparent reference to a place of worship of Vaishravana or Kubera, the god of wealth and king of Yakshas.[35] In addition to highlighting potentially positive references to Yakkhas in the literary tradition, modern commentators have proposed that the various species of pre-Vijayan inhabitants of Lanka enumerated in the Pali chronicles may in fact be the names of the tribes of the earliest peoples of the island. The *Mahāvaṃsa* itself leaves room for such an interpretation, recalling that a group of remote people of the island were descended from the children of Prince Vijaya and the Yakkhinī Kuvaṇṇā (Kuveni)—the Pulindā or the "people of the hills."[36]

From the point of view of the *Dīpavaṃsa* and *Mahāvaṃsa*, the recorded history of Sri Lanka begins with the visitations of the Buddha and the arrival of Vijaya. The chronicles say nothing about the historicity of the *Ramayana*, and nothing about the epic in relation to the island. Their authors were however almost certainly familiar with the Hindu epic, and the question as to whether a conscious choice was made to exclude the *Ramayana* in an effort to give primacy to Buddhist historical themes remains a subject of scholarly speculation (see Chapter 3, section 1). Modern Ravana enthusiasts have made use of the Yakkhas and Rakkhasas to suture the *Ramayana* to the Pali chronicle timeline, exploiting what may be traces of the epic left by these redactors in rendering their own, thoroughly Buddhist, vision of history. In the *Dīpavaṃsa*, the Buddha confines the resident demons of Lanka to another island, Giri Dipa, "Mountain Island," situated somewhere "in the great sea, in the midst of the ocean and of the deep waters, where the waves incessantly break; around it there was a chain of mountains, towering, difficult to pass; to enter it against the wish (of the inhabitants) was difficult."[37] Noteworthy here is the fortress-like quality to the island and its semantic resonances with the "inaccessible rock," the "triple peak" of Trikūṭa Mountain on which Ravana's fortress of Lankapuri is situated in the *Vālmīki* and other Indian *Rāmāyaṇas*. The *Mahāvaṃsa* also speaks of "Lankapura" as the residence of the "chief of Yakkhas," a city located somewhere within or nearby to the island of Lanka.[38]

A considerable amount of scholarly attention has been focused on the role of the *Mahāvaṃsa* in premodern and modern political life, emphasizing the fact that the chronicle contains such an early articulation of an ethno-religious ideal, in which the Sinhala people of Sri Lanka, sharing a common ancestry, are situated as custodians of the Buddhist religion and as heirs to the island's political domain. Indeed, the chronicles furnish a ready-made template for modern identity politics through their normative vision of Buddhist kingship, in which Sinhala (*sīhaḷa*) monarchs were obliged to defend the island and the Buddhist religion (*buddha sāsana*) against foreign usurpers, a role ascribed to the "Damiḷa" (Skt. *drāviḍa*) continental Indian Other. Although later Buddhist authors would muddy this Sri Lankan–Sinhala/Indian-Damiḷa semiotic (casting the Portuguese as *demaḷas*, "Tamils," for instance, in the context of Sinhala poems commemorating wars against the Conquistadors), racialist scholarship and political ideology imported to Sri Lanka by the British in the nineteenth century breathed new life into the identity tropes of Sri Lanka's premodern historiography.[39]

With an insistence on Lankan indigeneity, the Sinhala Ravana movement has today radically dislodged the Pali chronicles from their former place of centrality in Sinhala Buddhist political imagination. Ravana enthusiasts reject the proposition that Sinhala heritage traces back to Vijaya and his retinue, insisting that the Yakkhas were in fact Sri Lanka's original human inhabitants, established on the island long before any migration from India. There is even palpable hostility toward the *Mahāvaṃsa* on the part of some contemporary bricoleurs, who appeal to a panoply of other classical texts—including the Hindu Sanskrit epics, the Mahayana *Laṅkāvatāra Sūtra*, and vernacular Sinhala historiography—to compensate for what they claim to be the "distorted view" of Lankan antiquity advanced by the Pali *vaṃsas*. While the intensely positivist trawling of the literary archive undertaken by Ravana researchers leaves much to be desired in terms of interpretive methodology, their insistence on the incompleteness of the chronicle account of the island's distant past does reflect an actual concern on the part of monastic readers of the *Mahāvaṃsa* historically. Edward Upham, in collecting the manuscripts that would serve as the basis for the first English translation of the *Mahāvaṃsa* (published in 1833), allowed his informants to gather supplementary information from Sinhala texts such as the *Rājāvaliya* and *Rājaratnākaraya*, as well as from other manuscripts and oral accounts. George Turnour, who produced the second English translation of the

*Mahāvaṃsa*, disparaged interpolations in Upham's version as "mutilated abridgements" and "amplifications" on the grounds that they deviated from the core Pali text.[40] This overlooks the fact, however, that the monks and lay people providing the manuscripts for Upham *could have* merely given over a literal rendering of the Pali root text but chose instead to provide supplementary vernacular glossaries. Jonathan Walters and Matthew Colley observe that this was indeed "precisely the correct method for reading *Mahavamsa* according to *Vamsatthappakasini*, the *Mahavamsa* commentary upon which Turnour . . . claimed his authority."[41]

On its own, as an isolated physical document, the Pali text of the *Mahāvaṃsa* was in large part relegated as an object of veneration in Buddhist monasteries of the early nineteenth century (often kept on display in the main shrine).[42] "Reading" the *Mahāvaṃsa*, that is, making use of the text in order to learn about, teach about, or write new histories of the island, involved simultaneous readings from a commentary (*ṭīka*) on the text, as well as appeals to Sinhala vernacular sources (principally versions of the *Rājāvaliya*, *Saddharmālaṅkāraya*, *Rājaratnākaraya*, and *Pūjāvaliya*).[43] "Reading history" as an intertextual practice was in fact necessary, owing to the incomplete (and even sometimes contradictory) nature of the Pali *ur*-document of the *Mahāvaṃsa*. The implication is that, until it first appeared in print form and translation under the British, the *Mahāvaṃsa* itself was not conceived of as the singular, canonical source of the island's history. Vernacular historiography served as a necessary supplement. Regrettably, because the earliest European manuscript hunters were fixated on discovering the single most ancient (and thereby most authoritative) textual record of Indian Buddhism, they were uninterested in the sociology of *Mahāvaṃsa*-reading in Buddhist Viharas, even as they observed it firsthand.

Chapter 3 of this book traces the gestation of a crucial supplement to the early Pali chronicles—that of the historicity of the *Ramayana* as it relates to the island of Lanka—in late medieval and early modern vernacular poetry, topographical and historical works, and folklore. In collating the various oral traditions and miscellaneous Sinhala and Tamil documents linking landmarks with the activities of Rama, Sita, Ravana, and Hanuman in Sri Lanka, a highly localized and diffuse mythic topography begins to emerge. In Tamil Hindu oral and textual traditions, the establishment of the major temples of Munneswaram and Koneswaram (along with various other devotional sites on the island's east coast) is associated with both Rama and Ravana. Our earliest dateable Sinhala documents explicitly placing Ravana's domain on the island of Sri Lanka—the so-called "boundary books" or *kaḍayim pot*—locate Ravana's kingdom in the island's central west coast. In the south, stories of Hanuman dropping medicine to aid Lakshmana on his way back from the Himalayas at Unawatuna are remembered to this day, as are tales of Ravana's ruined fortress off the coast of Hambantota. The greatest confluence of local *Ramayana* mythologies occurs however in the central highlands—today the epicenter of the "Ramayana Trail."

In surveying these Sinhala textual and oral traditions, I will argue that the incorporation of the *Ramayana* into the Sinhala Buddhist historical imagination took place principally through informal means, over a long period of time, as the result of an exchange of texts across linguistic story-worlds. The source material for idiosyncratic Sinhala renditions of the epic appears not to have been high *kāvya*—Valmiki or Kampan—but rather highly colloquial variations on the epic popular in South India. While for example the author of the *Rāvaṇa Katāva*, the Kandyan era "Sinhala Ramayana," speaks of the inspiration for his work deriving from "Tamil teachers of long ago," the poem itself showcases themes from the *Mayil Irāvaṇaṉ Katai*, a popular Tamil folktale concerning Hanuman's adventures in Ravana's younger brother's subterranean realm of "Patala Lanka." The *Rāvaṇa Katāva* is composed in demotic Sinhala verse, its author betraying knowledge of Tamil village farming practices.

Suturing the *Ramayana* to the Pali chronicle account of Sri Lanka's distant past is, therefore, a significant triumph of "history from below." Several scholars have argued that the epic was originally intentionally excluded from the *Mahāvaṃsa* by its monastic authors, concerned as they were to emphasize the visitation of the Buddha as the genesis of the island's recorded history. This, if true, makes the more expansive "Ravana's kingdom" vision of Lankan antiquity incubated in popular imagination a subversive, alternative historical paradigm. As I go on to argue in Chapters 4 and 5, Ravana's kingdom continued to serve as a source of inspiration for Sri Lankan Buddhist authors in the nineteenth and twentieth centuries, culminating in the twenty-first century with the sublimation of the Pali chronicle account of the origins of the Sinhala people.

## 1.4 CHAPTER SUMMARIES

Chapter 2, "Moving Mt. Kailasa," beings by tracing the identification of the island of Sri Lanka with the "Lankapura" of the *Ramayana* epic. While "Lankapura" remained a mythical locale within the realm of literary imagination for Valmiki and other first millennium Sanskrit authors, the Cholas of the ninth century were the first to make a geographical equivalence between Ravana's kingdom and the island of Lanka as a domain of military conquest. The chapter goes on to explore the impact of various South Indian literary conventions on northern Sri Lankan literature, including the uniquely sympathetic rendering of Ravana in the temple histories (*talapurāṇams*) of Koneswaram (the famed Siva temple of Trincomalee), and the self-identification of the Arya Cakravartis rulers of Jaffna as "guardians of Rama's bridge" (*cētu kāvalaṉ*), the submerged isthmus spanning the Palk Strait from Mannar to the Indian mainland. I conclude by demonstrating avenues of transmission of Tamil impressions of Ravana's character, along with other themes from Tamil Puranas, into late medieval and early modern Sinhala literature.

Chapter 3, "The Many *Ramayanas* of Lanka," collates references to Ravana in Sinhala folklore, poetry, and topographical and historical prose texts from the fourteenth century to the British colonial period. I argue that formative Sinhala Buddhist impressions of Ravana—a number of which endure to the present day—were generated in large part through highly informal contexts; that is, through storytelling and the composition and augmentation of poetic verses, not as a derivation from the canonical sources or "high *kāvya*" which one might expect (the *Vālmīki Rāmāyaṇa* or Kampan's Tamil version of the epic). On this basis I argue that there is a precedent for the Sinhala Buddhist image of Ravana as *populist* in its orientation, as the establishment of Ravana's character in Sri Lankan imagination during the early modern period appears to have been the result of exchange between ordinary people—largely outside of the purview of courts, salons, and monastic colleges.

Chapter 4, "Ravana in Modern Sinhala Literature," examines renderings of the *Ramayana* in Sinhala poetry, drama and fiction from the late nineteenth century to the present. I explore the resurrection of the *Ramayana* alongside Buddhist themes in the Sinhala "neoclassical" literary revolution of the late 1800s, along with Ravana's role in the Hela Havula movement (led by a group of twentieth-century literati who advocated de-Sanskritization of the Sinhala language and traced an autochthonous heritage for the Sinhala ethnic group). The chapter reviews a number of radio, theater, television, and film productions of the *Ramayana* in the twentieth century offering a sympathetic treatment of Ravana which have hitherto escaped scholarly attention, concluding with an examination of the theme of ancient Sri Lanka as a prelapsarian paradise and repository of technological marvels in modern Sinhala and English fiction.

Chapter 5, "Terraforming the Past," follows the emergence of Ravana as a Sinhala Buddhist cultural hero in post-war Sri Lanka, including the use of his image by monastic activists, claims to his historicity made on the part of amateur and professional scholars, and the incubation of a "Hela-Yaksha" visual aesthetic and revisionist historical narrative on various online platforms. The title of the chapter derives from the "Ramayana Trail" and the destruction of Islamic property at the Dafther Jailani shrine complex, which I argue to be instances of the Sinhala Ravana narrative protruding into civic space to physically reshape monuments to the past. Sustaining the overall argument of the book that Ravana's image in Sri Lanka has been forged through essentially populist circumstances, I highlight the public, participatory dimension to the quest to excavate Ravana's kingdom in Sri Lanka today, along with the resurrection of pre-colonial mythic topography on the map of the Ramayana Trail.

Chapter 6, "A Bridge Too Close," summarizes evidence from previous chapters to illustrate the manner in which Ravana has historically functioned as an index of distance from the Indic world, as a symbol of Lankan political sovereignty, and as a metaphor for colonial loss. I argue that the revised "Yaksha descent" ethnic etiology of the Sinhala people and establishment of Ravana as a Sinhala Buddhist cultural hero represents more than a triumphalist, post-war fad, being instead an example of a revised palingenetic myth enabled by the digital age. The chapter concludes by outlining recent Tamil responses to the Buddhist appropriation of Ravana, along with efforts on the part of select groups of Sri Lankan Tamils and Sinhala Buddhists to employ Ravana as a conciliatory figure and potential symbol of shared Sinhala and Tamil ancestry.

As an appendix I have included a critical edition and translation of the *Rāvaṇa Katāva*, a c. seventeenth-century Sinhala poem narrating the essential plot of the *Ramayana* in 120 verses, based on manuscripts held in Sri Lanka and the United Kingdom. I include it here because the text has never before been published, and because it has been invoked by name by amateur scholars in support of fantastic and absurd claims. In addition to being the work closest to a real "Sinhala *Ramayana*," the poem contains a valuable snapshot of the diffuse *Ramayana*-related mythic topography circulating in Sinhala public imagination in the Kandyan period, revealing clear avenues of transmission of oral legends from Tamil to Sinhala (as discussed in Chapters 2 and 3).

## Notes

1. Damayanthi's words in Sinhala were: "*api budu baṇaṭa hīlā̆ vuṇu api yakku bolavu, äta, budu baṇaṭa hīlā̆ vuṇu yakku api*!" ("Api budubaṇaṭa hīlā̆ vecca api yakku bolav [Actor Anusha Damayanthi]," ANYT TV. Uploaded December 8, 2018, www.youtube.com/watch?v=zWS-8JbaYBs).
2. See Dileepa Witharana, "Ravana's Sri Lanka: Redefining the Sinhala Nation?" *South Asia: Journal of South Asian Studies* 42, no. 4 (2019): 781–795.
3. Banu Subramaniam, *Holy Science: The Biopolitics of Hindu Nationalism* (Seattle: University of Washington Press, 2019), 7.
4. See the discussion of Arisen Ahubudu's *Hela Deraṇa Vaga* in Chapter 4, section 3 of this text.
5. John Evans has recently supplied a quantitative sociological analysis of this dynamic in the United States, using metrics based on responses to survey questions, such as "we believe too often in science, and not enough in feelings and faith." Evans concludes that Protestant Christian skepticism toward the scientific community stems from (1) fear that scientists themselves have compromised motivations in performing their research and presenting their conclusions, and (2) concern over the moral implications of science (or, more accurately, *scientism*) dictating government policy (e.g., fear over the use of stem cells, limitation of personal liberties in the interest of reducing carbon emissions, fear over a slippery slope with respect to humanity "playing God" in the realm of genetically modified food, etc.). See chapter seven of John Evans, *Morals Not Knowledge: Recasting the Contemporary U.S. Conflict between Religion and Science* (Berkeley: University of California Press, 2018). For anthropological perspectives on the "post-truth" era in the United States, see contributions to Karen Ho and Jillian Cavanaugh (eds.), "What Happened to Social Facts?" Special section of *American Anthropologist* 121, no. 1 (2019).
6. Members of the Royal Asiatic Society of Sri Lanka have publicly spoken out against Ravana-oriented historical revisionism (see Chapter 5, section 2 of this text), as has Dr. Senarath Dissanayake, current Director General of the government Department of Archaeology (see Chapter 6 of this text).
7. On the influence of 1970s British social constructivist thought on philosophical defenses of native Indian science, see chapter one of Meera Nanda, *Prophets Facing Backward: Postmodern Critiques of Science and Hindu Nationalism in India* (New Brunswick: Rutgers University Press, 2003). The most vocal proponent of scientific

relativism and simultaneous Sinhala Ravana advocate is Nalin de Silva, Sri Lanka's current Ambassador to Burma, and former Professor of Mathematics and Dean of the Faculty of Science at the University of Kelaniya. De Silva draws copiously from the work of Paul Feyerabend in his defense of indigenous scientific methodology and modes of reasoning (see Chapter 6, section 2 of this book).

8. The story of this young lady's team of nine individuals searching for Ravana's treasure in the caves around Ella appears here: "Rāvana guhāvedī taruṇiyaṭa penvu venat mārgaya," *Hiru News*, March 30, 2016, http://www.hirunews.lk/129687/woman-goes-in-search-for-king-ravana. The interview is available on YouTube: "Rawana King will rise again with power," *NethTV*. Uploaded March 19, 2016, https://www.youtube.com/watch?v=lMmEu8jGNFk&t=9s.
9. William Mazzarella, "The Anthropology of Populism: Beyond the Liberal Settlement," *Annual Review of Anthropology* 48 (2019): 49; citing Eric Santner, *The Weight of All Flesh: On the Subject-Matter of Political Economy* (New York: Oxford University Press, 2016).
10. Sanjay Subrahmanyam, "Connected Histories: Notes Towards a Reconfiguration of Early Modern Eurasia," *Modern Asian Studies* 31, no. 3 (1997): 737.
11. As is the case in Hindutva discursive spheres in India, there is anti-secular, anti-liberal, and anti-urban rhetoric among Sinhala Buddhist nationalists today, directed at the "Colombo liberals" or "Kolumbians" who are accused of being out of step with the cultural and economic interests of the middle and working classes. I do not however see this anti-elitist discourse as essential to the Sinhala Ravana movement and give examples in Chapter 4, section 4 of the embrace of the historical Ravana narrative by upper-class, liberal, Anglophone Colombo circles.
12. Ernesto Laclau, *On Populist Reason* (New York: Verso, 2005), 67–124. For criticism of Laclau, along with a current overview of theories of populism in anthropology and political science, see William Mazzarella, "The Anthropology of Populism," 45–60.
13. The cultural essentialist, futurist, and millennial aspects of the twenty-first-century Sinhala Ravana movement invite comparison with other modern authoritarian imaginaries. Roger Griffin's "palingenetic ultranationalism" is a relevant descriptor of the Ravana phenomenon, as it represents a new myth articulating the rebirth of a nation and its people. Going so far as to list "Futurism" as a common trait of palingenetic ultranationalism, Griffin clarifies that twentieth-century fascism "offers to its followers not the prospect of returning to the idyll of a pre-modern society with its dynastic hierarchy and religious world-view intact, but rather of advancing toward a new order, one consonant with the dynamism of the modern world, yet able to purge it of the social, political, economic and spiritual malaise which liberal and socialist versions of modernisation have purportedly brought about." The twenty-first-century Sinhala Ravana movement does not conform therefore in every respect to Griffin's definition, as its promoters do offer "the prospect of returning to the idyll of a pre-modern society," as is characteristic of other South Asian archaic modernities. (Quotation in Roger Griffin, "Staging the Nation's Rebirth: The Politics and Aesthetics of Performance in the Context of Fascist Studies," in *Fascism and*

*Theatre: Comparative Studies on the Aesthetics and Politics of Performance in Europe, 1925–1945*, ed. Günter Berghaus [New York: Berghahn Books, 1996], 14.)

14. Sheldon Pollock, *The Language of the Gods in the World of Men: Sanskrit, Culture, and Power in Premodern India* (Berkeley: University of California Press, 2006), 7.
15. Gayatri Spivak, in asking whether or not "the subaltern can speak," cautions that attempts to resurrect the voices of marginal peoples of the past result in a kind of ventriloquism—the projection of the norms and expectations of the modern scholar, colonial operative, etc. (Gayatri C. Spivak, "Can the Subaltern Speak?" in *Marxism and the Interpretation of Culture*, ed. Cary Nelson and Lawrence Grossberg (London: Macmillan, 1988), 271–316).
16. In invoking the term "history from below," I am not arguing here that an alternative history of Sri Lanka based on the *Ramayana* was forged by a single social class or set of social classes, nor that such as vision of history was somehow an expression of class solidarity or a product of the oppression of "subaltern" groups.
17. Murray Rothbard, *For a New Liberty: The Libertarian Manifesto* (New York: Collier Books, 1973), 13.
18. In 2011, the Sri Lankan National Heritage and Cultural Affairs Ministry commissioned a sixth expansion of the chronicle, covering the period between 1978 and 2010, dedicated in large part to the accomplishments of Mahinda Rajapaksha during his first term as President (Mandana Ismail Abeywickrema, "The King and I," *The Sunday Leader*, April 10, 2011, http://www.thesundayleader.lk/2011/04/10/the-king-and-i-2).
19. Both the *Dīpavaṃsa* and *Mahāvaṃsa* begin their histories of the island with three visits by the Buddha Gotama who, the texts relate, soon after his enlightenment at the age of thirty-five, resolved to transport himself through the air to Lanka by means of his supernatural attainments, to cleanse the land of its malevolent, non-human occupants, such that his teachings (*sāsana*) might flourish there in the future. In the *Dīpavaṃsa*, the Buddha "sees" the island of Lanka and realizes it to be fit for the establishment of his *sāsana* while in his meditative trance under the Bodhi Tree, soon after obtaining enlightenment (1.17–18). The *Mahāvaṃsa* clarifies the timeline explaining that the Buddha made his first visit to Lanka on the full moon of the ninth month following his Buddhahood (3.19). On his first visit, the Buddha appears before an assembly of Yakkhas, driving them to the perimeter of the island by means of an expanding, superheating animal skin rug upon which he sat. He then by means of telekinesis brings another island ("Giri Dīpa") close to Lanka's shore, onto which the corralled Yakkhas and Rakkhasas disembark. Giri Dīpa is removed to a safe quarantine distance out into the ocean, the Buddha having effectively "interchanged the two islands for the (two kinds of beings), humans (*mānusā*) and Rakkhasas" (1.75). The Buddha's subsequent two visits to Lanka, according to both chronicles, involved his interaction with the resident Nagas—first resolving a disputation between the Naga king Mahodara and his nephew Cūḷodara, and subsequently preaching the *dhamma* on invitation from a Naga king named Maṇiakkhika. The Buddha's interaction with the Nagas of Lanka is the subject of chapter two of the *Dīpavaṃsa* and 1.44–84 of the

*Mahāvaṃsa*. The texts say that the Buddha's second and third visits took place in the fifth and eighth years after his enlightenment, respectively.

20. Lāṭa, or Lāḷa, a kingdom "between Magadha and Vaṅga," according to the *Mahāvaṃsa*.
21. See R. A. L. H. Gunawardhana, "The People of the Lion: The Sinhala Identity and Ideology in History and Historiography," in *History and the Roots of Conflict*, ed. Jonathan Spencer (London: Routledge, 1990), 45–87.
22. The *Mahāvaṃsa*'s account of Vijaya's Lankan colony amidst the Yakkhas is an instance of the "tale of the shipwrecked sailor" narrative motif, familiar from such diverse examples as Homer's *Odyssey*, the story of Sinbad the Sailor (from the Arabic *One Thousand and Ones Nights*), as well as other Asian Buddhist texts (including the Pali *Valāhassa Jātaka* and the seventh-century travel diary of Xuanzang). In the *Mahāvaṃsa*, the Yakkhiṇī Kuvaṇṇā takes the form of a hermit woman to entice Vijaya's crew of seven hundred men into the forest where they are imprisoned in a pit. Vijaya, recognizing the deceit, is able to capture Kuvaṇṇā in a noose, inducing her to marry him (at which time Kuvaṇṇā takes the form of a sixteen-year-old human girl). Kuvaṇṇā gives up her Yakkha brethren, who are slain by Vijaya (*Mhv* 7:1–38). Similar to the Pali chronicle version of the story, the *Valāhassa Jātaka* involves a group of five hundred sailors who are shipwrecked on the island of Tambapaṇṇi (i.e. Sri Lanka) (E. B. Cowell and W. H. D. Rouse (trans.), *The Jātaka; or, Stories of the Buddha's former births*, vol. II [London: Pali Text Society, 1973 (1895)], II.127–130 [no.196]). The proximity of the Vijaya colonization story to the *Ramayana* depiction of Lankapura in the imagination of the region is revealed in a version of the peopling of Sri Lanka collected by Xuanzang during his seventh-century South Indian sojourn. In this account, five hundred demonesses of Laṅkā living within an iron city seduce five hundred sailors accompanying the merchant prince Siṃhala. Siṃhala subsequently drives the demonesses into the sea, destroys their iron city, and rules Laṅkā as king. For discussion, see K. N. O. Dharmadasa, "The People of the Lion: Ethnic Identity, Ideology, and Historical Revisionism in Contemporary Sri Lanka," *Sri Lanka Journal of the Humanities* 15 (1989): 9; Gunawardana, "People of the Lion," 49ff.; Steven Kemper, *The Presence of the Past: Chronicles, Politics and Culture in Sinhala Life* (Ithaca: Cornell University Press, 1991), 56ff.; and John Holt, *Buddha in the Crown: Avalokiteśvara in the Buddhist Traditions of Sri Lanka* (New York: Oxford University Press, 1991), 50f.
23. Gail Sutherland observes that in the Pali Jātakas (the stories of the Buddha Gotama's former births), Yakkhas depart from their morally ambivalent depiction in Sanskrit literature to have their negative and malign traits amplified, embodying the "apotheosis of carnality, delusion, and ignorance" (*Disguises of the Demon: The Development of the Yakṣa in Hinduism and Buddhism* [Albany: State University of New York Press, 1991], 135).
24. On the conversion of Yakshas in early Buddhism, see Robert DeCaroli, *Haunting the Buddha: Indian Popular Religions and the Formation of Buddhism* (Oxford: Oxford University Press, 2004), 38–50. The *locus classicus* of "Yakkha conversion" in the Pali canon is the Ālavaka Sutta. For a discussion of the text, and for comments on

the enduring popularity of this text in Sri Lanka, see David Scott, *Formations of Ritual: Colonial and Anthropological Discourses on the Sinhala Yaktovil* (Minneapolis: University of Minnesota Press, 1994), 4f.

25. See Geoffrey Samuel, *The Origins of Yoga and Tantra: Indic Religions to the Thirteenth Century* (Cambridge: Cambridge University Press, 2008), 140–152. Yakshas and Nagas are depicted worshipping iconographic substitutes for the Buddha on the carved reliefs of Sāñcī, Bhārhut, and other early Indian Buddhist sites. See Vidya Dehejia, "Aniconism and the Multivalence of Emblems," *Ars Orientalis* 21 (1991): 48.
26. Kristin Scheible, *Reading the Mahāvaṃsa: The Literary Aims of a Theravāda Buddhist History* (New York: Columbia University Press 2016), 59.
27. The six species of non-human residents of Lanka named in the *Dīpavaṃsa* are Yakkhas, Pisācas, Avaruddhakas, Nāgas, Bhūtas, and Rakkhasas.
28. The author of the *Dīpavaṃsa* seems largely unconcerned with differentiating between Yakkhas and Rakkhasas, with the Buddha for example ordaining that "all the Rakkhasas shall dwell on Giri Dīpa" (*Dīpavaṃsa* 1.77), and following up in the very next verse to say that "the eager Yakkhas ran to Giri Dīpa" (1.78). The *Mahāvaṃsa* makes no specific mention of Rakkhasas at all, concluding its chapter on the Buddha's visitation of Lanka by highlighting his good will toward the island's "hosts of Asuras, Nāgas, and so forth" (*Mahāvaṃsa* 1.84).
29. Ravana is referred to as the "lord of the Yakshas" in the *Rāvaṇa Katāva* (see Appendix). He is likewise sometimes known as *yakṣādhipati* in Sinhala folklore (Nandadēva Vijēskēra, *Lankā Janatāva* (Colombo: S. Godage, 2015 [1955]), 9).
30. Somehow, upon Vijaya's arrival, Lanka remained home to at least one entire city of Yakkhas (Sirīsavatthu̧), one among whom, the Yakkhiṇī Kuvaṇṇā eagerly devised a plot to devour the new arrivals from India (see n.22, above). The seventeenth-century *Rājāvaliya* accounts for the presence of some Yakkhas at the time of Vijaya's arrival by explaining that: "apart from those Yakṣas who were sent to the island of Yakgiri, some had remained hiding in Laggala and Loggala in the forest of Tammännā" (A. V. Suraweera (trans.), *Rājāvaliya: A Comprehensive Account of the Kings of Sri Lanka* [Ratmalana: Vishva Lekha Publications, 2000], 17). The chronicle also includes a curious passage saying that King Mahasena (r. c. 277–304 CE) employed both men and Yakshas to construct his reservoirs: the men worked during the day while the demons labored at night (49).
31. On the place of *yakku* within Sinhala Buddhist cosmology, and their soteriological status, see Gananath Obeyesekere, "The Ritual Drama of the Sanni Demons: Collective Representations of Disease in Ceylon," *Comparative Studies in Society and History* 11, no. 2 (1969): 176f.
32. Methods of controlling Yakshas are advanced in Sinhala *mantra* and *yantra* books; poems associated with shrines to gods (*devālayas*) frequented by Sinhala Buddhists speak of protection from "the gaze of Yakkhas" (*yaku diṣṭi*) "befalling" (*helannē*) someone. For examples of the latter, see H. U. Pragñālōka (ed.), *Purāṇa Sivpada Saṅgrahāva* (Colombo: Government Press, 1952).
33. While the Yak Tovil rite protects against the malevolent influence of Yakshas, some Sri Lankan folklore relates that the Buddha's cleansing of the demonic denizens was

thorough and irreversible, explaining that he installed an invisible protective barrier (*sīma*) around the island, a kind of impenetrable force field. These oral legends explain that the malign influence of the Yakshas occasionally experienced by human beings (possession and physical illness) are therefore not a consequence of direct contact, but rather a result of the Yakshas' "gaze" (*bälma* or *diṣṭiya*) cast across the water to Sri Lanka from distant Giri Dīpa. See David Scott, *Formations of Ritual: Colonial and Anthropological Discourses on the Sinhala Yaktovil* (Minneapolis: University of Minnesota Press, 1994), 38–50. The ontological status of Yakshas remains ambiguous in Sinhala ritual life—the vocabulary used to describe their interference in human affairs suggests that these beings operate from afar (Scott's informants also explained that Yakshas can cast their disruptive "gaze" upon people by manifesting themselves as apparitions, including in the form of animal specters such as dogs and lizards), while by contrast the ritual space of the Yak Tovil implies that Yakshas are physically present during the rite in order to receive offerings made to them. For a catalogue of the varieties of Yakshas and their respective afflictions, see Paul Wirz, *Exorcism and the Art of Healing in Ceylon* (Leiden: Brill, 1954). For a detailed ethnographic account of the Yak Tovil rite, see Bruce Kapferer, *A Celebration of Demons: Exorcism and the Aesthetics of Healing in Sri Lanka* (Bloomington: University of Indiana Press, 1983). On the enduring popularity of Yak Tovil rites in southern Sri Lanka, including the configuration of discourse surrounding Yakshas within social attitudes restricting the mobility of women, see Alex Argenti-Pillen, *Masking Terror: How Women Contain Violence in Southern Sri Lanka* (Philadelphia: University of Pennsylvania Press, 2002), and Hege Myrlund Larsen, "Buddhism in Popular Culture: The Case of Sri Lankan 'Tovil Dance,'" PhD diss.: University of Bergen (2009). I am grateful to Eva-Alexandra Ambos for her insightful comments on this section.

34. *Mahāvaṃsa* 1.19.
35. *Mahāvaṃsa* 10.84–89. See S. Paranavitana, "Pre-Buddhist Religious Beliefs in Ceylon," *The Journal of the Ceylon Branch of the Royal Asiatic Society of Great Britain & Ireland* 31, no. 82 (1929): 303–307. In the Sanskrit literary tradition, Kubera (Vaishravana), Ravana's stepbrother, is known as the lord of the Yakshas (Sailendranath Samanta, "A Rare Image of Vaisravana from Kanchannagar, Burdwan," *Proceedings of the Indian History Congress* 27 [1965]: 49). This close family connection between the two species of demons may have been a source of justification for the proximity of Yakshas and Rakshasas in the premodern Sri Lankan literary imaginary. Henry Parker, writing in 1909, observed that Yaksha worship was practiced among upcountry Vedda (Sri Lanka's indigenous ethnic group) as well as by some Sinhala Buddhist villagers of the remote Uva Province, as an antidote to pestilence and disease (*Ancient Ceylon: An Account of the Aborigines and of Part of the Early Civilization* [London: Luzac & Co., 1909], 132–206). On Veḍda worship of ancestors transformed after death into *nā yakku*, see Gananath Obeyesekere, "Where Have All the Väddas Gone? Buddhism and Aboriginality in Sri Lanka," in *Hybrid Island: Culture Crossings and the Invention of Identity in Sri Lanka*, ed. Neluka Silva (London: Zed Books, 2002), 1–19.
36. Chapter seven of the *Mahāvaṃsa* explains that Vijaya and Kuvaṇṇā have two children, a son and a daughter, but that all three are promptly abandoned by Vijaya when

his mission of slaying the other Yakkha is completed. Kuvaṇṇā is subsequently killed attempting to return to her home city of Lankapura, at which point the two young children flee to the island's central highlands ("Malaya-raṭṭha," or the region of Samantakūṭa [Sri Pada]). The descendants of the exiled progeny of Vijaya and Kuvaṇṇā, the chronicle informs us, would come to be known as the Pulindā (*Mahāvaṃsa* 7.59–68).

37. *Dīpavaṃsa* 1.70.
38. The geography of the confinement of the Yakkhas according to the *Mahāvaṃsa* is less clear. The text leaves the spatial orientation of Giri Dipa undetermined, going on to speak of two other "Yakkha cities," Sirisavatthu and Lankapura. Sirisavatthu, also identified as the city of Yakkhas in the *Valāhassa Jātaka*, we can infer to be located somewhere on the island of Lanka, but Lankapura (Kuvaṇṇā's hometown and residence of the "chief of Yakkhas" (*Mahāvaṃsa* 7.33, 7.62)) is again spatially vague. Chapter 3 of this book treats the theme of a "second Lanka"—Ravana's capital of "Lankapura"—enduring as something of a free-floating *topos* in Sri Lankan literary imagination, sometimes located on the island of Sri Lanka itself, sometimes located offshore "on the way to India," and sometimes associated with a subterranean mirror-land of Lanka, a chthonic realm with entrances out in the sea connecting apertures amid the labyrinthine peaks of Sri Lanka's central highlands.
39. Although the term "Aryan" (or Pali *āriya*) does not denote any group of people or éthnos in either the *Dīpavaṃsa* or *Mahāvaṃsa*, modern commentators did not hesitate to superimpose the chronicles' Sīhaḷa–Damiḷa distinction onto the categories of "Aryan" and "Dravidian," newly minted in the European ethnic imagination.
40. Jonathan Walters and Matthew Colley, "Making History: George Turnour, Edward Upham, and the 'Discovery' of the *Mahavamsa*," *Sri Lanka Journal of the Humanities* 32, no. 1–2 (2006): 151.
41. Walters and Colley, "Making History," 151f.
42. This according to Rev. William Fox, who assisted Edward Upham with his translation (Walters and Colley, "Making History," 159, citing Edward Upham, *The Mahavansi, the Rájá-Ratnácari and the Rájá-vali* (London: Parbury, Allen, and Co., 1833), vol. 1, xii). George Turnour's assessment of the atrophied state of Pali learning in Sri Lanka by the early nineteenth century has been taken at face value by modern historians, although the actual situation appears to have been more complicated. Anne Blackburn (2001) documents the advanced Sanskrit and Pali curriculum of the Siyam Nikāya in the mid- to late-eighteenth century. It is possible however that the vibrant state of Pali learning at Kandy was not matched in more provincial settings. See also E. R. Gooneratne (ed.), *The Vimāna-vatthu of the Khuddhaka Nikāya (Sutta Piṭaka)* (London: Pali Text Society, 1886), xiv.
43. See G. P. Malalasekera, *Pali Literature of Ceylon* (Colombo: M. D. Gunasena, 1958 [1928]), 132ff., and J. E. Tennent, *Ceylon: An Account of the Island* (New Delhi: Asian Educational Services 2011 [1859]), vol. 1, 314. The *Pūjāvaliya*, first composed in 1266, was itself brought up to date to the eighteenth century (its appendix is known as the *Suḷu-pūjāvaliya*). The *Rājāvaliya* was also open to revision and known under various names until the late seventeenth century.

# 2
# MOVING MOUNT KAILASA

## 2.1 RAVANA THE SUBALTERN COSMOPOLITAN

Ravana is known to Hindus in India as the nemesis of Rama, an incarnation of the god Vishnu. The *Rāmāyaṇa* of Valmiki, regarded by tradition as the first major Sanskrit poem (*kāvya*), depicts Ravana as a despotic king of the powerful race of beings known as Rakshasas, who cruelly abducts the princess Sita in a disproportionate act of revenge for an injury committed to his sister, Shurpanakha. Paralyzed by his infatuation with Sita and blinded by hubris, Ravana ignores the better council of his brothers and goes to war with Rama, at the climax of which he meets his bitter end. While he serves the role of the villain in the epic, Ravana remains a complex character in a number of respects. He is, to begin, a liminal figure within the social landscape of the *Vālmiki Rāmāyaṇa*—a cosmopolitan and well-travelled individual but the ruler of a provincial fiefdom, the island citadel of "Laṅkāpuri." Ravana's lustful temperament and thirst for power are at their root attributed to a prenatal curse (a result of his mother, Kaikasi, approaching his father-to-be, Vishravas, at an inauspicious time, as he was performing a Vedic rite), although the demon-king's later-life military campaign against gods and men takes place amid a descent into tyranny during which Ravana gradually and willfully abandons the principles of *dharma* which inhibit the mistreatment of family, allies, and fellow sovereigns.[1] Subsequent renderings of the epic adapt Ravana variously—some reducing him simply to a two-dimensional foil for the heroic Rama, with other (particularly South Indian) versions offering a more balanced treatment of his character. In Kampan's famed twelfth-century Tamil version, Lankapuri is described as one among the most dazzling cities on earth, with Ravana its mighty, pious, and immensely learned ruler.[2] The same is true of the Telugu *Raṅganātha Rāmāyaṇamu*, which emphasizes the Rakshasa king's pious devotion to Shiva, along with his generosity, bravery, and skill in statecraft.[3]

While the character of Ravana is overwhelmingly perceived in negative terms by Hindus today—his defeat by Rama is commemorated in the annual

*Ravana's Kingdom*. Justin W. Henry, Oxford University Press. © Oxford University Press 2023.
DOI: 10.1093/oso/9780197636305.003.0002

festival of Dussehra—the demon-king remains a quiet hero for some in India. Throughout the Chota Nagpur Plateau, for example, we find instances of narrative reconfiguration of the *Ramayana* in which "the periphery is being 'centered'" (to quote Radhika Borde): the Bir Asur people of Netarhat, eastern Jharkand, revere the ancient "Asura king" as their distant ancestor, considering him a valorous, mighty, divine being who imparted *dharmic* knowledge of statecraft to Rama as he lay vanquished on the battlefield.[4] For many in central Chhattisgarh, Ravana is memorialized in the form of cement statues, where some Gonds also view him as a distant member of their family lineage (*vaṃśa*). Here locals perform *pūjā* to Ravana prior to the incarnation of his effigy during Dussehra, with some refusing to set fire to him during the ritual altogether.[5] The residents of Mandsaur, Madhya Pradesh also afford special honors to Ravana during Dussehra, requiring that Rama request Ravana's permission before delivering the *coup de grâce* during the ritual reenactment of the demon-king's defeat. (Mandodari, Ravana's wife, is also revered in Mandsaur, where she is remembered as a native of the region in oral tradition.[6]) Several Brahman sub-castes in India today celebrate Ravana as a learned ancestor (Ravana having been a "half-Brahman" through his father, Vishravas), including the Saraswat Brahmans of Uttar Pradesh and Kanyakubja Brahmans of Madhya Pradesh. Among these groups there is a tendency to reject Dussehra as an "anti-Brahman" ritual, and several efforts to establish shrines dedicated to the demon-king have been successful to date.[7]

Ravana became an emblem of the Dravidian movement for some from the first half of the twentieth century, where he served as a foil against the hegemony of the "Aryan north." Some in Tamil Nadu interpreted the archaeological finds at Harappa and Mohenjo-daro as evidence for a robust *pre*-Aryan civilization on the subcontinent, prefiguring by a century analogous claims made in support of Sinhala indigeneity and historical primacy in Sri Lanka.[8] Indeed, somewhat ironically given the fraught history of Tamil–Sinhala relations, a number of themes central to the Dravidian movement appear again in the present-day Sri Lankan Buddhist reclamation of Ravana. Both feature a revanchist view of the deep past, with Tamils postulating a now-submerged supercontinent ("Kumarikkaṇṭam" or "Kumari-nāḍu") extending outwards from Tamil Nadu, and Buddhists imagining a similarly expansive antediluvian Lanka. Both find in their respective deep antiquities a prelapsarian golden age of *dharmic* kinship, and mastery of the technical and literary arts. Both claim their respective languages—Tamil and Sinhala (or its prototype, "Hela")—to have been the most ancient in all the world, the "mother of all languages," and their respective homelands (Tamil Nadu and Sri Lanka) to be the "the cradle of human civilization."[9]

This chapter considers the process through which Ravana's abode of "Lankapuri" (or "Lankapura") came to be identified with the island of Sri Lanka, which I argue was a late first millennium South Indian innovation, sustained by the Arya Cakravartis kings of Jaffna. I argue furthermore that Sri Lankan Tamils innovated on the South Indian image of Ravana, rendering him a positive figure in the island's religious history—a fastidious devotee of Shiva and the original king of Sri Lanka, long before the arrival of Prince Vijaya. This chapter and the following work to identify specific points of interface whereby South Indian Puranic themes and legends relating to Ravana passed from Tamil to Sinhala speakers, among whom Ravana's moral character and heroism were further exalted. The final section of this chapter explores probable avenues of transmission from Tamil to Sinhala in elevated social spheres, by way of families of South Indian extraction who ascended in the royal houses of Sri Lanka's late medieval southwest, where Tamil and Malayalam speakers were employed as notaries and poets, and which maintained networks of religious patronage between Jaffna, Trincomalee, and Kotte. Chapter 3 examines more demotic texts, oral traditions, and points of social contact between Tamil and Sinhala speakers through which a thoroughly domesticated vision of Ravana's character developed in the Kandyan period (sixteenth to eighteenth centuries).

## 2.2 RAVANA'S LANKA IN INDIAN LITERATURE

There is little indication that Ravana's "city of Lanka" is intended to correspond with the island of Sri Lanka in the *Vālmīki Rāmāyaṇa*, where Ravana's "Lankapuri" is depicted as a citadel at the top of Trikuta Mountain—a fortress with impenetrable ramparts and moats.[10] Trikuta itself is described as an inaccessible rock rising from the midst of the ocean, 100 *yojana*s in breadth, its peak resembling that of Mount Kailasa.[11] Later first millennium Sanskrit renderings of the epic give no indication of a correspondence between Ravana's Lankapura and Sri Lanka, with some versions even making an explicit geographical distinction between the two islands.[12] South Indian religious literature also conforms to Valmiki's geographically vague and fanciful depiction of Lankapuri.

In the seventh-century hymns of Cuntarar, Ravana's "southern Lanka" is located somewhere "in the southern seas full of waves" (*tiraiyiṉār kāṭal cūḻnta teṉṉilaṅkai*), and is "full of broad roads made for strong chariots."[13] The Lanka of Kampan's famed twelfth-century Tamil version of the epic is again a fortified city jutting out of the ocean, "with the wide sea as its moat."[14] The *Kanta Purāṇam* (a Tamil adaptation of the Sanskrit *Skanda Purāṇa*) depicts "Ilaṅkaipuram" as a city somewhere far out amid the ocean, which sank during a fierce battle between Skanda and Vīravāku, resurfacing from the water some time afterward.[15] Subsequent South Indian poetry tended to be similarly equivocal on the whereabouts of Ravana's ancient domain.[16]

As Sri Lanka was known as "Lanka" from very early on (at least from the time of the *Dīpavaṃsa*), it would be surprising were there no conflation at all between the island and the "Lankapura" of literary fame. Indeed, we find precisely this in the fifth- or sixth-century *Vāyu Purāṇa*'s "description of Jambudvīpa's lands, islands, etc.," where "Malaya Dvīpa" ("the island of Malaya") is identified as home to "the city of Lanka," perched:

> on the beautiful ridge and peak of the mountain Trikūṭa decorated with different minerals. The mountain is many Yojanas in height. Its variegated precipices and caves resemble houses. The city has gold ramparts and archways. There are many mansions and palaces with turrets and gables of variegated color. It is a hundred Yojanas long and thirty Yojanas broad. It is flourishing and the people there are happy and gay.
>
> It is the abode of noble Rākṣasas who can assume various forms as they please. Know that to be the habitation of the enemies of Devas, proud of their strength. Free from all harassments, the city is inaccessible to human beings.
>
> In that island, on the eastern shore of the sea there is Gokarṇa, the great shrine of Śaṅkara (Śiva).[17]

Aspects of the *Vāyu Purāṇa*'s description are obviously less-than-empirical in nature, although some points of contact with the topography of Sri Lanka are apparent: the temple to Shiva at "Gokarna" corresponds to the Konesvaram temple at Trincomalee (see below in this chapter), and the name "Malaya" refers to the central administrative portion of Sri Lanka in the *Mahāvaṃsa* and subsequent chronicles.[18]

More direct identification of Sri Lanka with the abode of Ravana appears from the eighth century in South Indian inscriptional discourse recording territorial conquests over the island. The first known example is contained in the Kasakudi plates of Nandivarman. The *praśasti* boasts that the king's ancestor, Narasiṃhavarman I, was a "victorious hero, who surpassed the glory of the valor of Rama by (his) conquest of Lanka."[19] By the ninth century, the *Ramayana* began to take on substantial political and religious significance in South India, among both Shaivites and Vaishnavites.[20] Rama emerged as an ideal king[21] and a frequent standard of comparison in the literary works celebrating real-life military and political adventurers. In connection with this development, the Cholas standardized the equivalence between "Lanka" and Ravana's "city of Lanka" as they began making military headway onto the island in the early tenth century. A hymn celebrating the Citamparam Shiva temple complex attributed to a Chola prince named Kaṇṭarātitya (written during or some time before the year 907) eulogizes a recent victor, stating that, just as Shiva subdued Ravana, "the king of Lanka" (*ilaṅkaivēntaṉ*), "Cempiyaṉ, the just Cōḻa king of Uraiyūr, conquered both the hot-tempered tyrant of the [Pāṇḍyan] South and the king of Sri Lanka (*īḻam*)."[22]

Adversary Sinhala kings and their armies were likened to Ravana and his Rakshasa hosts. The Udayendram plates of Pṛthvīpati II (c. 919 CE) boast that when this king's ally, Parāntaka, "defeated the Pandya (king) Rājasiṃha, two persons experienced fear at the same time: the Lord of Wealth (Kubera) on account of the death of his own friend, and Vibhishana on account of the proximity of the Chola dominion to Sri Lanka."[23] The Tiruvālaṅgāḍu plates of Rājendra (c. 1017 CE) relate that his campaign in Sri Lanka was conducted even more efficiently than Rama's:

> Constructing a bridge across the water of the ocean with the
> assistance of able monkeys, the Lord of the Raghavas [Rama]
> killed with great difficulty the king of Lanka [Ravana]
> with sharp-edged arrows—
>
> [but] this terrible general of his [of King Rājarāja, Rājendra's father]
> crossed the ocean with ships and burnt the Lord of Lanka.
> Hence Rama is surpassed by him [i.e. by Rājendra].[24]

The depiction of Chola enemies as "Rakshasas" persisted until the twilight of the empire and was used in reference to Sri Lankans as well as continental adversaries.[25]

Sri Lankan Tamils seem to have openly accepted the identification of the island with the Lanka of the *Ramayana*, reversing however the negative and demonic connotations of their Chola predecessors. On analogy with Rama and Vibhishana, the Arya Cakravartis became themselves "guardians of the bridge," that is, protectors over the narrow, submerged isthmus connecting Rameswaram on the Indian continent with the island of Mannar.[26] In addition, the island ceased to be an "abode of Rakshasas" in Lankan Tamil literature. Instead, drawing from the Tamil Purana traditions of South Indian temples such as Citamparam and Rameswaram, Ravana was portrayed in a favorable light in northern Sri Lanka, remembered for his piety and foundational role at places of Shaiva worship across the island.

The seventeenth-century Setupati rulers of Ramnad and Sivaganga are the best known "protectors of the bridge," as their headquarters at Rameswaram and family name (*cētu pati*) suggest.[27] Lankan sources reveal that the title was in operation three centuries earlier on the opposite side of the "bridge," among rulers of the northern kingdom of Jaffna (who also traced their origin to Rameswaram in South India).[28] Early copper coins of the Arya Cakravartis, while borrowing their design from the mints of Polonnaruwa and Dambadeniya, were imprinted with the word *cētu*, "bridge," in Tamil lettering.[29] This, it would appear, is an abbreviated form of the title *cētu kāvalaṉ*, "protector of the bridge" (the same meaning as *cētu pati*). The *cētu* moniker also appears in a Tamil inscription commemorating an Arya Cakravarti military victory at Kotagama (only thirteen miles north-east of Dädigama, where Parakramabahu's capital lay at the time), most likely dating to the mid-late fourteenth century, when Jaffna exercised tax authority over the ports of the south.[30] The epithet appears later in connection with one Cekarāca Cēkaraṉ (most likely Pararāca Cēkaraṉ VI [r. c. 1478–1519] or his son, Caṅkili I) in a colophon of the *Cekarācacēkara-mālai*, an astrological work composed under his sponsorship:

Uniting the domains of southern Lanka,[31]
Uprooting [his opponents] as onlookers say, "O his glittering spear!" . . .
Ciṅkai Āriyan, protector of the bridge (*cētu kāvalaṉ*),
Lord of the Ganges, *tilaka* among the learned,
Teacher of many across the broad ocean,
Having no equal with respect to mastery of the triple Tamil,[32]
Cepparum Cekarāca Cēkaraṉ.[33]

A similar title appears in a colophon of the *Takṣiṇa Kailāca Purāṇam* belonging to the late fifteenth or sixteenth century:

> Bearing guardianship over the shore with its expansive bridge,[34]
> The one with his dark spear raised,
> Commander Ciṅkai Āriyaṉ,
> Cekarāca Cēkaraṉ who is ornamented with fame.[35]

As for the possible origin and significance of the *cētu pati* title, it is noteworthy that the submerged isthmus joining India and Sri Lanka makes the Palk Strait navigable at only two points: one near Rameswaram (this passage being only twelve feet at its deepest), and another off the coast of Mannar. For this reason, Mannar was a strategic asset with respect to the control of shipping in the region, one which fell within the territory of the Jaffna kingdom.[36]

## 2.3 RAVANA AND RAMA IN TAMIL TEMPLE LITERATURE

While the Arya Cakravartis identified themselves as "guardians of the bridge," Ravana and Rama appear ubiquitously as foundational figures in the Tamil temple myths and historiography of Sri Lanka's north and east. The characterization of Ravana as a *bhakta* of Shiva has deep roots in Indian literature. In the *Vālmīki Rāmāyaṇa*, the demon king reports to his brother Vibhishana that he has traveled to the Himalayas to undergo penance and win the favor of Shiva.[37] A popular theme of later South Indian temple imagery and Shaiva poetry, known in the Sanskrit Āgamas as the *rāvaṇa anugraha mūrti* (Shiva's manifestation (*mūrti*) as he delivers grace (*anugraha*) to Ravana), tells the story of Ravana's harassment of Shiva and subsequent subordination. It involves variations on a basic theme: Ravana was flying through the air on his chariot when his route was blocked by Mt. Kailasa. Arrogantly, he uprooted the mountain and began to toss it aside. Shiva interrupted Ravana, pinning him beneath the mountain. After being trapped for one thousand years, during which time he sings hymns of Shiva's majesty in apology, Ravana was released by Shiva, blessing him with a boon (long life, an invincible sword, or a *liṅgam* to worship).

The episode appears in chapter sixteen of the Uttara Kāṇḍa of the *Vālmīki Rāmāyaṇa*, after Ravana has won the *puṣpaka vimāna* from his half-brother

Kubera in battle. Shortly after it is commandeered, the aerial chariot stalls on route to Mt. Sharavana. There, Ravana and his retinue are approached by Nandi, who explains that his master, Lord Shiva, is disporting himself upon the mountain, for which reason it is inaccessible to all living beings, Rakshasas included. Heedless of the warning, Ravana laughed derisively (asking "who is this Shankara?"), prompting Nandi to issue a curse proclaiming that one day a monkey race will arise to destroy Ravana and his Rakshasa race. Undeterred, and believing Shiva to be responsible for arresting his newly acquired vehicle, Ravana lifted Mt. Kailasa and shook it violently. Shiva in response used his immense toe to press the mountain down upon Ravana's arms. Ravana's anguished cry was heard throughout the three worlds, for which reason, upon his release, Shiva bestowed upon him the name "Rāvaṇa," "the Reverberator" ("he who makes the worlds reverberate (*rāvita*) with his cries").[38] Some versions of Valmiki's text add a coda to this episode, in which Ravana asked Shiva for a boon of invincibility against humankind to round out those he had been granted already by Brahma. In response Shiva granted Ravana a great sword, the *candrahāsa*, although with it issued a warning: "This must not be treated with disrespect by you. If this is disrespected, then, without a doubt, it will return to me!"[39]

An early reference to the *rāvaṇa anugraha mūrti* appears in the *Kalittokai* of the Sangam corpus,[40] and afterward as a frequent literary motif in South Indian Sanskrit and Tamil works, often with variations on Valmiki's presentation of the episode. In the *Śiva Purāṇa*, Ravana cuts off nine of his ten heads as an act of penance, impressing Shiva sufficiently enough to win the boon of a personal *śiva-liṅgam* to worship.[41] The story is a steady motif of the seventh- and eighth-century Tamil Nayanar poets, and Ravana is mentioned in each of Appar's *patikam*s and many of Campantar's hymns.[42] Cuntarar describes Ravana as a mighty Rakshasa (*val arakkaṉ*), who regrettably misdirects all of his aptitude toward wicked ends. From the eighth century, an iteration of the *rāvaṇa anugraha mūrti* is depicted in South Indian temple reliefs in which a penitent Ravana, pinned beneath Mt. Kailasa, fashions a lute on which to sing hymns of praise to Shiva, using the tendons of one his severed arms as strings and his severed head as a sound box.[43]

South Indian Shaiva temple literature draws from the *rāvaṇa anugraha mūrti* and related stories in the *Śiva Purāṇa* to position Ravana as central to the establishment of a number of locations of devotional significance. The temple literature of Varañci (in Tamil Nadu) and Mahabaleswar (in Karnataka) invoke the story of Ravana's failed attempt to transport a Shiva *liṅgam* to Lanka, which first appears in the *Śiva Purāṇa*. In each case, Ravana accidentally lays down the *liṅgam* he has been given as a reward for his penance on route from the Himalayas to Lanka. When he attempts to pick it up again, he bends the *liṅgam* out of shape, causing it to appear like a cow's ear (a *go-karṇa*).[44] Significantly, "Gokarna" is also an early designation for the Koneswaram Temple of Trincomalee in Sri Lanka, where Ravana is regarded as an instrumental founding figure. The *Takṣiṇa Kailāca Purāṇam* gives a brief account of the *Ramayana*, the slaying of Ravana, and Rama's bestowal of the kingdom of Lanka to Vibhishana. Rama then prays to Shiva and attains a rarified mental state as a result of *darśan*.[45] Following his example, Vibhishana too worships at "the place of Gokarna," imploring Rama that they build a temple to Shiva at that spot.[46] Rama assents and construction begins. The temple is decorated with paintings of various Devas, including Ravana prominently (Vibhishana's devotion at the sight of the artwork is remarked upon, so the inclusion of Ravana seems to be out of respect for his fallen brother). Deities, including Indra and Vishnu, come to worship at the temple, and do so until Rama grants permission for them to return to their abodes. The text recalls a time when Ravana too sang sweet praise to Shiva on his *vīṇā* at Koneswaram (see Figure 2.1).[47]

Similar stories appear in the later written temple histories (*tala-purāṇams*) and oral traditions of other Shiva temples in northern and eastern Sri Lanka as well. The temple literature of Thiruketiswaram in Mannar recealls that Mayan, father-in-law of Ravana, had a temple built there to install a *śiva-liṅgam*. Rama is said to have later worshipped there on his return to India from Lanka.[48] The *tala-purāṇams* of Munneswaram (located on Sri Lanka's northwest coast) declare that the site gained prominence when Rama—returning to Ayodhya flying on the *puṣpaka vimāna* confiscated from Ravana—stopped to rest at an uninhabited spot. Determining that this would be a good place to worship Shiva, Rama dispatched Hanuman to India to retrieve a *liṅgam* for this purpose. When Hanuman tarried too long, Rama built his own *liṅgam* out of sand. Hanuman eventually returned with the *liṅgam*, only to have Rama hurl it away toward India in annoyance. Rama's sand *liṅgam* remained after the two of them returned to the continent, established as the first *liṅgam* to be worshipped at Munneswaram.[49]

The temple's origin story is in fact a very close facsimile of that of the Rameswaram Shiva temple, across the "bridge" of the Palk Straight in southern Tamil Nadu. The only discrepancy between the stories is that it was Sita, not Rama, who constructed the initial sand *liṅgam* of Rameswaram.[50]

**Figure 2.1** Ravana at Koneswaram Temple.—(Author's photo, May 2014)

Rameswaram's reputation as a place of devotional significance for Rama is present as early on as the *Śiva Purāṇa*, wherein Rama complains that Shiva's gift of invincibility to Ravana was inordinate, asking that he too be made invincible in battle against the demon king. Shiva grants this request, transforming himself into "the *liṅgam* named Rāmeśvara."[51]

Ravana is an ambiguous figure for Sri Lankan Tamil Hindus today. He is, to begin, regarded as a historical king of the island according to the surviving historical literature, as in the *Vaiyā Pāṭal* (a sixteenth-century chronicle of the Jaffna Kingdom) as well as the eighteenth-century *Yāḻppāṉa Vaipava Mālai*, which each begin their narration of the island's history with Vibhishana's receipt of Lankan kingship from Rama, whereafter Vibhishana "continued to reign up to and during the early part of the present *yuga*."[52] As is the case in South India, Shaiva-oriented Hindus in Sri Lanka have less theological stake in the antimony between Rama, an incarnation of Vishnu, and Ravana. Ravana is remembered not only as the architect of Koneswaram but also, in oral tradition, as the founder of a number of Shiva temples around Batticaloa.[53] The Rakshasa king's image as a model devotee to Shiva, attested in the Indian literary tradition, is amplified in its Lankan iterations. In the temple literature of Koneswaram, the sentiment of the *rāvaṇa anugraha mūrti* is inverted, making Ravana's feat of lifting Mt. Kailasa an act of extreme heroism and piety (rather than an act of antagonism). The eighteenth-century *Tirukōṇācala Purāṇam* gives the (still popular) story of Ravana's resolution to bring Koneswaram to his aged mother, Kanniya, who was nearby but too ill to make the journey to the top of the hill to worship. In the act of cutting away a portion of the hill, however, his sword broke, and Ravana was dragged into the sea (a vaulting cleft in the rock face at the temple premises is now called "Ravana's cut" (*rāvaṇa veṭṭu*) in reference to this incident). Realizing that his strength was inadequate for the task, Ravana turned instead to penance, pulling out his eyes and offering them as flowers to Shiva, pulling out the tendons of his arm to fashion a lute (*yāḻ*) on which he sang songs of devotion. Satisfied, Shiva restored Ravana's body, allowing himself to be transported along with his temple at Koneswaram to Kanniya. The Devas, worried that their regular worship at Tirumayilai would be interrupted, sent Vishnu to falsely inform Ravana of the death of his mother. Believing him, Ravana performed her funerary rites at the nearby hot springs at which she was residing, immediately after which Kanniya actually died.[54]

On the other hand, these positive dimensions of the demon-king's character exist only in adjunct to his role in Tamil versions of the *Ramayana* popular in Sri Lanka today (including the *Kampa Rāmāyaṇam*), where he is the abductor and cruel tormentor of Sita.[55] The *rāvaṇa anugraha mūrti* is depicted on the "Kailāca Vāhana" (one of the chariots paraded during Hindu temple festivals) in the form of massive sculptures depicting Shiva and Parvati sitting atop Mt. Kailasa, with Ravana beneath them playing a lute constructed of one of his twenty arms and ten heads.[56] In the forthcoming chapters, I make the case that a more complete inversion of Ravana's character—from treacherous villain to sympathetic hero—is accomplished in the Sinhala storytelling tradition. In demonstrating avenues of transmission from Tamil accounts of the *Ramayana* to Sinhala, I do however argue that the uniquely sympathetic image of Ravana was most likely incubated in Tamil Puranic and oral literature prior to this transfer. In an effort to make this case, Chapter 3 will follow the appearance of Tamil literary motifs in Sinhala poetry and folklore of the Kandyan era, including those of Ravana's devotion to his mother Kanniya, and those concerning Ravana's brother "Peacock Ravana" ("Mayil Irāvaṇaṉ" in Tamil). Characters and themes from Tamil iterations of the *Ramayana* finding their way into Sinhala are reminders of the longstanding tradition of literary exchange in Sri Lanka, representing only a single illustration of a broader pattern of cultural interface involving South Indian linguistic, aesthetic, and ritual influence in SriLankan Buddhist spheres.[57]

## 2.4 RAVANA'S LANKAN IMAGE

The geographical dimensions of ancient Lankapura are a preoccupation for modern Tamil and Sinhala political movements positing Ravana as a distant ancestor, with both parties claiming that their respective ancient domains were thousands of years ago many orders of magnitude larger than their present dimensions. Justification for such claims has been made on the basis of a literary motif—found in both Tamil and Sinhala texts—referring to a massive flood in deep antiquity of geologically consequential scale. In the South Indian Dravidian movement, the proposition that the land of Tamil Nadu was once a super-continent traversing most of what is now the Indian subcontinent was first inspired by a theory put forward in 1864 by British zoologist Philip Sclater, who sought to explain the presence of lemur fossils in Madagascar and India despite their absence in Africa and the Middle East. (As an explanation, Sclater proposed that a massive continent, which he dubbed "Lemuria," had long ago spanned the areas where lemurs are found today.) The suggestion that a prehistoric continent once stretched southward from the Indian subcontinent to occupy most of what is today the Indian Ocean was introduced to the Tamil reading public by way of British colonial administrators through the work of Ernst Heinrich Haeckel (1834–1919), who borrowed from the Lemuria thesis to support his own contention, contrary to Darwin's "African origin" hypothesis, that the very first anatomically modern humans evolved in Hindustan (the Indian subcontinent), from which they migrated outward through Eurasia and the South Pacific.[58]

In addition to the intuitive appeal of Haeckel's reverse migration theory (which positioned Indians as the first "conquering people" of prehistory), the Lemuria hypothesis found additional purchase in South India owing to its resonance with a well-known literary theme—first attested in medieval commentary on the Tamil Sangam corpus—concerning a series of floods which progressively diminished the coastal reach of the Tamil country. Nakkīraṉār, in his eighth-century commentary on the *Iṟaiyaṇār Akapporuḷ*, speaks of the "three Caṅkams" or literary academies of Maturai, Kapāṭapuram and "Upper Maturai" established by ancient Pāṇḍyan kings, which stood for 4400, 3700, and 1850 years, respectively, between the intervals of which each Caṅkam was sequentially lost by flooding from the sea.[59] Aṭiyārkkunallār elaborates in his twelfth-century commentary on the *Cilappatikāram*, explaining that forty-nine districts (*nāṭus*) of the Pāṇḍyan country were swallowed up by these successive floods, from the Paṉṟuḷi to the Kumari Rivers (implying that the ancient Pāṇḍyan kingdom extended a great deal farther south into the ocean than Cape Comorin, the present-day southernmost point of the Indian subcontinent). Later Tamil *tala-purāṇams* contain flood imagery as well, speaking of the survival of the temples with which they are associated through the most recent *pralaya*—the global flood inaugurating each "age of Manu."[60]

The scientific credibility lent by the Lemuria hypothesis to the motif of the loss of the three Caṅkams gave rise to a vision of Tamil dominion in deep antiquity of supra-regional extent, namely, a postulated kingdom of "Kumarināṭu"—a triangular continent which in its antediluvian state stretched from India to Madagascar to western Australia, the contours of which would receive increasing definition over the course of the twentieth century in the Tamil nationalist imaginary.[61] Forging an equivalence between Kumarināṭu and the ancient domain of Ravana required minimal effort on the part of Tamil commentators, who capitalized on the vexatious and underdetermined location of "Lankapura" in the Indian *Ramayana* tradition.[62] From the 1940s in Sri Lanka, Sinhala Buddhists associated with the "Hela Havula" ("Pure Sinhala Fraternity") movement produced a map of an ancient "kingdom of Lanka" with trans-hemispheric dimensions approximate to those of Lemuria/Kumarināṭu.[63] Somewhat ironically, twenty-first-century Sri Lankan researchers have appealed to one of the first published works in Tamil Nadu making an equivalence between Kumarināṭu and Ravana's kingdom, M. S. Purnalingam Pillai's *Ravana the Great* (1928), as they continue to embellish the Hela Havula account of Lankan geography in deep antiquity.[64] There are two passing observations to be made here: one concerning the remarkably parallel applications of the Lemurian hypothesis within two geographically adjacent twentieth-century South Asian indigenist–nationalist political imaginaries (Tamil and Sinhala). The second point—one which will be explored further in Chapter 5, section 4—concerns the fact that Purnalingam Pillai's *Ravana the Great* is now freely available in the public domain on the internet, making it in some sense unsurprising that the book would be haphazardly employed by contemporary Sri Lankan bricoleurs alongside so many other English language works of antiquated and speculative historiography circulating online. Placing these observations aside, however, we discover more nuanced questions relating to Sinhala–Tamil literary exchange historically through a closer look at other, pre-twentieth-century Sinhala sources invoked by present-day Sri Lankan Ravana enthusiasts as evidence for a prehistoric Lanka that was of substantially greater landmass.

These topographic and historical prose works, dating to the ascendant period of the Kingdom of Kandy (fl. sixteenth to eighteenth centuries), speak of the substantial reduction of Sri Lanka's size as a result of two catastrophic flood events: one occurring at the end of the war between Rama and Ravana, and the other in the early second century BCE. Sinhala works of the Kandyan period innovate on the Pali chronicles by introducing Ravana's reign as a historical epoch, one which ended 1,844 years prior to the enlightenment of the Buddha, narrating in addition that Ravana's "Lankapura" was flooded by the gods in retribution for his misdeeds, with "Ravana's fortress, twenty-five palaces, and 400,000 streets all overwhelmed by the sea."[65] Kandyan period Sinhala historical works introduce the flood motif again in relation to a later ruler of the island, Duṭṭhagāmaṇi's callous grandfather, King Tissa of Kalyāṇī (Kelaniya). These accounts expound upon the *Mahāvaṃsa*, which relates that Tissa cruelly put to death an agent of his younger brother, disguised as a Bhikkhu so that he might deliver a love letter to the queen. Enraged, the sea-gods caused the ocean to overflow the land, prompting Tissa to dispatch his daughter, Dēvī, alone in a golden vessel into the sea, to propitiate them. (Dēvī subsequently came ashore at Dondra in the southern kingdom of Rohaṇa, where she married King Kākavaṇṇa and gave birth to Duṭṭhagām aṇi).[66] The same texts add that the flood induced by Tissa's misdeed washed away a substantial portion of the island, reprising the retribution of the sea-gods following Ravana's demise. According to the *Vanni Rājāvaliya* (a modified version of the standard *Rājāvaliya*), even more of the eastern portion of the island was swept away by Araggat Deviyō (tutelary deity of the Kelaniya River), who was enraged by the king's Bhikkhu-cide: "Because of the unrighteousness of King Kälaṇitissa, a lakh of villages at Kälaṇiya, nine hundred seaports, four hundred and seventy fishing towns, twelve pearl diving towns and sixteen other towns belonging to Laṅkā were swallowed by the sea. Of the harbors, only Mannāra and Kaḍupiṭi Mādampē remained."[67] Historical works of the period emphasize that the contours of the island were of an altogether different proportion before Tissa's sin: the *Rājāvaliya* reveals that "eleven-twelfths of Sri Lanka were submerged by the sea."[68]

While story of a flood during the time of Kalyāṇa Tissa appears in the *Mahāvaṃsa*, the motif of the erosion of a major portion of Lanka over the course of one or more floods appears only much later (by the sixteenth century), at a time when other South Indian Puranic motifs also made an appearance in Sinhala literature and official documents.[69] From the fourteenth to the sixteenth centuries, Sinhala land grants (*sannas patra*), inscriptions, and poetic encomia (*praśasti*) associated with the courts of Gampola and Kotte innovated on stereotyped genealogies, declaring that their royal sponsors were descended from the lineage of Vaivasvata Manu (displacing Mahāsammata, a key dynastic figure in the Pali chronicle tradition, who was until then standardly named as the primordial monarch of Sri Lankan Buddhist dynastic chronology).[70] As will be discussed in detail in the following chapter, dramatis personae of the *Ramayana* also appear in Sinhala poetry, inscriptional discourse, and devotional life with regularity from the fourteenth century. Such an expanded, regionally cosmopolitan outlook in Sinhala literature and historiography was coincident with a sizable influx of South Indians into Sri Lanka as a response to demographic pressures on the continent, including the conquest of the Pandyan kingdom by the Muslim Khilji Dynasty in the first quarter of the fourteenth century. Buddhist political life on the island was simultaneously affected by continental Indian influence, notably within the Gampola Kingdom (1341–1406) and the court of Parakramabahu VI (r. 1410–1467) at Kotte. Gampola and the feudatories of the southwest and central highlands came to be dominated by two families of South Indian extraction—the Alakēśvaras (or Alagakkōṇāras) and the Meheṇavaras (or Mēṇavaras)—making Sinhala–Tamil bilingualism a routine aspect of courtly life in the island's predominantly Buddhist southwest.[71] The resultant influence of Tamil and Malayalam language, religion, and political culture on the kingdoms of late medieval southwestern Sri Lanka has been cataloged on a number of fronts.[72]

With respect to the transmission of literary themes across languages, occasionally the physical record provides a glimpse of the cross-fertilization process at work, as with the conspicuously Tamil-Malayalam names of the notaries of the courts of Gampola and Kotte (their status as transplants from a Tamil or Malayalam speaking environment also sometimes attested in their penmanship and notation of dates). The predominantly Buddhist courts of Sri Lanka's southwest did not conduct themselves in isolation from Tamil speaking regions of Sri Lanka during the late medieval and early modern periods, either. For seventeen years (between 1450 and 1467) Jaffna came under the rule of Kotte after being conquered by the son of Parakramabahu VI, Prince Sapumal, who along with his father was a generous patron of both Buddhist and Shaiva institutions indiscriminately.[73] Relevant to the specific question of the source of importation of Tamil Puranic themes and an interest in Ravana on the part of Sinhala speakers of Sri Lanka's southwest, there is also evidence that the Shiva temple at Koneswaram represented a significant religious destination for royals of Kotte. The *Kōṇecar Kalveṭṭu*, a seventeenth-century chronicle of Koneswaram, lists Prince Sapumal as a temple patron.[74] Fernão de Queirós, in his retrospective annal on the Portuguese conquest of Sri Lanka, describes a pilgrimage of Bhuvanekabāhu VII of Kotte (r. 1521–1551) to Shiva's abode at Koneswaram, where the king again retreated at the end of his life, ensuring that his "mortal remains were interred in Trincomalee where the sepulchres of ancient kings of the island were."[75] The significance of the temple to the kings of the southwest is again confirmed by Queirós when he describes the construction of a fort over its premises in 1622–1624, whereby the Conquistadors "turned into [a] defense of Christians that which was previously the abominable abode of his Idols and the honoured sepulchre of the Kings of Côta (Kotte) and of the others of Ceylon, or the urn of their ashes."[76]

The objective of this chapter has been to situate the reception of the *Ramayana* in Sri Lanka, in anticipation of a broader discussion in the forthcoming chapters concerning a more thorough domestication of the epic in the Sinhala literary tradition and public imagination. Here I have briefly discussed points of interface between Tamil and Sinhala speakers at the elite level of society, where Puranic themes and Tamil impressions of the historical status of the *Ramayana* in relation to the island of Sri Lanka may have been transmitted. Bilingualism, as well as cultural, religious, and literary exchange no doubt occurred in many social spheres of pre- and early modern Sri Lanka, a complete discussion of which is beyond the scope of this book. While the specific question of the transmission of the *Ramayana* has remained at a hypothetical level in this chapter, the following chapter will offer specific evidence for the Sinhala acquisition of Tamil impressions of Ravana at a more demotic level.

## Notes

1. For a treatment of Ravana's character in the *Vālmīki Rāmāyaṇa*, see Robert Goldman and Sally Sutherland Goldman's Introduction to *The Rāmāyaṇa of Vālmīki*, vol. VII, *Uttarakāṇḍa* (Princeton: Princeton University Press, 2017), 24–36. In the Āraṇya and Kiṣkindhā Kāṇḍas, Ravana is an obscure figure from the point of view of the main characters, with the whereabouts of his kingdom entirely unknown (prior to meeting Shurpanakha, Rama does not seem to have even ever heard of this provincial lord of the Rakshasas). By the Uttara Kāṇḍa, however, he is described as a mighty and learned king. If the Uttara Kāṇḍa stands as a later interpolation in which Rama was officially divinized, Ravana's elevation in status might be explained as an attempt to present him as a more formidable and worthy opponent. See R. Goldman and J. Masson, "Who Knows Rāvaṇa? A Narrative Difficulty in the *Vālmīki Rāmāyaṇa*," *Annals of the Bhandarkar Oriental Research Institute* 50, no. ¼ (1969): 95–98.
2. See P. S. Sundaram's translation in *Kamba Ramayanam: Sundara Kandam* (Tamil Nadu: Dept. of Tamil Development-Culture, 1989–1992), vv.1–79.
3. Shantilal Nagar, *Śrī Raṅganātha Rāmāyaṇa: Rendering into English from Telugu* (Delhi: B. R. Publication Corp., 2001), x.
4. Radhika Borde, "Did the Subaltern Speak?," in *Voices from the Periphery: Subalternity and Empowerment in India*, ed. Marine Carin and Lidia Guzin (London: Routledge, 2012), 281.
5. Joyce Burkhalter Flueckiger, "Standing in Cement: Possibilities Created by Ravan on the Chhattisgarhi Plains," *South Asian History and Culture* 8, no. 4 (2017): 461–477.
6. Aradhya Agnihotri, "Madhya Pradesh Towns Where Ravana Is Worshipped, His Death is Mourned," *Times of India* October 6, 2016, https://timesofindia.indiatimes.com/india/Madhya-Pradesh-towns-where-Ravana-is-worshipped-and-his-death-is-mourned/articleshow/54761295.cms; "In Sasural Mandsaur, Demon King Gives 'Permission' To Be Slain," *Times of India*, October 8, 2019, https://timesofindia.indiatimes.com/city/indore/in-sasural-mandsaur-demon-king-gives-permission-to-be-slain/articleshow/71484628.cms.
7. Siraj Qureshi, "A Dussehra Without Burning Ravana: This Brahmin Community in Agra Wants an End to Practice," *India Today*, October 12, 2016, https://www.indiatoday.in/india/story/raavan-vijay-dashmi-agra-saraswat-caste-brahmins-346178-2016-10-12; Neeraj Santoshi, "In MP's Ravan Village, The Demon King Is A Revered Deity," *Hindustan Times*, October 15, 2013, https://www.hindustantimes.com/india/

in-mp-s-ravan-village-the-demon-king-is-a-revered-deity/story-E5RYXcB30dt5Kv13nDdbEN.html.

8. M. S. Purnalingam Pillai, author of *Ravana the Great: King of Lanka* (Munnirpallam: The Bibliotheca, 1928), followed T. R. Shesha Iyengar and K. Subramania Pillai in making claims about the Dravidian implications of Harappa and Mohenjo-daro in *Tamil India* (Chennai: International Institute of Tamil Studies, [1927] 1999), 1–26.
9. On these claims in the Dravidian case, see Sumathi Ramaswamy, *Lost Land of Lemuria: Fabulous Geographies, Catastrophic Histories* (Berkeley: University of California Press, 2004), 113.
10. The Sundara Kāṇḍa of the *Vālmīki Rāmāyaṇa* describes Ravana's Laṅkāpuri as follows: "With its splendid white mansions, Lanka, set high on the mountain peak, looked . . . like a city in the sky. Hanuman gazed upon that city, built by Vishvakarman and protected by the lord of the Rakshasas, as if upon a city floating in the sky" (R. Goldman and S. Goldman, *Ramayana Book Five* [New York: NYU Press/JJC Foundation, 2006], 5.2.15–20 [73]).
11. R. Goldman et al., *The Rāmāyaṇa of Vālmīki: An Epic of Ancient India*, vol. VI, *Yuddha Kāṇḍa* (Princeton: Princeton University Press, 2009), sarga 30, vv.18–23 (195f.).
12. Sri Lanka, "the territory of the Siṃhalas" is identified as a separate location from Ravana's Lankapura in Rajashekhara's ninth- or tenth-century *Bala Rāmāyana*. The distinction between Simhala-dvipa and Trikuta Mountain is preserved in Bhoja's eleventh-century *Campū Rāmāyaṇa*. However, in the Yuddha Kanda appended later to the work by Laksmanasuri, Trikuta is referred to as "the torus of the lotus flower that is the island of Sinhala' (*siṃhala dvīpa kamala karṇikām*), in the *gadya* portion between verses 32 and 33. See Paramasiva Iyer, *Ramayana and Lanka*, part 1 (Bangalore: Bangalore Press, 1940), xi, xv. "Laṅkā" and 'Siṃhala' are listed as separate domains of the "southern division" according to Sanskrit topographical reckoning, including that of the *Mahābhārata* and Varahamihira's *Bṛhat-Saṃhita*. See J. H. C. Kern (ed.), N. Chidambaram Iyer (trans.), *Bṛhat-Saṃhita of Varaha-Mihira*, vol. 1 (Delhi: Parimal Publications, 2013), 14.11–16. On the geography of "Siṃhala Dvīpa" and "Laṅkā" in the *Mahābhārata, Markaṇḍeya Purāṇa*, the early eleventh-century *Tarikh al-Hind* of Al-Biruni, the *Golādhyāya Bhuvanakoṣa* of Bhaskaracarya, and the *Skanda Purāṇa*, see S. C. Paul, "Pre-Vijayan Legends and Traditions Pertaining to Ceylon," *Journal of the Ceylon Branch of the Royal Asiatic Society* 31, no. 82 (1929): 268–270.
13. M. A. Dorai Rangaswamy, *The Religion and Philosophy of Tevaram* (Madras: University of Madras, 1990 [1958]), 299.
14. See vv.3066–3067 of the *Araṇiya Kāṇṭam* of P. S. Sundaram's translation of the *Kamba Ramayanam*. Extensive description of Lankapura's geography is given in the *Cuntara Kāṇṭam* as well.
15. R. Dessigane and P. Z. Pattabiramin (trans.), *La légende de Skanda; selon le Kandapuranam tamoul et l'iconographie* (Pondichéry: Institut français d'indologie, 1967), 101ff.
16. In Venkatesha's fourteenth-century *Haṃsasandeśa*, Rama instructs his messenger bird to depart India "for the royal seat of the demon king Ravana on Trikuta Hill in

Lanka, the island country that appears and vanishes with the rising and falling ocean tides" (Steven Hopkins, *The Flight of Love: A Messenger Poem of Medieval South India by Veṅkaṭanātha* [Oxford: Oxford University Press, 2016], 56). Additional description of the island and city appears at vv.1.54–2.6 (the city of Lanka "stands on the sheer peaks of Suvela" [2.3]). The early fourteenth-century Keralan *Suka Sandeśa* references Rama's *setu* in the vicinity of Rameswaram (Sri Lanka is not explicitly mentioned) (N. P. Unni, *Sukasandesa of Laksmidasa* [Delhi: Nag Publishers, 1985], 35, 45).

17. G. V. Tagare, *Vāyu Purāṇa [Ancient Indian Tradition and Mythology Series, Purāṇas in Translation]* (Delhi: Motilal Banarsidass, 1987), 48.20–30. Because this description lies within the section of the text entitled the "description of Jambudvīpa's lands and islands, etc.," commentators have treated the location of "Malaya Dvīpa" ambiguously, with some identifying it with the southernmost tip of continental India (ibid., 312, n.3; S. Pathmanathan, *Facets of Sri Lankan History and Culture* [Colombo: Kumaran Book House, 2015], 550–554).
18. See *Cūlavaṃsa* 70.1–29, with notes in Geiger's translation.
19. E. Hultzch, *South Indian Inscriptions*, vol. 2 (Madras: Madras Government Press, 1891), no. 348.22. Chapter forty-seven of the *Cūlavaṃsa* confirms that a Lankan aspirant to the throne, Manavamma, was funded in his invasion of the island by one king Narasiṃha. Manavamma's second invasion was successful, and the chronicle dates his reign from 691 to 726 CE. Pallava inscriptions corroborate the war between Narasiṃhavarman I and Vallabha, the occupant of the Lankan throne deposed by Manavamma according to the *Cūlavaṃsa*.
20. On the significance of the *Ramayana* for fourteenth-century South Indian Vaishnava theology, see Ajay Rao, *Re-figuring the Rāmāyaṇa as Theology: A History of Reception in Premodern India* (Oxford: Routledge Press, 2015).
21. Paula Richman notes that, "in Tamil Nadu, the Thanjavur area has been closely associated with veneration of Rama as perfect king, especially during the Chola dynasty's imperial expansion" (Introduction to *Ramayana Stories in Modern South India: An Anthology* [Bloomington: Indiana University Press, 2008], 16).
22. Paul Younger, *The Home of Dancing Śivaṉ: The Traditions of the Hindu Temple in Citamparam* (New York: Oxford University Press, 1995), 216. For original text see *Tiruvicaippā* (§5, vv.7–8 (224–226).
23. W. M. K Wijetunga, *Sri Lanka and the Choḷas* (Ratmalana: Vishva Lekha Publications, 2003), 51–52.
24. R. S. H. Krishna Sastri, *South Indian Inscriptions*, vol. 3, part 3 (Madras: Madras Government Press, 1920), 398 (text) and 421 (trans.), v. 80. This inscription was written shortly after Rajendra's annexation of the northern portion of the island.
25. Rājendra Cōḷa III (r. 1246–1279) is remembered as "a very Rama of northern Lanka, renowned as the abode of the Vīra-rāksaṣas." K.A. Nilakantha Sastri comments: "this is clearly a reference to a campaign against the Śāmbuvarāyas, some of whom called themselves Vīra-rākṣasa and who held sway in the region of North Arcot" (*The Colas*, vol. 2, part 1 [Madras: University of Madras, 1975 (1937)], 202).
26. For a translation of the bridge episode in the Yuddha Kāṇḍa of the *Vālmīki Rāmāyaṇa*, see Goldman et al., *The Rāmāyaṇa of Vālmīki*: vol. VI, sarga 15 (154–156).

27. The earliest reference to any Setupati ruler in South India is from 1604 CE. See S. Thiruvenkatachari, *The Śetupatis of Ramnad* (Karaikudi: Dr. Alagappa Chettiar Training College, 1959), esp. 25–28.
28. A *ciṟappuppāyiram* of the *Cekarācacēkara-mālai* states that the Arya Cakravartis originated from Rameswaram, identifying them as belonging to the "Ganga" (*kaṅkai*) dynasty (S. Natesan, "The Northern Kingdom," in *University of Ceylon History of Ceylon*, ed. H. C. Ray, vol. 1, part 2, [Colombo: Ceylon University Press, 1960], 691).
29. F. Medis, "An Overview Of Sri Lanka's Mediaeval Coinage," *Journal of the Royal Asiatic Society of Sri Lanka* [New Series] 37 (1992/1993): 63–64, 67f. Medis speculates that the Tamil design (but not the *cētu* epigraph) was first copied from the "lion coins" of Parakramabahu I.
30. See A. Veluppillai, *Ceylon Tamil Inscriptions*, part 2 (Peradeniya: Royal Printers, 1972), 91–94, and S. Pathmanathan, *Ilaṅkait tamiḻc cācaṉaṅkaḷ (1300–1900)* (Colombo: Department of Hindu Cultural Affairs, 2013), 211–222.
31. *teṉilaṅkaipuri ticaitoṟu maruvum.* The use of *teṉ ilaṅkaipuri* to refer to "southern Lanka" exhibits continuity with the Chola designation of the island.
32. *muttamiḻ*, the three domains of Tamil composition according to the classical scheme: *iyal* (poetry), *icai* (song), and *nāṭakam* (drama).
33. Introduction to S. Patmanathan and K. C. Naṭarācā (eds.), *Takṣiṇa Kailāca Purāṇam*, vol. 1 (Colombo: Department of Hindu Religious and Cultural Affairs, 1995), xxi, citing a *ciṟappuppāyiram* of the *Cekarācacēkara-mālai*. Again, the king is referred to later in the body of the text as "Cekarāca Cēkaraṉ, utmost in learning, protector of the bridge (*cētu kāvalaṉ*)" (xxii). Pathmanathan gives a more complete citation in I. C. Irakunataiyar's edition of the *Cekarācacēkara-mālai*) in *Ilaṅkait tamiḻc cācaṉaṅkaḷ (1300–1600)*, 14, 220. On the dating of the *Takṣiṇa Kailāsa Purāṇam*, see Justin W. Henry, "Distant Shores of Dharma: Historical Imagination in Sri Lanka from the Late Medieval Period," PhD diss.: The University of Chicago (2017), 91–95.
34. *cētuvuyar karaik kāval pūṇṭvaṉ.*
35. *Takṣiṇa Kailāsa Purāṇam, Ciṟappuppāyiram*, i.
36. See C. S. de Silva and S. Pathmanathan, "The Kingdom of Jaffna up to 1620," in *History of Sri Lanka*, ed. K.M. de Silva, vol. 2 (Peradeniya: The University of Peradeniya, 1995), 105f.
37. Goldman et al., *The Rāmāyaṇa of Vālmīki*, vol. VII, *Uttarakāṇḍa*, sarga 13, vv.13–21.
38. Ibid., sarga 16, 1–31.
39. Ibid., 596, n.29.
40. See V. Murugan's translation in *Kalittokai in English* (Chennai: Institute of Asian Studies, 1999), 135 (no. 37).
41. See J. L. Shastra (ed. and trans.), *The Śiva-Purāṇa [Ancient Indian Tradition and Mythology Series, Purāṇas in Translation]* (Delhi: Motilal Banarsidass, 1970), 1366–1368.
42. See verses in S. Adi-p-Podi and T. N. Ramachandran, *Tirumurai the Sixth: St. Appar's Thaandaka Hymns* (Dharmapuram, Mayiladuthurai: Dharmapuram Aadheenam, 1995); see also Rangaswamy, *Religion and Philosophy and Tevaram*, 296. South Indian tradition explains this fact on the basis of Appar's insistence in a previous life that

Ravana sing praises to Shiva (David Shulman, *Tamil Temple Myths: Sacrifice and Divine Marriage in the South Indian Saiva Tradition* [Princeton: Princeton University Press, 1980], 322).

43. On eighth-century Pallava reliefs of Ravana lifting Mt. Kailasa at Kailāsanātha (Kāñcipuram) the Vaikuṇṭaperumāḷ Vishnu temple, and on the origin of the imagery at Mathurā in the fifth century, see Valérie Gillet, "Entre démon et dévot: la figure de Rāvaṇa dans les représentations pallava," *Arts Asiatiques* 62 (2007): 29–45.
44. In the Sanskrit *Śiva Purāṇa*, Ravana stops to urinate, entrusting the *liṅgam* to a cowherd who is unable to hold it for the duration (Shastra, *The Śiva-Purāṇa*, 1366–1368). In addition to being a name of the forest in which Shiva practiced his penance according to the Sanskrit Puranas, "Gokarna" (Tamil: *kōkaṇṇam*), is a place name associated historically with at least three Indian temples: Mahabaleswar, Kedaram in Bengal, and the Gokarna Temple of Mahendra Mountain in Kalinga (S. Pathmanathan, *Hindu Temples of Sri Lanka* [Colombo: Kumaran Book House, 2006], 57–58). Gokarna is also mentioned as the name of a mountain of uncertain location in the Sundara Kāṇḍa of the *Vālmīki Rāmayana* (Goldman and Goldman, *Ramayana: Book Five*, 5.34.73 [206]).
45. *Takṣiṇa Kailāsa Purāṇam, Tirunakarac carukkam*, vv.1–8.
46. Ibid., v.10.
47. Ibid., v.12, 15.
48. S. Arumugam, *Some Ancient Temples of Sri Lanka* (Colombo: Ranco Printers and Publishers, 1980), 36; K. Vaithianathan, "Thiruketheeswaram Temple and the Port of Mantota," in *Thiruketheeswaram Papers*, ed. K. Vaithianathan (Colombo: privately printed, 1960), 19–20. Vaithianathan adds that, according to local tradition, "Arjuna, the hero of Mahabharatha and the kinsman and disciple of Lord Krishna, also visited Thiruketheeswaram in the course of his pilgrimage to the South."
49. The story is found in the *Srī Muṉṉēśvara Māṉmiyam* (eighteenth or nineteenth century), as well as in the *Dakṣiṇa Kailāsa Mahātmyam*, a (most likely modern) Sanskrit work glorifying the Hindu temples of the island (Pathmanathan, *Hindu Temples of Sri Lanka*, 243–244; Rohan Bastin, *The Domain of Constant Excess*: Plural Worship at the Munnesvaram Temples in Sri Lanka [New York: Berghahn Books, 2002], 45). Many Shaiva temples on Sri Lanka's east coast also claim to be locations at which Rama stopped to perform religious rites in memory of the departed on his return to Ayodhya (Arumugam, *Some Ancient Temples of Sri Lanka*, 20, 75).
50. See Shulman, *Tamil Temple Myths*, 50f., and G. Sethuraman, *The Saiva Temple of India: A Study on Ramesvaram Temple* (Delhi: Sharada Publishing House, 2013), 25. In some accounts of the establishment of Rameswaram, Hanuman is dispatched to Varanasi or Mt. Kailasa to fetch a *liṅgam*. Philip Lutgendorf also records a rarer variant of the story, "in which the Śaiva brāhman Rāvaṇa is summoned from Laṅkā (sometimes accompanied by Sītā) to officiate as priest in the *sthāpanā* ritual" ("Hanumān's Adventures Underground: The Narrative Logic of a *Rāmāyaṇa* 'Interpolation,'" in *The Ramayana Revisited*, ed. Mandakranta Bose [New York: Oxford University Press, 2004], 152).
51. Shastra, *The Śiva-Purāṇa*, 1381–1384. Ramanathasvami Kovil at Rameswaram is one of twelve *jyotiliṅgam* temples throughout India, where Shiva is worshipped as a

physically manifest beam of light, represented by ancient *liṅgams*. The Sanskrit *Liṅga Purāṇa* also prefigures later Tamil temple literature, saying that Rama established a *lingam* at the seashore at Rameswaram after killing Ravana. The motif of Rama expiating the sin of killing Ravana at Rameswaram was known and clearly significant in Jaffna by the Portuguese period (Fernão de Queyroz, *The Temporal and Spiritual Conquest of Ceylon*, trans. S. G. Perera (New York: AMS Press, 1975 [1930], I.58). On Indian literature referencing pilgrimage to "Rama's bridge," see Phyllis Granoff, "Rama's Bridge: Some Notes on Place in Medieval India, Real and Envisioned," *East and West* 48, no. 1/2 (1998): 93–115. The story of the bridge's construction is the subject of Pravarasena's seventh-century *Setubandha.* Shankara's disciple Padmapada visits the bridge (at Rameswaram, after visiting Citambaram) in the *Śankaradigvijaya.* Other accounts of pilgrimages to the *tīrtha* of Rama's *setu* are later, from the sixteenth century onwards.

52. The resident Rakshasas departed the island upon Vibhishana's death, "from fear of foreign subjugation." See C. Brito, *Yalpana-vaipava-malai, or, The History of the Kingdom of Jaffna* (New Delhi: Asian Educational Services, 1999 [1879]), 1; and *Vaiyā Pāṭal,* vv.12–13. Dagmar Hellmann-Rajanayagam gives a comparative study of the two texts in "*Yāḻppaṇa Vaipava Mālai, Kailāya Mālai* und *Vaiyāp Pāṭal*: Kulturelle Wahrnehmungen in der historischen Literatur der Jaffna-Tamilen," *Zeitschrift der Deutschen Morgenländischen Gesellschaft* 164, no. 2 (2014): esp. 473. The eighteenth-century *Maṭṭakkaḷappu Pūrva Carittiram*, a Tamil history of Batticaloa, traces Lankan monarchy from Ravana's reign to the arrival of Prince Vijaya, saying (uniquely) that Rama remained to rule over Lanka instead of returning to Ayodhya after the battle. See *Maṭṭakkaḷappu Pūrva Carittiram*, ed. S. E. Kamalanathan and Kamala Kamalanathan (Colombo: Kumaran Book House, 2005), 1–4. This text is also known as the *Maṭṭakkaḷappu Māṉmiyam.* The text also says that the island's Shaiva religion dates from the time of Ravana, preserved until the arrival of Prince Vijaya.
53. Dennis McGilvray, "Mukkuvar vannimai: Tamil caste and matriclan ideology in Batticaloa, Sri Lanka," in *Caste Ideology and Interaction*, ed. Dennis McGilvray (Cambridge: Cambridge University Press, 1982), 72.
54. C. Sivaratnam, *Outline of the Cultural History and Principles of Hinduism* (Colombo: Stangard Printers, 1964), 255f. For the version of this refiguring of the *rāvaṇa anugraha mūrti* as it appears in the *Takṣiṇa Kailāsa Purāṇam*, see chapter six of the text, the *Tarucaṉāmuttic carukkam*, vv.103–135. Until recently, Ravana's mother was herself worshipped at the hot springs which bear her name several kilometers from Koneswaram. For a nineteenth-century account of this practice, see Tennent, *Ceylon*, vol. 2, 496f.
55. The *Kampa Rāmāyaṇam* is taught as a standard component of Tamil literature courses in secondary schools and universities in Sri Lanka today (A. Shanmugadas, "A Study of the Tamil Writings on Ramayana in Sri Lanka," *Padmam: Professor S. Pathmanathan Felicitation, Volume*, ed. V. Kanagaratnam et al. [Jaffna: Bavani Pathippakam, 2004], 259). On the Colombo "Kampaṉ Kaḻakam," see P. Sanmugeswaram et al., "Reclaiming Ravana in Sri Lanka: Ravana's Sinhala Buddhist Apotheosis and Tamil Responses," *South Asia: Journal of South Asian Studies* 42, no. 4 (2019): 16f.

56. Ibid., 12.
57. For an overview of secondary literature, see Justin W. Henry and Sree Padma, "Lankapura: The Legacy of the Ramayana in Sri Lanka," *South Asia: Journal of South Asian Studies* 42, no. 4 (2019): 727, n.2.
58. See Ramaswamy, *The Lost Land of Lemuria*, 101–112.
59. David C. Buck and K. Paramasivam, *The Study of Stolen Love: A Translation of Kaḷaviyal eṉṟa Iraiyaṉār Akapporuḷ with Commentary by Nakkīraṉār* (Atlanta: Scholars Press, 1997), 4–6.
60. David Shulman argues that these recollections of a primordial deluge in South India issue possibly from a shared source, participating in an archetypal theme of "renewed creation which follows upon the deluge" ("The Tamil Flood-Myths and the Caṅkam Legend," *Journal of Tamil Studies* 14 [1978]: 10f.). The *Maṇimēkalai* (c. sixth century) recalls the destruction of the port city of Pūkar in a massive deluge (even though a village by that name still exists at the mouth of the Kaveri River).
61. The name "Kumarināṭu" was first applied to the hypothetical dominion of the ancient Pāṇḍyas by V. F. Suryanarayana Sastri in 1903 (Ramaswamy, *The Lost Land of Lemuria*, 104f.). On the superimposition of regional topography, rivers, mountains, and cities on the imagined map of Kumarināṭu, see ibid, p.130.
62. On sympathetic treatment of Ravana in the context of the Dravidian movement, and on the imagined geographical extent of his kingdom in Tamil literature of the period, see K. V. Zvelebil, "Ravana the Great in Modern Tamil Fiction," *Journal of the Royal Asiatic Society of Great Britain and Ireland* no. 1 (1988): 126–134. The Sangam flood motif intersects with the legend of Ravana in Kacciyappar's c. fourteenth-century *Kanta Purāṇam*, which identifies Lanka (*ilaṅkai*) as an island far out into the ocean which was long ago lost to the waves (*Kanta Purāṇam* 3:4; cited in Alexander McKinley, "Making Lanka the Tamil Way: A Temple History at the Crossroads of Landscapes & Watersheds," *South Asian History and Culture* 11, no. 3 [2020]: 264).
63. See K. N. O. Dharmadasa, "A Nativistic Reaction to Colonialism: The Sinhala-Buddhist Revival in Sri Lanka," *Asian Studies: Journal of Critical Perspectives on Asia* 12, no. 1 (1974): 169. Arisen Ahubudu cites Alexander Kondratov's revived Lemuria thesis as his inspiration for a Lankan supercontinent of deep antiquity (*The Story of the Land of the Sinhalese (Helese)* [trans. of *Hela Deraṇa Vaga* (2005) by Nuwansiri Jayakuru] [Colombo: Stamford Lake House, 2012], 4–7).
64. Purnalingam Pillai's book appears often as a source cited by Sri Lankan "Ravana researchers."
65. Suraweera, *Rājāvaliya*, 15f., 21. The flood of Ravana's kingdom appears in contemporary Sinhala topographical works (*kaḍayim pot*) and poetry also, see discussion in Chapter 3, section 2 of this text.
66. *Mahāvaṃsa*, 22.13–22.
67. *Vanni Rājāvaliya*, 37. The text explains that Kelaniya was further inland from the sea at that time.
68. Suraweera, *Rājāvaliya*, 26. The *Lakvidiya*, a short Kandyan period Sinhala work on the origins of occupational caste and the administrative divisions of the island, records more precise and even greater dimensions of loss: "This Sri Lanka, first

inhabited by Yakshas and then by human beings during the time of the Buddha Gautama, was at that time seven hundred *yojanas* in circumference. Then, during the days of Kälaṇitissa, because the king caused the death of an innocent Thēra by putting him in a cauldron of boiling oil, the grief-stricken gods angrily submerged the king's territory with the waves of the ocean in order to destroy the world using their divine power. At that time, nine islands surrounding Laṅkā, twenty-nine districts, 35,504 villages together with great seaports, tanks, fields, gem mines, numerous living beings (legless, two-legged, four-legged, many-legged), structures such as *cētiyas*, shrine rooms, and monastic residences were all washed into the sea. Kälaṇiya, which was formerly seven hundred *gāvutas* away from the sea, now is at a distance of only one" (adapted from H. A. P. Abeyawardana's translation in *Boundary Divisions of Mediaeval Sri Lanka* (Mattegodagama: Academy of Sri Lankan Culture, 1999), 172, 208). The calculation runs that Sri Lanka extended 2,100 miles further west into the ocean than it presently does.

69. The *Mahāvaṃsa* (22.18–20) mentions a flood during the time of Tissa of Kalyāṇī as a result of the wrath of the gods, but not any erosion of land.
70. See Henry, "Distant Shores of Dharma," 70–77.
71. Both families, with their practice of matrilineal succession and stated connections to the city of Vañci, most likely emigrated from Kerala, perhaps sometime in the thirteenth or early fourteenth century.
72. For a list of references, see n.57 above in this chapter.
73. See Henry, "Distant Shores of Dharma," 79–82, 126–137.
74. The *Kōṇēcar Kalveṭṭu* numbers "Puvaṉēka-kayavāku" among the seven or eight historical patrons of Koneswaram, designating him "a member of our clan" (*eṅkaḷ kulattu*) (*Kōṇēcar Kalveṭṭu*, 110).
75. "From Calane he was taken to Cota, and thence to Triquillmale, where he had prepared his resting place, all making reverence to him in their fashion, for they say he died a great pagan" (de Queyroz, *Temporal and Spiritual Conquest*, vol. 1, book 2, 271, 296).
76. Ibid., vol. 2, book 4, 734–737.

# 3
# THE MANY RAMAYANAS OF LANKA

## 3.1 THE PRESENCE AND THE ABSENCE OF THE RAMAYANA

Anyone looking into the reception of the *Ramayana* in Sri Lanka is confronted with a paradoxical literary record. On the one hand, we hear of no Sinhala or Sri Lankan Tamil *Ramayana*, and the early Pali chronicles (the third- or fourth-century *Dīpavaṃsa* and fifth- or sixth-century *Mahāvaṃsa*) say nothing of the historicity of the epic, and nothing about it in relation to island. Noted historian Ananda Guruge goes so far as to proclaim that Sri Lanka "is unique among the countries of Southeast and South Asia in that the Ramayana neither has been nor is a part of the living cultural tradition."[1] All of this is despite the fact that Sri Lanka would seem a prime candidate to be the "southern Lanka" featured so centrally in the story, an association which indeed many Indians came to make over the centuries (see Chapter 2). On the other hand, the *Ramayana* was clearly known by Sinhala speakers from early on in Sri Lanka, its presence attested in the inscriptional record[2] as well as in Kumaradasa's sixth-century Sanskrit rendering, the *Jānakīharaṇa*.[3] Allusions to the epic appear in Buddhist historical works and medieval Sinhala poetry, and oral legends associate landmarks throughout the island with Rama, Sita, Hanuman, and Ravana. An overly sleepy person may be jokingly nicknamed "Kumbhakarna" by Sinhala speakers today, some of whom refer to the island's long-ago pre-Buddhist era as the "Ravana *yuga*."[4]

This chapter surveys late medieval and early modern Sri Lankan written sources relating to the *Ramayana*, tracing the gradual incorporation of Ravana's kingdom into Sinhala poetry, topographia, historical works, and folklore. Positive treatment of the *Ramayana* as a source of literary inspiration, moral instruction, and historical information marked a departure from traditional Sinhala Buddhist monastic attitudes toward the epic, which was (likely intentionally) excluded from the island's Pali chronicles,[5] and which furnished an enduring object of consternation for author monks.[6] Buddhist resistance to the *Ramayana* is documented as far back as the fourth or fifth

*Ravana's Kingdom*. Justin W. Henry, Oxford University Press. © Oxford University Press 2023.
DOI: 10.1093/oso/9780197636305.003.0003

century, when Buddhaghosa refers to the "Theft of Sita" (*sītā haraṇa*) as a "pointless story" (*nirattha kathā*), categorizing it along with the *Mahābhārata* as mere "senseless babble."[7] This appraisal is carried over in the c. twelfth-century Sinhala *Amāvatura* and fourteenth-century *Saddharmaratnāvaliya*, the latter of which speaks of "stories such as those about Rama and Sita" as hindrances to the realization of Nirvana.[8]

A less censorious attitude toward the epic begins to emerge in the late medieval period, which, as noted in the previous chapter, coincides with the appearance of Sanskrit and Tamil Puranic imagery in royal inscriptional discourse and encomia, no doubt at least the partial result of the ascent of several families of South Indian extraction in the ruling houses of Sri Lanka's southwest.[9] In the sphere of these royal courts from the fourteenth century, Vishnu, Vibhishana, and Lakshmana appeared among the "god kings" (*devi rajjuruvan*) or "warrant guardians" (*varan deviyō*) invoked as protectors of the realm, deputized by the god Shakra who had received permission to do so from the Buddha Gotama himself.[10] Recognition of the *Ramayana* narrative appears in this context in the fourteenth-century Sinhala *Mayūra Sandeśaya*, in which the author directs his peacock courier to Vibhishana's shrine at the Kelaniya Raja Maha Vihara (a Buddhist temple outside modern Colombo). The messenger bird is here to proclaim in supplication:

> I have come to worship at your splendorous feet, O Lord Vibhishana!
> May you, for the duration of this *kalpa*, watch over and ensure tranquility
> for the king [Bhuvanekabāhu V]
> Who is the pinnacle of all auspiciousness, his Queen, and the three brothers[11]
> Who show such might and resolve, and the many officers
> and ministers of all of them!
> Give them victory as was given to Rama, son of Dasaratha, and his army,
> such that he could extend his dominion in all ten directions!
> Grant them greater prosperity than is known even to Shakra, Vishnu,
> and to all the other gods whose dominion reaches
> in all the ten directions![12]

Indeed, Vibhishana's *devālaya* at Kelaniya and Vishnu's at Devinuvara (where he is locally known as Upulvan) would continue to feature as the points of departure and/or destinations of later Sinhala messenger poems (with one or both appearing prominently in nearly all of such poems until the eighteenth century).[13] Other Sinhala messenger poems (*sandeśa kavi*) make use of Rama's heroism as a simile-ready stock trope, a go-to *upamāna* with which the military prowess of a patron could be exalted. Superimposing the landscape of the *Ramayana* onto native soil, the author of the *Kōkila Sandeśaya* (c. 1450) describes the city of Jaffna as one in which:

> Lord Rama, King of the Gods, flourishes. In his body he shines with the color of the ocean as if it has struck thereon when the great bridge (*mahat setuva*) was constructed with great effort to convey the vast armies for battle against the Ten-necked One (Ravana).[14]

While *sandeśas* represent an elevated literary genre—composed by literati (in many cases, by Buddhist monks) and intended for audiences at the courts of Gampola and Kotte—the poems also offer a glimpse into the realm of circulation of epic stories among ordinary Sinhala speakers of the day. The *Girā Sandeśaya* (c. 1450–1460) presents a scene in which travelers visiting a rest house in the coastal town of Välitoṭa (modern Balapitiya) relate amongst themselves such legends:

> There were stories of Rāma and Sītā
> —passed along from person to person—
> the essence of which is given in various poems and dramas,
> and which are old, frivolous (*misadiṭu* = *mithyādṛṣṭi*) stories.[15]

While the author of this poem, most likely a student of the famed scholar monk Sri Rahula, cleaves to conservative monastic attitudes regarding the suitability of the epic as a subject of conversation among lay Buddhists, he betrays to us that the *Ramayana* was familiar to his contemporaries at large. Other hints regarding the popularity of the epic come from the *Sidat Sañgarā*, a fourteenth-century work on Sinhala grammar and poetics, which gives the short sentence "Rama slew Ravana" (*ravuḷā märī ramraja*) as an example of an "-ā" ending accusative case.[16] The common idiosyncratic Sinhala rendering of Ravana's name—*rāvaṇā*, ending with a long "ā"—may be a relic of its usage in verse composition, where short "-a" ending words are often arbitrarily lengthened for the sake of meter.

The remainder of this chapter considers additional references to the *Ramayana* in Sinhala verse and prose works of the fifteenth to seventeenth centuries, on the basis of which I argue that an elevation of Ravana's character took place both as a result of his domestication as a perceived historical king of the island, and as a result of interface with Sri Lankan Tamil Hindus who had already independently generated a sympathetic image of this traditional villain, as discussed in the previous chapter. I argue that formative Sinhala Buddhist impressions of Ravana—a number of which endure to the present day—were generated in large part through highly informal contexts; that is, through storytelling and the composition and augmentation of poetic verses, and not as a derivation from the canonical sources or "high *kāvya*" which one might expect (the *Vālmīki Rāmāyaṇa* or Kampan's Tamil version of the epic). On this basis, I argue that there is a precedent for the Sinhala Buddhist image of Ravana as *populist* in its orientation, as the establishment of Ravana's character in the Sri Lankan imagination during the early modern period appears to have been the result of exchange between ordinary people—largely outside of the purview of courts, salons, and monastic colleges.

## 3.2 THE RAMAYANA IN SINHALA LITERATURE AND FOLKLORE

The central characters of the *Ramayana* would go on to have independent mythological careers in Sinhala folklore and ritual texts, which incorporate a number of epilogues, sub-narratives, and variations on the epic unique to Sri Lanka. A prime illustration is the Kohom̆bā Kankāriya, a Sinhala dance drama, originally performed in the context of a ritual propitiating the deity Kohom̆bā. Kohom̆bā Kankāriya is significant in the present-day as the basis for curriculum in "Kandyan dance," now promoted as traditional Sri Lankan performance art through official state channels.[17] The *Kohom̆bā Yakkama*, the metrical text to which the drama is set, most likely took its final form in the vicinity of Kandy in the seventeenth or eighteenth century, although its core is tracible to the fifteenth-century court of Parakramabahu VI.[18] The frame story involves the plight of Paṇḍuvasdeva, Prince Vijaya's nephew and successor to the throne of Lanka, who had been cursed by the Yakkhiṇī Kuveṇi as revenge for having been so callously abandoned by Vijaya. The resulting terrible ailment which confined Paṇḍuvasdeva to his bed[19] could only be alleviated by foreign medical expertise, for which reason an Indian Prince named Malaya had to be brought over to the island by means of a subterfuge.[20] The story of Malaya's pedigree consumes a large portion of the text, beginning with an idiosyncratic story outline of the *Ramayana*, necessary because, as we learn, Malaya is Princess Sita's son. In this version, Rama has left Sita alone in the forest for seven years such that Rama might expiate the ill effects of having come under the influence of the planet Saturn, during which time he wandered about in the guise of an elephant. Sita, alone and vulnerable, was in the interim abducted by Ravana and taken to Lanka, where she promised him that they could be wed once her vow of chastity expired in three months. Rama, at the end of his seven years of penance, discovers Sita missing and enlists the help of Valin to retrieve her (Hanuman does not appear in the story), securing their alliance by killing the king of apes who had eloped with Valin's wife.

With several magical boons assured him by Rama (who is also simply called Vishnu in the text), Valin proceeds to Lanka and to Ravana's park, where Sita is being kept. Here, significantly, it is Sita who orders the guards to apprehend Valin, as his antics disrupt the pleasant time she is having with Ravana in his royal garden. The guards, so ordered, wrap Valin's tail with cloth, dip it in oil, and set it ablaze, leading to Valin's escape and the burning of the city. After Valin returns Sita to India, she conceives a child with Rama. Left at home as Rama attends an assembly of the gods, Sita is visited by Uma, who asks about her time in Lanka and about the appearance of Ravana. Sita sketches for her a portrait of Ravana on a plantain leaf, which is promptly discovered by Rama upon his return home. In a jealous fit, Rama orders his brother (here simply called "Saman") to take Sita out to the forest and behead her. Saman feigns completion of the task, leaving Sita near a hermitage in the Himalayas and returning with the blood of an animal on his sword. Helpless again in the forest, Sita is aided by the compassionate sage Vālamīga (Vālmīki), who builds her a leaf-hut by the pond of his ashram. Taking refuge there, Sita gives birth to her son, sometime later in one instance leaving him alone in the hut while going to forage nearby. Hearing the cries of the infant, Vālamīga enters the hut to discover the child lying on the ground. Unable to touch the child as a result of his Brahmacarya vow, the sage instead takes a lotus from the pond and throws it on the bed, where it transforms into a second, identical baby boy.[21] Having returned home and taken up the baby on the bed to nurse him, Sita is shocked and confused to find another baby crying beneath the bed. Beseeching Vālamīga for an explanation, the sage recounts what had happened to Sita's disbelief. Demanding proof, Vālamīga reproduces his miracle, this time creating a third child from a blade of sacrificial grass (*ītaṇa*), which Sita promised to suckle at the end of her finger. These three children, named Sañdaliñdu, Mala, and Kistrī,[22] were raised by Sita to the age of seven when they departed to the Malaya country (Kerala, the Malabar coast), where they established their reputations as royals, and came to be known as the "Malaya triplets."[23]

The Kohoṁbā Kankāriya, both as text and performance, serves as a reminder of the significant channel of cultural influence from southwestern India to Sri Lanka.[24] In the *Kohoṁbā Yakkama*, true to her name and in keeping with continental *Ramayanas*, Sita is born of a furrow in a ploughed field and discovered by King Janaka. Oral tradition identifies the corpus as having been transmitted by Ravana himself, in keeping with Sinhala impressions of the ancient king as a master of *mantras* and esoteric knowledge.[25] The *Kohoṁbā Yakkama* is also an example of the tendency in Sinhala literature and folklore to elevate Ravana at the expense of Rama, perhaps in an attempt on the part of Buddhist writers to, in John Holt's words, "cut Viṣṇu down to size," rendering him less of a transcendental deity in order that he might be absorbed within the Sri Lankan Buddhist deistic pantheon (the *deva-sāsana*, of which the Buddha is the head).[26]

A memorable instance of domestication of the epic comes in the derivation of the name of the kingdom of Sītāvaka (1521–1594), a feudatory which at its height encompassed much of the island's present-day Northwestern, Western, and Sabaragamuwa Provinces. The *Sītāvaka Haṭana*, a Sinhala poem written c. 1585 at the court of King Rajasinha I, relates that long ago "the noble king Ravana" secured his dominion over the whole of Lanka by massacring the competing feudal lords, ordering his men to fill a pot with the blood drawn from each of them.[27] A single one among his adversaries managed to escape into the jungle, where he contrived to fill a pot full of blood from his leg and leave it where Ravana's troops might find it, in hopes that this would satisfy them. After this duke had done so and fled to safety, the pot remained until some years later it was discovered by a group of farmers ploughing their field, where to their surprise the blood in the pot had transformed into a healthy baby girl. The perplexed farmers sought out an explanation from a nearby forest sage, who told them of Ravana's purge of the nobility, revealing himself to be the girl's father, and bestowing on her the name of "Sītā" ("furrow"). So, the poem explains, the Kingdom of Sītāvaka derived its name from this local event.[28]

The similarity of the *Sītāvaka Haṭana*'s rendition of Sita's birth to a common variation found in a number of Jain, Sanskrit, and Indian folk versions of the *Ramayana* serves as a reminder of the permeability of storyworlds in South Asia: in the *Vasudeva-hindi* of Sanghadasa, the *Uttara Purāṇa* of Gunabhadra, and the *Devi Mahābhagavata Purāṇa*, Sita is conceived by Ravana's wife, Mandodari, after Ravana collected the blood of a number of ascetics in a pot and induced her to drink it. (In these versions, fearful of a prophecy that Ravana will be destroyed by the baby child's future husband, Ravana and Mandodari abandon the infant Sita, whereafter she is discovered buried in the earth by Janaka, as in the *Vālmīki Rāmāyaṇa*.[29]) Beyond taking inspiration from Indian versions of the epic, the *Sītāvaka Haṭana* like other roughly contemporary Sinhala works embeds *Ramayana* episodes within the landscape of Sri Lanka, participating in a domestication of the epic which, as I argue below, would have enduring effects on Sinhala impressions of the island's history and topography. Legends associated with Sita in Ravana's custody endure in the vicinity of Sītāvaka's capital (modern Avissawella), including those concerning a cave where she was held captive ("Sītā Leṇa"), a nearby waterfall where she bathed ("Sītā Pīlla"), and a bend in the river (a tributary of the Kelaniya Ganga) where she disported.[30] Ravana's Lankan kingdom is given greater contour in the *Srī Laṅkādvīpayē Kaḍayim* ("Boundaries of the Island of Sri Lanka"), a short Sinhala prose work on the topography and administrative divisions of the island which circulated under a variety of titles, including the *Meraṭa Kaḍayim Pota* and the *Rāvaṇa Rājāvaliya*.[31] The bulk of the *Srī Laṅkādvīpayē Kaḍayim* is devoted to a description of the twenty-eight districts (*raṭa*s) of the Māyā Raṭa (central and southwestern Sri Lanka).[32] This text describes man-made boundary markers (*kaḍayim*) along with natural features and topography of the island. The physical descriptions of various towns and districts are supplemented with local lore and toponymic etymologies (*nirukti*s, "folk etymologies") explaining their histories, along with remarks on the dispositions of their inhabitants. The *Srī Laṅkādvīpayē Kaḍayim* is Buddhist in orientation throughout—naming temples, Bodhi trees, and other sites of devotional significance, and remarking on the degree of piety of the residents of various towns and districts. Its content and locus of geographical concern (in the island's southwest) indicate that the "Boundary Book" developed out of a prior text, the mid-fourteenth-century *Kurunāgala Vistaraya*, taking its final form in the late fifteenth century (at Kotte) or sometime in the sixteenth century (at Kandy).[33] Variations between recensions indicate that the text was recopied and modified locally over the course of the following several centuries. Its broad circulation in monastic collections suggests that it was viewed as a useful reference work, something like a short encyclopedia on the island's geography and places of historical interest. This is significant in light of the text's picture of the earliest history of the island, which represents a significant break from the Pali chronicles. The *Srī Laṅkādvīpayē Kaḍayim* begins with a short invocation to the Buddha, followed immediately by an account of the birth of Ravana: "The four *yugas* are those of Kreta, Treta, Dvapara and Kali. In this *yuga* which is one among those four, Pulasti along with the Asura Kanya gave birth to the king named Ravana."[34] The text continues with an account of his errant reign, during the course of which:

> he deviated from the law of kings (*rājadharma*)—without protecting the religious orders, without paying respects to gods, the Buddha, monks or Brahmins—he instead levied taxes on them, demanding something even from recluses and the Pacceka Buddhas (*pasē budun*) living at the top of Nandamūla Mountain. Thus he established one hundred kingdoms in Lanka, subordinated the Indian rulers, imprisoned the rulers of the *dēva*-world, *asura*-world, *garuḍa*-world, [and] *nāga*-world and levied tributes from them. He captured the kingly planets of moon and sun and forced them to serve him by shedding their light over his city.[35]

After a brief account of Ravana's reign and his defeat by Rama, the text goes on to explain that because of the demon king's wickedness, a massive flood engulfed the island after his demise, reaching all the way to Badulla and Kandy. We learn furthermore that Ravana's ancient citadel once lay to the north of the present shores of the island, between Mannar and Tuttukudiya (on the southern tip of India).[36] The *Srī Laṅkādvīpayē Kaḍayim* enumerates several other locations associated with the *Ramayana* war and Ravana's kingdom scattered throughout Sri Lanka's coastal southwest: Mädavelāna-rājjya, west of Dambadeni, where "breadfruit chips were made for King Ravana"[37]; Rā-gama, so named because infants drank toddy (rā) during the time of Ravana; Attanagalu, where Rama handed sovereignty of Lanka over to Vibhishana, and where a queen, prince, merchant and royal tutor were allowed to settle with their entourage by Rama at the conclusion of the war;[38] and several principalities ruled over by vassals during Ravana's time.[39]

In their recent analysis of the text, Jonathan Young and Philip Friedrich usefully situate the *Srī Laṅkādvīpayē Kaḍayim* in the context of Sri Lanka's late medieval southwest, discerning a "moral topography" superimposed upon the *kaḍayim*'s description of the various towns and cities of the central southwest (the "Māyā Raṭa"). They recognize the author's positive evaluation of the residents of the established centers of monastic learning and political power of the fourteenth and fifteenth centuries, wherein the cities of

Gampola ("Siňduruvana Raṭa"), Kelaniya, Attanagalu, and Matale are home to "virtuous persons" (*sat purusayō*), where "devoted and intelligent people" conduct themselves. This is contrasted with the settlement of the northern frontier of the Māyā Raṭa—the districts on the border of the Pihiṭi Raṭa along the Deduru Oya river basin, whose denizens are exemplary in deceit, lust, greed, and trickery.[40] Following from this observation, Young and Friedrich locate two messages intended for the established political elite of the island's southwest in the *kaḍayim*'s moral landscape. The first is a deployment of the destruction of Ravana's kingdom as an allegorical cautionary tale—a reminder that the fate of the kingdom of Dambadeniya (fl. thirteenth century) could befall either Gampola or Rayigama, if their citizens were to stray from *dharma* (in a religiously neutral sense), as had the demon-king of long ago. The second message reflects anxiety on the part of the elites of Gampola and Rayigama toward the ascendent political class of merchant and mercenary guilds, such as the *aiññūṟṟuvar*, originally of South Indian extraction. The morally ambivalent status of the northern districts containing "10,000 merchant towns" (*paṭunu gam*), still in the fifteenth-century vassals of the greater principalities of the southwest, is according to Young and Friedrich expressive of disruptive forces on the horizon, from which "political challenges to kingdoms in the southwest could be and were launched, incursions that were clearly read as threats to normative models of Buddhist kingship by authors in Māyā Raṭa's hinterland."[41]

Allegory aside, the *Srī Laṅkādvīpayē Kaḍayim* offers an important reference point with which to plot the gradual incorporation of Ravana's kingdom into Sinhala Buddhist conceptions of the island's distant past. The text signals that, contemporary with the emergence of literary references to the *Ramayana* in Sinhala poetry, oral legends concerning specific events described in the epic were beginning to find their way into written historiography and topography. The precise origins of the superimposition of the geography of the *Ramayana* onto Sri Lanka are impossible to trace, although there are intimations that such associations were being made centuries prior to the redaction of the *Srī Laṅkādvīpayē Kaḍayim*. "Polonnaruwa," the central seat of power from the late eleventh to thirteenth centuries, derives from "Pulastya Nagara" (Pali: Pulatthi-nagara)—Pulastya being the grandfather of Ravana and, according to the *Mahābhārata* and Sanskrit Puranas, the progenitor of all Rakshasas.[42] By the fifteenth century, the poets of Parakramabahu VI's court at Kotte had expanded upon the traditional genealogy of the island's Buddhist kings, deriving their patron's royal pedigree not from Mahasammata (the primordial king of the Pali *Aggañña Sutta*) but from Ikshvaku through to Dasharatha and Rama.[43] Influentially, the seventeenth-century Sinhala *Rājāvaliya*, the most cited vernacular chronicle among Sri Lankans today, assigns an exact date to Ravana's reign—1844 years before the Buddha's enlightenment.[44]

## 3.3 RAVANA'S MOUNTAIN ABODE

While *Ramayana* legends are found all throughout the island, myths concerning Ravana's capital city and the grove where he imprisoned Sita are clustered in Sri Lanka's remote highlands. Legends endure of the battle between Rama and Ravana in the vicinity of Mt. Laggala in the Knuckles Range, a mountain which locals believe to be the very basis for the name of the island, "Lak-gala," "Mt. Lanka."[45] The greatest concentration of Ravana *topoi* however appears further south, amid the mountains and hills lying between Nuwara Eliya, Sri Pada, Ella, and Balangoda. We can infer a number of reasons for this. In the westernmost quadrant of this "Ravana diamond," Sri Pada ("Adam's Peak") has functioned as a multi-religious pilgrimage attraction for centuries, offering a panorama of the surrounding landscape concerning which Hindus and Buddhists on their way to the summit no doubt traded legends and verses. The complex geology and natural beauty of the region—containing Sri Lanka's highest peaks, waterfalls, escarpments, plateaus, and a network of underground caves—stirred the imagination of Sinhala poets of the Kandyan era, among whom the misty expanse of what is now Horton Plains National Park secured its place as Ravana's pleasure grove, "Aśoka Vāṭika." As will be discussed further in the following chapter, the remote central highlands remain a fixation among modern Ravana enthusiasts who seek his treasures in the region's labyrinthine caverns. Discoveries of a heavy concentration of paleolithic human settlements (dating as early as 5800 BCE) in the southern corner of this region (around the Kalthota escarpment) now kindles speculation over the identity of the island's pre-historic people, including their equation with the "Yaksha tribe" of Ravana's alleged era.[46]

The high-elevation town of Nuwara Eliya—famous for its sprawling tea plantations—is today the epicenter of the "Ramayana Trail," home to the Seetha Amman Temple which receives busloads of Indian Hindu tourists daily (see Chapter 5). The current, renovated temple was opened in January 2000, over the site of a much smaller shrine, built by Indian Tamil plantation workers sometime shortly after Nuwara Eliya become a major outpost of tea production in the mid-1870s.[47] It is generally assumed that the locations associated with Sita and Ravana in this region came into vogue around this time, late inventions of the Tamil Hindu workers who staffed the region's plantations.[48] The *Srī Laṅkādvīpayē Kaḍayim* along with other Kandyan period "boundary verses" suggest to the contrary that centuries earlier locals had placed Ravana's great capital city here.[49] One Kandyan era *kaḍayim* poem traces the hills and rivers of the "upper Hävāhäṭa," a district bounded in the west by "Samanala Peak" (Sri Pada), and including the "mighty peak of Talāgala" (Pidurutalāgala, Sri Lanka's highest mountain), where to the east of Mt. Hakgala (just south of Nuwara Eliya) lies "the top of Sita Mountain (*sītā kaňdu*)," near to "Ravana's rock."[50] This mythic topography apparently endured in oral memory into the nineteenth century: while the area around Nuwara Eliya was virtually uninhabited in the reports of the earliest British expeditions,[51] Major Jonathan Forbes in his 1833 memoire gives an extensive entry on Nuwara Eliya and Sita Ella, calling the area "famous in the Ramayana and the most ancient Hindu legends by the appellation of Asoka Aramiya."[52] Forbes relates what his informants told him regarding the stretch of hills from Hakgalla (a mountain overlooking what is now Sita Eliya) to Adam's peak (a distance of thirty-seven kilometers as the crow flies), remembered by locals as the "pleasure-grounds of Ravana" (see Figure 3.1).

Charles Pridham, writing in 1849, fills out more of the legendary terrain of the region:

> In Upper Ouva, adjoining the rocks of Hakgalla, are the Nandanodiyana (pleasure grounds) and Asoka Aramaya (Asoka groves) of Rawana, which are Sanctified to Hindoo pilgrims, by the events of the Ramayan and the traditions of Rama and Seeta, which are still preserved by the Brahmins of Kataragama. This district included within the steep ranges of mountains in ancient legends, called the walls Rawana's garden, which extended from Samanala [Sri Pada] to Hakgalla, and from Pedrotalla-galla to Gallegammạ Kandé [Galle]. At the northern end Hakgalla mountain, the Seeta Talawa (plain of Seeta), where the goddess is said have been concealed with Trisida, the niece of Rawana, who was her sole companion. Hanuman, eluding the vigilance of the guards, contrived to penetrate their bower, and having delivered to Seeta the ring of Rama, with assurances that her release would be effected, he proceeded to set fire to the neighbouring forests. It was this conflagration which cleared Neuwara-ellia and other plains in this region

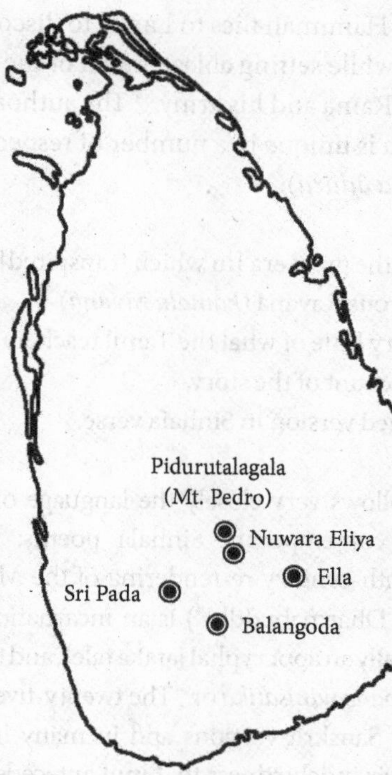


**Figure 3.1** The 'Ravana Diamond' of Sri Lanka's central highlands.—(Author generated image)

of genii [sic], according the Hindoo and Cingalese legends, and rendered them barren of useful productions.[53]

This legend, related through Pridham's local informants, is in fact an outline of a Kandyan period poem known as the *Rāvaṇa Katāva* (perhaps seventeenth century). The text is significant for a number of reasons, and it stands out for its essentially complete (although idiosyncratic) rendering of the "story of Rama and Sita"—making it is the closest approximation to a "Sinhala Ramayana" that has come down to us. The *Rāvaṇa Katāva* has never been published in print, for which reason I have included a translation based on the manuscripts available in public archives as an appendix to this book. The poem of some 120 Sinhala quatrain verses relates Rama's refusal of the advances of Ravana's sister, Surpanakha, whose nose Rama subsequently cuts off. Ravana abducts Sita in retaliation and keeps her captive in the central mountains of Sri Lanka. Hanuman flies to Lanka to discover Sita, is captured by Ravana, and escapes while setting ablaze much of the island, with further destruction wrought by Rama and his army.[54] The author credits the inspiration for the poem, which is unique in a number of respects, as deriving from "Tamil teachers" (*demala äduru*):

> Regarding the close of the great era [in which transpired] the war
> involving prosperous Ravana (*kamala rāvanā*)—
> Since we now know very little of what the Tamil teachers [knew],
> Unable to give a full account of the story,
> I will narrate an abridged version in Sinhala verse.[55]

This apologetic caveat follows very closely the language of introductory verses found in two roughly contemporary Sinhala poems: the *Mahāpadaraňga Jātakaya*, a late seventeenth-century re-rendering of the *Mahābhārata* in which Yudhisthira's character ("Dharmabuddhi") is an incarnation of the Bodhisattva (making the work essentially an apocryphal Jataka tale), and the *Vētālan Katāva*, an adaptation of the *Vetāla-pañcaviṃśatika* or "The twenty-five stories of the goblin" (famous in a number of Sanskrit versions and in many Indian vernaculars).[56] Both poems mention their indebtedness to Tamil antecedents, with the *Vētālan Katāva* referring to the basis of the composition as "a story belonging to the Tamil scholars of long ago" (*poraṇin demaḷ[a] ädurange katāvē*).[57]

The title of the poem itself is suggestive of the shift in perspective to that of an indigenous, Lankan mode—this Sinhala *Ramayana* is not a *Ram Kathā* but a *Rāvaṇa Katāva*, wherein a substantial portion of the dramatic narrative takes place from Ravana's point of view.[58] Ravana's relationship with his brothers is the subject of considerable dialogue, the conflagration of Lanka is described in extended detail, and the agony of Ravana upon seeing his kingdom ruined casts him as an almost tragic victim. Ravana is described as "one possessing great merit" (*maha pin äti*),[59] and in an impassioned plea from his brother Kumbhakarna imploring him not to go to war with Rama, the virtuous deeds of his life are recounted:

> O Ravana—who on that day brought the stone chariot speedily to your mother!
> O Ravana—who heard the plea of your dear wife [asking you] to create a son!
> O Ravana—do not go [to battle] with Rama and do not dispatch your sons!
> O Ravana—whose mother said that there is no other amid the three worlds
> to replace you![60]

The narrative of the poem is at times disjointed, partially a consequence of what appears to have been the author's attempt to integrate local legends regarding Ravana, Sita, and Hanuman. The author demonstrates knowledge of the *kaḍayim* book account of the extent of Ravana's kingdom, stating that he possessed "one hundred cities within this domain," and in the detail of Ravana's city being consumed by a flood.[61] The "garden of Sītāvaka" is mentioned as the location where Sita and Ravana first disembarked in Sri Lanka the day after she was abducted.[62] The poem furnishes an etiological myth for the origin of Horton Plains, a largely deforested tract stretching south from Nuwara Eliya to Aluthnuwara, explaining that no vegetation grows here as a result of Hanuman's destructive rampage, during which he rooted up all the trees and plants before him in the course of his escape. Novel to the *Rāvaṇa Katāva* is its conclusion, in which Ravana is not slain by Rama, but lives on to resettle with his few surviving soldiers amid the ruins of his citadel (*rāvanapura*), in what is today the Province of Uva, so named, according to these verses, after the sound of Ravana's dolorous cry upon witnessing the destruction of his kingdom:

Defeated, King Ravana summoned his army around him
Arms interlocked, their strength exhausted, the Asuras trudged on
Searching along the path he found a bit of hilly ground
Hopping from one dry spot to another Ravana and his loyal forces
    bore themselves up.

. . .

He rambled on sorrowfully gazing at the devastation of the city
Pacing about inconsolably as he saw all the various places that had been lost
There on the side of the mountain as he walked round the foot
    of the sole remaining tree
And in so doing the "land of ūva" came into being on that day.

Rama and his monkey allies, having reduced Sri Lanka to ruin
To their minds [a victory] as sweet as the taste
    of the choicest fruits of the forest
But walk behind the rock where the forces of the city
    of valorous Ravana stood

There you will find the "land of ūva"—the area adjacent to that
rooted up by Hanuman.

So King Ravana taking along his mighty army settled
at the garden there
[Harvesting] fruits [so delicious] it was as if they were gifts from heaven;
That garden, the place uprooted by Hanuman, became "Nuwara Eliya"
Where Ravana's army was laid to waste by the arrows of Upulvan.[63]

In addition to securing a definite location for Ravana's hoary domain, the author of the poem domesticates the ethnic identity of the "Asuras" in a verse describing the devastating first volley of Rama's bowmen:

In the east stood ready a thousand rows of archers
Ready with a thousand laks of arrows
Shining like lightening as they flew
Slaughtering and laying waste to the Sinhalas by the hundreds as they came.[64]

The *Rāvaṇa Katāva* goes on introduce a theme which figures importantly in twenty-first-century impressions of the topography of Ravana's Lankan kingdom—the suggestion that deep below his mountain citadel lay a vast underground lair, its entrances still discoverable amid the caves of the central highlands. In the course of the story, Hanuman, when captured by Ravana's guards, is led through an iron door "down a thousand steps into a chasm within the earth." The entrance to this subterranean portion of Ravana's kingdom was "concealed not far from Strīpura," and is called simply "Pātāle," "the underworld." (Strīpura, "the women's city" or Ravana's harem, we infer, remains on the map of the modern Ramayana Trail as the "Strīpura Caves," a cluster of caverns near the town of Kiriwanagama, nine kilometers east of Nuwara Eliya.) In the poem, Ravana then commands that Hanuman be offered as a sacrifice at the temple of Kali:

Deep beneath Lanka—endowed with *tejas*, power and might
Her lovely form inordinately pleasing to the mind
Resides Mahā Kālī, the woman who grants all that one desires
Within her temple where she receives regular worship—

Her legendary temple (*kovila*) which was infused with incense
Amid its wooden beams a place of many sacrifices
Where various scented coverings and banners were laid out
—here Hanuman was to be led inside.[65]

Marched off to the temple on Ravana's orders, Hanuman volunteers to enter Kali's shrine willingly, excitedly suggesting that the guards bring as many offerings of their own as they can, to make it a magnificent *pūjā*. Locked within the sanctum, a ravenous Kali emerges to first consume the piles of food brought by Ravana's troops, into which Hanuman had burrowed himself. With Kali full and incapacitated, Hanuman lets out an immense breath propelling him through a gap in the ceiling, where Kali had knocked a tile loose with her tongue. The episode reveals a probable source of influence on the poem in the form of a supplement to the *Ramayana* known in many Indian vernaculars in which Ravana has an additional brother—Mahīrāvaṇa or Ahirāvaṇa, who inhabits his own "subterranean Lanka" (*pātāḷa laṅkā*).[66] In Tamil South India this brother is known as "Peacock Ravana,"[67] his story recounted in numerous vernacular retellings of the epic, and whose enduring popularity is attested in the subject chosen for the third Tamil film ever made: *Mayil Irāvaṇaṉ* (1918).[68] In these iterations, Ravana is the king of the "southern Lanka," and his younger brother, Peacock Ravana, the sovereign of "Patala Lanka," a cavernous underground realm, its point of entry the stalk of an enormous lotus growing out of the middle of the ocean.[69]

In the *Mayil Irāvaṇaṉ Katai*, an early modern Tamil prose rendering of the tale, Ravana desperately appeals to Mayil Irāvaṇaṉ ("Peacock Ravana") to devise a plan to capture Rama and Lakshmana when he learns that his generals, his brother Kumpakarṇaṉ, and his dear sons have been slain in battle. Alerted to the threat, Rama and Lakshmana secure themselves in an impenetrable fortress fashioned out of Hanuman's coiled tail, its only entrance through his mouth and only exit through his ear. Unable to enter Hanuman's tail by force, Peacock Ravana takes on the guise of Vibhishana to gain passage and abduct the two brothers. The plot discovered, Hanuman makes haste to Patala Lanka to rescue Rama and Lakshmana from the sacrificial altar of Bhadra Kāḷi, Peacock Ravana's "family deity." There with the help of his long-lost son (Maccavallapaṉ, employed as a guard of the Kali temple) and Peacock Ravana's younger sister (Tūrataṇṭikai, a secret devotee of Rama), Hanuman is able to return Rama and Lakshmana to the world above. (Hanuman informs Kali—addressing her as the "great goddess of the earth"—that her younger sister Sita is being held captive above-ground, and that the three of them must be set free to save her.) Hanuman stays behind to battle Peacock Ravana, whose life-force he discovers is contained within five giant beetles dwelling deep within the caves at the furthest limits of his realm; Peacock Ravana is defeated when Hanuman finally discovers and crushes the beetles.[70]

One gets the sense throughout the *Mayil Irāvaṇaṉ Katai* that Patala Lanka represents a kind of inverted, negative image of terrestrial Lanka. While the story has nothing negative to say about Ravana (he only appears in the introductory frame narrative), Peacock Ravana is a wicked, fratricidal, master of the dark arts, reviled as a *caṇḍāḷa* by his younger sister Tūrataṇṭikai. Peacock Ravana's domain resembles his older brother's, with, for example, its own pleasure grove made of coral (the homologue of Ravana's Aśoka Vāṭika). Bhadra Kāḷi is the sister of Sita—each an embodiment of the earth goddess Bhūmi, one above ground and one below, we presume—and is also referred to as "the Pattiṉi of Patala Lanka."[71] The goddess Pattini has for centuries been a mainstay in Sri Lankan religious and ritual life—the only female warrant guardian (*varan deviyō*) of the island's Buddhist courts, and still today frequently honored with a *devālāya* on Buddhist temple premises. Rites of worship associated with Pattini were from the late medieval period essential in Sinhala village agricultural ritual. (As a reminder of another point of contact with the South Indian Tamil world, the goddess Pattini was herself originally Kannaki of the *Cilappatikāram*, still depicted holding her anklet aloft in her right hand in Sinhala Buddhist art and statuary.[72]) The Patala Lanka in this Tamil spin on "Hanuman's adventures underground" was then easily grafted onto a Sinhala *Ramayana* (or "Rāvaṇa Katāva") set in the cavernous mountains of Sri Lanka's central highlands. It would seem therefore that the "Tamil teachers" (*demala äduru*) mentioned at the outset of the *Rāvaṇa Katāva* were not, as we might expect, the greatest poets known from that literary tradition (specifically, that is to say, there is no indication that the *Rāvaṇa Katāva* was inspired in any way directly by Kampan's *Irāmāvatāram*). The *Mayil Irāvaṇaṉ Katai* is rather the written version of a story that circulated widely in Tamil oral tradition—a fun adventure featuring Hanuman, and precisely the kind of tale likely to have permeated the Tamil-Sinhala linguistic membrane of the Kandyan world at the level of ordinary people.

A final hint at the multilingual story-world out of which the *Rāvaṇa Katāva* emerged comes through repeated references to Ravana's aerial vehicle, here called his *gal rata* or "stone chariot."[73] Kumbhakarna's recollection of Ravana bringing the stone chariot speedily to his mother is however somewhat confusing—this is not an event recognizable from other *Ramayanas*, nor from the Sri Lankan Tamil *tala-purāṇams* of Koneswaram (where it is not his *chariot* that Ravana brings to his ailing mother but a portion of *Mt. Kailasa*). A sense then emerges of an author who possessed some indistinct knowledge of the famous episode associated with Koneswaram, who went on to conflate the extracted portion of Shiva's mountain with Ravana's routine vehicle. If the *Rāvaṇa Katāva* was, as we assume, written by a Sinhala speaker somewhere in upcountry Sri Lanka in around the seventeenth century, with some (although perhaps not extensive) knowledge of versions of the *Ramayana* and images of Ravana circulating among his Hindu contemporaries, then it makes sense that we would encounter inexact reproductions of impressions of Ravana popular among Sri Lankan Tamils.

## 3.4 THE SURVIVAL OF RAVANA'S KINGDOM IN POPULAR IMAGINATION

The significance of the perdurance of Ravana's kingdom in Sri Lankan popular imagination will become apparent throughout the following two chapters, which explore the demon-king's legacy as a literary figure in modern Sri Lanka, along with unremittingly positivist interpretations of the literary record seeking to resurrect Ravana as a historical king of deep antiquity. I have above in this chapter parenthetically noted instances of centuries-old Sinhala literature and folklore being preserved (or resuscitated) in the "Ramayana Trail," and will in this concluding section continue to build the case that the events of the *Ramayana* had secured a place amid Sinhala Buddhist perceptions of Sri Lanka's distant past well before Ravana's twenty-first-century revival.

Crucial early testimony to the status of Ravana's kingdom in Sinhala Buddhist historical imagination comes in the *Temporal and Spiritual Conquest of Ceylon* by Fernão de Queirós, a Jesuit chronicler, which is a reflection on 150 years of Portuguese dominion in Sri Lanka. Queirós, who never himself visited Sri Lanka, wrote from Goa in the 1680s, basing his work on firsthand accounts and correspondence of Portuguese agents, collected since their arrival in Sri Lanka in 1506. The informants of the Portuguese clearly perceived the *Ramayana* as a seminal event of the island's past, with the version of events related by them intersecting in places with the Sri Lankan Tamil *tala-purāṇam* tradition.[74] In the legendary series of events related by Queirós, Ravana returned to Sri Lanka with Sita in tow, whereupon he first "took to the port of Triquilimalê [Trincomalee]; and inhabiting and cultivating the land, they gave it the name 'Lancave' which means distant and delightful land."[75] Rama's bridge, too, is described in factual terms, with Queirós relating that Rama sought Ravana "with a powerful army, and making a bridge for his passage across the shoals of Chilaõ and the Island of Manâr, had marched as far as Palachêna, near the port of Negombo."[76] Following the defeat of the Rakshasas, the retrieval of Sita, and the immolation of Ravana's headquarters at Seytavâca (Sītāvaka), in the account of Queirós informants as in the standard rendition of the epic, Rama returned north to his own land. In commemoration, "heathendom built the pagode of Raman-coir (Rameswaram) on a small island, which is the beginning of those shoals, and is separated by the channel Vtiar [sic]."[77]

The version of events related to Queirós has an odd alternative ending, although one which is noteworthy in its correspondence with the *Rāvaṇa Katāva*, and insofar as it still circulates among Sinhala Buddhists today:

> [Ravana], seeing himself defeated and dishonored, carried away by his feelings, hid himself in the lands of Mayogâma in the borders of Sofragaõ and bewitched the gold and silver from the mountains, that they might never more be seen or found. . . . In one of these mountains, they say, he fell asleep, and is still sleeping, believing that he who offers a sacrifice of the husk of a *nêle mari* (*nêle* is rice in the husk) and of the oil of the coco, will wake him and heal him of the wounds which so many centuries ago he received in battle.[78]

Queirós' account concludes with the remaining Magi (Rakshasas) going on to live another 372 years on the island until, apparently, they were expelled by Prince Vijaya and his party. During this time, they built "sumptuous edifices, of which no memorial is found except for a labyrinth in the country of Biligal-Corla in the village of Columbua, which means the abode or dwelling-place of nymphs." The collocation in Queirós' account of the Hindu temples at Koneswaram and Rameswaram, together with Sītāvaka and the allusion to Ravana's subterranean lair, suggest that by the time he was writing Sri Lankan impressions of the events of the *Ramayana* consisted in a well-forged alloy between sites of significance to Tamils in the northern kingdom and Sinhala speakers of the island's southwest.

By the late nineteenth century, Sinhala Buddhist authors spoke comfortably of the historicity of Ravana's kingdom, as well as the terrain of Sita's captivity specific to the Nuwara Eliya region. The anonymous author of one lengthy Sinhala prose rendering of the epic from this time, dating probably to the 1880s or 1890s, preserved on ola leaf at the University of Peradeniya Library, mentions what he or she understood to be a longstanding oral tradition associated with Sita around the vicinity of Nuwara Eliya:

> A number of places are found in Sri Lanka famous for their connection with the memory and name of Sita Devi: Sita Falls, Sita Lake, and so on. . . . In the short distance between Nuwara Eliya and Haggala, the ancient places where an Indian princess known as Sita Devi was kept are heard by way of stories passed down through word of mouth (*mukhya paramparā kathāven*). Sita Devi, wife of the venerated Indian king Rama, was kept confined in the palace of the king named Ravana, who himself belongs to the lineage of guardians of Lanka during the era of kings (*laṅkāvē rajakala rāksa gōtrayaṭa ayat rāvanā*).[79]

The author goes on to take a familiar cartographic tour of the vicinity of Sita's upcountry area of incarceration, including one intriguing local legend still known to the people of Nuwara Eliya:

> In the town of Sita Eliya there are the ruined remains of a temple to Shiva (*naṭabunu vū īsvarālayak*)—a *kovil* which is now decrepit and in which the various statue images . . . have gone to a thorough state of decay. It is located on the ridge atop the mountain which is above the waterfall there. Taking this place as a starting point, I'll list now the places which can be found here relating to the time of Sita Devi, strewn throughout the three domains of Lanka[80]: the place where King Ravana cast water, the place where his head was struck upon the rock by the princess—here amid the wild trees where warm water flows upon the slope is Sita Lake. In the vicinity there is a rock where moon-like Rama searched for his wife, where waves of elephants patrol, where Sita was held at the command of importunate (*akala*) Ravana. Entering into that rock by way of the door and making your way across the ledge, not far from Sita Lake there is a rock named Koṇḍagala, where it is said that Sita would comb her hair. There is amid the cold climate of

> Nuwara Eliya a variety of small black balls (*kaḷuguli vagayak*) possessing the taste of a similar kind of food of the Himalayas, and which sometimes upon seeing the villagers will pick up, and, having grilled them in fire and broken them open with their feet, call them "Sita cakes" (*sītā käta*).[81]

The legend that Ravana kept Sita captive in the vicinity of Nuwara Eliya endures in region today, along with an explanation for the origins of the common marble sized ferrous rocks littering the rock slopes ("the variety of small black balls"), which are said to be the fossilized remains of rice-flour cakes given to Sita by Ravana for refreshment. Tamil speakers of Nuwara Eliya call the rocks *rāvaṇa mōtakam* ("Ravana's rice cakes"); Sinhala speakers, in further association with this legend, explain that nearby Mt. Haggala derives its name from Ravana's food offerings to Sita, *aggalā* being the word for a dessert made of flour and jaggery (akin to Indian *laddu*).[82] For the author of this nineteenth-century Sinhala *Ramayana*, such accounts "passed down through word of mouth" were, if not accurate in every detail, still rooted in some historical truth. The author avers that "Sita Devi was in Sri Lanka many thousands of years ago,"[83] and clarifies on the final folio that what is here recorded—"that ancient tale of the Ramayana" (*e rāmāyanaya purāna* [sic])—"is found in Lankan history" (*laṅkā itihāsaye labāgannā*).[84]

Oral memory of Ravana and Sita were preserved by lay and monastic Buddhists alike in the upcountry, as attested in Ven. Davuldena Gñānissara's 1987 Sanskrit poem *Yatidūtam* ("The Messenger Monk"). Ven. Gñānissara (1915–2017) was born in the village of Davuldena in the upcountry district of Badulla, going on in later life to become the Chief Prelate or Mahānāyaka of the Amarapura Nikaya, one of Sri Lanka's three Buddhist fraternities. At the age of twelve he was ordained at the nearby Thapovanārāma Vihāra in Sapugolla, half-way between Badulla and Nuwara Eliya, in the heart of Uva Province and the Ravana diamond. *Yatidūtam* is an fascinating work in its own right, a modern example of *sandeśa kāvya* in which the messenger, an unnamed junior monk, is directed to travel from his remote upcountry monastery to Colombo in a Jaguar car, in order to beseech the prelate of the Vidyodaya Pirivena to order the island's patron deities to protect the nation against the Liberation Tigers of Tamil Elam (President J. R. Jaywardene, his family, and a number of other ranking politicians receive extended *praśasti*s in the poem). Gñānissara instructs his envoy en route to:

> worship at the town called Sītāloka (Sītā Eliya), which is very cool and which is known throughout the land for its beauty by way of its many people and palaces—the place which was long ago the citadel of Ravana, Lord of Lanka, where for several years Sita was subjected to cruel treatment in the Ashoka garden.[85]

Acknowledging the devotional significance of the place for Tamils, he goes on in the following verse to say:

> On a rocky area in that town, nearby to the Sītā River, may your eyes be graced by the splendor of "Sītā Devī Temple," built by faithful Tamil people (*bhaktihotoḥ draviḍajanatā*), which is decorated with various murals, and where the sound of the jingling of anklets rings out perpetually. (v.52)

Like the author of the nineteenth-century Peradeniya prose *Rāmāyaṇaya*, Gñanissara adds local color to his description:

> There is a popular story about this place regarding Sita, the daughter of Janaka and wife of Rama, who bathed along with her friends in a certain lotus-pond which is upon the summit at a densely wooded place upon the mountain peak—a pond which is even today watched over by Asuras. (v.42)

Gñānissara urges the messenger monk on his way to pass through Divirumpola (another stop on the twenty-first-century Ramayana Trail), the place where Sita "entered into the middle of a fire showing the purity of her soul."[86]

Another cluster of *Ramayana* sites appears on the southern coast of the island, in the vicinity of Hambantota. The *Rāvaṇa Katāva* gestures to the legends of this region, briefly mentioning an escape attempt by Sita and her retrieval by Ravana. While imprisoned at the pleasure grove somewhere in the central highlands, "not far from Samanala Mountain," Sita one day ran off:

> In order to bathe at Hambantoṭa rock
> Where she found herself encircled by a net of flames
> Within which Ravana caught sight of her
> Jumping in [he swam] to where he saw the hair of her head.[87]

Today, not far to the east along the coast from the port city of Hambantota, eleven kilometers offshore amid the Great Basses Reef are a series of atolls, the largest of which is simply named "Ravana." Local lore here usurps the highland claim to Ravana's citadel, maintaining that the atolls are the remains of the peaks of Lankapura after his capital and the balance of the island were swept away by the sea. Associated folklore is attested in the writings of R. L. Brohier,[88] as well as in a later-life travelogue of Leonard Woolf, a civil servant in British Ceylon from 1904 to 1911 and husband of author Virginia Woolf. Woolf returned to the island in 1960 to travel with a Sri Lankan friend who had served under him as a provincial revenue officer; the details of their reunion and travels around the southern coast were later related to Wijesinghe Beligalla and published in 1995. Their informants identified a number of landmarks which transposed Ravana's domain onto the stretch of coast around Hambantota: Ravana's palace was located at Usangoda (fifteen kilometres west of Hambantota); Velipatanvila (in Usangoda, now home to the luxury Ravana Garden Hotel) was a landing strip for his flying machine; Abarana Ella (a waterfall in Hambantota) was Ravana's harem, where his concubines tragically committed suicide upon learning of their king's defeat at the hands of Rama.[89] Travelling further west along the coast, Rhumassala Kanda in Galle is remembered as a portion of the mountain transported to the island by Hanuman, containing the medicinal herb needed to cure a wound sustained by Lakshmana in battle.[90] (This recalling an episode contained in the *Vālmīki Rāmāyaṇa*, in which Hanuman hastens to the vicinity of the mountains Chandra and Drona to retrieve the rare Sanjeevani plant—unable to identify it, he transports the entire mountain back to Lanka.[91])

Finally, another set of legends centers in the remote mountains of the Knuckles Range north of Kandy, there espoused by locals who self-identify as descendants of the "Yaksha clan." The notion that a contingent of the island's pre-Vijayan inhabitants survived in the island's central interior is at least a millennium and a half old, attested in the *Mahāvaṃsa* account of the flight of the Yakkhiṇī Kuvaṇṇā's two children to the "Malaya-raṭṭha."[92] Here villagers today identify Mt. Laggala as the site of Ravana's ruined citadel, an association for which there is a two-hundred-year-old pedigree. When Maj. Jonathan Forbes visited the region on an expedition in 1832, he recorded this verse recited by his guide:

> Here stern Ravan was vanquished, and in that dread hour
> Lakagalla was rent by the conqueror's power,

> It was Rama's keen shaft cleft the mountain in twain,
> And Lak'galla's bright lake made a desolate plain.[93]

In their recent survey of the present-day legends of Meemure (a small village near Mt. Laggala), Tharaka Ananda and Charmalie Nahallage note that the villagers of Meemure identify as descendants of King Ravana, calling themselves members of the *yakṣa gōtraya*, the "Yaksha clan." A local deity, Kälē Baṇḍāra (not to be confused with the god Däḍimuṇḍa, also called Baṇḍāra Deviyō), villagers believe to have been the grandfather of Ravana, an ancient king of the island.[94] Ananda and Nahallage further report:

> According to the inhabitants of Meemure, king Ravana and his strongest *yaksha sena athma* (souls of the Yaksha armies) were there to protect the village. They have very strong fear of, and faith in, the Lakgala Mountain where they believe the souls of these armies live . . . In the Meemure village many of the *devivarayo* and *yaksha pirivara* (groups of Yakshas) are considered supernatural beings who were once human.[95]

The authors also record three verses, "well known among the older generation in Meemure," which identify Laggala as the place where Ravana kept Sita hidden, explaining that the mountain itself showed Rama the path to her during his rescue mission.[96] In the town of Ranamure, opposite Meemure at the base of the northern slope of Mt. Laggala where some residents also believe themselves to be descended from the "Yaksha clan," Baṇḍāra Deviyō is identified directly with Ravana, and is today venerated in this capacity during the annual festival of "Rāvaṇā Yakkama."[97]

***

In a demonstration recorded for television broadcast by The Royal Institution of Great Britain in January 1992, biologist Richard Dawkins explained to his studio audience the most probable course of the evolution of the animal eye. Postulating that the organ began as a small patch of photoreceptive skin cells, around which a protuberance to focus light gradually developed, Dawkins concludes that, far from being an impossible or improbable adaptation, eyes likely evolved independently in many species, and may even have been lost and regained in single species due to selective pressures over the course of time:

> Eyes can evolve at the drop of a hat. And in fact, if we look around the animal kingdom, there are lots of eyes dotted around—each of them is different, many of them work on completely different principles, and they have evolved quite independently of each other, many times over.[98]

In Sri Lanka, there is more than one Ravana's citadel, more than one Aśoka Vāṭika, more than one "Sita Falls." Landmarks of intrigue or arresting beauty—misty mountain peaks, labyrinthine networks of caves—invited narrativization from locals and passersby, for whom familiar "stories of Rama and Sita" provided a natural source of inspiration. Like the animal eye in Dawkins' account, *Ramayana* topographies in Sri Lanka developed independently and idiosyncratically, tailored in conformity with the landscape onto which they were superimposed. We hear today of a Lankapura at Nuwara Eliya, Avissawella, Hambantota and Laggala, but how many others must there have been? How many local *kaḍayims*, legends, and verses were passed down for generations but never came to the attention of travelogue writers, ethnographers, or manuscript editors? In addition to the Sinhala examples outlined in this chapter, there are legends associated with Rama's activity preserved in Tamil speaking regions of the island, concerning which future ethnographic research remains a desideratum.[99] The *Srī Laṅkādvīpayē Kaḍayim* itself contains an implicit recognition of the complex mythic stratigraphy of Ravana's kingdom in Sri Lanka, giving a detailed description of a portion of the ancient king's domain in the vicinity of Kurunegala, but only vaguely gesturing to the location of his ancient citadel as being now underwater, somewhere in the ocean between Mannar and Tuttukudiya.

The seductiveness of the *Ramayana* as a template for emplaced mythmaking surely owed to the fact that, in the first place, the epic is a fun story (*too fun* from the point of view of the Buddhist monks who for the better part of 1500 years spoke censoriously of it[100]), and, secondly, owing to the fact that the *Buddhist* landscape of Sri Lanka was already severely overdetermined by the monastic chronicle and commentarial traditions. The opening chapter of the *Mahāvaṃsa* records the specific locations visited by the Buddha Gotama during his three trips to the island, the basis of what would later be incorporated into the *solos-mahāsthāna* or "sixteen great places," foci of Buddhist devotional traffic in Sri Lanka still to this day.[101] By contrast, the *Ramayana*s of India left the contours of Ravana's Lankapura—a mountain citadel somewhere in the southern ocean—free to be discovered and expounded upon by any who chose to do so. Certainly Sri Lankans were not unique in making the *Ramayana* their own—local cities are identified with Ayodhya and other significant places described in the epic in Javanese, Malaysian, Vietnamese, Cambodian, and Thai versions as well.[102] The Sri Lankan case is unique however in the extent to which such emplacement remained at the level of informal storytelling, never canonized or hypostatized until the unveiling of the map of the Ramayana Trail by the Ministry of Tourism in 2008—a map that reflects a highly diffuse *Ramayana* topography generated by centuries of local myth-making.

In its treatment of vernacular Sinhala iterations of the *Ramayana*, this chapter works to overcome a fixation on the Pali chronicle tradition which has led scholars until now to focus solely on the *absence* of the epic from the Sri Lankan Buddhist literary record. Heinz Bechert, for instance, argues that the Mahavihara authors of the *Mahāvaṃsa* consciously excluded any historical narration derived from the *Ramayana* in order to maintain the primacy of Sinhala Buddhist political and religious life in the text.[103] Richard Gombrich similarly maintains that the absence of the *Ramayana* in Pali historiography reflects Theravada Buddhist hostility toward its Brahmanical Hindu values.[104] Steven Collins offers a novel argument to suggest that there was no need for a *Ramayana* among Sri Lankan Buddhists because the Pali *Vessantara Jātaka* was able to serve as a kind of substitute, being a narrative made up of the same basic story-matrix.[105] My discussion above does not necessarily contravene the arguments of Bechert and Gombrich, who are certainly correct in recognizing occasional hostility toward non-Buddhist ritual and theology on the part of medieval Sri Lankan monastic authors.[106] My intention is here to highlight the fact that, alongside monastic opprobrium toward the Hindu epics, we can reconstruct a keen interest among lay Buddhists in relating the landscape of the island to the *Ramayana*, received as it was by them through informal channels, bypassing any conservative censorship on the part of Buddhist monks intent on preserving the *Mahāvaṃsa*'s strict historical chronology (wherein Sri Lanka's history begins with the Buddha Gotama and with Prince Vijaya, forebearer of all subsequent Sinhala kings).

## Notes

1. Ananda Guruge, "Sri Lankan Attitude to the Ramayana: A Historical Analysis," *Indological Taurinensia* 19–20 (1993–1994): 131.

2. The names of several of lay donors related to "Rama" are attested in epigraphs recording gifts to the Buddhist Sangha dating from the third century BCE to the first century CE, including Ramadataya (Rāmadattā, a queen) and Sona, son of Ramajhata (Rāmajāta, a village or clan headman) (S. Paranavitana, *Inscriptions of Ceylon, Containing Cave Inscriptions from 3rd Century B.C. to 1st Century A.C. and Other Inscriptions In The Early Brāhmī Script* [Colombo: Department of Archaeology, 1970], vol. 1, 3, 62). An inscription dating to the first year of the reign of Sena II (c. 846 CE) mentions two officers of the king named Kaṇṇā (Kṛṣṇa) and Rāvaṇā (S. Paranavitana, "Viyaulpata Pillar-Inscription," *Epigraphia Zeylanica* IV.4, no. 21 [London: Oxford University Press, 1937], 176–180).
3. See introduction to K. C. Swaminathan, *Jānakīharaṇa of Kumāradāsa* (Delhi: Motilal Banarsidass, 1977).
4. G. Obeyesekere and A. Tissa Kumara's introduction to the *Rāvaṇa Rājā*valiya (Colombo: Godage International Publishers, 2005), 9. The term "Rāvaṇa yugaya" in this sense appears at v.8 in the c. seventeenth-century *Rāvaṇa Katāva*, see translation in Appendix.
5. See Heinz Bechert, "The Beginnings of Buddhist Historiography: *Mahavamsa* and Political Thinking," in *Religion and Legitimation of Power in Sri Lanka* (Chambersburg, PA: Anima Books, 1978), 1–12.
6. While the *Mahāvaṃsa-Cūlavaṃsa* draws from the epic to furnish similes and allusions, it denies the *Rāmāyaṇa* and *Mahābhārata* status as "historical works" (*itihāsa*). See *Cūlavaṃsa* 64: 42–44. The *Cūlavaṃsa* refers to "the Rāmāyaṇa and Bhārata" as "worldly stories" (*lokiyā kathā*), giving Duṣyanta's exploits (i.e., in the *Śakuntalā*) as an example of "itihāsa." In the Sanskrit commentarial tradition, the *Vālmīki Rāmāyaṇa* was traditionally regarded as *kāvya* (in fact the *ādi-kāvya* or "first poem"), and the *Mahābhārata* as *ākhyāna* or "story literature" (Gary Tubb, "Śāntarasa in the 'Mahābhārata,'" *Journal of South Asian Literature* 20, no.1 [1985]: 143). The *Harivaṃśa* section of the *Mahābhārata* is classified by the tradition as *itihāsa* or "legendary history." For a list of allusions to the *Ramayana* in the *Mahāvaṃsa/Cūlavaṃsa*, see C. E. Godakumbura, "Rāmāyaṇa in Śrī Laṅkā and Laṅkā of the Rāmāyaṇa," *Journal of the Royal Asiatic Society of Sri Lanka* [New Series] 59, no. 2 (2014): 61f.
7. References occur in Buddhaghosa's *Papañca Sūdanī* and *Sumaṅgalavilāsinī*. See Alastair Gornall, *Rewriting Buddhism: Pali Literature and Monastic Reform in Sri Lanka, 1157–1270* (London: University College London Press, 2020), 146 and 164, n.10.
8. A. Seneviratne, "Rama and Ravana: History, Legend and Belief in Sri Lanka," *Ancient Ceylon: Journal of the Archaeological Society of Ceylon* 5 (1984): 229. The *Saddharmaratnāvaliya* takes this statement from Buddhaghosa directly. Gurulugomi's c. twelfth-century *Amāvatura* declares "pointless stories such as the *Mahabharata* and *Ramayana*" (*barata rāmāyaṇādi nirarthaka kathā*) to be, like the teachings of the "lowly Nigaṇṭhas," "neither practical nor re-examinable." See Udaya Meddegama's translation in *Amavatura: The Flood of Nectar* (Colombo: Central Cultural Fund, 2006), 98; Sinhala text in *Amāvatura*, 93.
9. See discussion in Chapter 2, section 4 of this text.

10. On Vishnu-cum-Rama's ascension in the Sinhala Buddhist pantheon, see John C. Holt, *The Buddhist Viṣṇu: Religious Transformation, Politics, and Culture* (New York: Colombia University Press, 2004). On Vibhishana as a guardian deity, and on the history of his *devālaya* at the Kelaniya Raja Maha Vihara, see Sree Padma, "Borders Crossed: Vibhishana in the Ramayana and Beyond," *South Asia: Journal of South Asian Studies* 42, no. 4 (2019): 747–767. A record of an inscription at the Sabaragamu Saman Dēvāle dating to c. 1449 identifies Saman as Lakshmana. S. Paranavitana argues that this identification was made on the basis of homophony between "Lakṣmaṇa" and "Las-Saman," a possible Sinhala epithet of Saman as "god of the (the Buddha's foot-) print." See S. Paranavitana, "God of Adam's Peak," *Artibus Asiae* [Supplementum] 18 (1958): 27f. The *Jinakālamālinī*, a Pali work written in Chiang Mai in 1516, remarks that the island of Laṅkā was protected by four powerful divinities: Sumanadevarāja, Rāma, Lakkhaṇa, and Khattagāma (i.e., Kataragama, Skanda). See S. Paranavitana, "Religious Intercourse between Ceylon and Siam in the 13th–15th Centuries," *Journal of the Ceylon Branch of the Royal Asiatic Society* 32, no. 85 (1932–1934): 192f. There are other later occasional literary equivalences made between the god Saman and Lakshmana, as in the c. seventeenth-century *Rāvaṇa Katāva* (see Appendix and below in this chapter), the *Rāma Rāvaṇa Yuddhaya*, and the mid-eighteenth-century *Śirōpādaya nohot Saman Devi Varṇāva*. While we are not justified in assuming this association to be widespread, Alexander McKinley records a conversation with a present-day Kapurala of the Sri Pada Hatton-Trail Saman shrine wherein the priest made a clear association between Saman and Lakshmana ("Mountain at a Center of the World," PhD diss.: Duke University (2018), 156–162).
11. The Alakeśvara brothers of Rayigama: Alagakkōnāra (Alakeśvara), Äpā (Vīrabāhu), and Dēva Swāmi (see *Mayura Sandēśaya*, ed. R. A. Liyana Āracci [Colombo: Samayavardhana Pothala Samāgama, 2007], vv.66–71, 155).
12. *Mayura Sandēśaya*, v.38. The poem was written at some point between 1360 and 1391, probably by a Buddhist monk of Dharmakīrti's school at Gaḍalādeniya.
13. See Justin W. Henry, "South Indian Influence, Religious Cosmopolitanism, and Multilingualism in Sinhala *sandeśa* Poetry," *Linguistic and Textual Aspects of Multilingualism in South India and Sri Lanka [Collection Indologie 147, NETamil Series 8]* (Pondichéry: École Française d'Extrême-Orient/Institut Français de Pondichéry, 2021), 759.
14. Translation in E. T. W. Sumanasuriya, "A Critical Edition of the *Kokilasandesaya*," PhD diss.: University of London (1958), v.258.
15. *Girā Sandeśaya*, v.114. Other conversation at the rest house described in the poem includes discussion of the Buddha's virtues, making tales of Rama and Sita frivolous by comparison.
16. James Gair and W. S. Karunatillake, *The Sidat Saṅgarā: Text, Translation and Glossary* (New Haven, CT: American Oriental Society, 2013), sūtra 4.5 (40f.).
17. For a historical and ethnographic study of the canonization of Kohom̆bā Kankāriya as intangible cultural heritage, see Susan Reed, *Dancing the Nation: Performance, Ritual, and Politics in Sri Lanka* (Madison, WI: The University of Wisconsin Press, 2010).

C. E. Godakumbura clarifies that the text of the *Kohom̆bā Yakkama* was known only to performers of the Kohom̆bā Kankāriya rite in a few upcountry villages, and it was not by any means widespread in oral tradition (Godakumbura, "Rāmāyaṇa in Śrī Laṅkā," 56).

18. On the dating of the *Kohom̆bā Yakkama* and related literature, see Anurudha Seneviratne, "Kohom̆bā Kaṅkāriya: A Traditional Ritual in the Hill Country of Sri Lanka," in *Studies in South Asian Culture*, Vol. II [Senerat Paranavitana Commemoration Volume] (Leiden: E.J. Brill, 1978), 205–214.
19. *Divi dos*, the name of Paṇḍuvasdeva's affliction, means either "the leopard disease" or "the disease of one's life."
20. The story of Rāhu taking the form of a boar to lead Prince Malaya to Lanka also appears in the seventeenth-century *Rājāvaliya*, where there is an allusion to Malaya's parentage by Sita in referring to him as "the prince brought up by the queen who took flight on a peacock machine (*monara yaturu*, or (alt. ms.) *dan̆ḍumonara yantraya*)." *Rv*, 172; see Suraweera, *Rājāvaliya*, 20. Another Sinhala poem which relates the story, the *Malayarāja Kathāva*, explains that the curse fell to Panduvasdeva because he had in assuming kingship taken up the sword of his predecessor Vijaya (Seneviratne, "Kohom̆bā Kaṅkāriya," 205f.).
21. Seneviratne argues sensibly that this origin story of the Malaya children is derivative of that of Kusa and Lava, the twin sons of Rama and Sita who appear in the *Ramayana* ("Kohom̆bā Kaṅkāriya," 209).
22. "Kistrī," metathesis for "Kit-śrī."
23. A summary of the plot along with excepts and translations of the *Kohom̆bā Yakkama* are given by C. E. Godakumbura in "The Rāmāyaṇa: A Version of Rāma's Story from Ceylon," *The Journal of the Royal Asiatic Society of Great Britain and Ireland* 1 (1946): 14–22. Mudiyanse Disanayaka compiles a number of verse works related to Kankāriya rites, accompanied by an analysis of literary figures contained in them in his *Kohom̆bā Yak Kaṅkāriya Kāvya Sāhityaya* (Colombo: Godage International Publishers, 2018 [1998]). A list of manuscripts related to *Kohom̆bā Kankāriya* preserved in the Hugh Nevill Collection of the British Library is given by Tissa Kariyawasam in his study of ritual ("The Rāmāyaṇa and Folk Rituals of Sri Lanka," *Journal of the Royal Asiatic Society of Sri Lanka* [New Series] 59, no. 2 [2014]: 102).
24. Keralan impact on pre- and early modern Sinhala literature, music, and drama is a subject on which a good deal more scholarly work is yet to be done. Anurudha Seneviratne and James Sykes have, for instance, both observed similarities between the form and original applications of *Kohom̆bā Kaṅkāriya* and Keralan Kathakali, both "enactments of legends" performed in village settings through extended performances, taking an entire day or even days. See Seneviratne, "Kohom̆bā Kaṅkāriya," 211; James Sykes, "The Musical Gift: Sound, Sovereignty and Multicultural History in Sri Lanka," PhD diss.: The University of Chicago (2011), 193, n.81. On the relationship between Keralan Kaḷarippayaṭṭu and related forms of martial arts in Sri Lanka, see Chapter 6, section 1.
25. This according to one of Beryl De Zoete's informants in the 1950s (*Dance and Magic Drama in Ceylon* [London: Faber and Faber, 1957], 165).

26. Holt, *The Buddhist Viṣṇu*, 141.
27. The phrase "noble king Ravana" (*pavara rāvaṇa niriňdu*) appears twice at v.125 in the *Sītāvaka Haṭana*.
28. *Sītāvaka Haṭana*, vv.125–132.
29. Suvira Jaiswal, "Historical Evolution of the Ram Legend," *Social Scientist* 21, no. 3/4 (1993): 91. On other versions of the epic in which Ravana features as Sita's father, see A. K. Ramanujan, "Three Hundred Rāmāyaṇas: Five Examples and Three Thoughts on Translation," in *Many Rāmāyaṇas: The Diversity of Narrative Tradition in South Asia*, ed. Paula Richman (Berkeley: University of California Press,1991), 35–37; and contributions to K. S. Singh and Birendranath Datta (eds.), *Rama-katha in Tribal and Folk Traditions of India* (Calcutta: Anthropological Survey of India; Seagull Books, 1993).
30. Gamini de S. G. Punchihewa, *A Lost Medieval Kingdom of "The Lion King"* (Ratmalana: Vishva Lekha, 2003), 75f., 102.
31. The *Srī Laṅkādvīpayē Kaḍayim* is edited and translated by H. A. P. Abeyawardana in his *Boundary Divisions of Medieaval Sri Lanka* (Mattegodagama: Academy of Sri Lankan Culture, 1999). Abeyawardana lists twelve manuscripts as sources. The *Meraṭa Kaḍayim Pota* and the *Rāvaṇa Rājāvaliya* are edited by Gananath Obeyesekere and Ananda Tissa Kumara in *Rāvaṇa Rājāvaliya saha Upat Kathā* (Colombo: Godage International Publishers, 2005). The *Srī Laṅkādvīpayē Kaḍayim* is attributed to one Giratalane Unnanse by popular tradition (A. Kulasuriya, "The Minor Chronicles and Other Traditional Writings in Sinhalese and their Historical Value," *The Ceylon Historical Journal* 25 [1978]: 23).
32. Māyā Raṭa makes up along with Pihiṭi and Ruhuṇu (Rohaṇa) Raṭa-s the traditional three-fold geographical division of Sri Lanka (together constituting the island as the *Tri Siṃhaḷa*). The term is first attested in an inscription of Niśśaṅka Malla (r. 1187–96) (D. M. de Zilva Wickremasinghe, "Galpota Slab-Inscription," *Epigraphia Zeylanica II* [London: Oxford University Press, 1928], 106 [§B line 8]). "Tisīhala" first appears in the fourteenth-century portion of the *Cūlavaṃsa* (81.46; cf. 81.15, n.4). By the fifteenth century, these divisions no longer corresponded to any actual domains of political control, adding to the evidence that the *Srī Laṅkādvīpayē Kaḍayim* is concerned principally to tell a story of the island's imagined past rather than to document geographical realia.
33. On the composition and probable dating of the *Srī Laṅkādvīpayē Kaḍayim*, see Henry, "Distant Shores of Dharma," 55–58, there referred to as the "standard *kaḍayim*."
34. *Srī Laṅkādvīpayē Kaḍayim* (text in Abeyawardana, *Boundary Divisions*, 155). All published recensions of this text agree in their phonetic rendering of "*rāvaṇā*," in keeping with a curious but widespread middle period Sinhala orthographic choice.
35. See Abeyawardana's translation in *Boundary Divisions*, 191, and *Rāvaṇa Rājāvaliya*, 33.
36. The seventeenth-century *Rājāvaliya* makes the same assertion as to the location of Ravana's citadel, now lost to the sea (Suraweera, *Rājāvaliya*, 25f.). There are several avenues of interpretation open in considering this single aspect of the expanded scope of the island's ancient past in the *Srī Laṅkādvīpayē Kaḍayim* and *Rājāvaliya*. Placing

Ravana's capital city somewhere between Sri Lanka and the subcontinent may have been an attempt to hedge between the location of Ravana's "Lanka" as Sri Lanka itself, and the traditional, nondescript representation of "Lankapuri" (situated at the peak of Trikuta Mountain, somewhere in the southern sea) in Indian *Ramayana* literature.

37. *Srī Laṅkādvīpayē Kaḍayim*, translation in Abeyawardana, *Boundary Divisions*, 199.
38. Ibid., 196.
39. Kumburugomu Raṭa (near modern Katuṇayake), "a royal city in the age of Ravana" (ibid., 194; *RRv*, 37); Kuruṇāgala, over which a certain king ruled during Ravana's time (ibid., 200); Kalyānapura (Kelaniya), the residence of Vibhishana (ibid., 195).
40. Jonathan Young and Philip Friedrich, "Mapping Lanka's Moral Boundaries: Representations of Socio-Political Difference in the *Ravana Rajavaliya*," *South Asia: Journal of South Asian Studies* 42, no. 4 (2019): 775.
41. Ibid., 777.
42. Polonnaruwa is called "the Kalinga city of Pulastipura" in the inscriptions of Niśśaṅka Malla (r. 1187–1196) (Wickremasinghe, "Galpota Slab-Inscription," 106 [§B, line 7]; "Prīti-Dānaka-Maṇḍapa Rock-Inscription," *Epigraphia Zeylanica II* (London: Oxford University Press, 1928), 169–171 [lines 8 and 36]).
43. Henry, "Distant Shores of Dharma," 74–76.
44. Suraweera, *Rājāvaliya*, 15f. The *Rājāvaliya* also expands on the *Srī Laṅkādvīpayē Kaḍayim*'s flood episode, remarking that a major portion of the island was eroded when the flood receded, with "Ravana's fortress, twenty-five palaces, and 400,000 streets all overwhelmed by the sea" (21).
45. T. Ananda and C. Nahallage, "Unique Religious and Cultural Practices as Evident in the Kandyan Village of Meemure," in *Selected Papers from the International Conference of the Humanities 2015*, ed. K. Herath and D. Fernando (Faculty of Humanities, University of Kelaniya, 2016), 74.
46. See discussion of the work of Raj Somadeva in Chapter 5, section 2. Somadeva et al. review the finds associated with paleolithic settlements around Kalthota in *Kaltota Survey—Phase I* (Colombo: Postgraduate Institute of Archaeology (PGIAR), University of Kelaniya, 2015), 1–4.
47. Sir Edward Barnes built a sanatorium for soldiers on the Nuwara Eliya plateau, which in 1847 brought Samuel Baker, who established "Baker's Farm," a nearly exclusively European enclave in Nuwara Eliya. The first roads to Nuwara Eliya were macadamized in 1874 (S. N. Breckenridge, *The Hills of Paradise: British Enterprise and the Story of Plantation Growth in Sri Lanka* (Colombo: Stamford Lake Publication, 2001), 191–194).
48. See for example Rohan Bastin, "Hindu Temples in the Sri Lankan Ethnic Conflict," *Social Analysis: The International Journal of Social and Cultural Practice* 49, no. 1 (2005): 49.
49. The *Srī Laṅkādvīpayē Kaḍayim* speaks of the island being inundated by the sea following Ravana's defeat, involving a flood which reached all the way to Mahānuvara (Kandy), Badulla and Alutnuvara (Abeyawardana, *Boundary Divisions*, 203).
50. H. U. Prajñāloka Himi, *Purāṇa Sivpada Saṅgrahāva* (Colombo: Government Press, 1952), 7. Liyanwela and Diyaheruma are some twenty kilometers north of Nuwara

Eliya, bordering what is now Victoria Randenigala Rantembe Sanctuary. Mā-oya, along with the Mahaweli one of the "boundaries of Upper Hēvāhäṭa," is located to the northwest of these towns.

51. In his *An Account of the Interior of Ceylon, and of Its Inhabitants: With Travels in That Island* (London: Longman, Hurst, Rees, Orme and Brown: Paternoster-Row, 1821), John Davy relates that Nuwara Eliya was devoid of inhabitants, being a domain of wild animals and overlaid with elephant dung: "All I could collect from the natives with me amounted to this—that the Pattan was never inhabited, and that, except for the passing traveler, it is visited only by two descriptions of men—by the blacksmiths of Kotmalé, who come in the dry season to make iron, and by the gem-renter and his people in quest of precious stones" (480). Sita Eliya, the small hamlet home to the Seetha Amman Temple today, first appears in the official census only in 1881 (it is not registered in the census of 1871). Sita Eliya's population in both 1881 and 1891 was forty people (A. C. Lawrie, *A Gazetteer of the Central Province of Ceylon*, vol. II [Colombo, G.J.A. Skeen, 1898], 795).
52. Jonathan Forbes, *Eleven Years in Ceylon, Comprising Sketches of the Field Sports and the Natural History of That Colony, and an Account of Its History and Antiquity*, vol. II (London: Richard Bentley, 1840), 114; see extensive entry on 128–132.
53. Charles Pridham, *An Historical, Political and Statistical Account of Ceylon and Its Dependencies*, vol. I (London: T. and W. Boone, 1849), 23f., n.2. During her time on the island at the turn of the twentieth century, Constance Gordon-Cumming compiled a number of *niruktis* of place names in the Nuwara Eliya region: Yakka-galla, Deewuran-gaha ("the tree of the oath"), Malegawa-tenne ("the palace-flat" where Ravana once had a palace), Nanda-nodiyana (Ravana's "pleasure ground") (*Two Happy Years in Ceylon*, vol. 1 [London: Chatto & Windus, 1901], 149). Sita Ella ("Sita Falls") and the legend of Hanuman are given on page 134. An elaborate *Ramayana* mythology of the Nuwara Eliya region is recounted by Donald Obeyesekere in *Outlines of Ceylon History* (Colombo: The Times of Ceylon, 1911), 3f.
54. For a summary, see K. D. Somadasa, *Catalogue of the Hugh Nevill Collection of Sinhalese Manuscripts in the British Library*, vol. 5 (London: The British Library, 1993), 196f.
55. Appendix, *Rāvaṇa Katāva*, v.3.
56. The *Vetāla-pañcaviṃśatika* appears in the *Bṛihatkathā* of Kshemendra and the *Kathāsaritsāgara* of Somadeva, and in Tamil in the *Vētāḷa Katai* and *Vikkiramātittaṉ Katai*. Kamil Zvelebil notes that "the story (or stories) of *Bṛhatkathā* might have been popular in [the Tamil] country at least from [the] 8th c. onwards" (*Lexicon of Tamil Literature* [Leiden: E.J. Brill, 1995], 551).
57. *Vētālan Katāva*, v.39. See also C. E. Godakumbura, "The Dravidian Element in Sinhalese," *Bulletin of the School of Oriental and African Studies* 11, no. 4 (1946): 840f.; and C. E. Godakumbura, *Sinhalese Literature* (Colombo: The Colombo Apothecaries' Company, 1955), 178–182.
58. On local Indian *Ramayanas* referred to as *Ram Kathās* or "stories of Rama," see Paula Richman's introduction to *Ramayana Stories in Modern South India: An Anthology* (Bloomington: Indiana University Press, 2008), 11–18.

59. Appendix, *Rāvaṇa Katāva*, v.64.
60. Ibid., v.53.
61. Ibid., vv.108–110.
62. Ibid., v.25.
63. Ibid., vv.111–115.
64. Ibid., v.58.
65. Ibid., vv.84–85.
66. For a survey of Indian versions of the epic featuring Mahīrāvaṇa/Airāvaṇa see D. B. Kapp, "The 'Ālu Kuṟumba Rāmāyaṇa': The Story of Rāma as Narrated by a South Indian Tribe," *Asian Folklore Studies* 48, no. 1 (1989): 124, and Lutgendorf, "Hanumān's Adventures Underground," 149–163. On the etymology of *mahī-* and *ai-rāvaṇa*, see W. L. Smith, "Mahīrāvaṇa and the Womb Demon," *Indological Taurinensia* 10 (1982): 218.
67. In the preface to his translation of the *Mayil Irāvaṇaṉ Katai*, Kamil Zvelebil works to explain Mayil Irāvaṇaṉ's name through South Indian impressions of the peacock as a "bellicose bird" (as the conveyance and theriomorphic form of Murugan, the god of war), as well as on account of the use of the peacock's blue-green color as a simile for the ocean (Mayil Irāvaṇaṉ's "Pāṭāla Laṅkā" is only accessible through its entrance located somewhere in the remote southern sea). See Kamil Zvelebil, *Two Tamil Folktales: The Story of King Mataṉakāma; The Story of Peacock Rāvaṇa* (Delhi: Motilal Banarsidass, 1987), xli–xlii.
68. Ibid., xlvf. Regrettably no copy of this film seems to have survived in any archive.
69. Ibid., 183.
70. See Zvelebil's translation in ibid., 173–219.
71. Ibid., 190.
72. See Gananath Obeyesekere's study in *The Cult of the Goddess Pattini* (Chicago: University of Chicago Press, 1984). A Sinhala adaptation of the *Cilappatikāram* is known under the title *Pattini Hālla*, see Peter Silva, "The Influence of Dravida on Sinhalese," DPhil Diss.: Oxford University (1961), 18. Silva cites a 1941 edition of the text by D. A. De S. Epa; there is another as well: D. P. R. Samaranayaka (ed.), *Pālaňga hālla saha pattini hālla* (Colombo: M. D. Gunasena, 1959).
73. The *Rāvaṇa Katāva* does not refer to Ravana's vehicle as the *puṣpaka vimāna* (as it is often in Sanskrit), nor as the *daňḍu-monara* or "wooden peacock" as it is called in Sri Lanka today (see Chapter 5, section 3 in this text).
74. For this portion of his chronicle, Queirós drew from the records of Captain Antonio Monis Baretto, dispatched to Colombo by Francis Xavier to continue working to convert Bhuvanekabahu VII to Roman Catholicism. On Queirós' sources for the *Temporal and Spiritual Conquest of Ceylon* in general, see Tikiri Abeyasinghe, "History as Polemics and Propaganda: An Examination of Fernao de Queiros, 'History of Ceylon,'" *Journal of the Royal Asiatic Society Sri Lanka Branch* [New Series] 25 (1980–1981): 39–45.
75. de Queyroz [Queirós], *Temporal and Spiritual Conquest of Ceylon*, I.8.
76. Ibid.

77. Ibid., I.9.
78. Ibid., I.9.
79. *Rāmāyaṇaya*, ff.83–84.
80. The "three domains of Lanka" presumably refer here to the traditional political division of the island into the northern "Rāja Raṭa," the central "Māyā Raṭa," and the southern "Rohaṇa (or Ruhuṇu) Raṭa." See n.32, above.
81. *Rāmāyaṇaya*, ff.84–86.
82. Thanks to Sandaresee Sudusinghe for demystifying the bit about "the variety of small black balls" with some connection to Sita by telling me about her field trip to with Prof. Raj Somadeva to Nuwara Eliya, who on that occasion pointed out the ferrous marbles and the legends associated with them. I am grateful to Krishantha Federicks for help with this difficult portion of the text. The detail concerning the Tamil version of this legend I learned from an online presentation by Dr. Shantha Kumar, Assistant Director of Education, Sri Lankan Ministry of Education ("Rama's Journey in the land of Ravan," Ayodhya Research Institute, Department of Culture, December 18, 2020, https://www.youtube.com/watch?v=G0lvR4vYAmE).
83. *sītā dēvi laṅkāvē siṭiyē dänaṭa avuruda dās ganananakaṭa peradīya* (f.87a).
84. Ibid., ff.87a–b. The only clue as to the author's identity is that he or she says that they hail from "Kitul Lähäragama," which I am unable to place.
85. *Yatidūtam*, v.51.
86. *yasmin sītā janakatanayā darśayantyātmaśuddhiṃ| paunaḥ punyaṃ śapathamakarodvahnimadhyaṃ praviśya* (*Yatidūtam*, v.30).
87. Appendix, *Rāvaṇa Katāva*, v.29.
88. R. L. Brohier, *Seeing Ceylon in Vistas of Scenery, History, Legend, and Folklore* (Colombo: Lake House, 1965), 217; *Discovering Ceylon* (Colombo: Lake House, 1973), 241f.
89. Witharana, "Ravana's Sri Lanka," 783, n.6., citing Vijēsiṃha Beligalla, *Lenārḍ Vulf Samaga Gamanak* (Colombo: Godage International Publishers, 1995).
90. C. G. Uragoda remarks: "Even today the large majority of the drug plants used in Ceylon are the same as those currently used in the neighboring mainland. The realization of this fact may have given rise to the popular legend that certain forested hills, e.g. Doluwakanda and Rumassalakanda [at Unawatuna], from which certain drug plants are often collected, are only fragments of a part of the Himalayas that was carried over to Ceylon by the mythical monkey-king, to provide drugs for wounded in the Rama–Ravana battle" (*A History of Medicine in Sri Lanka* [Colombo: Sri Lanka Medical Organization, 1987], 16). See also S. Abeywickrema et al., "The Distribution of Indigenous Medicinal Plants of Ceylon," in *Proceedings of the International Symposium of Medicinal Plants [Kandy 1964]* (Colombo: Government Press, 1966), 41.
91. The episode occurs in the Yuddha Kāṇḍa of the *Vālmīki Rāmāyaṇa*. See Goldman et al., *The Ramayana of Valmiki*, vol. VI (Princeton: Princeton University Press, 2009), sarga 40, vv.30–31 (228).
92. *Mahāvaṃsa* 7.59–68; see Chapter 1, section 3.

93. Forbes, *Eleven Years in Ceylon*, vol. II, 104. See also Forbes' full account of the legends of Ravana related by the people in the Laggala region (99–104).
94. Ananda and Nahallage, "Unique Religious and Cultural Practices of Meemure," 73.
95. Ibid., 77.
96. Ibid., 74. Folk poetry documented in the mid-twentieth century gives an account of the people of the region as being descended from Kuveni's son, Jīvahatta, who according to one set of verses is identical with the god Kälē Baṇḍāra. Interestingly the poem says that he "spoke both learned Tamil and thorough Sinhala" (*igena demaḷa muḷu siṅhala bāsāva da kiyaminnē*), and that he is worshipped in stone *kovils* ("Kälē Baṇḍāra Deviyangē Vittiya," in Prajñāloka Himi, *Purāṇa Sivpada Saṅgrahāva*, 53f.).
97. Ariyadasa, "Rāvaṇa dēvatvayen pudana 'yakkama' ṭa giyemu." Residents of Ranamure have their own set of folklore relating to Mt. Laggala and the battle between Rama and Ravana. Ariyadasa reproduces a Sinhala verse recited to him while on assignment relating the events of the *Ramayana* to the topography of the region, with its last line conforming to a theme in the *Rāvaṇa Katāva* regarding the permanent effects of Hanuman's act of arson: "it is because of Hanuman that today the island of Lanka is dark [in color]" (*hanumā nisā ada lakbima aňduru vuṇā*).
98. "Growing Up in the Universe: Climbing Mount Improbable," *The Royal Institution Christmas Lectures*, season 26 episode 3. Originally broadcast on BBC 4, January 1992.
99. Locations in the vicinity of Jaffna are identified in connection with Rama's activity: "Tiruvaḍinilai," where an impression of his footprint remains visible; "Villūṇḍi," where he once stopped with his bow (S. Pathmanathan, *Facets of Sri Lankan History and Culture* [Colombo: Kumaran Book House, 2015], 554). Ronit Ricci gives an example of what we might call an "isolate" Lankan *Ramayana*—a *Ramayana* germane to a small community which does not seem to have influenced, nor to have been influenced by, other Sri Lankan versions of the epic—in referring to a version performed by Indonesia-Malay Muslims living in colonial Ceylon in the eighteenth and nineteenth centuries (*Banishment and Belonging: Exile and Diaspora in Sarandib, Lanka and Ceylon* [Cambridge: Cambridge University Press, 2019], 155f.).
100. Opprobrium toward the Hindu epics is carried through to the nineteenth century by a poem published in 1863 by Don Philip de Silva Āpā Appuhāmi (famous as the author of one of the first printed Sinhala astrological almanacs, the *Āpa Pañcāṅga Lita*): "The *Ramayana* and *Bharata*—two tales which are in their entirety mere prattle, and whose words are altogether vacant—this much concerning these two works should be known to any wise person" (*rāmāyana bara ta| ätaḷuva deḍum mulu ta| kīmut bas nira ta| yutuva deyaňgin danuva niyava ta*). First published in the December 1863 issue of a Sinhala language serial, *Sārārtha Pradīpikāva* (9), with Āpā's commentary to follow in February 1864 (32). Thanks to Buddhika Konara for this reference.
101. S. L. Kekulawala, "The Religious Journey into *Dhamma (Dharmayātrā)*: Buddhist Pilgrimage as an Expression of Religiousness," in *Religiousness in Sri Lanka*, ed. John R. Carter (Colombo: Marga Institute, 1979), 56; Lynn de Silva, *Buddhism: Beliefs and*

*Practices in Sri Lanka* (Colombo: self-published, 1974), 173–177. The Sri Lankan Buddhist chronicle tradition from its inception was keen to describe the topography of the island. One-quarter of the *Mahāvaṃsa* is dedicated to King Duṭṭhagāmiṇi's reclamation of the northern kingdom from the Indian usurper Eḷāra, throughout the course of which the terrain of Duṭṭhagāmiṇi's campaign (from southern Rohana north to Anuradhapura)—the distance between various rivers, cities, and landmarks—is given in considerable detail (that is to say, the medieval *kaḍayim* genre did not invent Lankan Buddhist cartography).

102. Santosh Desai, "Ramayana—An Instrument of Historical Contact and Cultural Transmission between India and Asia," *The Journal of Asian Studies* 30, no. 1 (1970): 6.
103. Bechert, "The Beginnings of Buddhist Historiography," 1–12.
104. R. Gombrich compares Valmiki's *Rāmāyaṇa* with the Pali *Dasaratha* and *Vessantara Jātakas*, dating the *Jātakaṭṭhakathā* to the early first millennium, "perhaps as late as the 5th century" ("The Vessantara Jātaka, The Rāmāyaṇa, and the Dasaratha Jātaka," *Journal of the American Oriental Society* 105, no. 3 [1985]: 434).
105. Steven Collins, "What is Literature in Pali?" in *Literary Cultures in History: Reconstructions from South Asia*, ed. Sheldon Pollock (Berkeley: University of California Press, 2003), 649–688.
106. Antagonism between Buddhist monks and Shaivites in Sri Lanka no doubt owes to a host of historical factors, with Sinhala Buddhist identity shaped in part by a common language (Sinhala) and a rhetoric of political manifest destiny reinforced by clear geographical borders—the physical shores of the island itself. Charles Hallisey argues that intensive efforts were underway—in South India from around 900 CE and in Sri Lanka from around 1000 CE—to persuade lay people to exclusively support either Shaivism or Buddhism. In the Sri Lankan Buddhist case, this involved in part "ideological distance" from the Indic world, reinforced by Buddhist symbols (such as the Buddha's relics), Buddhist institutions, and ideals of Sinhala Buddhist monarchy exclusive to the island. Evidence for such competitive antagonism on the part of Buddhist monks comes in the form of twelfth-to-fourteenth-century Sinhala Buddhist prose works and poetry (some intended for broad lay audiences), a number of which exclusively advocate Buddhist forms of worship, affirm the efficacy of Buddhist apotropaic rituals, and occasionally deride Shaiva and Vaishnava theology and practice. See Charles Hallisey, "Devotion in the Buddhist Literature of Medieval Sri Lanka," PhD diss.: The University of Chicago (1988), 176–192.

# 4
# RAVANA IN MODERN SRI LANKAN LITERATURE

## 4.1 THE *RAMAYANA* AND THE SINHALA NEOCLASSICAL MOVEMENT

In the 120 years prior to his twenty-first-century revival, Ravana maintained a steady, if understated, presence in Sri Lankan literary output, where he stands at the center of a tension within the Buddhist nationalist imaginary over the very origins of the Sinhala people. For those who found the proposition of an exogenous origin for the island's Buddhist people (as in the account enshrined in the *Mahāvaṃsa*, in which the "Sīhaḷas" hailed from north-eastern India), Ravana symbolized an alternative possibility—that of an indigenous legacy of Lankan human habitation, deriving from the "Yaksha tribe" of deep antiquity. Ravana's fortunes as a subject of literary attention over the past century and a half are implicated in other, more complex negotiations regarding the place of continental Indian classical literature, drama, dance, and music in the Sinhala cultural sphere; that is, at formative junctures in the canonization of perceptions of Sinhala cultural authenticity.

This chapter follows Ravana's incarnation as both a literary and historical figure over the past century, first as inspiration to the architects of the "neoclassical" Sinhala literary revolution, and subsequently as palladium of the Sinhala indigenist nationalist movement, which claimed the demon-king as a progenitor of Sri Lanka's Buddhist people. I go on to explore Ravana's kingdom as a signifier of Sri Lanka as Edenic paradise in later Sinhala and English novels, a trope which, I argue, has in recent years transcended its literary confines to manifest within the imaginations of real-life policy makers and treasure hunters. Ravana's liminal status in the twentieth century as simultaneously a literary character and historical personage, along with instances in the twenty-first century of authors claiming to have discovered mysterious texts documenting the existence of the Yaksha tribe, I account for as a phenomena assuaging an *anxiety of incompleteness* plaguing a segment

*Ravana's Kingdom*. Justin W. Henry, Oxford University Press. © Oxford University Press 2023.
DOI: 10.1093/oso/9780197636305.003.0004

of Sri Lanka's Buddhist population—an anxiety surrounding the proposition that the Sinhala people were descended from Indian emigrees two-and-a-half millennia ago, rather than from a native population of the island.

The emergence of independent publishing firms in the late nineteenth century coincided with a period of intense experimentation in music, dramatic theater, and literature, as Sri Lankan authors worked to forge novel media with aesthetic and thematic dimensions attractive to the public at large. While literature and drama taking Sri Lanka's ancient Buddhist kings as their subject matter attained canonical status as the first "modern national" tokens of their respective genres in the eyes of later Sinhala commentators, such works were not fully representative of the broad palette of source materials used by the authors and artists of this period. Beyond Pali and Sinhala works cleaving to the essential meta-narrative of the *Mahāvaṃsa* (in which valiant Sinhala monarchs repeatedly defend the Buddha *sāsana* from foreign "Damiḷa" usurpers), authors sought inspiration from Tamil and Indian Sanskrit works as well. The Sri Lankan Sanskrit revival took place in two, for the most part independent domains: one centered at the newly established Buddhist monastic colleges of the Colombo suburbs, and another in the secular realm of urban theatre, music, and print. At the Vidyalankara and Vidyodaya Pirivenas, prominent faculty edited and translated Sanskrit works on medicine, astrology, jewelry-making, and architecture, and also published a number of primers, grammars, and Sanskrit-Sinhala dictionaries (*kośa*s) in an effort to provide educators and interested members of the public with the tools necessary to revive Sanskrit learning, which many monks viewed as an integral part of traditional Buddhist education.[1] Scholar monks simultaneously composed original *aṣṭaka*, *śataka*, *campū* and *sandeśa* poems on the life and ministry of the Buddha, essential Buddhist philosophy, and in commemoration of key episodes in the religious history of Sri Lanka.[2] Philologically inclined monks both competed with one another and supported one another's efforts. Ratmalane Dharmarama earned legendary status for his close reconstruction of the Sanskrit text of cantos 1–15 of Kumaradasa's *Jānakīharaṇa* based on a Sinhala commentary available to him in 1890 (manuscripts of the original text subsequently discovered in India confirmed the accuracy of Dharmarama's interpolation).[3]

Contemporary with the reclamation of Sanskrit philology at the Buddhist *piriveṇa*s was what might be characterized as a Sinhala "neoclassical" revolution in literature, drama, and music in the Colombo arts scene. Enabled by printed editions of classical texts from India, Makalandavage John de Silva

(1857–1922) wrote popular Sinhala stage adaptations of the *Ramayana*,[4] the story of Nala and Damayanti (*Nala Rāja Caritaya*, 1887), Kalidasa's *Abhijñāna Śakuntalā* (1904), Harsha's *Ratnāvalī* (1906), and *Nāgānanda* (1919), as well as a version of the *Uttara Rāma Carita* (1906) which followed the original Sanskrit text very closely.[5] Beyond the works of Kālidāsa there was an interest in the life of the poet himself, attested in Simon De Silva Senaviratne's 1887 drama *Kālidāsa Nṛtya Pota* (subtitled in English "The Historical Tragedy Entitled 'Kalidas' "), and Heṭṭiyākandagē Joseph Andrew Fernando's 255 stanza biographical poem, *Kālidas Caritaya*, published the same year. Particular interest in Kalidasa can perhaps be explained in part through a legendary account of the poet's later life (traceable to a fifteenth-century Sinhala work, the *Pärakumbā Sirita*) relating that Kalidasa traveled to Sri Lanka on invitation of the poet-king Kumaradasa, ultimately to die tragically there. The fact that the life of Kalidasa found a modern, Sinhala print rendering three years before the life of the Buddha (Weragama Punchi Bandara's 1890 *Saṃbuddha Caritaya*) gives some indication of the atmosphere of excitement surrounding the rediscovery of a pan-Indo-Lankan literary heritage taking place in Colombo at the time.

There is a great deal to say regarding the late nineteenth century as a formative phase for the very notion of "modern Sinhala literature"—a period of inchoate literary experimentation, involving competition and synthesis between *haut culture* and village/folk traditions, drawing inspiration from a variety of continental and traditional Sri Lankan sources. The multiform treatment of the *Ramayana* in this literary moment is exemplary of these dynamics; it was viewed as a quintessential subject for Sinhala composition by authors of this period, who found inspiration in native and Indian Sanskrit tradition, as well as from Tamil and Sinhala variations on the epic. Excitement at this time over the rediscovery of a continental Sanskrit literary tradition intersecting with Sri Lanka is attested in Calutantrige Don Bastian Jayaweera Bandara's 1886 *Rāmāyaṇaya hevat Rāvaṇā Saṅhāraya*, a three-hundred-page Sinhala prose rendering of the epic, subtitled in English, "Adventures of Rama, or, the Destruction of Ravana." In addition to being a novelist and playwright, Bastian (1852–1921) was a leading publisher and journalist of his time, a temperance advocate, an instrumental figure in the establishment of Buddhist Sunday schools in Sri Lanka, as well as the founder of the first Sinhala daily newspaper (*Dinapatā Pravṛti*) in 1895.[6] Bastian's *Rāmāyaṇaya* is exemplary of the late nineteenth-century neoclassical Sinhala renaissance and instrumental to its legacy for several reasons. The first is that, despite the fact that Don Bastian identifies the *Vālmīki Rāmāyaṇa* as his template[7], his *Rāmāyaṇaya* is in fact a genuine work of local synthesis, containing an extended episode of Rama and Lakshmana's captivity in the subterranean abode of Ravana's brother, Mayil Rāvaṇa ("Peacock Ravana") (see Figure 4.1)[8]. While not a part of the *Vālmīki Rāmāyaṇa*, the Peacock Ravana story circulated among Sinhala Buddhists from the Kandyan period, and it seems to have been available to Bastian through a Tamil iteration, as it had been for the author of the *Rāvaṇa Katāva*[9] (see Chapter 3, section 3).

The subtitle of Bastian's prose work itself—*Rāvaṇa Saṅhāraya*, "the destruction of Ravana"—continues a trend begun centuries earlier and

Figure 4.1 Cover image from C. Don Bastian's *Rāmāyaṇaya hevat Rāvaṇa Saṅhāraya* (1886).

amplified in subsequent twentieth-century Sinhala renditions of the epic: a re-orientation away from the heroism of Rama and toward a defense of Ravana, remembered as a historical king of the island and defender of its shores. While Bastian's later works drew from European and local Buddhist themes for their subject matter, Ediriweera Sarachchandra has noted the influence of Bastian's *Rāmāyaṇaya* specifically on A. Simon de Silva and Piyadasa Sirisena, "the fathers of the Sinhala novel," both writing at the turn of the twentieth century.[10]

Continental literary influences were supplemented with musical ones as well. The Hindustan Dramatic Company's performance of an Urdu play (*Inder Sabha*) in Colombo in 1877 was the first inspiration for a unique modern genre of Sinhala theatre: *nurti*, derived from Sanskrit *nṛitya*, "expressive dance." Calutantrige Don Bastian was himself the first to popularize the *nurti* style for a Sinhala audience, having attempted a stage version of the *Rāmāyaṇaya* before meeting critical success with his productions of *Romalin*, *Romeo and Juliet*, and *Franklow and Ingirlee*.[11] For Bastian, "the father of *nurti*," north Indian musical accompaniment capitalized on an already popular trend, with two dramatic companies from Bombay (the Hindustan Dramatic Company and K. M. Baliwala's Elphinstone Dramatic Company) making routine visits to perform in Colombo between 1882 and 1913.[12] Nurti style, with its use of *rāga* and *tāla*, came at this time to displace *nāḍagam*, a Tamil South Indian dramatic musical style popular among Sinhala performers from the mid-eighteenth century onward. (In the twilight of its reign on the stage, one *nāḍagam* production of the *Ramayana* in Sinhala was composed by R. J. F. Varnakulasuriya, *Rāmāyanaya hevat Rāvanā Nāḍagam*.[13]) For John de Silva, heir to Bastian's role as Colombo's premier theater producer, *nurti* represented more than simply a fad but a chance to reunite Sinhala audiences with what he understood to be their north Indian, Aryan heritage.[14] De Silva began his career adapting foreign plays into Sinhala (including Sanskrit dramas as well as Shakespeare), subsequently choosing to dramatize the heroic kings and seminal events from Sri Lankan Buddhist history and becoming the nation's foremost playwright by the early twentieth century.[15] De Silva was, like Bastian, a passionate defender of Buddhism, directing his work to a largely middle-class Colombo urban audience, to whom, as K. N. O. Dharmadasa explains, he "extolled the virtues of the past, contrasting them with the "degradation" of the present and exhorting his audience to follow the examples of their forebearers."[16] De Silva's "Danno Budungē," a musical excerpt from his *Sirisaṅgabō Charitaya*

(1903), went on to become a venerated song among Sri Lankan Buddhists, sung daily in public schools and often at state functions. While his later work drew inspiration from Buddhist pietism and historical instances of Sinhala resistance to foreign domination, he explains in the preface to his 1886 *Sītā Haraṇa* ("The Theft of Sītā") that, despite being Hindu, the *Ramayana* is significant for "the many facts it shows related to ancient Sri Lanka," knowledge concerning which had been lost to present day Sinhala people.[17]

De Silva would later revisit Ravana to make him a marker of Sinhala indigeneity in a 1912 poem about Adam's Peak. This mountain in the central highlands—also known as Sri Pada (the "Holy Foot")—has historically been Sri Lanka's most active and multi-religious pilgrimage destination, drawing Buddhists, Hindus, and Muslims to its summit onto which a decorative stone footprint is hewn. Buddhists venerate it as the footprint left by the Buddha during a visit to the island, Hindus believe it to be Shiva's, and Muslims believe it to be Adam's. De Silva, in his *Śrīpāda Śatakaya*, acknowledges the footprint as belonging to the Buddha, reinforcing the incorrectness of the Muslim view by clarifying that the island's earliest inhabitants were in fact descended from *Ravana*, not Adam:

> In this earthly world, the Lord of Sages had placed
> his sacred foot in four places
> One lotus-foot [among the four] in the Moors' Mecca
> They say that [on Sri Pada] it is Adam's sacred foot;
> because of that error, [its true significance] is hidden.
> Where in a hundred homes of this Lanka is there an awareness of that?
>
> On this island, the kin of Adam and his wife appear [according to Muslims],
> Though in fact it was Ravana who showed those skills in this land,
> Making Shem, Ham, and Japheth [merely] kings appearing in the Bible . . .[18]

With De Silva having elsewhere advanced the view that the Sinhala people are descended from "Aryan" (i.e., originally Indian) stock, one might be disinclined to attribute much significance to the verse above, at least with respect to the playwright's conception of Lankan human habitation millennia before the Buddha's time.[19] From the early 1880s, however, Buddhist publications floated the notion that Ravana was in fact an early Sinhala (*hela*) monarch, long before the time of the Buddha. *Lak Miṇi Kirula*, an early Sinhala newspaper, carried a feature on the island's history in 1881 stating that the island of Lanka was "a powerful kingdom even before the advent of Vijaya," ruled over by king Ravana with his council of ten elders in 2837 BCE.[20] Other publications of the era also naturalized the imagery of the *Ramayana* for a pro-Buddhist, pro-independence readership. The editors of a Sinhala magazine inaugurated in July 1926 entitled *Rāmasäraya* explained their title choice of "Rama's arrow"—the weapon which had slain the evil Ravana—as a metaphor for righteous Buddhist activities with the potential to establish world peace.[21]

The turn of the twentieth century was a formative moment not just for modern Sinhala literature, but also for the Sri Lankan Buddhist national imaginary more broadly speaking. Opposing narratives concerning the original peopling of the island, competing visions over the future of national sovereignty, and even divergent opinion regarding the nature and derivation of the Sinhala language played out in the public sphere at this time, often finding expression in literary form. Defenders of the position that the Sinhala people and their language were native to Sri Lanka came to self-identify as the Hela Havula movement, a designation coined in 1941 by linguist, poet and cultural critic Munidasa Cumaratunga (1887–1944) and his associate, author Rapiyel Tennakoon (1899–1965).[22] The group's name "the Pure Sinhala Fraternity," reflects its members' mission to canonize an official form of the Sinhala language free from the influence of Sanskrit—*hela* being a rendering of the word "Sinhala" germane to the tradition of verse composition in a register of the language free of any consonant clusters resembling Sanskrit or Pali. Cumaratunga and Tennakoon believed this rarified Sinhala to be its pure and original form—native to Sri Lanka along with its earliest speakers—characterizing the language therefore not simply as another Indo-European or "Aryan" derivative of Sanskrit, but rather as *sui generis* and indigenous to the island of Sri Lanka.[23]

A means of backdating the earliest human habitation of Sri Lanka to an era before that of Prince Vijaya and the Buddha Gotama was understandably welcome to those advancing such a nativist linguistic ideology, resulting in further elevation of Ravana from the domain of the literary and the mythological to that of the historical and empirical. In a 1941 essay published in his English language journal *Helio*, Cumaratunga at once undermined the colonization myth of the *Mahāvaṃsa* and subverted the traditional moral valances of the *Ramayana*. Cumaratunga here celebrated Ravana for resisting the invading armies of India, rendering Vibhishana a traitor for acquiescing to vassalage under Rama. From his point of view, Prince Vijaya, who appeared on the scene several millennia later, was little more than a foreign invader:

> It is a slur on the Sinhalese nation to say that the arch robber Vijaya and his fiendish followers were its progenitors. Many thousands of years before their arrival we had empires greater and mightier than any other nation could claim to have had.[24]

Tennakoon took up this theme in the very next edition of *Helio* in a piece entitled "The Hidden History of the Helese." Here he followed Cumaratunga in calling Prince Vijaya the "leader of [a] gang of robbers" and the "grandson of a highway robber," dismissing the proposition that the Sinhala people were descended from Aryans on the grounds that Europeans had imputed racial connotations to the term which were irrelevant to its original usage.[25] Tennakoon's first poem *Vavuluva* ("Bat Language"), written in 1939 and for which Cumaratunga supplied the preface, proffers a re-rendering of the *Ramayana* fully in keeping with the Hela Havula worldview. In this version, framed as a conversation between a male bat (Vavula), and female *drongo* bird (Kävidiya), Ravana's sister, Shurpanakha, is blameless in her initial interaction with Rama and Lakshmana (the catalyst for Sita's abduction in conventional iterations of the story). Instead of shamelessly flirting with the two brothers and assailing Sita, the "beautiful and friendly woman" Shurpanakha is the victim of Rama and Lakshmana's crass derision, subsequent to which Sita desires to herself go voluntarily to Sri Lanka to meet Ravana.[26] The title of the poem is a reference to the range of motion of a bat's head: like the auger of a hand-held drill, the head of the bat rotates in one direction before jerking backwards in the opposite direction. This image, in chapter twenty-seven of the poem, functions as a metaphor for the attitudes of the directors of the Royal Asiatic Society's Sinhala dictionary project, initiated in 1926 and headed by a Sri Lankan, Sir D. B. Jayatilaka. The accusation implicit in *Vavuluva*, commentators explain, is that the editors of the dictionary project focused their readings of classical Sinhala texts in a single-minded direction, working in a reactionary way ("spinning their heads about in the opposite direction") when they encountered criticism from local scholars (i.e., Cumaratunga and the Hela Havula). Cumaratunga's criticism of the dictionary project centered on the choice to hire German philologist Wilhelm Geiger (1856–1943) as a consultant. Cumaratunga alleged first that Geiger, as a foreigner, had an impoverished understanding of the Sinhala language, and second, that the Royal Asiatic Society had uncritically accepted his assertion that Sinhala was an Indo-European language derived from Sanskrit.[27]

## 4.2 RAVANA ON STAGE AND SCREEN

The *Ramayana* went on to have significant, if not altogether uniformly sustained, relevance in Sinhala literature and drama in the twentieth and twenty-first centuries. Wimal Abhayasundara (1921–2008), who in later life established his celebrity as a four-time recipient of the State Literary Award of Excellence, wrote and produced a musical stage piece for Radio Ceylon entitled *Mandōdarī* in 1960, dramatizing the friendship between Sita and Ravana's wife, Mandodari. In this piece, Mandodari sympathizes with Sita who is imprisoned in the highland mountains of Sri Lanka, reassuring her that no harm will come to her from Ravana, and that she will work to set her free. When at the conclusion of the play Ravana is finally knocked unconscious to the ground, Mandodari weeps over his body, proclaiming his virtues.[28] Abhayasundara went on to compose a full-length opera entitled *Laṅkādhīsa Rāvanāyanaya* ("The Epic of Ravana, Lord of Lanka"), highlighting the demon-king's pietism, valor, and intellectual acumen. The play opens with a recapitulation of the episode, famous to Sri Lankan Tamils, of Ravana's quest to replace his mother Kanniya's Shiva *lingam*. Shiva intervenes as Ravana cuts off his heads one by one as a display of devotion to the god, promising Ravana that a *lingam* will be gifted to him soon and that his name and memory will endure through the ages.[29] The opera highlights Rama and Lakshmana's aggression toward Shurpanakha (who is "violated and tortured"), Ravana's kind treatment of Sita, the traitorous disposition of Vibhishana, along with Ravana's military tact, erudition, and virtue. The opera concludes with the tearful lamentation of Rama as he regrets the fact that he slew Ravana, confessing to his ill-treatment of Shurpanakha.[30] In his introduction, Abhayasundara explains the motivation of his previous radio opera, commenting on the fact that Mandodari was not only a woman of pure caste (*kulaya*) and great wealth, but also equal to or exceeding Sita in beauty and intelligence.[31]

Subsequent stage productions include Gamini Gunawardena's *Rama and* Sita (1964)[32] and Arisen Ahubudu's production of *Sakviti Rāvaṇa* ("Ravana the Wheel-turning King") in the early 1980s, which presents Ravana as the progenitor of the Hela people and as having ruled the subcontinent of deep antiquity, "some two thousand years prior to the Greeks."[33] Playwright and director Dayananda Gunawardena, considered one of the fathers of modern Sinhala theater along with Ediriweera Sarachchandra, Sugathapala de Silva and Henry Jayasena, in 1984 wrote and produced *Madura Javanikā* ("The sweet curtain"), which he billed as a "docu-drama" or dramatization of Sri Lankan cultural history, beginning from the age of Ravana (in an interview Gunawardena spoke of the *Mahāvaṃsa*'s incomplete rendering of Sinhala cultural history).[34] *Madura Javanikā* returned to the stage at Colombo's Lionel Wendt Theater in March of 2015,[35] joining other productions in a twenty-first-century Ravana renaissance of sorts. In 2008, percussionist Pabalu Wijegoonewardane wrote a ballet entitled *Mahā Rāvaṇa* (2008) based on the Mahayana *Laṅkāvatāra Sūtra* (which features the Buddha in dialogue with Ravana when he was Lord of Lanka).[36] In June 2018 the University of Colombo's Ballet Opera unveiled "Ravana: The Legend Untold," at the Nelum Pokuna Mahinda Rajapaksha Theatre, Sri Lanka's largest arts venue. The debut of the ballet, which was based on Bhadraji Mahinda Jayatilaka's "historical novel" *Śrī Rāvaṇṇā Puvata* [sic] (discussed below), saw a number of state officials in attendance, including the heads of the Ministry of Buddha Sasana, the Ministry of Higher Education and Cultural Affairs, and the National Institute of Education.[37] Another contemporary stage rendering of the epic, *Rāvaṇa Sītābhilaṣaya* ("The Romance of Ravana and Sita"), ran at the Lionel Went Theatre in Spring 2019, co-written by director Namel Weeramuni and University of Colombo professor emeritus, former ambassador, and prominent public academic J. B. Disanayake.[38] In this version, the massive battle between the forces of Rama and Ravana is omitted—instead, Rama makes his way to Lanka after Sita is abducted and on the spot asks her to undergo the fire test to prove that she had been faithful while captive. Ravana chivalrously intervenes, telling Sita she has no need to undertake such a trial, and that he would go to war against Rama if it meant protecting her from such humiliation. Sita implores Ravana not to do so, at which time Ravana's mother appears in a fiery spectacle, identifying herself as "Lō Mātā," "the Mother of the Earth." Lō Mātā explains that she knows of Ravana's love for Sita, and in the dramatic climax removes her heart and hands it over to Sita, thus averting war and sanctioning the romance between the two characters.[39]

*Rāvaṇa Sītābhilaṣaya* was in fact J. B. Disanayake's second *Ramayana*-inspired script. The first he wrote and produced as a high school senior at Colombo's Ananda College, inspired after seeing a production of Ediriweera Sarachchandra's *Manamē* in November 1956. In 2016 Disanayake published his original script along with an afterward recounting his excitement at seeing Sarachchandra's landmark of Sri Lankan theater, which he acknowledges as the first "truly modern" Sinhala play, containing Buddhist subject matter and employing traditional Sinhala musical and theatrical styles. Reflecting on his adolescent debut as a playwright, Disanayake recalls that, like *Manamē*, he wanted his play to be based on the story of a king (*rāja kathāva*) but that, as Sarachchandra's protagonist was born in India, he wished instead to cast a main character born in Sri Lanka. This was the inspiration for the choice of Ravana, and for titling his play *Rāvaṇa, Gīta Nāṭakaya* ("Ravana, the musical drama"). Two aspects of Disanayake's later life reflections emerge as significant. The first is that Disanayake avers the probable historicity of Ravana as a king of the island, pointing out that "Laṅkāpura" is a name of Sri Lanka in the *Mahāvaṃsa*, and saying that "while others believe King Ravana to be merely a mythic figure, I myself do not think so." He explains to the contrary that the "Indian *Ramayana*" is "not our version of the story," and that Sri Lankans have every right to be proud of their ancient king, calling Ravana "a son of Lanka" (*laṅkā putrayek*).[40] The second is the place that Disanayake affords the story of Ravana in relation to the revolution in Sinhala theater of the 1950s, of which he was an enthusiastic spectator. From Disanayake's point of view both as a young man and in later life, Ravana was a character from Sri Lanka's past who urgently merited theatrical representation. *Rāvaṇa, Gīta Nāṭakaya* follows the *Ramayana* narrative in a more familiar way than does *Rāvaṇa Sītābhilāṣaya*, ending with the battle between Rama and Ravana and Ravana's death. In this truncated but more conventional form, Disanayake's play in fact resembles the plot of *Manamē*, Sarachchandra's own invention, in which a prince, traveling back to his home in Benares having married the daughter of his teacher in Takshila, is confronted by a Hunter King of the forest. The Hunter King demands that the Benares prince hand over his bride, after which they battle, and the prince of Benares is slain. After his death (enabled by a momentary act of compassion toward the Hunter King on the princess' part), the Hunter King successfully seduces the princess and wins her romantic affection before ultimately abandoning her.[41] We see in the basic outline of *Manamē*, therefore, a dramatic outline similar to *Rāvaṇa Sītābhilaṣaya*, which boldly renders Ravana not just a righteous king but also, ultimately, romantically successful—a "country gentleman" as lord of the relatively provincial Lanka.

Ravana has in recent years come to prominence on the small and silver screens in Sri Lanka as well. A lighthearted family comedy entitled *Sītā*

*Maṅ Āva* ("Sita, I'm home!") directed by Jayasekara Aponso debuted in September 2013 but was forced into a limited theater run. A contingent of fifteen Buddhist monks representing the Ravana Balaya—"Ravana's Force," a political action group with ties to the Bodu Bala Sena—crashed the red-carpet premier at the Ritz Cinema in Borella, disrupting the screening and demanding that the title of the film be changed. Ven. Ittǟkandē Saddhatissa, the secretary and spokesperson for group, explained to the media that because Ravana was a great king of Sri Lanka, no one has a right to portray him in a comedic light, and that the Ravana Balaya would declare war on the film unless the names of its three characters (Ravana, Rama, and Sita) were changed.[42]

Derana TV's popular *Rāvaṇa* serial was, as of June 2020, in its seventy-first installment (production has paused due to the COVID-19 pandemic). Set 4,500 years ago during an invasion of Sri Lanka by the despotic "Deva tribe" of India, the tele-drama follows the story of Ravana summoned by the Munis of Polonnaruwa, in order to take back the "Hela kingdom" which belongs rightfully to the "Yaksha tribe" (the program's subtitle is "The uprising of the Yakshas against foreign intervention").[43] Transposing the terrain of northern Sri Lanka into deep antiquity,[44] *Rāvaṇa* sports a fantasy aesthetic with elaborate sets, costumes, CGI graphics, and no shortage of fight scenes. The show employs a broad palette of Puranic myth and contemporary supplements to tell the story of the world of the Yaksha tribe, where we discover the application of Ayurvedic remedies to resurrect the dead, subterranean energy crystals, motorized vehicles, and characters and themes taken from the *Mahāvaṃsa*, the *Ramayana*, and even the grail romances of King Arthur (only the rightful heir to Lanka can remove the coronary sword [*candrahāsa*] from the stone at Sigiriya into which it is embedded).[45]

Parallels between Derana's *Rāvaṇa* and the first major serialized television broadcast of the *Ramayana* in Hindi demand some comparative observations. In *Politics after Television* (2001), Arvind Rajagopal highlights the epistemological rupture generated by Doordarshan's *Ramayan* (1987–1990)—involving at once a transgression of the Indian state's secular mandate in the realm of broadcasting, and a confluence of trends in economic liberalization and Hindutva ideology intersecting to form what Rajagopal refers to as "a new visual regime."[46] For Rajagopal, *Ramayan* interpellated the nation's Hindi speaking audience on an unprecedented scale, working to forge a "syndicated Hinduism" or a sense of Hindu solidarity through television viewership.[47] There are of course a number of significant contrasts between

Derana's *Rāvaṇa* and Doordarshan's *Ramayan*. Doordarshan is a state-run enterprise, owned by the Broadcasting Ministry of India, while Derana is a private broadcasting company (albeit one featuring programming resonant with Sinhala nationalist ideology).[48] Whereas Rajagopal postulates *Ramayan* to have been a catalyst for the tidal wave of Hindutva grass-roots activity culminating in the 1992 Babri Masjid demolition, Derana's *Rāvaṇa* debuted a decade after the end of Sri Lanka's civil war, fulfilling public demand for a televised version of the epic tailored to public tastes (well after the Sinhala Ravana revival was underway).[49] The production of Derana's *Rāvaṇa* is therefore better accounted for as a fulfillment of consumer demand, rather than as a form of state-orchestrated propaganda art. *Rāvaṇa* does however resonate with Rajagopal's characterization of *Ramayan* as a program, "drawing on myth and devotionalism to portray a golden age of tradition that was yet ahead of the modern era in statecraft and warfare," and likewise makes an effort to "appeal to diverse social groups"—not in the case of *Rāvaṇa* "under a symbolic rubric that could be tied to the banner of Hindu assertion," but under a banner of *Sinhala Buddhist* assertion.[50] *Rāvaṇa*, like Doordarshan's *Ramayan*, addresses and interpellates its audience directly, with the narrator in every episode making use of the possessive plural to refer to the ancient kingdom of the island as *apē hela deraṇa*, "our Hela world."

## 4.3 RAVANA'S LIMINAL STATUS IN HISTORY AND HISTORICAL FICTION

There is a mirror dimension to some of Ravana's contemporary literary and dramatic appearances mentioned above. While these examples drawn from stage and screen have no pretensions of portraying true events, often self-consciously embellishing and retooling the traditional *Ramayana* story, the authors and producers in some cases very explicitly advance empirical claims regarding the historicity of Ravana's kingdom in other venues. While, for instance, *Rāvaṇa* the serial is billed simply as entertainment drama, in 2017 Derana TV hosted a twenty-four-part series on the "historical Ravana" featuring (mostly amateur) scholar guests in roundtable discussions on the evidence associated with the historicity of the demon-king. Arisen Ahubudu and J. B. Disanayake have outside of their literary work publicly advanced the suggestion that Ravana was a great Sri Lankan king. Ahubudu (1920–2011) was one of the most celebrated literary figures of the twentieth century among Sinhala Buddhists, as an essayist, playwright, and poet, and a vocal participant in the Hela Havula movement. Mentioned above as the author of *Sakviti Rāvaṇa*, Ahubudu also composed the lyrics for *Laṅkā Laṅkā Pembara Laṅkā* ("Lanka, Beloved Lanka"), recorded in the late 1940s by Sunil Shantha to go on to become a radio classic. The song references Bali, Taru (Tāraka), and Ravana as great rulers of the island, together with Gämunu (Duṭṭhagāmiṇī) and Vijayabāhu.[51] As an advisor to the presidential administration of Ranasinghe Premadasa (1989–1993), Ahubudu successfully lobbied for the erection of a massive statue of Ravana at the rear entrance to the Kataragama temple complex.[52] In 2005 he published *Hela Deraṇa Vaga* ("Description of the Hela World") through the Central Cultural Fund, the government agency under the Ministry of Buddhasasana, Cultural and Religious Affairs which, among other things, manages heritage preservation and sponsors authoritative translations of Sinhala classics. Here Ahubudu dismisses the *Mahāvaṃsa* narrative of the peopling of the island on the grounds that it overlooks Sri Lanka's "pre-historical age" (*pūrva aitihāsika yugaya*), which he says Indians have been clever to recover for their own heritage from the *Mahābhārata* and *Rāmāyaṇa.* His bibliography ranges from Ptolemy and Faxian, to Ibn Battuta and Helena Blavatsky, to Ernest Heinrich Haeckel and Heinrich Schmidt. References to the lost continent of Lemuria and some dubious programming aired on the US History Channel are likewise invoked. Throughout the course of the book, Ahubudu argues that some of the first hominids, sun worship, and the world's earliest alphabet all originated in Sri Lanka. In his forward, Ahubudu recalls a verse from Munidasa Cumaratunga's *Hela Miyäsiya* (1941) on the tragedy of the subjugation of Sri Lanka under colonial rule, which, both Ahubudu and Cumaratunga maintain, obscures the glory of the ancient Sinhalas in global memory:

*nuvaṇa nuvana* *dī*
*vimasata nibäṅ* *dī*
*häma raṭa agä* *dī*
*heḷayaṭa para* *dī*

Though once in the eyes [of all the world]
Idolized and respected
A pinnacle among nations
The Helas were defeated.[53]

Historiography was admittedly a departure from the customary output of Arisen Ahubudu, who is remembered today primarily for his literary accomplishments. *Hela Deraṇa Vaga* is noteworthy, however, as an index to the longevity of the Hela Havula view of the island's distant past, as well as in its explicitly positivist methodology. Shrinat Ganevanta, in his introduction to the book, remarks on Ahubudu's commitment to the "Rankean method," laying bare the evidentiary facts of his textual archive while abstaining from any metahistorical commentary.[54]

J. B. Disanayake, by contrast, has enjoyed half a century as a public intellectual in Sri Lanka as one of the founders of the Department of Linguistics at the University of Colombo, author of numerous books on Sri Lankan culture, and a frequent interviewee in Colombo newspapers and on television. It was thus with academic bona fides that Disanayake produced *Understanding the Sinhalese* (1998), in which he speculated about an alternative, native-autochthonous origin of the Sinhala people.[55] While *Understanding the Sinhalese* hedges with third person qualifiers in gesturing toward the island's pre-Vijayan civilization ("some people believe . . ."), in *Lanka: the Land of Kings* (2007) Disanayake advances a more definite account. He names Ravana as the first king of the island, going on to fill in the details of additional monarchs prior to Prince Vijaya.[56] In a recent newspaper feature on "Sri Lanka as a multilingual society," Disanayake went on record stating that among the historical languages of the island is that of the Yakkhas, "used by Princess Kuveni whom Vijaya married," as well as "the language used by the ethnic group known as the Rakkhasas, who were considered descendants of King Ravana."[57]

While Ahubudu and Disanayake compartmentalized their creative and historical/investigative endeavors, more genre-porous works also populate the Ravana-themed Sinhala bibliographical archive. D. F. W. Kalu Aracci's *Ravuḷu Haṭana* ("The Ravana War," 1973) is something akin to *Ramayana* "fan fiction," with the first half of the novel devoted to an alternative prequel to the standard epic. Here amid a cast of characters nowhere found in Valmiki's version, Kalu Aracci introduces a novel ethnic geography of pre-Buddhist Sri Lanka (Asuras reside in the western portion of the island, and Yakshas, Rakshasas and Nagas each have their own domains), writing furthermore of Ravana's indefatigable efforts to enforce a ban on the sacrifice of animals and women (not *sati* but actual sacrifice) among the Brahmins of his vassal states in India. Subsequently we learn that King Dasharatha has been cursed on account of his compassionless slaughter of sixty elephants in a Vedic ritual, that Shurpanakha is in fact Sita's close friend in whom she has confided that her marriage with Rama is loveless, and that, following the conclusion of the war and death of Ravana, the people of Sri Lanka despise Vibhishana as a traitor and resent the fact that he has acceded to the throne.

Better known is Bhadraji Mahinda Jayatilaka's "historical novel," *Śrī Rāvaṇṇā Puvata* (1997). While the work is ostensibly a dramatized recapitulation of an ancient legend (Jayatilaka refers to his book as a *katāva*), the preface mentions the author's fortuitous encounter with several Ayurvedic physicians who supplied him with additional information about Ravana and medicine. Jayatilaka supplies a chart of Ravana's genealogy at the outset of the book (descent from Pulasthi, etc.), and proclaims on the rear cover:

> As we are *yakku* ourselves, Ravana's name is immortal to us. Born as Surya Yakshas, we live within the trees and vines. After death, we nourish the trees and vines—the very trees and vines through which we live . . . Therefore, we who are as sons of the Surya Yakshas must live like the *yakku* before us and protect the forests. For so long as there are trees, so long as the sun and moon both shine—so long too shall our Yaksha lineage live on (*apē yakṣa parapurat jīvat venavā*).[58]

The phrase which appears here, "we ourselves are Yakshas" (*api yakku tamā*), also sported on the book's first edition front cover, is semantically identical to the defining slogan of the twenty-first-century Sinhala Ravana movement (*api yakku bolavu*). Beyond the ostensible format of *Śrī Rāvaṇṇa Puvata* as a novelization of Valmiki's classic—a *katāva* for the modern age—Jayatilaka promotes an almost hylozoic view of the Lankan biome, in which the very bodies of the Yaksha ancestors of the Sinhala people are a sustaining life-essence. Naturally, in Jayatilaka's telling, Ravana is a sympathetic character, even (prior to the incident with Shurpanakha) expressing concern for Rama and Sita's fertility issues upon learning that the exiled couple was childless, suggesting that his court ministers send some "Yaksha medicine" (*yakungē behetak*) to help the princess conceive.[59]

Adding to the hyperabundance of alleged physical and textual evidence for Ravana's kingdom (discussed further in the following chapter) is a final literary genre, that of sheer invention. The purveyors of allegedly newly uncovered ancient documents—most notably T. R. Mirando Obeyesekere and Ven. Mānāvē Vimalaratana—have been deeply influential in the modern Ravana movement, their work copiously cited (even in official government publications), and widely shared on social media and YouTube. T. R. Mirando Obeyesekere (1940–2020) is, for many Sri Lankans, synonymous with Ravana scholarship. Author of over fifty books, Obeyesekere received a great deal of public exposure from the early 2000s through features in a number of leading Colombo newspapers (including *Maubima*, *Laṅkādīpa*, and *Daily Mirror*).[60] An amateur scholar himself, Obeyesekere's late-life career profited from the conflation of his own identity with that of two other people: Gananath Obeyesekere, Professor Emeritus at Princeton, and A. H. Mirando, who earned his PhD from the University of London's School of Oriental and African Studies in 1968, and whose columns arguing for the historicity of the *Ramayana* appeared in the *Daily News* throughout the 1980s.[61] Mirando Obeyesekere styled himself "Dr" and "Ācārya" ("professor," although he had no academic affiliation and it is unclear where he earned his doctoral degree), and was identified by the press as "one of Sri Lanka's foremost anthropologists," a cringe-worthy attribution from the point of view of Gananath Obeyesekere, who now lives in retirement in Kandy and with whom Mirando bears no relation.[62]

Mirando Obeyesekere applies boilerplate positivist analysis of standard source material (the *Vālmīki Rāmāyaṇa*, the *Rājāvaliya*, and Sinhala *kaḍayim* books) in service of his sensational claims: Ravana possessed a jet powered airplane, nuclear power, intercontinental ballistic missiles, and so on. We are told that Ravana was the inventor of the world's first violin, ruled over a "Lanka" eight times its current size, and belonged to "Yaksha tribe" (*yakṣa gōtraya*) from whom the Sinhala people are descended. The Yaksha tribe had a global footprint in antiquity, with a colony in ancient Palestine "which often faced rivalries from border countries Jordan, Iraq and Egypt" (a Yaksha settler named "Moses" defiantly remained in the region to establish a family lineage). Western treasure hunters trek to Obeyesekere's secluded home in Matale to solicit information from him, he says.[63] Although his writings have had an outsized influence on the twenty-first-century Ravana revival, at risk of boring the reader through redundancy I will abstain from rehearsing them all here. Relevant to the discussion in this chapter are the several texts to which Obeyesekere appeals which are preserved only, he says, in his private collection. These include the *Rāvaṇa Vata* (containing hitherto unknown information on the history of Sigiriya),[64] several Sinhala poems and instructional manuals on Angampora (a putative traditional Sri Lankan martial art), and a poetic work which Obeyesekere refers to as the *Rāvaṇa Kathāva*. Obeyesekere has offered a photograph of the cover folio of the latter, although no proof of its contents, claiming that the original text was written on golden plates, later copied to palm-leaf and passed down as a family heirloom.[65]

While we are not privy to any direct quotations from the *Rāvaṇa Kathāva* in Obeyesekere's works, he does reproduce some verses from several author texts (none of which are attested in the archival record) in a recent book on "The Ancient Art of Angampora."[66] Obeyesekere gives what he claims to be the final verses of an ancient Sinhala poem entitled the *Aňgam Purāṇaya*, combining principles of Buddhist pietism with devotion to Ravana, here elevated to the status of a martial deity. The following alleged portion of the text constitutes the "oath" (*divi*) taken by practitioners of the "Angam craft" (*aňgam śilpaya*), which was used as a method of restraining the mind by even gods and the Buddha:

*satun märīmen vaḷaki* *mu*
*matpän pānayen vaḷaki* *mu*
*durācāra kisi nodaki* *mu*
*aňgam deviyan namadi* *mu*

We refrain from the killing of animals
We refrain from drinking intoxicating beverage
We distance ourselves from any and all immoral pursuits
Prostrating ourselves before the Lord of Martial Arts

*rāvaṇā deviyō apa suraki* *navā*
*saturan säma dena pänalā ya* *navā*
*aňgam karuvan pinumgasa* *navā*
*mihikata ada keḷimaḍalak ve* *nevā*

Lord Ravana protects us
As all enemies leap away
Those who perform *aňgam* strike gracefully
Today amid the earthen circle of combat

*api āpasu duvannē* *näta*
*saturan ḷaṅ vennē* *näta*
*api biya haňdunannē* *näta*
*aňgama vikuṇanne* *näta*

We never run off in retreat
Enemies fear being close
We ourselves know no fear
Without ever selling our services

Obeyesekere goes on to quote from another mysterious text, the *Aňgam Śilpa Purāṇa*, reinforcing the moral uprightness of Angampora practitioners in keeping with the Five Precepts of Buddhism, along with the awesome spectacle of this ancient art:

*ihaḷa pelē aňgam* *karu*
*kisiviṭa nokiyayi horu* *boru*
*deviyan haṭa men garu* *saru*
*karanu mänavi movunaṭa* *garu*

Practicing *aňgam* upon the high steps
Those who never steal and speak no lies
With respect and prosperity like that of the gods
As one should rightly respect them

*siṅhalayāgē* *aňgam*
*ḍōlayagē häḍi* *suňgam*
*hela diva bäbalena* *aňgam*
*muḷu lova hellu* *aňgam*[67]

That martial art of the Sinhalas
Together with the fierce beating of the *ḍola* drum
The martial art which shines throughout the island of the Hela people
The martial art which shakes all the world.

While readers might not be overly impressed with the elementary quality of Obeyesekere's fragments, Angampora has in recent years undergone a revival among Sinhala Buddhists in Sri Lanka, who identify Ravana's descendants as custodians of this tradition (see Chapter 6, section 1). Angampora performers feature in the annual procession to Ravana that has been taking place since 2014 at a Buddhist temple in the Colombo suburbs, the Pannapitiya Devram Vihara, during which two enormous shields (*maha peli*) carried in carts are used as gongs, with participants sounding giant war drums (*rana bera* and *yuda bera*) as an image of Ravana is paraded around the temple grounds.[68] Those reconstructing the prehistory of Angampora characterize it as a defense technique developed by the ancient Yakshas (by King Taraka, several millennia prior to Ravana, to be precise), passed on through Ravana's grandson's, Raviśailāsa and Keveshasta.[69]

A complete vision of the world of the prehistoric Yaksha people is furnished by Ven. Mānāvē Vimalaratana, a resident monk at the Sri Jayasurama Aramaya temple in Meegalewa (twenty-six kilometers south of Anuradhapura). Vimalaratana has authored a series of books disclosing the contents of a mysterious manuscript known only to him, the *Vargapūrṇikāva*, a text which he claims records the history of the Sri Lanka's "Yaksha tribe" (*yakṣa gōtraya*), preserved orally until the eighteenth century when it was committed to palm-leaf.[70] The *Vargapūrṇikāva* allegedly supplies a complete dynastic chronology of the lineage descended from Raviśailāsa, Ravana's grandson, in addition to a description of the accomplishments, customs, and laws of the Yaksha people. The text gives some vivid and fine-grained description, including accounts of the clothes and ornaments worn by Yaksha women (captivating to the eye but not overly erotic, Vimalaratana clarifies). Vimalaratana in fact devotes a fair number of pages to his claim that in Ravana's time, women were socially equal to men, holding high elected office, and able to renounce in the Buddhist Sangha.

Vimalaratana supplies excerpts from the *Vargapūrṇikāva*, and extensively reproduces the runes and ideograms which he says make up the Yaksha script (all verified by way of ancient epigraphs found throughout the island, he tells us in another of his recent books on newly discovered and reinterpreted inscriptions, complete with photographs).[71] Vimalaratana repeatedly stresses the incompleteness of the *Mahāvaṃsa*'s account of the earliest history of the island, claiming that Buddhism was introduced to Sri Lanka by the Buddha Gotama himself (thus bypassing the Pali chronicle's involvement of the Indian king Ashoka). We are assured that the Yaksha people had their own Buddhist scripture, a sermon delivered *in situ* by the Buddha, preserved in the *yakṣabāsāva* as the "Viśakumbhana Sutta." On the *Vargapūrṇikāva*'s telling, the Yakkha princess Kuveni was in fact the daughter of Sri Lanka's first nun, a woman named Kavilāśapāli. Vimalaratana accuses the *Mahāvaṃsa* of its own revisionism, denying that Kuveni was seduced by Prince Vijaya, saying that instead she lived a chaste and celibate life to eventually become a nun herself.[72] Naturally the Yaksha language, from which

Sinhala is originally derived, bears no connection to Sanskrit, Pali, nor any other Indian dialect.[73]

Vimalaratana's more bizarre claims include those of diplomatic connections between the Yaksha people and extraterrestrials, from whom Ravana learned advanced medicine, electromagnetic science, and jet propulsion. (Contact between South Asians and "celestial beings" is in Vimalaratana's mind confirmed in the *Aggañña Sutta*, a canonical Pali account of anthropogenesis.[74]) In connection with this, according to Vimalaratana, Yaksha women's clothing fashion included a number of head ornaments made of a kind of leaf called *dälissa*, worn in arrangements determined by the position of the sun and planets, so as to minimize the damaging impact of radiation from outer space (*grahaloka valin*) on their complexion. (As we speak of "tin foil hat" conspiracy theorists, we might characterize Vimalaratana as a "*dälissa* leaf" historical revisionist.)

In failing to make the textual sources for their claims available for public scrutiny, Mirando Obeyesekere and Mānāvē Vimalaratana pay no heed to the dictum that extraordinary claims require extraordinary evidence. Nonetheless, they remain the most widely cited "Ravana researchers" in Sri Lanka today, their work even having attained state recognition on some occasions. Vimalaratana has appeared as a guest on radio programs, televised "expert panels," and Ravana related public events.[75] Several Facebook groups entitled "Vargapūrṇikāva" featuring Sinhala nationalist content have collectively attracted nearly 50,000 followers. His *Vargapūrṇikāva* has been cited by credentialed scholars (see Chapter 6, section 2) and is quoted in literature distributed by the Sri Lankan Air Force in support of the claim that the island is home to an indigenous martial arts tradition dating back over 30,000 years.[76] Mirando Obeyesekere, whose work has been cited in support of the Ministry of Tourism's "Ramayana Trail" (see Chapter 5, section 2), found himself publicly honored in August 2014 by the Minister of Culture and Arts for his contributions to Ravana scholarship at a ceremony held in the Colombo National Museum.[77] Obeyesekere's Ravana advocacy has been posthumously enabled by YouTube: one of his final interviews, uploaded March 12, 2019, attracted 82,000 views by March 25, and had garnered a total of over 300,000 as of December 2020, ten months after his death.[78]

In their reconstruction of the sociology of the "*yakṣa gotraya*" of Lankan antiquity, Obeyeskere and Vimalaratna work to fulfill the Hela Havula view that the (original) Sinhala language was wholly *sui generis*, unrelated to Sanskrit or to any other Indo-European language. This concern to circumscribe the origins of Sinhala language, culture, and ethnicity within Sri Lanka's shores is a vivid token of what Arjun Appadurai refers to as the *anxiety of incompleteness* which so often plagues nationalist imaginaries. Appadurai discusses this concept in reference to the "national ethos" found nearly universally among discourses of the nation today:

> No modern nation, however benign its political system and however eloquent its public voices may be about the virtues of tolerance, multiculturalism, and inclusion, is free of the idea that its national sovereignty is built on some sort of ethnic genius.[79]

Appadurai gives the example of Samuel Huntington's accusation that Hispanic people have been reluctant to assimilate into American culture (which Huntington views implicitly as Euro-Protestant) as a reminder that such cultural essentialism is not limited to "dark Baltic states, raving African demagogues, or fringe Nazis in England and northern Europe."[80]

In quests for ethnic origins, the anxiety of incompleteness lends itself to grandiose, hyperdiffusionist theories concerning the influence of a nation's cultural genius. Early Hela Havula activists saw the influence of Sinhala language throughout the ancient world, claiming that Greek *helios* ("sun") is derived from *hela* (the people of the solar race), and that "Madagascar" derives from Sinhala *mäda gas kara*, "the middle place [of the world] with an abundance of trees."[81] Such philological inference on the basis of sheer homophony in service of establishing a supra-regional Lankan sphere of influence in deep antiquity is reminiscent of a mode of cognition that Richard Landes calls "semiotic arousal." In his discussion of the numerological, steganographic, and divinatory proclamations of millenarian charismatic leaders, Landes defines semiotic arousal as an interpretive framework in which "anything means something, and free association becomes an impeccable and convincing system of meaning."[82]

The following chapter discusses evidence for Ravana's historicity adduced through the suspension of any contextualization or counter-perspective, in examples relating to the interpretation of epigraphs, etymologies of Sri Lankan place names, and references in classical Sanskrit literature. Here I would like to consider the relationship of semiotic arousal to the vexatious writings of Mirando Obeyesekere and Mānǟvē Vimalaratana, which purport to offer definitive textual proof of the grandeur of Ravana's Hela-Yaksha world, but which cannot be substantiated as anything more than literary invention. Obeyesekere and Vimalaratana, two of the most prominent but by no means the only twenty-first-century Sinhala Ravana enthusiasts to have produced ancient documents with fantastic contents,[83] ask readers to accept their evidence without any hermeneutical constraints, like the prophets and charismatics whom Landes describes. The persuasive potential of evidence and argumentation generated in this mode depends of course upon a receptive audience—in the case of millenarian charismatics, this involves an audience primed with millennial expectation. In the case of the twenty-first-century Sinhala Ravana phenomenon, the anxiety of incompleteness which plagued a minority subset of Sinhala nationalists for a century found expression in Sri Lanka's Buddhist population at large, heightening the susceptibility of the reading public to semiotic arousal as well as, relatedly, generating an appetite for a style of analysis and production of evidence that might be called *literary hypertrophy*, involving the conflation of what Dominic LaCapra refers to as documentary and "worklike" modes of literary production.[84]

The attitudes of Mirando Obeyesekere and Mānāvē Vimalaratana are an extreme example of this phenomenon—for these two authors, all ancient texts describing Ravana's kingdom can be gleaned for empirical evidence, with the question of their status as works of imaginative literature (as "worklike" on LaCapra's definition) never coming into play. (The fact that Obeyesekere and Vimalaratana leave no room to account for authorial imagination in the works they cite as documentary evidence is of course an irony of the greatest degree because their own writing is prolifically, if not entirely, imaginative). By contrast, Arisen Ahubudu and J. B. Dissanayaka more neatly distinguish their own "worklike" portrayals of Ravana, representing him imaginatively in *Ramayana*-themed musical, dramatic, and literary works, while elsewhere arguing for his historicity by appealing to what they interpret to be documentary elements of Sanskrit, Pali, and Sinhala literary works. Ahubudu and Dissanayaka's output stands alongside a third variety of literary hypertrophy—works which are genre-porous and, as such, undefinable using conventional bibliographical designations, such as B. M. Jayatilaka's *Śrī Rāvaṇṇa Puvata* (a "historical novel" written primarily as dialogue but framed in its front matter and back matter with historiographical pretensions).

## 4.4 RAVANA'S LANKA AS LOST PARADISE

Sri Lanka, as an island with a terrain increasingly difficult to access as one travels further into the interior from the coast, furnishes an ideal setting for tales of adventure and expedition. Sri Lanka's topographical mystique juxtaposed with its geographical centrality amid Indian Ocean trade networks made the island a subject of literary fascination for centuries. Travelogues written by Europeans grew to constitute a substantive genre during the colonial era, with Robert Knox's account of his escape from captivity in Kandy lending inspiration to Daniel Defoe's *Robinson Crusoe* (1719).[85] A number of scholars have noted an often preferential, romanticized attitude toward Sri Lanka in the imagination of British imperialists who by the nineteenth century had secured dominion over most of the South Asian subcontinent. Sujit Sivasundaram explains that in this context:

> The apparatus through which Ceylon was unified under a centralized regime of what Indian observers expressly declared to be "colonialism" set in motion a discursive and intellectual way of thinking and writing of this space as a romanticized and sexualized island, a lost Eden, and a place which was very different to the barren and Hindu mainland. The island's Buddhism was seen to hold a key to the mainland's past, and this religious system was thought to have lessened the force of some of the norms of society in India, such as caste or gender oppression.[86]

Surveying colonial-era British travelogues which included visits to Sri Lanka, Sharae Deckard notes that writers often "commented that Ceylon was more perfectly 'Oriental' than other countries which they visited on their Grand Tour of the empire."[87] The "veritable paradise of Ceylon" was in the view of these authors home to the egalitarian and pacifist religion of Buddhism. The Sinhalese people, both men and women, were exoticized as "graceful" and "sensual," with the occasional practice of polyandry becoming a fixation for foreign visitors which confirmed in their eyes "the emasculation of Sinhalese men," while "fulfilling fantasies of promiscuous native women."[88] British Ceylon was in this sense a paradise "discovered" and incorporated through the organs of the empire at large, a tropical Eden awaiting the enjoyment of European tourists while at the same time, like all colonial properties, a repository of natural wealth subject to orderly extraction. While Sri Lanka was represented as a contemporary paradise in this way, it was in addition imagined as host to a once greater civilization, the "classical" Buddhist kingdom of Anuradhapura, reconstructed through archaeological expeditions of the late 1800s.[89] Sri Lanka's lost hydraulic civilization furnished confirmation for the British of a broader thesis concerning a golden age of South Asian antiquity, the apogee of Indian literary production, creative flourishing, and political dominion which had fallen into decline over a millennium and a half prior.[90]

One discerns at the heart of the twenty-first-century Sinhala Ravana imaginary a response toward, and reappropriation of, colonial impressions of Sri Lanka as a lost paradise in the senses outlined above. Literary and putatively historical impressions of Ravana's kingdom are structured around the themes concerning fantastic material and technological wealth awaiting discovery, mitigating the extraction of native resources by foreign powers, and the promise of restoring an Edenic Hela-Yaksha society (sometimes involving the return of King Ravana himself). Significantly, the Ravana revolution displaces another fully articulated vision of a prelapsarian past which for decades served as a template for Buddhist modernity among Sinhala nationalists. In the years following Sri Lankan independence in 1948, development discourse was inspired by a model based on the hydraulic agricultural society of ancient Anuradhapura, in which social and economic life were governed by a harmony between "temple, tank and paddy field."[91] Unsatisfied with a vision of the halcyon past based principally on accomplishments in irrigation engineering, the archaic modernity of Hela-Yaksha society bypasses "hydraulic culture" (*vari saṃskṛtiya*) to celebrate a broader spectrum of alleged native innovations in medicine, mathematics, and the technical arts.

The theme of Ravana's kingdom as lost paradise along with that of the specter of colonial extraction have perhaps no clearer literary instantiation than in Susitha Ruwan's popular Sinhala novel *Rāvaṇa Meheyuma* ("Ravana Mission," 2011).[92] The sci-fi thriller takes place over a twenty-four-hour period, its plot proceeding from the accidental discovery of the ruins of Ravana's palace, deep within the hills of Horton Plains. The hero is Gotabaya Rajapaksa, Sri Lanka's Secretary of Defense, who embarks in a race against time to save the site from the United States Air Force (the US government has learned of the palace through a CIA tip-off and dispatched jet fighters to destroy it, eager to rob Sri Lanka of this 10,000-year-old cultural heritage monument). Naturally, the palace contains proof of Ravana's advanced technology, his aircraft, and of Sri Lanka's status as the *fons et origo* of world culture. Rajapaksa personally treks through the rugged terrain to reach the palace in the nick of time, and, with the help of a Colombo journalist, is able to set up a live television broadcast in order to verify to the world that the palace and its fantastic treasures are indeed real. Ruwan's 2015 follow up work, *Rāvaṇa Meheyuma 2*, follows along similar lines, telling the story of the discovery of the ruins of an ancient city on the ocean floor off the coast of Mannar by a Chinese oil-seeking venture. Sri Lankan archaeologists called to investigate speculate that the site may in fact be the lost city of Atlantis based on a reference to the city of "Āṭānāṭa Pura" found in the canonical Pali Buddhist literature. The villain this time around is Blake Splinter, who joins the investigative team claiming to be professor of archaeology at the University of Birmingham in the UK. Splinter learns along with the Sri Lankan scholars leading the excavation that, during Ravana's time, the island's inhabitants possessed powered flight, craft outfitted for space travel, and that some of the significant geography of India mentioned in the Sanskrit epics was in fact located in Sri Lanka ("Asura Bhāvana" and "Laṅkāpura" were located at Horton Plains, "Mahā Meru" is Sri Pada). The team is taken hostage on the oil rig by four of the Chinese expeditionary employees, whom we discover to be in league Blake Splinter—not actually an academic but in fact a professional treasure hunter. Freed by a team of army commandos clandestinely radioed by the captive Lankan archaeologists, the protagonists dive to discover a "Rosetta Stone" inscription amid the sunken ruins, confirming (in corresponding Hela and Egyptian hieroglyphs) that Sri Lanka was universally regarded in deep antiquity as "the center of the world."[93]

The "Ravana Mission" series brings into focus much of the ethos of the Sinhala Ravana movement. The narrative of both books is structured by themes of colonial loss and post-colonial exploitation, post-civil war triumphalism, and the necessity of Lankan sovereignty. *Rāvaṇa Meheyuma (1)* was first published in 2011, when steps were in motion within the United Nations Human Rights Council to investigate possible war crimes committed by the Sri Lankan government. The United States Department of State support for the investigation, which would ultimately result in a UNHRC resolution in 2015, did not go unnoticed by the Sri Lankan media. Ruwan's novels at the same time work to reclaim the subgenre of "Sri Lankan science fiction" from the orientalist gaze of its inventor, Arthur C. Clarke (who himself lived as British expatriate in Sri Lanka from 1956 until his death in 2008). Clarke's celebrated *The Fountains of Paradise* (1979) takes place in the near future on the equatorial island of "Taprobane," its plot centered on the efforts of an obsessive engineering genius, Vannevar Morgan, to build a "space elevator" capable of launching cargo ships into earth's orbit. Morgan's ideal site for the massive catapult is "Sri Kanda," a mountain sacred to the people of Taprobane and overseen by the island's highest ranking Buddhist clergy. Initially denying Morgan permission to excavate the mountain, the monks abandon Sri Kanda when a freak weather event deposits a massive swarm of yellow butterflies on its slopes, in apparent fulfilment of the ancient prophecy that the mountain would topple when butterflies stormed its gates. (Sri Kanda is of course Clarke's fictional homologue of Sri Pada, where according to Buddhist legend droves of butterflies flock seasonally at the end of their short lifespan, in order to worship the Buddha's footprint.) Free to carry out his project, Morgan strips Sri Kanda of its ancient Buddhist edifices in a dramatic conclusion, suggesting the victory of western rational progress over local superstition.[94] In Susitha Ruwan's novels, the premise of *The Fountains of Paradise* is inverted—rather than abandoning Buddhist tradition to achieve technological fulfillment, lost technology lies *hidden within* the sacred mountains themselves. No compromise is required as Sri Lanka is at once both traditional *and* rational—essentially Buddhist, morally and perhaps militarily superior to the West heir to a once great civilization concerning which agents of neo-colonial powers have only conspired to plunder and obscure.

Colombo architect Sunela Jayewardene's *The Line of Lanka* (2017) elevates the quest for Ravana's kingdom to a truly liminal genre: part travelogue, part crash-course in Sri Lankan history, part adventure novel, featuring lush prose descriptions of Jayewardene's hiking trips through remote corners of the island with her husband and friends. Drawing from the legends of locals they encounter along the way and supplemented with her own imagination, Jayewardene weaves a series of fantastic theories surrounding the pre-history of the island, a number relating to the time of Ravana. The title of the book derives from the arrangement of the auxiliary shrines to the god Saman centered around his seat at Sri Pada, also known as Samantakūṭa, "Saman's Peak." These are the *devālaya*s at Ratnapura, Deriyangala, Mahiyangana, and Bulthombe, which lie along two axes, intersecting with one another at Sri Pada at near perfect right angles. A host of inferences follow based on this presumed geomancy, the significance and relation to one another of which is, however, not in every case clear. We learn that the "arrow" plotted by the axes of the Saman shrines points directly to Fua Mulaku, an atoll in the southern Maldives where the possible ruins of Buddhist temples have been unearthed, and whose residents speak a dialect closer to Sinhala than is standard Dhivehi (Sinhala and Dhivehi are related languages). Jayewardene explains that an axis at an eighty-six-degree-angle relative to the equator (precisely the angle of the south–west to north–east running axis of the Saman shrines) is significant in the *Sūrya Siddhānta*, a famed Sanskrit astronomical treatise, representing an ancient cartographical equivalent to the Prime Meridian, thereby making Sri Pada the "Greenwich" of the ancient world.[95] Jayewardene goes on to explain that Sri Pada was marked as geographically significant by ancient map makers because, the reader is informed, it possesses the lowest geomagnetic energy of any place in the world.

*The Line of Lanka* blends local lore with positivist readings of legendary events to produce a fantastic picture of the technological and engineering capacities of ancient Sri Lanka. On Jayewardene's understanding, not only did colonial archaeologists dismiss King Dutugemunu's island-spanning highway (the *kalugal bämma*) and Sri Lanka's premodern steel forging industry as native fantasies, but in their underestimation of local accomplishments in deep antiquity failed to adequately prime us today for the magnitude of what we might find if we dig deep enough. According to her, the original identity of Saman was Rama's brother Laksman (see Chapter 3, section 1), venerated millennia ago for restoring the alkaline pH of the soil in the southern highlands (the vicinity of Saman's shrines) after it was decimated by missiles launched in the conflict between Rama and Ravana. References to the marine archaeology in the Gulf of Cambay ("the lost city of Dwaraka"), David Davenport's speculation that Mohenjo-Daro was destroyed in an atomic blast (a description of which is supposedly found in the *Mahābhārata*), and the "Yonaguni monument" of Okinawa are invoked to encourage open-mindedness on the part of the reader with respect to the mysteries of the past.[96] *The Line of Lanka* has been well-received among Colombo readers, shortlisted for the prestigious Gratiaen Prize, and serves as a reminder that Ravana mania is not restricted to the Sinhala speaking literary and media spheres, having gained currency among English speaking urbanites as well.[97]

## 4.5 CONCLUSION

In the imaginations of Mirando Obeyesekere and Susitha Ruwan, the relationship of native Hela genius to foreign powers is necessarily antagonistic, with the threat of extraction and exploitation always looming. Their view of the historical relationship of indigenous Lankans to outsiders—a view representative of that of the twenty-first-century Sinhala Ravana imaginary at large—echoes that of Munidasa Cumaratunga and the Hela Havula, who disparaged the suggestion that the Sinhala people were descended from Prince Vijaya, the "robber baron" from India. As illustrated in the previous chapter concerning medieval and Kandyan era impressions of Ravana's kingdom, however, variegated and nuanced views also circulated in the twentieth century alongside more radically nativist ones. This was the case for W. A. de Silva, two-time President of the Ceylon National Congress, for whom Ravana's ancient Lankan kingdom offered a multivalent allegory for the global political situation of 1938. Writing in that April's edition of the *Journal of the Young Men's Buddhist Association*, as the storm clouds of war were gathering in Europe and as Sri Lankans were realistically imagining a future for their nation with the yoke of colonialism lifted, De Silva cast Ravana's hoary domain as an empire with both exploitative and civilizing tendencies:

> Ravana the King of Rakshasas had a vast Empire which he and his proud people ruled from their island home. Countries as far as the Himalayas and the Godaveri were under his sway and protection.
>
> *The Rakshasas were not colonists, but were imperialists. They exercised power and whenever they subjected a people they protected them and exploited them.*
>
> The wealth of their out-living possessions drifted to their Island, till it became extremely rich and powerful at the expense of their dominions.
>
> The Aryans who were gradually coming down from the north were conquerors pure and simple. Wherever they went they exterminated the aboriginal tribes and occupied their land as the Western Aryans did at a later period in such places as North and South America, Australia and South Africa.[98]

De Silva clarifies that the Rakshasas were an advanced race on many fronts, skilled artisans and weapons specialists, pioneers in science with "mathematicians of note and architects and medicine men," and "well versed in the use of fire and gas" to power machines. Echoing the legends of Koneswaram, he explains that, "in the arts of peace, too, [the Rakshasas] took no mean part. Ravana himself was a great devotee who had practised Yoga till he was able to extract the secrets of nature."[99] Just like the British at the twilight of their empire, however, Ravana and the Rakshasas were ultimately blighted by hubris and overextension:

> At this period people of Lanka lived intensively. In that very intensity there was a seed of destruction. The bubble of life was swelled in an ever

> increasing splendour of colour and shape. It was pricked by the fortunes of a war. It burst hardly leaving any vestiges of its former pride of place. Today the plains of Uva, the beautiful and undulating *patina* are shown as the country that was burnt by Hanuman, the faithful ally of Rama.[100]

The Rakshasas of Sri Lankapura were then for De Silva a relatively (although not altogether) benevolent imperial outfit of Asiatic antiquity. They, like the British, were bearers of the standard of civilizational progress, and, as the British of his day were about to, met with the same end as do all decadent empires in the model of epochal history. Whatever lessons the ancient Helas might hold for modern readers, the true villains of pre-historic South Asia were on De Silva's view the ancestors of the global hegemon of the early twentieth century, the bellicose "Aryans" of north India whose conquest was of the most reckless and exploitative sort. Citing the *Vālmīki Rāmāyaṇa*, De Silva explains that the crowning achievement of Rakshasa technological prowess was looted by Rama upon his departure—Ravana's aerial vehicle, or "Pushpika Vimana." De Silva's implicit parallel between the Aryans of Ayodhya and the "Western Aryans" (European colonial powers) presages Jawaharlal Nehru's observations a decade later concerning the intentional dismantling of Indian manufacturing capabilities at the hands of the British, as part of a strategy to make colonial subjects dependent on foreign imports.[101] Although the *Mahāvaṃsa* narrative continued to dominate Sinhala Buddhist nationalist ideology for the duration of the century, De Silva's historical vignette establishes the currency of Ravana's kingdom in the public imagination by the 1930s, attesting to the allure of a vision of the distant past that left space for an autochthonous race of Sri Lankans long before the time of the Buddha Gotama.

While it is of course true that a great deal of the twenty-first century reconstruction of Ravana's ancient Lankan kingdom depends on straightforward positivist readings of classical Sanskrit, Pali, and Sinhala works, I wish to argue here in addition that Ravana's image as inherited by modern Sri Lankan authors supplies a template which tends to blur the distinction between the legendary and the empirical. As discussed in the previous chapter, from centuries ago commentators invoked historical narration derived from the *Ramayana* to supplement the narrative lacuna of the *Mahāvaṃsa* with respect to Sri Lanka's earliest inhabitants—a strategy of historical interpolation upheld in the nineteenth and twentieth centuries by those who viewed "descent from Vijaya" as an ignominious account of the origins of the Sinhala people. Beyond the convenience of the *Ramayana* as a temporal adjunct to the Pali chronicle timeline, the idiosyncratic topography of Ravana's kingdom as related in Kandyan era Sinhala accounts—with the island's central highlands positioned as a Yaksha sanctuary, the point of entry to a massive subterranean extension of Lankapura—is saturated with potential for stories concerning expeditions to recover the treasures of the ancient Helas. This potential is actualized in the twenty-first century in literary form, as in Susitha Ruwan's *Rāvaṇa Meheyuma* series, in the form of claims regarding the recovery of physical evidence of Ravana's kingdom (discussed in the following chapter), and in the public imagination at large, wherein the lost treasures of Ravana's kingdom have in recent years stirred the imagination of the entrepreneurial and the adventurous. GoPro-captured video of spelunkers exploring "Ravana's caves" in the island's central highlands have garnered millions of views on YouTube. A Google search for "Ravana's body found in Sri Lanka" turns up articles and videos from a number of Indian news outlets and tabloids reporting the discovery of "Ravana's mummified body" alongside a splendid cache of burial goods made of gold and jewels (photos included). We are informed that the find took place in 2019 in the Rangala region of the Knuckles Mountain Range of the island's north-central highlands, with the articles citing as their source the "International Ramayan Research Centre" and Sri Lanka's Ministry of Tourism.[102] While such sensationalism smacks of commercial intentions (tourism in Sri Lanka suffered a serious dip as a result of the April 2019 Colombo Easter Bombings), earlier stories surfaced in Colombo newspapers of explorers trespassing in remote areas in search of Ravana's treasure. One such report from July 2011 reads like the setup to a Susita Ruwan novel: three well-equipped expeditionary diggers were taken into custody by the Kandy Range Vice Squad after having excavated a tunnel forty feet long over the course of several weeks. According to the police report, the trio believed that they could find precious items buried by Ravana in the remote hills of Rattota near Matale, and they were led by a man "alleged to be an archaeologist with overseas training."[103]

This chapter examined Ravana's understated although significant literary career in Sri Lanka over the past century, highlighting the manner in which premodern Sanskrit, Pali, and Sinhala sources have inspired both Ravana-centric updated dramatizations and novelizations of the *Ramayana*, as well as positivist readings seeking textual evidence for Ravana's historical kingdom at the expense of any consideration of the source material's genre or "worklike" dimensions. I have in this chapter also followed others in arguing that the unique geographical situatedness of Sri Lanka—as an island with close cultural and linguistic ties to the Indian subcontinent, and with its mountainous central interior—has influenced literary paradigms and tropes, notably those concerning Sri Lanka as an "island paradise" and a guarded repository of wealth, resources, and archaeological discoveries related to civilizational antiquity. Chapter 5 goes on to explore the gestation of further contours of Ravana's kingdom in the public imagination in the twenty-first century, facilitated by the sharing of images and ideas on social media, blog sites, and YouTube.

## Notes

1. Following on the disruptions of colonial transfer of power and the fissiparous re-alignment of the Buddhist Sangha through new ordination lineages imported from Thailand and Burma, an epicenter of classical language education emerged in the Parama Dhamma Chetiyāramaya Pirivena, which was founded by a single dedicated monk with a small endowment from a handful of lay benefactors in 1841 in Ratmalana, just south of Colombo. Some of the first students at the fledgling Chetiyāramaya Pirivena were two monks of the Siyam Nikaya who would themselves go on to establish the major monastic colleges of their day: Ratmalane Dharmarama, founder of Vidyalankara Pirivena, and Hikkaduwe Sri Sumangala, founder of Vidyodaya Pirivena, and a teacher of T. W. Rhys Davids (founder of The Pali Text Society) and Col. Henry Steel Olcott, co-founder of the Theosophical Society.
2. On themes such as the life of the Buddha, Prince Siddhartha's wife Yasodhara, and King Ashoka's son Mahinda. Private printers supported in the dissemination of some of these works and subsequently, after Sri Lanka's independence in 1948, a number were published by the Sri Lankan Cultural Ministry.
3. C. E. Godakumbura, "A Note on the Jānakīharaṇa," *The Journal of the Ceylon Branch of the Royal Asiatic Society of Great Britain & Ireland* [New Series] 11 (1967): 96f.; F. W. Thomas, "The Jānakīharaṇa of Kumāradāsa," *The Journal of the Royal Asiatic Society of Great Britain and Ireland* April (1901): 253–280.
4. John de Silva produced two *Ramayana* plays in 1886: a longer and more complete version of the story simply entitled *Rāmāyaṇa*, and a shorter one focusing on the drama of Sita's captivity and rescue entitled *Sītā Haraṇa, hevat, "Ginigat" Rāmāyaṇaya*. De Silva explains that he subtitled the play *Ginigat ("Gone to the fire") Rāmāyaṇaya* to commemorate a Colombo theater (the "Kolamba Malvattē Puṣpamandiraya") which had years earlier been destroyed by a fire (John de Silva's preface to *Sītā Haraṇa, hevat, "Ginigat" Rāmāyaṇaya* [Colombo: Śāstrāloka Press, 1886], i).
5. See vol. 1 of Sunil Ariyaratne's compilation of *The Complete Plays of John de Silva* (Colombo: Godage International Publishers, 2008 [1992]).

6. K. N. O. Dharmadasa, *Language, Religion and Ethnic Assertiveness: The Growth of Sinhalese Nationalism in Sri Lanka* (Ann Arbor: University of Michigan Press, 1993), 127.
7. Don Bastian gives a précis of European scholarship on the *Vālmīki* and *Kampa Rāmāyaṇas* at the time, mentioning August Wilhelm Schlegel's 1829 edition and Latin translation of the *Rāmāyaṇa*, "Señor Garsio's" Italian translation, Clarisse Bader's work in French, along with Pramada Das Mitra (ix–x of the preface to the 1886 edition of *Rāmāyaṇaya hevat Rāvaṇā Saṅhāraya*). He mentions receiving, in July 1869, "a very hard to find book in English published in Benares containing the last chapters [of the epic]." He does not mention Ralph T. H. Griffith's 1870–1874 translation, the first complete translation of Valmiki's text in English.
8. Section 13 of Sri Lanka's Intellectual Property Act No 36 of 2003 states that the duration of copyright of printed books extends seventy years after the death of the author/copyright holder. C. Don Bastian died in 1921. https://www.lawnet.gov.lk/intellectual-property-2/.
9. The "Mayil Rāvaṇa" portion of the story appears on pages 224–244 of Don Bastian's *Rāmāyaṇaya*, throughout which he gives only one cryptic reference in a footnote to an alternate reading "in another book" (227). Commentators have misidentified the source of the "Peacock Ravana" episode as Kampaṉ's *Rāmāyaṇa*, no doubt a result of the fact that Don Bastian mentions in his preface a partial Sinhala translation of that text made by Don Jerenimus Vīraśēkara Abhayaguna-wardhaṇa in 1841. In reality, Don Bastian must have had either a manuscript version of "Peacock Ravana" available to him, or possibly a printed Tamil text (Kamil Zvelebil was unable to trace the earliest editions of the *Mayil Irāvaṇaṉ Katai* printed in Tamil Nadu, hypothesizing that they would have been available as early as the 1850s–1860s, see preface to *Two Tamil Folktales*, xxviv). Beyond the references to "Mayil Rāvaṇa," proper names such as "Rāmasvāmi" and "Sītāparamēsvari" further suggest that Don Bastian had among his sources at least one Tamil reference.
10. Ediriweera Sarachchandra notes the direct influence of Bastian's work on the form and style of their early short prose romances, with others noting the reproduction of the theme of "exile of the couple to the forest" in Piyadasa's *Jayatissa and Rosalind* (1906) (*The Sinhalese Novel* [Colombo: M.D. Gunasena, 1950], 67, 81f.). Beyond works related to Ravana and the *Ramayana* by significant authors of the Sinhala neoclassical renaissance there are others which have long since fallen into obscurity. K. R. Perera's 330 verse poem entitled *Rāvanā Yuddhaya* (1893) combines a Pali Jataka story (the "Dasaratha Jātaka") with Vālmīki's epic (and was popular enough to merit reprinting in 1902). See Tissa Kariyawasam, "Religious Activities and the Development of a New Poetical Tradition in Sinhalese, 1852–1906," PhD Diss.: University of London (1973), 465f.
11. Sykes, *The Musical Gift*, 220.
12. Garrett Field, *Modernizing Composition: Sinhala Song, Poetry, and Politics in Twentieth-Century Sri Lanka* (Berkeley: University of California Press, 2017), 22.
13. Music and lyrics included in R. J. F. Varnakulasuriya, *Rāmāyanaya hevat Rāvanā Nāḍagam* [two parts] (Colombo: Sastraloka Press, [n.d., c.1923]).

14. Field, *Modernizing Composition*, 23–25.
15. John de Silva's later plays included *Sirisaṅgabō Caritaya* (1903), *Srī Vikrama Rājasiṅha* (1906), *Valagambā* (1907), *Dutugämunu* (1910), *Mahānāma* (1910), *Alakeśvara* (1913), *Devanampiya Tissa* (1914), *Vessantara* (1916), *Vihāra Mahā Devi* (1916), *Paraṅgi Haṭane* (1917) on war with the Portuguese, and *Käppeṭipola* (1917) on the 1818 Kandyan Rebellion against the British. For an overview of de Silva's theatre career and political activities, see Sarath Amunugama, *The Lion's Roar: Anagarika Dharmapala and the Making of Modern Buddhism* (New York: Oxford University Press, 2019) 379–412.
16. Ibid., 129.
17. de Silva, *Sītā Haraṇa, hevat, "Ginigat" Rāmāyaṇaya*, i. De Silva also mentions that the first Sinhala translation of the *Kampa Rāmāyaṇa* was done by one "Sīnigama Sthavira," perhaps Sīnigama Dhīrakkhanda, chief incumbent at the Dīpaduttāramaya Vihāra in Kotahena from 1845–1858. I have been unable to trace this reference.
18. Adapted from McKinley, "Mountain at a Center of the World," 241, translating de Silva's *Śrīpāda Śatakaya*, vv.14–15.
19. De Silva explains in the introduction to his *Śrī Vikrama Rājasinghe* that he established the Arya Subodha Drama Society in 1902 to reunite the Sinhalese with their Arya-Sinhala Buddhist heritage, commenting elsewhere that it was for this reason that he viewed it as important to reconnect the Sinhala people with north Indian classical music. See Field, *Modernizing Composition*, 23–25.
20. N. Wickramasinghe, *Sri Lanka in the Modern Age: A History* (Oxford: Oxford University Press, 2014), 90f. No copies of *Lak Miṇi Kiruḷa* seem to have survived in archival collections, although there is an excerpt from the first edition in Kalukondayāvē Prajñāśekharābhidhāna's compendium of early Sinhala periodicals (*Siṅhala Puvatpat Saṅgarā Itihāsaya*, vol. 1 [Colombo: M.D. Gunasena, 1965], 365–372). I am grateful to Mr. Buddhika Konara for pointing this out to me and for this reference.
21. June and August 1929 excerpts from *Rāmasäraya* reproduced in Kalukondayāvē Prajñāśekharābhidhāna, *Siṃhala Puvatpat Saṅgarā Itihāsaya*, vol. 6. (1969), 2897f.; and *Siṅhala Puvatpat Saṅgarā Itihāsaya*, vol. 7 (1970), 3275f.
22. Harshana Rambukwella, *The Politics and Poetics of Authenticity: A Cultural Genealogy of Sinhala Nationalism* (London: University College London Press, 2018), 39.
23. From the point of view of Hela Havula, then, the abundant Pali and Sanskrit lexicon attested in Sinhala historically were merely later "accretions" to the language as it existed in its pure and original form. Doubt regarding the status of Sinhala as a derivative of Sanskrit was pronounced early on by James De Alwis in his 1852 translation of the *Sidat Saṅgarā*, a fourteenth-century Sinhala grammar. De Alwis concluded that Sanskrit and Sinhala are related only insofar as they are both cognates of a considerably earlier, now lost parent language (*The Sidath Sangarawa* [Colombo: William Skeen, Government Printer, 1852], xxxviii–xlviii).
24. Dharmadasa, *Language, Religion and Ethnic Assertiveness*, 262, citing *Helio* 1.7–8 [1941], 56. Excoriating the Brahmin "enemies of this country" who refuse to acknowledge the splendor of Ravana's ancient domain of Lanka, Munidasa Cumaratunga showcases his own knowledge of Sanskrit vocabulary to relate the story of the

ancient king in a Sinhala-language primer published in 1933 (*Śikṣāvatāraya sahita Śikṣāmārgaya* [Colombo: Department of Cultural Affairs, 2009 (1933)], 11–14).

25. See quotations in Field, *Modernizing Composition*, 38, citing "The Hidden History of the Helese: IV," *Helio* 1.9–10 (November 1, 1941), 77–78. We may note that Tennakoon is largely correct in blaming the British for superimposing racial attributes upon the vocabulary of the *Mahāvaṃsa*, which does not employ the term "Ariyan" (*āriya*) as an ethnonym. See Gunawardhana, "The People of the Lion," 46–86.
26. Summary in Field, *Modernizing Composition*, 44.
27. Ibid., 45–47.
28. "Mandōdarī," in Wimal Abhayasundara, *Niṣādī* (Colombo: S. Godage, 1959 [2006]), 237–248. I am grateful to Garrett Field for informing me of this opera and for sharing the original Radio Ceylon recording.
29. Wimal Abhayasundara, *Laṅkādīsa Rāvanāyana* (Colombo: S. Godage, 1999), 226.
30. Maya Muni (Mayāsura) then rebuilds the decimated kingdom of Lankapura and the opera concludes with a panegyric to Ravana.
31. Abhayasundara, *Laṅkādīsa Rāvanāyana*, 33.
32. Gamini Gunawardena's play *Rama and* Sita (1964) features an extended, flirtatious scene between Ravana and Sita (several months into Sita's captivity in his fortress) as they whimsically reminisce about their childhood pets and pastimes. A fair portion of the play is devoted to exploring Ravana's religious and romantic turmoil, in discussion with Sita, Vibhishana and Kumbakarna. This rendering of the epic features no final battle between Ravana and Rama—rather, with his palace surrounded and learning that he has been betrayed by Vibhishana, Ravana decapitates himself before he can be taken. (Gamini Gunawardena [1964]. *Rama and Sita: A Play* [privately printed, no publication information]). I thank Tissa Jayatilaka for informing me of this play.
33. Arisen Ahubudu, "Siṅhalayāṭa hisat hadavanat dena sinhala avurudda," *Rāvaya* (April 1987): 4.
34. Natasha Fernandopulle, "From Nari Bena to Gajaman Puwatha: Remembering theatre veteran Dayananda Gunawardena," *Sunday Times*, July 5, 2009, http://www.sundaytimes.lk/090705/Plus/Sunday timesplus _11.html. Dayananda Gunawardena's script was self-published in 1984 as *Madura Javanikā hevat Siṅhala Vaṅśaya*.
35. "Soul Quest at Lionel Wendt." *Sunday Observer*, March 15, 2015, http://archives.sundayobserver.lk/2001/pix/PrintPage.asp?REF=/2015/03/15/mon50.asp.
36. N. M. Kalugampitiya, "Rāvanā & Sinhala Buddhism: A Strained Relationship Ridden With Contradictions," *Colombo Telegraph*, July 29, 2015. https://www.colombotelegraph.com/index. php/ravana-sinhala-buddhism-a-strained-relationship-ridden-with-contradictions/#_ftn3.
37. "The First public show 'Ravana: The Legend Untold.'" University of Colombo official webpage, June 2, 2018, https://cmb.ac.lk/first-public-show-ravana-the-legend-untold.
38. Dilshan Boange, "A New Twist to an Olden Tale," *Sunday Observer*, September 23, 2018, http://www.sundayobserver.lk/2018/09/23/arts/new-twist-olden-tale.

39. Thanks are owed to Ravi Ratnasabapathy for taking me to see *Rāvaṇa Sītābhilāṣaya* in February 2019 and to Nayomi Maḍhupani for helping to decipher portions of the recording of the performance.
40. Afterward to J. B. Disanayake's *Rāvaṇa, Gīta Nāṭakaya* (Maharagama: Sumita Prakāśayō, 2016 [1957]), n.p.
41. For a critical appraisal of Sarachchandra's play, see Suwanda Sugunasiri, "Sexism in Sarachchandra's 'Maname,'" *Journal of South Asian Literature* 29, no. 2 (1994): 123–146.
42. " 'Sītā maṅ āvā' ṭa bādhā," *BBC Sinhala*, September 14, 2013, https://www.bbc.com/sinhala/sri_lanka/2013/09/130914_jayasekara; "Rāvaṇā bala mōḍa siṅhala grāmīya bauddhayan andayi," *Sri Lanka Guardian*, September 17, 2013, http://www.sinhala.slguardian.org/2013/09/blog-post_17.html. See discussion of the Ravana Balaya in Chapter 5, section 1 of this text.
43. *Rāvaṇa: vidēśiya mädihat vīmaṭa erehiva yakbayangē näṅgī sitīma*. Episodes are free to view on YouTube and on Derana TV's website, http://www.derana.lk/Ravana-Teledrama?page=1.
44. The ashram of Viśravas Muni (Ravana's father) is Isurumuniya at Anuradhapura; the ashram of Pulastya, Ravana's grandfather, is at Polonnaruwa; Sigiriya is the "sky palace" of Kubera, which Ravana is to inherit.
45. For reference to the *candrahāsa* in the Uttara Kāṇḍa of the *Vālmīki Rāmāyaṇa*, see Chapter 2 of this book, n.39.
46. See introduction to Arvind Rajagopal, *Politics after Television: Religious Nationalism and the Reshaping of the Indian Public* (Cambridge: Cambridge University Press, 2001), 1–29.
47. Ibid., 245.
48. A recent example of Derana's programming promoting Sinhala nationalist ideology was the network's choice to air a Chinese government funded documentary alleging that the COVID-19 virus was spread internationally by Muslims ("China Spearheads Anti-Muslim Propaganda Campaign in Sri Lanka Amid Coronavirus Fears," *Colombo Telegraph*, April 30, 2020, https://www.colombotelegraph.com/index.php/china-spearheads-anti-muslim-propaganda-campaign-in-sri-lanka-amid-coronavirus-fears/). Gotabaya Rajapaksha's "Presidential Task Force to build a Secure Country, Disciplined, Virtuous and Lawful Society," formulated in June 2020, includes Dilith Jayaweera, the head of the Derana media network, as a member of its board ("Gota's Junta Consolidates After SC Ruling: Task Force for Disciplined Society Ready for Action," *Colombo Telegraph*, June 3, 2020, https://www.colombotelegraph.com/index.php/gotas-junta-consolidates-after-sc-ruling-task-force-for-disciplined-society-ready-for-action/).
49. Indian *Ramayana* serials aired in syndication in Sri Lanka were not positively received by Sinhala Buddhist viewers.
50. Rajagopal, *Politics after Television*, 15.
51. Garrett Field, "Commonalities of Creative Resistance: Rapiyel Tennakoon's *Bat Language* and Sunil Santha's 'Song for the Mother Tongue,'" *Sri Lanka Journal of the Humanities* 38, no. 1/2 (2012): 15. Ahubudu also names Pulatisi (Pulastya, Ravana's

grandfather), Dämasiri (Guruḷugomi), Rahal (Tōṭagamuvē Śrī Rāhula) and Kumaratu (Munidasa Cumaratunga) together as great sages of Lanka.

52. K.N.O. Dharmadasa, personal communication, July 22, 2016.
53. Forward to Ariesen Ahubudu [sic], *The Story of the Land of the Sinhalese (Helese)* [trans. of *Hela Deraṇa Vaga* (2005) by Nuwansiri Jayakuru] (Colombo: Stamford Lake House, 2012), xii.
54. Ibid., vi–vii.
55. J. B. Disanayake, *Understanding the Sinhalese* (Maharagama: Sumitha Publishers, 2012 [1998]). For his speculation in *Understanding the Sinhalese*, Disanayake refers readers to a book written by a colleague of his at the University of Colombo (although in the Psychology unit of the Faculty of Medicine), Vijaya Dissanayake's *Rāvana-Vijaya Mithyāvan da?* ["Are Ravana and Vijaya Myths?"] (Colombo: Sarasavi Publishers, 1981). Disanayake embarks on his own deeply positivist reading of the Sanskrit epics and Pali chronicles, explaining that some believe the Yakshas, Rakshasas, Nagas (and possibly also *devas*) to have been tribes inhabiting the island prior to Vijaya's arrival. The discussion is bracketed by summaries of speculative theories of other scholars (S. Paranavitana, Ananda Guruge, and others).
56. "Mani Akkhika" was "king of the Nagas"—this Disanayake reconstructs from the reference in the *Mahāvaṃsa* to a Naga king (Maṇi Akkhika), who invited the Buddha and five hundred of his fellow monks to preach the Dhamma "in the Kalyāṇī country" (*Mahāvṃsa* 1.71–76). The "Nāgas" Disanayake interprets as one race of people in pre-Vijayan Sri Lanka, with the "Yakkhas" constituting another—again he deduces from the first chapter of the *Mahāvaṃsa* that the king of the Yakkhas prior to Vijaya's arrival was an individual named Citta Raja (J. B. Disanayake, *Lanka: The Land of Kings* [Maharagama: Sumitha Publishers, 2007]).
57. J.B.Disanayake, "Multilingualism for Advanced Communication," *Daily News*, February 22, 2018, http://www.dailynews. lk/2018/02/22/features/143600/multilingualism-advanced-communication.
58. Rear cover of the 2013 edition of B. M. Jayatilaka, *Śrī Rāvaṇṇā Puvata: Hela Yak Parapurē Katāva* (Jā-Äla: Samantī Pot Prakāśayō, 2013 [1997]).
59. Ibid., 163.
60. The bulk of Obeyesekere's books are on Sinhala literature and cultural heritage, although his list also includes such intriguing miscellaneous titles as *Plato's Kāvya Darśa*. Seven of his books contain "Ravana" in the title, with several others relating to the ethnic heritage of the Sinhala people as descended from "Yakshas."
61. Noted historian A. P. Guruge offered rebuttals to A. H. Mirando's arguments in an editorial exchange between the two which took place between 1983 and 1988 in the *Daily News*. References to this debate, along with a summary of Mirando's views on the historicity of the "Ravana *yuga*" are included in A. H. Mirando, *Siṅhalayangē Mūlārambhaya* (Colombo: M.D. Gunasena, 1992). Mirando's 1968 SOAS PhD dissertation, supervised by A. L. Basham, is a commendable piece of scholarship on Kandyan era Sinhala literature, later published as *Buddhism in Sri Lanka in the 17th and 18th Centuries with Special Reference to Sinhalese Literary Sources* (Dehiwala: Tisara Press, 1985).

62. Personal communication with Gananath Obeyesekere, November 2014. For Gananath Obeyesekere's published comments on Mirando Obeyesekere's scholarship, see *The Buddha in Sri Lanka: Histories and Stories* (London: Routledge, 2017), 38, 144–146. Mirando Obeyesekere was often identified as a "renowned anthropologist" in his newspaper interviews.
63. A representative set of Mirando Obeyesekere's claims are found in a collection of English translations of a series of interviews which first appeared in *Maubima*, a Sinhala daily newspaper (Nandana Tennekoon and Mirando Obeysekere, *Ravana, King of Lanka* [Colombo: Vijitha Yapa, 2013]). See also his obituary: Dhammika Seneviratna, "Piraviya nohena hidäsak tabāgiya ācārya mirāṇḍō obēsēkara," *Dinamiṇa* [online], February 26, 2020.
64. Mirāṇḍō Obēsēkara, "Rāvaṇā raju yaḷi nägiṭi," *Laṅkādīpa* [online], July 23, 2014.
65. I have included an edition and translation of the *Rāvaṇa Katāva* on the basis of the manuscripts available in public archives as an appendix to this book, partially for the sake of demystifying this Kandyan period Sinhala poem. The text I have recovered does not correspond to Obeyesekere's—there is no mention of any jet powered aircraft or ballistic missiles.
66. Miranḍō Obēsēkara, *Śrī Laṅkāvē Purāṇa Aňgam Śāstraya* (Jā-Äla: Samanti Pot Prakāśayō, 2015).
67. Ibid., 19.
68. Deborah De Köning, "The Ritualizing of the Martial and Benevolent Side of Ravana in Two Annual Rituals at the Sri Devram Maha Viharaya in Pannipitiya, Sri Lanka," *Religions* 9, no. 250 (2019): 12–14.
69. Ajanta Mahantaāracci, *Aňgampora: Heḷayē Saṭan Rahasa* (Nugegoda: Serenity Publishing House, 2017 [2013]), 20–27.
70. Mānāvē Vimalaratana, *Yakṣa gōtrikayangē aprakaṭa toraturu*, 1st ed. (Mahagalkadawala: self-published, 2008 [2001]); 2nd rev. edition (Jā-Äla: Samanti Pot Prakāśayō, 2016); *Yakṣa gōtriya bhāṣāva saha ravi śailāśa vaṃśa kathāva* (Jā-Äla: Samanti Pot Prakāśayō, 2017 [2012]).
71. Mānāvē Vimalaratana, *Yakṣa gōtrika sel lipi saha anāväki* (Jā-Äla: Samanti Pot Prakāśayō, 2016).
72. Mānāvē Vimalaratana, *Yakṣa gōtriya bhāṣāva saha ravi śailāśa vaṃśa kathāva* (Jā-Äla: Samanti Pot Prakāśayō, 2017), 20.
73. Ibid., 105–108.
74. Ibid, 49f. On the *Aggañña Sutta*'s account of "beings of pure luminescence" gradually acquiring corporeal bodies, see Steven Collins, "The Discourse on What is Primary (*Aggañña Sutta*): An Annotated Translation," *Journal of Indian Philosophy* 21, no. 4 (1993): 301–393.
75. Witharana, "Ravana's Sri Lanka," 788.
76. "The Misty Corridors of Traditional Anganpora [sic]." Sri Lankan Air Force official webpage, www.airforce.lk/angampora.php. See discussion in Chapter 6, section 1 of this text.
77. This August 2014 ceremony also honored two other Sinhala Ravana promoters, Suriya Gunasekara, former Secretary of the All Ceylon Buddhist Congress, and actor and martial arts enthusiast Palitha Galappathi (Witharana, "Ravana's Sri Lanka," 788).

78. "Mirando Obesekara Talks About Ravana," *Vishwa Karma*, March 12, 2019, https://www.youtube.com/watch?v=CaGRGFRi1CE&t=167s.
79. Arjun Appadurai, *Fear of Small Numbers* (Durham, NC: Duke University Press, 2006), 3.
80. Appadurai reminds us furthermore of the terrifying potential consequences of the anxiety of incompleteness: "Numerical majorities can become predatory and ethnocidal with regard to small numbers precisely when some minorities (and their small numbers) remind these majorities of the small gap which lies between their condition as majorities and the horizon of an unsullied national whole, a pure and untainted national ethnos. This sense of incompleteness can drive majorities into paroxysms of violence against minorities" (ibid., 3).
81. See Chapter 2, section 4 of this text. Ahubudu advances both the Lankan-Lemurian supercontinent hypothesis and the *helios-hela* equivalence in his *The Story of the Land of the Sinhalese (Helese)*, 4–7, 41.
82. Richard Landes, "Millenarianism and the Dynamics of Apocalyptic Time," in *Expecting the End: Millennialism in Social and Historical Context*, ed. K. Newport and C. Gribben (Waco, TX: Baylor University Press, 2006), 19.
83. Any discussion of fabricated documentary evidence in the realm of Sri Lankan historiography must include mention of the extraordinary claims made by Senarath Paranavitana (1896–1972) at the twilight of his career, having spent a lifetime establishing his reputation as a trailblazing scholar and as Sri Lanka's most preeminent archaeologist and epigraphist of the twentieth century. Paranavitana's final three books took as their source material "interlinear inscriptions" which he claimed to have discovered slyly indited between the lines of notable, previously catalogued ancient epigraphs of northern Sri Lanka. These unnoticed lithic palimpsests, he claimed, contained references to, along with long quotations from, significant lost works, mostly in Sanskrit, confirming some of the more speculative historical theories that Paranavitana had advanced late in life. We learn of lost works establishing Sri Lanka as a cosmopolitan hub of the ancient and medieval world (belonging to the Abhayagiri monastery of Anuradhapura and royal library of the Śrī Vijaya empire at Sumatra), of supplements to medieval Indian inscriptions, and of Lankan scholarly connections to the Greek and Roman worlds. See A. W. P. Guruge, "Senerat Paranavitana as a Writer of Historical Fiction in Sanskrit," *Vidyodaya Journal of Social Science* 7, no. 1–2 (1996): 157–160.
84. LaCapra defines the "documentary" aspects of a text as those which situate it "in terms of factual or literal dimensions involving reference to empirical reality and conveying information about it." This he contrasts with the "worklike" dimensions of a text which "supplement . . . empirical reality by adding to and subtracting from it." The worklike "thereby involves dimensions of a text not reducible to the documentary, prominently including the roles of commitment, interpretation, and imagination" (*Rethinking Intellectual History: Texts, Contexts, Language* [Ithaca: Cornell University Press, 1983], 30).
85. See chapter six of Sarojini Jayawickrama, *Writing that Conquers: Re-reading Knox's "An historical relation of the island of Ceylon"* (Colombo: Social Scientist's Association, 2004).

86. Sujit Sivasundaram, *Islanded: Britain, Sri Lanka, and the Bounds of an Indian Ocean Colony* (Chicago: University of Chicago Press, 2013), 14.
87. Sharae Deckard, "Exploited Edens: Paradise Discourse in Colonial and Postcolonial Literature," PhD diss.: University of Warwick (2007), 217.
88. Ibid., 218.
89. See discussion in Chapter 5, section 1 of this text.
90. See David Kopf, *British Orientalism and the Bengal Renaissance* (Berkeley: University of California Press, 1969), 22–42.
91. See Jonathan Spencer, "Introduction: The Power of the Past," in *Sri Lanka: The History and Roots of Conflict*, ed. Jonathan Spencer (London: Routledge, 1990), 10. On the origins of the Sinhala term *vari saṃskṛtiya*, "hydraulic culture," with Edmund Leach, see H. L. Seneviratne, *The Work of Kings: The New Buddhism in Sri Lanka* (Chicago: University of Chicago Press, 1999), 261.
92. Susitha Ruwan, *Rāvaṇa Meheyuma* (Colombo: Sarasavi Publishers, 2013 [2011]). Ruwan is a Colombo area medical doctor and online gaming enthusiast.
93. Susitha Ruwan, *Rāvaṇa Meheyuma 2* (Colombo: Sarasavi Publishers, 2015).
94. Sharae Deckard comments that Clarke's *The Fountains of Paradise* "enacts a neo-imperial fantasy through the science-fiction genre" ("Exploited Edens," 245).
95. Chapter one of the *Sūrya Siddhānta* does afford cartographic significance to "Laṅkā," the "haunt of the *rākṣasa*," implying the literary "Laṅkāpura" rather than the island of Sri Lanka. See commentary on chapter one, verses 50 and 62 in Ebenezer Burgess' translation ("Translation of the Sûrya-Siddhânta," *Journal of the American Oriental Society* 6 (1858–1860), 141–149, 173f., 184f.).
96. Jayewardene further claims that the geographical precision with which Saman's shrines are placed amid mountainous terrain is evidence of aerial surveillance capability, and also that Ravana's labyrinth of caves radiating from Duvili Ella represent tunnels too perfect to have been naturally formed.
97. On Ravana as a reverential subject in the Colombo art world, see Witharana, "Ravana's Sri Lanka," 787. Ravana's mechanical flying peacock, or *dan̆du-monara*, which serves as an all-important index of the lost technology of Hela-Yaksha civilization today (see Chapter 5, section 3 of this text), has featured in other recent English language fiction published abroad for international audiences. In Paul Cooper's *River of Ink* (London: Bloomsbury Publishing, 2016), an historical novel told from the point of view of a thirteenth-century court poet, King Parakramabahu Pandyan has a treasured toy mechanical peacock in his bed chamber (36). In *Heaven's Edge* (New York: Grove Press, 2002), Romesh Gunasekera generates a dystopian future for a paradisal tropical island fraught with civil war (left unnamed but obviously modelled on Sri Lanka), to which the novel's protagonist, a first-generation immigrant living in the UK, returns in search of his heritage. After a sequence of harrowing experiences during his trip, Marc, the main character, discovers the mechanical flying peacock at the end of the novel, using it to escape to the secluded mountain region of Samandia (i.e., Samanta-kūṭa, the novel's analogue of Sri Pada).
98. W. A. de Silva, "Sri Lankapura, the city of Ravana," *The Buddhist [Quarterly Journal of YMBA]* 8, no. 12 (1938, April): 241 (italics in original). For de Silva's biography, see M. B. Ariyapala, "W.A. de Silva Memorial Lecture," *Journal of the Royal Asiatic Society of Sri Lanka* [New Series] 41 (1996): 205–210.

99. de Silva, "Sri Lankapura, the city of Ravana," 242.
100. Ibid., 242.
101. Jawaharlal Nehru, *The Discovery of India* (London: Meridian Books, 1947), 247–253.
102. A number of outlets carried the story, one example at: "Ravana's dead body found after 10,000 years in this cave of Sri Lanka," *News Track*, October, 21 2018, https://english.newstracklive.com/news/ravanas-dead-body-found-after-10-000-years-in-this-cave-of-sri-lanka-sc54-nu-54616-1.html.
103. L. B. Senaratne, "Arrested While Digging for Ravana's Treasures." Another story regarding a team of nine individuals searching for Ravana's treasure in the caves around Ella appeared in March 2016 ("Rāvana guhāvedī taruṇiyaṭa penvu venat māargaya," *Hiru News*, March 30, 2016, http://www.hirunews.lk/129687/woman-goes-in-search-for-king-ravana).

# 5
# TERRAFORMING THE PAST

## 5.1 THE QUEST FOR HELA-YAKSHA CIVILIZATION

The legend of Ravana sleeping deep within Sri Lanka's mountains—attested 350 years ago by Fernão de Queirós and still current among Sinhala Buddhists[1]—captures an essential theme within the present-day Sinhala Ravana imaginary: the latent potentiality of the island's prehistorical civilization. Today, the proposition that the technological treasures of the ancient Hela-Yaksha civilization lay buried somewhere amid Sri Lanka's central highlands has transcended its status as lore, parable, or literary device to inspire real life expeditions and excavations, on the part of both amateurs and certified experts. The prospect of recovering from deep antiquity procedural knowledge relating to medicine, mathematics, astronomy, and engineering is already familiar to us as a dimension of Hindutva discourse in India, in recent years sanctioned by Prime Minister Narendra Modi himself through fantastic claims regarding ancient Indian mastery of plastic surgery and genetic science.[2] "Archaic modernity" is Banu Subramaniam's term for such visions foreseeing the augmentation of modern society with knowledge recovered from the distant past, which in the Indian case has involved a rejection of the incompatibility of religion and science, along with a rejection of the characterization of Hinduism as "ancient, non-modern, or traditional." Subramaniam points out that twenty-first-century Hindutva has instead "embraced capitalism, Western science, and technology as elements of a modern, Hindu nation."[3] The impulse to reclaim India's status as an originally and essentially advanced civilization—thoroughly "rational" as evidenced in its scientific and technological accomplishments—can be understood as an attempt to subvert an ideological metanarrative of the European colonial enterprise, involving, in Gyan Prakash's words, "the triumph of universal reason over enchanting myths."[4]

The discursive construct of "great civilizations" of antiquity—measurable in extent, comparable in their scale and influence, recoverable although

*Ravana's Kingdom*. Justin W. Henry, Oxford University Press. © Oxford University Press 2023.
DOI: 10.1093/oso/9780197636305.003.0005

rigorous investigation—is of course itself largely a product of European intellectual modernity, coincident with the emergence of the discipline of archaeology. Heinrich Schliemann's pioneering excavations of Troy were followed by others which captured the public imagination: Howard Carter's discovery of the tomb of Tutankhamun, Arthur Evans' work at Knossos, and, in India, the discovery of Mohenjodaro and Harappa in the early 1920s (billed as India's own "lost civilization"). The "lost ancient city" of Sri Lanka was Anuradhapura, the seat of political power on the island from the third century BCE to the tenth century CE, excavated under British supervision throughout the 1880s and 1890s to become one of the most photographed archaeological sites in South Asia at the time.[5] Anuradhapura presented a rare confluence of archaeological and textual data, in which the events recounted in the *Dīpavaṃsa* and *Mahāvaṃsa*—themselves unique as historical documents predating by centuries any similar chronicles from India—could be corroborated by archaeological research.

New means of probing subterranean and submarine depths in the nineteenth century allowed explorers to conceptualize on a scale beyond even that of recorded civilizational history, and to penetrate into the realm of "deep time." Geology and paleoarchaeology would go on to flourish as established disciplines, emerging from what was at its inception an intensely imaginative scientific milieu, in which the intrepid promised to recover the "lost continents" of Greek and Indian mythology.[6] In keeping with Hindu and Buddhist notions of cyclical world ages, one conceptual iteration of "deep time" is found in the Pali chronicles, wherein the *Dīpavaṃsa* depicts the island of Sri Lanka as periodically (over the course of hundreds of thousands or millions of years) undergoing a civilizing process involving the visitation of a series of Buddhas. The *Dīpavaṃsa* asserts that, just as the Buddha Gotama dispelled the Yakkhas, Rakkhasas, and Bhutas, each of his three predecessors (Kakusandha, Konāgamana, and Kassapa) rescued the island from some calamity—fever, drought, and the ruinous contest of two competing kings.[7] In advancing such a conception of deep time, the Pali chronicle account leaves some ambiguity as to the pre-Vijayan status of Lanka with respect to human habitation. On the one hand, the chronicles speak of no human inhabitants on the island at the time of Vijaya's arrival, only of the Buddha's expulsion of the resident demons to render Lanka suitable for human flourishing.[8] On the other hand, the ancient presence of Yakkhas and Rakkhasas—although clearly not regarded as human beings in Pali literature—has invited a variety of positivist interpretations on the part of modern commentators.

The *Mahāvaṃsa* itself bridges the genealogy of the mythic Yakkhas with the human species in a well-known episode from its seventh chapter. Here Prince Vijaya, following his marriage and alliance to the daughter of the chief of the Yakkhas, has two children with the Yakkha princess Kuveni (Kuvaṇṇā). Vijaya promptly abandons the three of them, however, with Kuveni soon thereafter killed attempting to return to her home city of Lankapura, and the two young children fleeing to the island's central highlands ("Malayaraṭṭha," or the region of Samanta-kūṭa [Sri Pada]). The descendants of the exiled progeny of Vijaya and Kuveni, the chronicle informs us, would come to be known as the Pulindā or "people of the hills."[9] Modern commentators saw in this vignette a proto-historical recollection confirming the long-established human habitation of the island, finding an equivalence between the "Yakkhas" of the *Mahāvaṃsa* and the Vedda, Sri Lanka's non-Sinhala, non-Tamil ethnic group.[10] Henry Parker's proposition that the Yakkhas of the *Mahāvaṃsa* were in fact aboriginal tribes was reproduced in several essays by Senrat Paranavitana, which became oft-cited references for subsequent positivist readings of the Pali chronicles and other classical Indian literary works throughout the twentieth century.[11]

In the twenty-first century, the "Yaksha heritage" of the Sinhala people has emerged as a defining shibboleth within Sri Lanka's Ravana renaissance. "Api yakku bolau" or "we belong to the Yaksha tribe" is now a recognizable refrain, a rallying cry for supporters of the current Rajapaksha regime (see Chapter 1), with several popular Facebook groups named after the slogan.[12] "Yakku Talks" is one of the most popular Sinhala pop-culture and general interest Facebook pages, with over 820,000 followers as of August 2021.[13] The ethnicization of Ravana and his "Yaksha tribe" has correlated with his *Buddhicization* as well. In an act of sheer invention on the part of twenty-first-century Sinhala Ravana enthusiasts, Ravana is depicted as having been a Buddhist devotee himself, the anachronism resolved by insisting that he was converted by "some Mahayana Buddha."[14] Paperbacks on "historical Ravana" cluttering the shelves of Colombo publishing houses clarify that the ancestral king lived during the age of the Buddha Kashyapa (the Buddha previous to Gotama and the third of the present *kalpa*), even though we may note that the time scale suggested by the canonical Pali *Buddhavaṃsa* make this proposition difficult to reconcile with the "Ravana *yuga*" (most often cited as having been between 8,000 and 4,000 years ago).[15]

Nowhere else is the Buddhicization of Ravana more visible in Sri Lanka today than with the contingent of activist monks who have (quite literally) taken up the king as their banner. "Ravana's flag" was first flown by Buddhist monks following the sudden death of Rev. Gangodawila Soma in Russia in 2003. A charismatic preacher likened during his lifetime to Anagarika Dharmapala, the nineteenth-century Buddhist reformer, Rev. Soma died at age fifty-five of a heart attack while visiting St. Petersburg to accept an honorary doctorate from the Russian government. Although no foul play was suspected or implied by officials at the time, Rev. Soma's death spawned elaborate conspiracy theories within the Sri Lankan media, all involving a plot on the part of "Christian fundamentalists" to murder the internationally known monk. A monastic political action group, the Jathika Sangha Sammelanaya (a forerunner to the Jathika Hela Urumaya, which claimed nine seats for Buddhist monks in the 2004 Sri Lankan Parliamentary election), distributed a flier with an image of the Sri Lankan flag and a verse entitled "Ravana's Congregation" (*rāvanna käla* [sic]). The vitriol of the short poem establishes a tone sustained by subsequent Ravana-inspired monastic agitators, proclaiming that Rev. Soma had "sacrificed his life for the sake of the nation," "having unveiled the nakedness of the murderous ruling bastards, and of the paltry cows of the [Christian] clergy!"[16]

The centrist coalition government to which the poem directed its ire was that of Chandrika Kumaratunga (President, 1994–2005) and Ranil Wickremasinghe (Prime Minister, 2001–2004), displaced in November of 2005 by the election of Mahinda Rajapaksa as President and leader of the Sri Lankan Freedom Party. Underwriting *Rāvanna Käla* was public frustration over the perceived impotence of the Kumaratunga administration in its treatment of the Liberation Tigers of Tamil Elam (LTTE), anger which translated into a mandate for the Rajapaksa regime to reverse course on a 2002 permanent cease-fire agreement, ramp up military efforts to reclaim the island's east coast, and ultimately to bring Sri Lanka's twenty-six-year civil war to a conclusion in May 2009. Rajapaksa's 2005 and 2010 presidential campaigns foregrounded imagery suggesting that his administration's prerogative was the restoration of a Sinhala Buddhist state, with a decisive victory over the LTTE providing the context for new discourses of post-war activism focusing on the alleged subversive threats of Muslims and Christians.[17] Such concerns were rallying points for the political action groups composed of Buddhist monks which have ascended to public notoriety in post-war Sri Lanka, most vocally the Bodu Bala Sena ("Sinhala Power Force"), Sinhala

Ravaya ("Sinhala Echo"), and Ravana Balaya ("Ravana's Force"), all of whom Nirmal Dewasiri characterizes as exemplary of the nation's "new Buddhist extremists."[18]

The Ravana Balaya, members of which interrupted the 2013 screening of *Sītā Maṅ Āva!* (see Chapter 4, section 2), is led by Ven. Ittākandē Saddhatissa, and was until recently known as the "Ravana Bala Kaya" ("Ravana's Brigade").[19] Ven. Saddhatissa makes explicit the group's chartered mission to secure a national government prioritizing Buddhism over minority religions, stating in a 2014 interview:

> Any nation where there is a majority of a certain religion, it should have the priority in that country . . . If you take countries like England, for example, the parliament has very close connections with the church. Kings and queens take their vows in the church. Why can't Buddhists of Sri Lanka have the same power? Why can't Buddhists be closely associated with the government? This culture has been present in Sri Lanka for so many centuries, where kings had a close relationship with the temple.[20]

The Ravana Balaya gained notice in 2013 for staging a 250 kilometer "pilgrimage" from Kataragama to Colombo to present a petition to then President Mahinda Rajapaksa insisting that the government stop spending resources on the certification of Halal meat.[21] The group has since then demanded that Muslim refugees from Pakistan be closely monitored by the government,[22] advocated a ban on imported Tamil films, threatened to throw eggs at Sri Lankan cricketers defecting to Indian teams,[23] and interrupted a number of Christian Evangelical prayer meetings in Polonnaruwa (responding to alleged complaints over pastors converting Buddhists and Hindus in the area).[24] The Ravana Balaya's opposition to cow slaughter on Buddhist humanitarian grounds recapitulates a hot-button issue for Indian Hindu nationalists, with obvious implications for Muslims who eat beef but not pork.[25]

A principal concern of the Ravana Balaya is the preservation and memorialization of historical sites bearing significance to the Sinhala Buddhist heritage, from their point of view. The most contentious such site at present is Kuragala, a town in the remote hills of the island's south-central highland, seat of the devotional cult of Muhiyadeen Abdul Qadir al-Jilani (1078–1166). Al-Jilani was a Persian Sufi mystic whom local Muslims believe to have visited Sri Lanka during the twenty-five-year gap in his recorded biography, having spent this time meditating for twelve years in a secluded cave at Kuragala, while looking out a small aperture in the rock toward Mecca. Interest in the site was renewed in the late nineteenth century through the Muslim merchant community of nearby Balangoda, with an open-air mosque—Dafther Jailani—constructed in 1922. On the basis of second-century Brāhmī inscriptions noted in the area, from the 1970s claims began circulating that Dafther Jailani had in fact been built on the ruins of an ancient Buddhist temple, spurring demands that the government step in to intervene against Muslim destruction of a Buddhist archaeological heritage site. Under the authorization of the Archaeological Department, the state's Ministry of Cultural Affairs proceeded to build a "reconstruction" of a small reliquary mound at the summit of the hill above the cave associated with al-Jilani. The dagoba was left unfinished due to the successful legal intervention of the chief trustee of the Dafther Jailani shrine, H. L. M. Aboosally, at the time Member of Parliament for the Balangoda constituency.[26]

The campaign to reclaim Kuragala for Sinhala Buddhists intensified again in 2013, when, at a rally in Kandy on March 17, Bodu Bala Sena leader Rev. Galagodatte Gñānissara told the crowd to "get ready to celebrate Wesak [the most important annual Buddhist holiday] at Kuragala!" Supported by the Sinhala Ravaya and Ravana Balaya, the Bodu Bala Sena publicly advocated that Dafther Jailani be dismantled and relocated to the town of Balangoda, thus leaving the disputed premises free for archaeological exploration and, eventually, reclamation as an active Buddhist devotional space.[27] The following month, Gotabaya Rajapaksa, at the time Secretary of Defense (currently the nation's President), intervened ordering the Defense Ministry to clear the Dafther Jailani shrine's four-acre premises of all buildings except for standing Muslim tombs and the mosque itself. The justification was the establishment of an "archaeological zone" for the Department of Archaeology to freely excavate the area related to the putative second-century Buddhist Vihara, a project which necessitated the dismantling of Muslim administrative offices, storerooms, pilgrim shelters, tea shops and commercial structures.[28] By May, the Governor of the Western Province expressed worry that the Bodu Bala Sena might follow through on its threat to bus thousands of Buddhists to the site to finish the demolition job themselves.[29]

Buddhist monastic activists had, by the end of 2013, successfully instigated the relocation of two other Sri Lankan mosques. The first was the fifty-year old Masjidul Kairiya in Dambulla which in April 2012 was stormed by a mob two thousand strong, led by a contingent of Buddhist monks. A decision was shortly thereafter handed down by the nation's Prime Minister (serving simultaneously as Minister of Cultural Affairs) to relocate the Dambulla Masjidul Kairiya to another area of the city, with the original grounds of the mosque along with surrounding Muslim residences declared a Buddhist "sacred area" by the Urban Development Authority.[30] In August 2013 monks belonging to the BBS and Ravana Balaya led an attack on the night of Eid against a congregation of Muslims worshipping in a newly built mosque in the Grandpass area of Colombo, seriously injuring the resident Imam and moving on to harass neighboring Muslim homes. Exercising its authority to adjudicate in matters related to the ownership of property housing places of worship, the Ministry of Buddha Sasana and Religious Affairs determined in a ruling similar to that of the Dambulla case that the new Grandpass mosque could be relocated to the nearby grounds, where another mosque already stood.[31]

Alongside monastic agitators lay Sinhala Ravana enthusiasts have also championed the Buddhist reclamation of Dafther Jailani. In February 2015, a popular Facebook group, "Rāvaṇa Parapura" ("Ravana's Lineage") shared a video of Gotabaya Rajapaksa's 2013 visit to the shrine showing him in a confrontation with mosque trustees as he explained the need for the establishment of an "archaeological zone." The video, which currently boasts over thirteen thousand views, bears a caption calling Rajapaksa "our minister, who is the roar of the lion at Kuragala!" and repeatedly reinforces the point that "the Sinhala people were here long before the Arabs came."[32] Online forums claim that "Ravana researchers" have gone even further, undertaking archival work to break the Buddhist temporal barrier regarding the antiquity of Sinhala heritage at the site, demonstrating that it has been occupied for millennia.[33] Claims that the area around Kuragala was a portion of Ravana's domain (including the Buddhist temple at which he worshipped, the "Lanka Pabbatha Vihara") circulate online on "research forums" and blogs[34], and have also recently been upheld by several high-profile members of the Buddhist clergy. Delthota Dhammajothi Thero, chief incumbent of the Pilavala Galedanda Purana Vihara (near Kandy), stated in a 2013 newspaper interview that archaeological evidence supports the claim that Kuragala was inhabited since King Ravana's time.[35]

Parallels between Dafther Jailani at Kuragala and the Babri Masjid at Ayodhya, India are of course difficult to overlook. Both involve the forceful occupation of Muslim devotional space by members of a religious majority (Buddhists and Hindus, respectively), claims on the part of these majorities to crucial knowledge concerning the religious artefacts attesting to the primacy of their own tradition at the sites, and the eventual adjudication of religious property by state archaeological commissions and courts. Kuragala does stand out as unique from Ayodhya in one respect, however. Because there already was some Buddhist inscriptional evidence at the site (the significance of which is debated but the historical authenticity of which is not), and because the state sanctioned Buddhicization of Kuragala is already well underway, invoking Ravana as proof of Sinhala precedence seems like a redundant instance of evidentiary overkill. It is, I would like to suggest, an instance of Ravana serving as a plenary signifier in the historical sense, and an instantiation of the narrative that the material remains of his kingdom serve as the bedrock and ultimate *terminus post quem* of any archaeological research into Sri Lanka's deep antiquity.

## 5.2 THE RAMAYANA TRAIL

In further defense of Sri Lanka's sacred places, the Ravana Balaya has stepped in to advocate for the ancient king on Sri Lanka's recently opened "Ramayana Trail." The locus of the controversy was a small, remote Buddhist temple, Divurumpola (fourteen kilometers southwest of Nuwara Eliya), advertised to Indian tourists as the place where Sita underwent her *agni parīkṣa* to prove her chastity.[36] When it was revealed that the Indian government had secured approval from Sri Lankan officials to construct a temple to Sita on the temple premises, the Ravana Balaya held a public media event to declare that the group would not permit the building of a shrine in memory of Sita with Indian funds unless a statue of Ravana was constructed first.[37] The idea of attracting Indian Hindu tourists by way of *Ramayana*-related sites had been around since the 1990s, although it was not until the nation's civil war drew to a close that the Ramayana Trail as fully envisioned could be actualized.[38] The Trail was first unveiled in January 2008 at a ceremony in New Delhi by the Sri Lankan Tourist Development Board, and boasts a circuit of locations throughout the island each with some putative connection to the "historical Ramayana."[39] Targeting potential Indian vacationers to Sri Lanka, the Trail contains over fifty destinations, including the areas where Sita was kept captive, the battlefield between Rama and Ravana, and various locations associated with the activity of Hanuman. In addition to being celebrated as a reciprocally beneficial economic arrangement between India and Sri Lanka, the initiative was billed as a diplomatic program, involving periodic visits between government officials of the respective nations to check up on the mutual benefits of the project, the sponsorship of several Hindu temples in Sri Lanka by the Indian government, and culminating in what Narendra Modi recently referred to as "Ram diplomacy" between India and Sri Lanka.[40]

The first major public event related to the Ramayana Trail on Sri Lankan soil took place in July 2008, when, on invitation from the Sri Lanka Tourism Development Authority, a Chennai-based couple, D. K. and D. K. Hema Hari, gave a presentation on historical evidence for the historicity of the *Ramayana* at the Galle Face Hotel. The Haris, proprietors of the "Bharat Gyan research institute," spoke to an audience of Buddhist monks, Hindu religious leaders, journalists, government officials, and members of the general public. The Haris returned three months later to give a similar presentation at the Colombo Chinmaya Mission, outlining their findings and making available a book published by Bharat Gyan along with a film (distributed as a DVD), both the book and the film entitled *Ramayana in Lanka*.[41] The film bore the imprimatur of the Minister and Deputy Minister of Tourism of Sri Lanka, and was produced and narrated in the style of similar promotional videos on the ancient cultural attractions of Anuradhapura, Polonnaruwa, and Dambadeniya available in malls, gift shops, and information offices throughout the country. The launch corresponded with the visit of His Holiness Pujya Swami Tejomayananda, Head of the Chinmaya Mission Worldwide, to deliver a spiritual discourse on the subject of the "Tulsi Ramayana."[42] Some of Sri Lanka's leading scholars, both Sinhala and Tamil, lent their names to the project.[43]

The cartography of the Ramayana Trail as unveiled in 2008 anticipated an imminent end to the nation's civil war—at the time in its twenty-fifth year—outlining points of interest throughout the island including several in the extreme north of Nagadeepa and Jaffna. The imagery of *Ramayana in Lanka*, showcasing various highlights on the Ramayana Trail, is harmonious, ecumenical, and optimistic. The introduction to the film, narrated over images of a South Indian Hanuman temple festival, speaks of the importance of the *Ramayana* to both India and Sri Lanka, and the "extensive research" which has proven the historicity of the epic "without question" (a brief interlude then flashes an image of Shree Chandrasekaran Swamigal, of the Sri Panchamuga Anchaneyar Temple [Ramapuram, near Chennai]). The closing credits are played over a group of Tamils singing "Rāma Rāma Jaya Rāja Rām, Rāma Rāma Jaya Sītā-Rām" accompanied by a Mridagam drummer—a *bhajan* somewhat alien to the Sri Lankan Hindu context but warmly familiar to continental Indian Vaishnavas. In describing the locations of Ravana's capital in the central highlands, Tamil residents are featured alongside a Buddhist monk speaking of the historicity of the abduction of Sita, giving the impression of the acknowledgement of a prior Hindu (or at least shared) heritage of deep antiquity on the island.

The epicenter of the Ramayana Trail lies in the upcountry district of Badulla, which includes a list of attractions mentioned in the *Rāvaṇa Katāva* and related Kandyan era Sinhala text and legends (Ella, Stripura Caves, Horton Plains, and Hakgala Kanda as the location of Ravana's botanical garden; see Chapter 3). With the Trail now operational, the foremost attraction for Indian Hindus in this area has become the Seetha Amman Temple of Nuwara Eliya, a small city in the tea-producing central mountains, nestled forty-two kilometers southeast of Kandy. Billed as the site of the "Aśoka Vāṭika" (the garden where Ravana kept Sita prisoner mentioned in the *Vālmīki Rāmāyaṇa*), the temple received busloads of Indian visitors daily by 2019. Depressions in the rock by the bank below the temple are believed to be those of Hanuman, with the black mud seen in portions of the riverbed attributed to residual ash from the conflagration of Ravana's palace upon Hanuman's departure.[44]

The Ramayana Trail appears to have been a modest commercial success, although the full circuit of destination sites remains more advertising rhetoric than a realizable vacation plan (many of the sites are in remote areas lacking supplementary attractions).[45] The most popular stops listed on the trail for Indian tourists are Nuwara Eliya (home to the Seetha Amman and Shri Bhakta Hanuman Temples), the Sri Anjaneyar Temple to Hanuman in Mount Lavinia, and the Kelaniya Raja Maha Vihara (a Buddhist temple in the Colombo suburbs featuring shrines to Vishnu and Vibhishana).[46] A number of private tourism companies and Hindu religious associations in both Sri Lanka and India offer week-long, all-inclusive package vacations around the Trail, including the Bengaluru International Society for Krishna Consciousness and promoters working in conjunction with the Sri Lanka Chinmaya Mission.[47] The Ramayana Trail now has an Indian leg operated under the Indian Railway Catering and Tourism Corporation, where for Rs. 15,000 passengers can take a sixteen-day, all-inclusive journey by train from Delhi to Ramesvaram. The "Sri Ramayana Express" stops first at Ayodhya before traveling on to other "prominent sacred places associated with the life of Ram," giving passengers the option to purchase an additional

**Figure 5.1** Lakshmana, Rama, and Sita at the Seetha Amman Temple, Seetha Eliya.—(Author's photo, February 2019)

package to complete the Ramayana Trail in Sri Lanka (billed separately, departing from Chennai airport).[48] In January 2020 a proposal was raised at the World Ramayana Conference in Jabalpur to promote a pan-Southern Asia Ramayana circuit, bringing in India, Nepal, Thailand, Cambodia, and Indonesia on a collaborative international government initiative.[49]

Nira Wickramasinghe has noted that, in its inception, the strategy of constructing the Ramayana Trail differed from that of Indian heritage recovery projects over the past four decades, in which "there was often collusion between the interests of scholars associated with the Archaeological Survey of India (ASI) and popular histories, a forum strongly supported by the Baratiya Janata Party (BJP) and Sangh Parivar."[50] By contrast, the putative evidence used to chart the Ramayana Trail came through much more nebulous and informal channels. Neil Kiriella, the first Chairman of the Ramayana Trail Executive Committee,[51] also oversaw the Sri Lanka Heritage Foundation, an NGO promoting Ramayana tourism and research. Under this arrangement, the public face of the Sri Lankan Ministry of Tourism's Ramayana initiative was simultaneously charged with collecting and publishing essays written by "independent researchers," including among them Mirando Obeyesekere and Kiriella himself. Claims by these authors

Figure 5.2 Hanuman's 'footprints' at the Seetha Amman Temple, Seetha Eliya.—(Author's photo, February 2019)

regarding the historicity of the *Rāmāyaṇa* extended beyond Sri Lanka, including assertions that Ravana was the first to discover nuclear power, and that millennia ago he controlled vassal states in South America and Southern Europe.[52]

Other conceits of the Ramayana Trail are likewise familiar from claims which have now circulated in India for some time. We are told that the narrow, submerged isthmus extending from Mannar to Ramesvaram on

**Figure 5.3** Sita's 'fire test' at the Divurumpola Raja Maha Vihara.—(Author's photo, February 2019)

the Indian mainland is the remains of the bridge that Rama and his monkey allies constructed to cross over to Lanka. We are told that the civilization of the subcontinent seven millennia ago had developed astounding technological capabilities—intercontinental ballistic missiles, advanced medicine, and powered flight. In the *Ramayana in Lanka* film, a Buddhist monk representing the remote upcountry Kappitipola Vihara, Ven. Chandra Jothy Thera, claims that he and his monastic colleagues possess a model of

Ravana's "peacock flying machine" (*dan̆ḍu-monara yantara*), which "studies have shown could have actually flown." The book and film etymologize a number of locations in the central highlands in relation to Ravana's aviation needs: Veragantoṭa is interpreted as "the place of aircraft landing," Gurulupotha is understood as "parts of birds," interpreted to mean an "aircraft repair center." A prevailing motif in not just Ramayana Trail promotional literature but in Sinhala Ravana discourse at large is the notion that the ruins of the plateau-top palace at Sigiriya, conventionally dated to the fifth century, were once a part of Ravana's central terminal for take-off and landing. (Sigiriya now dominates a Google Images search for "Ravana's palace.")

Such fantastic propositions drew criticism from credentialed Sri Lankan historians and archaeologists, inspiring a number of vituperative op-eds in Colombo newspapers and culminating in a 2010 symposium hosted by the Royal Asiatic Society, to which a number of "historical Ravana" advocates were invited.[53] Susantha Goonatilake, along with a number of other distinguished academics in attendance, accused Kiriella and his associates of engaging in government sponsored pseudo-scholarship, pointing out the absence of any training on their part in archaeology and epigraphy. Attendees highlighted among other things Kiriella's unverified assertion that his Executive Committee had "reinterpreted" certain known inscriptions (and discovered certain additional ones), concluding that some dated to as early as 17500 BCE. Beyond pointing out fanciful reconstructions and implausible readings of catalogued epigraphs, panelists noted that an apparent associate of Mr. Kiriella—a taxi driver, one Mr. Pathiraarchchi—had painted some of the inscriptions in question in preparation for photography.[54]

Several points relevant to the overall thesis of this book emerge here. As Hugh Urban has recently discussed, the promotion of spiritual tourism in India has been instrumental to the consolidation of Hindu heritage, vocally supported in a number of contexts by the BJP government. Narendra Modi himself has cast the issue of developing religious tourism in a competitive economic light, arguing that *yātrā* (pilgrimage) and *pīṭha*s (Hindu holy sites) could do for India what the *ḥājj* has done for Saudi Arabia:

> The pilgrimage—yatras—to religious places are very important for 125 crore (1.25 billion) Indians and thus, developing them as tourist spots could strengthen the Indian economy, but the rulers of this country have . . . ignored development of the Indian religious places as tourist

> spots . . . The development of Mecca and Medina as religious places has strengthened the economy of that country, but we have ignored the values of our cultural heritages.[55]

In contrast to the Indian government's active role in developing sites for Hindu religious pilgrims, and in contrast to the complicity of Indian state research institutions in authorizing "popular histories," the emergence of the Ramayana Trail in Sri Lanka came about in a somewhat grassroots fashion. The Sri Lankan government has done relatively little in terms of development or attempts to corroborate historical claims related to the trail's attractions. In an interview in 2010, the Director General of the Sri Lanka Tourism Development Authority, Seenivasagam Kalaiselvam, stated that he did not view it as the government's job to do any such corroboration, saying that his department would promote the trail "as long as people believe in the presence of historical sites."[56] The Hindu temples which furnish the trail's main attractions have been constructed by Hindu donors (many of them Indian) over the past twenty-five years. The Ramayana Trail as a hypothetical circuit of destinations aggregates folklore tradition both Sinhala and Tamil, and it draws on imagined landscapes both centuries old and contemporary, making the Trail an example of a commercial instantiation of populist history.

While the Ramayana Trail came under scrutiny from credentialed scholars at its inception, there have been major efforts over the past decade to elevate the popular legends underwriting the Trail to the status of serious academic hypotheses. Leading the charge is Raj Somadeva, Professor of Archaeology at the University of Kelaniya, who, as a specialist in paleoarchaeology, has directed excavations throughout the island over the past fifteen years. Somadeva has translated his research into public-facing scholarship through op-eds and frequent interviews, and is also a defender of Buddhist precedence at Kuragala.[57] He is currently one of two academics on the board of the Presidential Task Force for Archaeological Heritage Management in the Eastern Province, formulated in June 2020.[58] The thrust of Somadeva's agenda is to the push the boundaries of Sri Lanka's civilizational history further into the distant past, claiming that the island has been inhabited for 125,000 years (substantially earlier than the date of 38,000 BP provided under the current scientific consensus[59]), that an advanced, literate civilization may have existed in Sri Lanka for millennia, and that Buddhism was practiced on the island for centuries prior to the arrival of Arahant Mahinda in the third century BCE. The latter claim rests on a deeply positivist reading of the Pali chronicles, with Somadeva insisting that ancient frescoes and inscriptions which he and his team have discovered near Balangoda corroborate the *Mahāvaṃsa*'s recollection of the Buddha's conversion of the Yakkha and Naga tribes to Buddhism over 2500 years ago.[60] Consonant with broader twenty-first-century Sinhala Ravana discourse, civilizational autonomy underwrites Somadeva's messaging. The arrival of Buddhism in Sri Lanka did not require Indian mediation by way of the missions of Asoka, as it was introduced directly by the Buddha himself. Megalithic burial monuments of northern Sri Lanka are unconnected to those of South India, we learn.[61] Somadeva's understanding of the nature of the civilization of the Yakkhas and the Nagas is itself also intensely populist in design. Confronted in a 2014 newspaper interview with a question over the fact that Yakshas and Nagas appear not just in Sri Lankan Buddhist texts also but in others from India, China, and Central and Southeast Asia, Somadeva denied that his postulated Yakkha-Naga society derived from the "Great Indian Tradition" of panregional Sanskrit literature, replying:

> You are talking of the tradition taken by the super-structure of the society; kings, ministers, the Buddhist clergy, not the common people. The common people had separate traditions, thinking and behaviour patterns.[62]

Somadeva does not himself speak of the specific proposition that Ravana was an historical king, although his putative reconstruction of "Yakkha and Naga culture" is an obviously adjacent discourse. Sinhala Ravana enthusiasts have unsurprisingly embraced Somadeva's work as evidence for their position, viewing his paleoarchaeological indigenism as a tacit endorsement of their even more grandiose historical worldview.[63]

## 5.3 DAŚĀNANA RĀVAṆA: A MASTER OF SCIENCE AND MEDICINE

Ravana has always been a multifaceted character in his literary incarnations, portrayed from the beginning as a complex and cosmopolitan individual by Valmiki, the *ādi-kavi* himself. Ravana's academic talents are central to his image as a historical king of Sri Lanka, where today he is celebrated as a great astrologer, mathematician, engineer, musician, and medical doctor—as a master of the *śāstra*s corresponding to modern scientific disciplines, as well as an adept of esoteric and martial arts (*tantra* and *aṅgampora*). The prevailing assumption, even among some academics, is that Ravana had always been perceived in this way by Sri Lankans.[64] Anuradha Seneviratne in a 1984 essay on Sinhala folklore speaks of the popular recollection of Ravana as a prehistoric king of the island, along with his:

> valour and intelligence; ten heads for his learning and wisdom. He was also a master of music. The musical instrument known as the Rāvanahasta or Rāvana vīnā is his invention. His knowledge of medicine is highly regarded and respected. The medical texts such as *Nādīprakāsa*, *Kumāratantra*, and *Arkaprakāsa* are attributed to him. He was so powerful and courageous that Rama could kill him only by divine intervention.[65]

A review of the archival record however produces no evidence that these Sanskrit medical works circulated in Sri Lanka prior to the late nineteenth century, nor is any special association between Ravana and Ayurveda found in Sinhala palm-leaf manuscripts on medical science.[66] The perception of Ravana as a master of Ayurveda and other technical *śāstra*s appears in fact to be another exemplary instance of the cosmopolitan derivation of his contemporary image, in this case closely connected to emerging discourses of scientific modernity in India.

Sanskrit medical texts, sometimes with corresponding Sinhala translations, were reproduced en masse by Sri Lankan printers in Colombo, Kandy, Galle, and Dondra from 1886 onwards, including the *Yogaśataka*, *Nāḍi Prakāśa*, and portions of the *Suśruta Saṃhitā*.[67] A major influx of Sanskrit medical works to the island came with the establishment of the first modern Ayurvedic institutions: Siddha Ayurveda College in Jaffna, founded in 1925 by Ayurvedic physician J. Bastiampillai; the College of Indigenous Medicine in Colombo; and the Sri Lanka Siddhayurveda College in Gampaha (the latter two both established in 1929). The freshman staff of these colleges acquired their training at the Ashtanga Ayurveda Vidyalaya in Calcutta, some under the direct tutelage of its co-founder and principle, Kaviraj Jamini Bhushan Roy. In the decades to follow, the Sri Lanka Siddhayurveda College maintained a special relationship with the Ashtanga Ayurveda Vidyalaya, to which graduates were regularly admitted for post-graduate studies.[68] Bengal, as the intellectual center of British colonial India, was home to the first English medical school in Asia (Calcutta Medical College), and was the locus of subsequent efforts to modernize traditional Indian medicine. Curriculum at the Astanga Ayurveda Vidyalaya was enhanced by a robust publication industry generating print editions of Sanskrit medical works, inaugurated by Gopalchandra Sengupta's compendium *Āyurveda Sārasaṃgraha* in 1871.[69] J. O. M. Obeyesekera, proprietor of the Free Oriental Medical Library and author of the first major printed treatise in Sinhala on Ayurveda (*Āyurveda Vyākaraṇaya*, 1906), recounts the Sanskrit titles with the benefit of which he completed his research, procured in India by him and by his associates.[70] His list includes the *Kumāra Tantra*, whose authorship was attributed to Ravana according to the Bengali manuscripts from which the first Indian print editions were compiled.[71] Full editions of other Sanskrit works attributed to Ravana would follow. A Sri Lankan edition of the *Arka Prakāśa*, a c. sixteenth-century Sanskrit work on herbal medicine, was published in Colombo in 1945.[72] Like the *Kumāra Tantra*, the text contains in its first chapter a dialogue between Ravana and Mandodari in which some herbal preparations are described. The state's Department of Ayurveda, established in 1961, sponsored the publication of full Sanskrit editions and Sinhala translations of additional Indian medical texts, the introductions to which explain the transmission of Ayurveda from the gods to the later Rishis and Munis, including finally to Pulastya (Ravana's grandfather), who introduced medicine to Sri Lanka, and Agastya (Ravana's uncle), who introduced it to South India.[73]

The proposition that medical science in Sri Lanka dated back to Ravana appears to have been naturalized in a short period of time. In his 1947 presidential address to the Ceylon Branch of the British Medical Association, Dr. E. M. Wijerama began with an extensive historical background of medicine in India, beginning with the Vedas (taking "Ayurveda" to be "one of the four Vedas") through to the period of the "two outstanding medical personalities" of Caraka and Sushruta (Wijerama identifies Sushruta, the great surgeon, as a contemporary of Rama and Ravana). Wijerama relates that the earliest record of medicinal learning relating Ceylon involved "a medical conference held somewhere in the Himalayas, summoned by the great Dhanvantari," at which:

> Ceylon was represented by Sage Pulastiya and King Ravana, both physicians of great repute. It was whilst returning from this conference that Ravana is believed to have espied Seetha and committed an act which was not quite professional and which led to the first Indo-Ceylon conflict.[74]

For contemporaries of Wijerama, evidence of Ravana's erudition in medical science served to confirm hypotheses regarding the advanced state of technical knowledge in general belonging to Sri Lanka's pre-Buddhist inhabitants. In the introduction to his 1970 dictionary of medical terms, Kiriällē Ñāṇavimala (a Buddhist monk and prolific textual scholar of his day) lists the Sanskrit treatises authored by Ravana (*Kumāra Tantra*, *Arka Prakāśa*, *Nāḍi Prakāśa*, and *Uḍis Tantra*), going on to discuss the tribes which dominated the island millennia ago, the Devas, Yakshas,[75] and Nagas. Ñāṇavimala laments the fact that these peoples were later vanquished at the hands of Vijaya and his retinue, as with them the technical arts (*śilpa śāstra*) of Sri Lanka's ancient civilization were irretrievably lost. He explains that with the importation and translation of Sanskrit medical treatises from India, Sri Lanka had in the twentieth century entered a new golden age of medical knowledge, similar to Ravana's in ancient times. Ravana was, according to Ñāṇavimala:

> An author from a medical lineage respected throughout the world, who issued royal commands from his chief capital at Pulastipura, crest-gem of the medical lineage of the great sage Pulasti, Ravana Lord of Sri Lanka, foremost among doctors of the world. The opinion of some Indian pundits is that he reigned 1207 years prior to Vikrama Samvatsa (57 BCE). The *Rājāvaliya* states that he lived 1844 years prior to "the year of the Buddha." Following from this, one can come to the conclusion that he who bore the epithet "Dasis"—owing to the ten crowns he possessed by ruling the ten lands of India (*dambadiva dasa deśayak*)—lived some time prior to 4000 years ago. From mentions of the use of "nāga arrows" and "fire arrows" during the Ravana-Rama war, one perceives that during that period in Sri Lanka there existed an industrial era (*karmānta yugayak*) similar to present day Europe, owing to the various machines and sciences (*yantra-sutra atin*). Thus we recognize that King Ravana was in possession of an industrial nation (*kārmika raṭak*). It is mentioned that each of his brothers possessed aerial vehicles (*ahas yāna*).[76]

Drawing in a bit of Sri Lankan Tamil mythic geography, Ñāṇavimala speaks of Ravana "guarding his *tapas* at Gokarṇa Āśram, where he lived pleasing Brahma in order to obtain a boon," and where he also may have practiced Ayurveda.[77]

The attribution of the initial importation of medical science to Sri Lanka by way of Ravana endures in the twenty-first century in popular imagination as well as in official state publications. The University of Colombo's Institute of Indigenous Medicine (the institute descended from the original College of Indigenous Medicine established in 1929) today boasts a web homepage recapitulating the main bullet points of E. M. Wijerama's 1947 address, explaining the traditional belief that Ravana represented Sri Lanka "at a medical symposium at the base of Himalaya in India," and that he was the author of "Arkaprakasya, Nadivignanaya, Kumarathanthraya and Udishathanthraya."[78] The government Ministry of Health, Nutrition and Indigenous Medicine's 2016–2017 Performance Report gives the following note: "It is believed that traditional Sinhalese practice of medicine runs back to a history of some 6,000 years. It is believed that King Ravana who ruled this country in ancient times was a clever medical practitioner and his era is believed to be a period with much advancement in all aspects of the practice of indigenous medicine in this country."[79]

The most ubiquitous image of Ravana in his twenty-first-century Sri Lankan revival is that of him aboard a flying vehicle known as the *daňḍu-monara* or "wooden peacock." Depictions of the *daňḍu-monara* vary in their aesthetic, running the gamut from Da Vinci-esq, roughshod wood paneled, foot-powered mechanical contrivances, to others sporting a sleek burnished metal hull and futuristic propulsion nacelles, inspired by graphic-novel and fantasy art. Illustrations of such a vehicle—often featuring the neck and head of a peacock carved into its bow—adorn the covers of Sinhala paperbacks purporting to tell the "unknown history" of king Ravana, are shared in online forums and on Facebook, and can even be found on the covers of history books intended for use by secondary school children.[80] The Ravana Aviation Kite Association holds an annual competition on Colombo's Galle Face Green for enthusiasts to use their imaginations in reconstructing the design of Ravana's *vimāna*.[81] The Sri Lankan National Air Force Museum in Ratmalana now features a model of the ancient king's aerial chariot hanging from the rafters. In the mountain town of Ella—today a major tourist-hub, believed to have once been the lair of the demon-king—amidst the *daňḍu-monara* billboards, Ravana themed hotels and cocktail menus, for $20 US you can take a spin on the "Flying Ravana" zipline. In June 2019, Sri Lanka successfully launched its first research satellite into low orbit around the earth, the "Ravana One."[82]

In Indian tradition, the demon king memorably possesses an aerial vehicle in the *Vālmīki Rāmāyaṇa*—his *puṣpaka vimāna*, originally a gift from Brahma to Kubera, described as a structure "enclosed by golden columns" with "gateways of lapis and gemstones," housing "trees that bore whatever was desired as their fruit." Some manuscripts of the poem extend the description to say that the *puṣpaka vimāna*:

> moved with the speed of thought and was steered by its owner's will. It could take on any form at will and could fly through the sky. Its staircases were of gemstones and gold, and its raised platforms of burnished gold. It was a celestial vehicle, indestructible and a perpetual delight to the eye and the mind.[83]

We are however given no specifics of the *puṣpaka vimāna*'s mechanics in Valmiki's text, nor any suggestion that it resembles a peacock (or a bird) in design. Indeed, *vimāna*s, which are essentially flying castles, are a stock literary trope found in many Hindu, Buddhist, and Jain texts dating back in some cases more than 2000 years.[84]

The *dañḍu-monara*, by contrast, is in all instances depicted as a winged contraption, conforming in outward appearance to feasible expectations of aeronautical capability. While the "wooden peacock" has a centuries old heritage in Sri Lanka, its association with Ravana appears to be a late-nineteenth-century innovation, significant insofar as it offers another instance of the literary cosmopolitan genealogy of Sinhala Ravana, in this case extending well beyond the Indic world. The *dañḍu-monara*'s quite late association with Ravana is one clue among others suggesting that the image of the flying wooden peacock arose independently of Indian *Ramayana* tradition—in fact its origins most likely lie within Euro-Arabic-Indic stories involving "fountain houses" and "mechanical gardens" complete with robotic fish, birds, and other animals, developing out of literary exchange between the Fatamid, Byzantine, Abbasid, and north and central Indian empires of the late first millennium.[85] This trade in "wonders and marvels" would have involved translation between Latin, Greek, Arabic, and Sanskrit. Mechanized fountains, human and animal automata, along with descriptions of winged flying machines are found in such famed Sanskrit texts as the *Pañcatantra* (a seminal collection of folktales) and the eleventh-century *Kathā Sarit Sāgara* ("Ocean of the Streams of Stories").[86] In India the genre was related to a technical treatise by the poet-king Bhoja (fl. 1025), the *Samarāñgaṇa Sūtradhāra*, which includes a chapter on machines blurring the lines between the magical and the technical in its descriptions of elaborate plumbing, automatically refilling oil lamps, motorized menageries, robotic soldiers, and alchemically enabled combustion engines. Here Bhoja includes some specific instructions on the construction of flying machines:

> Having built a great bird made of light wood, with a fine, tightly knit outer covering, and placing within its belly a mercury mechanism (*rasa-yantram*) functioning as a receptable for a blazing fire,
>
> Through the power of that mercury (*pāradasya śaktyā*) and the force of the air released from the wings [of the bird] flapping in unison, a man mounted atop it may travel a great distance through the sky, painting pictures [amid the clouds], his mind altogether serene.[87]

Bhoja offers here a fantastic—perhaps even technologically prescient—scene, leaving us to imagine fiery jet engines and either an intricate form of contrail skywriting, or, a more romantic (if less physically plausible) sport of cloud-crochet.

Mechanical contrivances appear from around this time in Pali Buddhist texts as well, memorably as golems guarding the relics of the Buddha. This motif appears first in an eleventh-century text from Burma, the *Loka-paññati*, a Pali translation of a now lost Sanskrit work (the *Loka-prajñapti*).[88] The story contained in the *Loka-paññati* begins with a mechanically inclined man of Pāṭaliputta, who hears of an industry in the faraway land of Roma (Rome) of constructing mechanical people, employed to carry out various tasks in the realms of manual labor and policing (farming, apprehension of criminals, execution). Determined to become proficient in this technology and to import the craft to India, the young man dies arranging that he should be reborn in Rome. Having done so, in his new life he marries the daughter of the master robot-maker, learns the secrets of the trade, and mounts a daring escape from Rome with the schematics for golem design sewn into his thigh. Although he is hunted down and killed by mechanical sentinels, his body is returned to Pāṭaliputta, where his son is able to recover the instructions. The son is then commissioned by King Ajātasattu to build a contingent of mechanical guardians for the relics of the Buddha in his possession, and then deploys them to guard the relics in an underground chamber, above which a reliquary mound (*thūpa*) is built. Many years later, the site is discovered by King Asoka (Ajātasattu's grandson), who requires the services of the robot-maker's aged son to disarm the golems (here known as *purusa-yantas*, "machine people"). A similar story, this time with the god Shakra commissioning Vishvakarma to construct a mechanical booby trap to protect the Buddha's relics, appears in a thirteenth-century Sri Lankan Pali work, the *Thūpavaṃsa*, also adapted into a Sinhala text of the same name. Shakra, concerned about the vulnerability of the relics recently enshrined by King Ajatashatru, arranges that Vishvakarma would:

> set up a contraption with a number of figures of ferocious animals and setting up inside the relic chamber (another contraption) which made the wooden figures bearing crystal colored swords revolve with the speed of the wind, he had it all joined to one pin, had a rampart of granite in the form of a "brick-ball" built, and having it covered on top with a single (stone slab), had earth thrown in, the ground leveled, and a granite *thūpa* established upon it.[89]

A token of this broader literary genre concerning mechanical contrivances, the wooden flying machine is attested in Sinhala in a thirteenth-century poem, the *Dańḍumonara Kathāva*, or "the Tale of the Wooden Peacock." While the Sinhala name for the device (the "wooden peacock," *dańḍu-monara*) is unique, the basic story motif and concept of the bird-machine is found throughout India in various regional literature and oral traditions. The *Dańḍumonara Kathāva* recapitulates key aspects of a story known early on in Sanskrit by way of the *Pañcatantra* to tell of a carpenter's son assisting a prince in building a mechanical bird, with the prince then using the contraption to travel to a distant kingdom and seduce a princess.[90] Variations on this story appear in a number of Sinhala folk tales, as recorded by Henry Parker in his *Village Folk Tales of Ceylon* (1910).[91] In these tales the design of the peacock is given some visual contour: its wings flap to produce lift, powered by the operator "peddling" (*padinavā*) from his cockpit seat, with three ropes (attached to ailerons?) controlling direction and pitch,[92] see Figure 5.4).[93]

While the *dańḍu-monara* made its way to late-medieval-period Sri Lanka by way of the literary circuit connecting the island to the Indian subcontinent, it continued to inspire within popular imagination into the modern period. The *Rājāvaliya* mentions that Prince Malaya, whom we learn was Sita's son in the *Kohoṁbā Yakkama* (see Chapter 3), was "brought up by the queen who took flight on the peacock machine."[94] The Galle Face Hotel adopted the *dańḍu-monara* as its insignia in 1864, commissioning a relief rendering of

**Figure 5.4** 1921 cover image of U. D. Johannes Appuhamy's "The Story of the Wooden Peacock," based on a traditional Sinhala folk tale.

the flying peacock on the hotel's exterior wall which stood until recent years. The *Dańḍumonara Kathāva* was among the traditional Sinhala works edited for print publication in the early days of this endeavor,[95] with the story of the prince using the mechanical flying craft to elope with his princess continuing to inspire poetic renditions of the tale into the twentieth century.[96] Martin Wickremasinghe (1890–1976)—the poet, novelist and essayist whose enduringly popular works inspired by his own rural upbringing approximate him as something of the "Mark Twain" of the island nation—published a children's story (*Dan̆ḍumonaraya*) based on the centuries-old fable in 1932.[97]

How then did the flying mechanical peacock come to be associated with Ravana? Or, how did the *dan̆ḍu-monara* come to replace the *puṣpaka vimāna* in Sinhala literature and folklore? The *Rājāvaliya* intimates that the *dan̆ḍu-monara* had replaced Ravana's *vimāna* for at least some Sinhala speakers by the seventeenth century, Sita's famous "flights" being (first) her abduction to Lanka and (afterward) during the return to Ayodhya onboard the commandeered aerial conveyance. An explicit co-location of Ravana and the mechanical flying peacock comes in the late-nineteenth-century Peradeniya Library *Rāmāyaṇaya*, wherein Rama and Laksman watch helplessly as Ravana flies off with Sita aboard the *dăṇḍu-monaraya* (the verbs associated with the motion and operation of the craft here are "sailing" [*yātrā* [sic] *kalēya*] and "peddling" or "rowing" [*yantraya pädaviya*]).[98] The author takes a moment to describe Ravana's "wooden peacock machine," saying that it was "a vehicle large in size, several stories in height, and that it could be operated at Ravana's will."[99] Collating the evidence suggests that Ravana's *dan̆ḍu-monara* was the product of local synthesis of literary traditions in the Kandyan period, in a context where stories like the *Dan̆ḍumonara Kathāva* and "stories of Rama-Sita" were, as the author of the Peradeniya Sinhala *Rāmāyaṇaya* herself puts it, "passed on by word of mouth." It is possible that Ravana came to be paired with this particular vehicle by way of a semantic conflation involving the name of his subterranean young brother, Peacock Ravana. As attested in the *Rāvaṇa Katāva*, Peacock Ravana was known by Sinhala speakers since the Kandyan era, resurrected in Sri Lanka's neoclassical literary revolution in C. Don Bastian's *Rāvaṇa San̆hāraya* (1886), the first printed Sinhala version of the *Ramayana* (see Chapter 4, section 1), which includes a version of the Peacock Ravana story.[100] In the absence of a *Ramayana* literary canon, and in a context in which Sinhala storytellers had a maximal degree of freedom to rework dimensions of the story (Mt. Kailasa becomes Ravana's "stone chariot" in the *Rāvaṇa Katāva*, for instance), the *dan̆ḍu-monara* as a long-established motif of oral fable furnished an intuitive substitute for Ravana's hoary conveyance.

## 5.4 RAVANA AND GLOBAL ALTERNATIVE MEDIA

As these examples reinforce, the twenty-first-century Sinhala Ravana movement's insistence on an ancient, purely autochthonous Lankan civilization and language stands in ironic contrast with what is in fact a broadly international as well as religiously and linguistically cosmopolitan set of source material. Chapters 2, 3 and 4 of this book explored avenues of literary transmission between Sri Lanka and India, highlighting the linguistic, geographical, and genre diversity of the repertoire of sources used to produce a uniquely sympathetic "Sri Lankan Ravana" in both the Tamil and Sinhala cases. Here I suggest that the cosmopolitan nature of Ravana has been upheld in the twenty-first century—this time as a product of digital bricoleurs—as freedom of access to information through the internet has given myth-makers an unprecedented capacity to disseminate augmented narratives and images of their hero of Lankan antiquity. The online incubation of Sinhala Ravana is, I would also contend, a continuation of the *populist* mode in which the demon-king acquired his *sui generis* Sri Lankan literary image in the first place. While in the medieval and early modern context Sinhala speakers formed their impressions of Ravana through storytelling and other informal contexts of literary exchange, today Ravana-related content is shared freely on blog sites, discussion fora, and webpages—generating content shared on Facebook pages dedicated to Ravana, the "Yaksa tribe," and Sinhala ("Hela") consanguineous heritage (as well as of course on the walls of individual users).

Such internet platforms have been crucial to the development of the visual aesthetics of the Ravana and his "Yaksha tribe," with creative renderings showcased in YouTube music videos featuring songs dedicated to Ravana (including Ranwala Balakaya's "Yakku Bolau"[101]), on Facebook pages and posts related to Angampora, and in online fan art. The Yaksha tribe features women in red bandanas and leggings, skillfully acrobatic, martially capable, and fearlessly swallowing fire. Men are shirtless and have long hair and often beards, with sarongs girded at the knees, reminiscent of the stereotyped appearance of the Vedda or indigenous hunter-gathers of Sri Lanka. Perhaps the best-known living embodiment of the Yaksha aesthetic is Anoj De Silva, an Ayurvedic physician, wellness guru, and political commentator who claims to be descended from King Ravana and therefore rightful heir to his kingdom. Video interviews with De Silva are featured on a popular Facebook "Yaksha tribe" themed page, "Vargapurṇikāva," in which De Silva denounces democracy as a "disease" and calls for the restoration of the great Hela monarchy of antiquity.[102] He flirted with the possibility of running for President during the November 2019 election, courting the approval of the Bodu Bala Sena (the politics of whom were previously discussed).[103] De Silva has made felicitous use of social media to promote his brand, having garnered over fifty-four thousand followers on Facebook[104] and sixty-five thousand subscribers on his YouTube channel, "Laankeswara Media."

Ravana's flying mechanical peacock—the *dan̆ḍu-monara*—continues to stand as a synecdoche for the cosmopolitanism of the Sinhala Ravana phenomenon in the internet era, where the aerial conveyance has evolved from its rugged wood and rope design to a sleek, futuristic craft, attributed with motility beyond that of the most advanced engineering today. The equivalence made between the *dan̆ḍu-monara* and the *vimāna*s of classical Indian literature, along with the claim that Ravana's vehicle was capable of extra-planetary travel, both appear to be innovations of the last several decades, and, like so many other aspects of Sinhala Ravana, the product of literary invention and exchange which first took place far beyond Sri Lanka's shores. While, as explained above, references to the *dan̆ḍu-monara* may be traced back to the thirteenth century in Sri Lanka, the more contemporary details surrounding Ravana's flying craft are easily traceable to Dileep Kanjilal's 1985 *Vimana in Ancient India* (including the proposition that the thrusters are powered by a "mercury vortex engine," a theme which originates with Bhoja's *Samarāṅgana Sūtradhāra*).[105] Kanjilal—a close personal friend of Erich Von Däniken (author of *Chariots of the Gods*, 1968) and regular attendee of European Ancient Astronaut Society meetings throughout the 1980s—was an architect of the "ancient technology" historical paradigm in India and principal advocate for the authenticity of the *Vaimānika Śāstra* (a short Sanskrit text on aeronautical engineering of doubtful origin, first brought to print in 1973, and now a *locus classicus* in Ufological circles worldwide).[106] Kanjilal's book itself has been available online since the early 2000s, and Sinhala Ravana bricoleurs remain hard at work relating the fanciful reconstructions of flying technology from alleged ancient Sanskrit texts to the Sri Lankan situation. Indeed, the list of (mostly Indian Sanskrit) texts provided by Sri Lankan "Ravana researchers" as evidence for advanced ancient mechanical technology in the region (including the *Ṛgveda Saṃhita*, *Viṣṇu Purāṇa*, *Samarāṅgaṇa Sūtradhāra*, and the *Vaimānika Śāstra*) corresponds very closely with those tallied by Kumar Kanjilal in his *Vimāna in Ancient India*.[107]

Contributors to Ravana blogs offer reinterpretations of early Sinhala inscriptions, circulate images of alleged lithic carvings of motorized aircraft, and offer revised etymologies of a number of village names supposedly having to do with the maintenance of Ravana's mechanical peacock. Inspired by Hindu epics and Puranas, twenty-first-century bricoleurs supply an entirely novel dynastic history for the ancient Hela-Yaksha civilization: before Ravana there reigned King Taraka, Vishravas Muni, Pulastya, and Kubera, with whom Ravana jostled for control of the kingdom. Ravana's sons and grandsons through Indrajit, Ravishailasa, and Keveshasta, continued his legacy (Vibhishana, considered a traitor to his Yaksha brethren, is usually left out of these accounts). Popular Ravana blogs circulate fantastic science claims on their accompanying Facebook pages where they are further disseminated and embellished. Hyperdiffusionist narratives populate the Sinhala Ravana imaginary, insisting that the ruins of the plateau-top palace at Sigiriya, conventionally dated to the fifth century, was Ravana's central terminal (with other hubs in South and Central America at what are now identified as the ruins of the Maya and Inca).[108] There is presently an ongoing battle between two camps of editors over the English language Wikipedia entry on Sigiriya, with Ravana enthusiasts working to foreground the palace's "legendary past," and another more empirically minded faction inclined to omit such a section entirely.[109] Ravanalankapura.wordpress.com is the most trafficked Ravana forum, with over five hundred thousand hits as of October 2019. The site is unambiguous regarding the political implications of historical evidence for Ravana's great civilization, boasting a subsection entitled (in English): "Ravana is a hero for Sinhala nationalists."[110]

Within the digital ether out of which Sinhala Ravana's profile has emerged dwell other prophetic, conspiratorial, and downright bizarre ideas constitutive of the global alternative media multiverse. Speculation about the lost history of Ravana's kingdom circulates alongside blog posts on the "Mayan Prophecy" concerning the end of the world in 2012.[111] Ravana enthusiasts claim that a mysterious circular geometric engraving at the Ranmasu Uyana ancient royal park of Anuradhapura is not, as archaeologists have identified it, an astrological chart, but rather a "stargate" or inter-dimensional portal.[112] Ravana's Lankapura was in fact the lost city of Atlantis.[113] The Yakshas or pre-Vijayan inhabitants of Sri Lanka were the product of interbreeding between Aryans and extraterrestrials.[114] Proof that the September 11, 2001 terrorist attacks were the work of Ravana can be glimpsed in a cloud of dust manifest in the form of his face in video footage from the NYC World Trade Center collapse.[115] In its detailed exposition of a theory of primordial sun worship, Susitha Ruwan's *Rāvaṇa Meheyuma 2* (see Chapter 4) shows influence from the conspiracy theory documentary *Zeitgeist* (2007), immensely popular in right-libertarian circles in the United States. In an example of the "pizza effect" at play along the transnational, multi-lingual alternative media highway, top-selling amateur historian Suriya Gunasekara cites a 1998 American History Channel program referencing the *Vaimānika Śāstra* as evidence for Ravana's *dan̆ḍu-monara*.[116]

Out of the Pandora's Box of academically marginal ideas which have found a wide audience in the internet era come the extraordinary claims of Ven. Meevanapalane Siri Dhammalankara Thero, relevant to this discussion insofar as they represent the most extreme imaginable view of Lankan Buddhist autochthony. An elderly Amarapura Nikaya monk currently residing at the Ananda Maitreya Sangaraja Meditation Center in Balangoda, Ven. Dhammalankara has since the early 1980s promoted the notion that the life and ministry of Siddhartha Gotama—the Buddha Gautama—took place on the island of Sri Lanka. Ven. Dhammalankara's manifesto, now widely available as a PDF online, is a short book entitled *Apa Upan Mē Hela Bima Budun Upan Jambudvīpayayi* ("This land of the Helas in which we were born is the "Jambudvīpa" in which the Buddha was born"), in which he claims that the redactors of the Pali *Mahāvaṃsa* misinterpreted a number of the place names relating the Buddha's biography. Most crucial among these errors he insists was the confusion of the name of the land of Siddhartha Gotama's birth, concerning which "Deva Hela" was misread as "Jambudvīpa" (that is, "Sri Lanka" was misread as "India"). While according to Ven. Dhammalankara the original, much older "Sinhala (Hela) *Mahāvaṃsa*" is now lost, there remains a supplementary text known as the *Hela Vaṃsa Kathā* (a text which scholars have not seen) containing the correct geographical information. According to Dhammalankara, a careful examination of place names throughout northern Sri Lanka confirms the amended map provided by the *Hela Vaṃsa Kathā*, corresponding to the names of the locations throughout Magadha where the seminal events of the Pali Suttas took place.[117] Ven. Dhammalankara now enjoys a large audience on YouTube, where his sermons and Q&A sessions have garnered tens of thousands of views. He too is an advocate of "historical Ravana," claiming curiously that the Ravana whom we know from the *Ramayana* was the *seventh* in a lineage of *cakravartin* kings, all named Ravana.[118] Ven. Dhammalankara's radically nativist perspective has been adopted by some Sinhala Ravana promoters who reject the miracles described in the *Mahāvaṃsa*, along with the notion that the Buddha Gotama expelled Sri Lanka's Yakkhas and Nagas, calling such supernatural characterizations of the Buddha "the real myth."[119]

## 5.5 CONCLUSION: "OUR HELA WORLD"

In *The Language of the Gods in the World of Men* (2006), Sheldon Pollock discerns "two complementary paradigms of Western thinking about culture-power formations" emerging out of the European intellectual milieu of the nineteenth century, products of related developments in the fields of history, philosophy, and political science, as well as the consolidation of Western nation states and the success of global colonial enterprises. The two paradigms are those of "civilization" and "nation," concerning which Pollock explains that:

> the former is the usual conceptual framework for understanding cosmopolitan culture and imperial polity, the latter for understanding vernacular culture and national polity. Both frameworks share assumptions about autochthony, but in constituting it they employ opposite historiographical practices. The theory of civilization, or as it is called here, civilizationalism, needs historical scarcity; nationalism, by contrast, requires historical surplus. No civilization wants its origins searched, and every nation does.[120]

Pollock uses these concepts to define a spectrum of modern discourse about "culture" in which the geographically largest and conceptually least determined pole consists of "civilizations," with "the nation" occupying the opposite pole of the spectrum as the "smallest complete unit of culture and power."[121] "Theories of civilization"—in a broad sense, from nineteenth-century orientalist applications of the term to present-day, security-state discourse—treat civilizations as discrete cultural formations, often possessing unique, irreconcilable values (Pollock refers to Samuel Huntington's "clash of civilizations" thesis as "civilizationalism"), and depend upon a view of their initial genesis as "autochthonous" or springing forth from a formative, localized moment of cultural genius. Theories of nations, too, "typically ignore complexity, heterogeneity, and historical process," but distinguish themselves from theories of civilizations insofar as nations represent not just categories of analysis but also "categories of practice." By this Pollock means that discourses and ideologies of national belonging (nationalisms) summon us to action, treating "the nation" to which one belongs as a citizen as a touchstone of personal identity, an object of reverence, and as a geographically circumscribed integral polity (in need of defense).[122]

While I do not intend to critique Pollock's taxonomy of civilization v. nation, I will contend on the basis of the previous discussion in this chapter and the previous that, first, the cultural unit of "the nation" as Pollock defines it appears insufficient to contain the ambitious historical imaginary of the Sinhala Ravana movement; and, second, that Sri Lankans today *do* want the origins of their "Hela-Yaksha civilization" searched. The refrain designating Ravana's ancient domain, *apē hela deraṇa*, "our Hela world" (heard for example on each installment of Derana TV's popular ongoing serial, *Rāvaṇa*), is polysemic in its referent—it may refer to the island of Sri Lanka, while simultaneously gesturing to a Lankan cultural footprint in deep antiquity, global (indeed, *civilizational*) in its extent. A visual illustration of the hegemonic centrality of Ravana in the historical imagination of Sinhala Buddhists today appears on the cover of Arisen Ahubudu's *Hela Deraṇa Vaga* ("An Account of the Hela World," 2005), a short book available for purchase at the Central Cultural Fund, published under sponsorship from the Sri Lankan National Library. Ahubudu (1920–2011), essayist, playwright, poet, and co-founder of the Hela Havula movement, was one of the most celebrated literary figures of the twentieth century among Sinhala Buddhists. The illustration depicts Ravana flying through the sky in his mechanized peacock, beneath him an oval image of the globe split open like an egg across the Prime Meridian. A map of Sri Lanka emblazoned with a Swastika ascends upward from the fissure, with several other glyphs floating amid the ether.[123] The image provincializes not just Europe but the entirety of the non-Sri Lankan world. Ravana enthusiasts tell us that traces of the influence of Hela-Yaksha civilization are attested at the great pyramids of Egypt, at the ruins of the Maya and Inca in Central America, and in ancient Babylon. The new "prime meridian" positioning Sri Lanka at the center of the ancient world for Ravana enthusiasts today is derived from the *Sūrya Siddhānta*, a famed Sanskrit astronomical treatise, which does in fact mention Laṅkā, "the abode of Rakshasas," as a location of cartographic interest.[124]

Contrary to Pollock's insistence that "no civilization wants its origins searched," Sinhala Ravana enthusiasts have excitedly embraced the quest for empirical evidence related to their Hela Deraṇa. "Historical scarcity" of documentary evidence relating to Ravana's kingdom has been overcome through profligate literary invention and imaginative archaeology and epigraphy, as discussed in Chapter 4. Such a compensatory impulse as a response to historical scarcity is, I suggest, a novel and recent development related to the populist information logic of the digital age (because so much of the Sinhala

Ravana movement has taken place in extra-academic contexts, I am reluctant to characterize such discourse as "historiographical practice"). Expeditions in search of Ravana's lost treasure, kite-building contests to reconstruct the *dañḍu-monara*, exhibitions putatively reviving the native lost martial art of Angampora, and the emergence of a Hela-Yaksha visual aesthetic through various online fora are all examples of the public, participatory dimension of the reclamation of Ravana's kingdom. An exemplary instance of the representation of such an endeavor as a collective national effort comes in the Civil Aviation Authority of Sri Lanka's recent call for any documents relating to the legend (*purāvṛttaya*) of Ravana's mechanical flying craft. The agency, which in its normal capacity regulates the nation's airports and civilian air traffic, convened a workshop in July 2019 from which participants concluded that Ravana—not the Wright Brothers—was in fact the world's first aviator. It was on this basis that the Civil Aviation Authority of Sri Lanka (CAASL) put out an advertisement in Colombo newspapers in July 2020 asking for the help of the general public with information on the design of the ancient king's aircraft, which they hoped to obtain through rare "books, documents, etc." As of one week after the initial solicitation, the CAASL had received over one hundred citizen submissions.[125]

To be clear as well, the project of recovering Ravana's kingdom is explicitly cast as "civilizational" discourse by Sri Lankans today, who speak of the "Hela-Yaksha civilization" in English, and of Ravana's lost *śiṣṭācāraya*, the Sinhala word used to translate English "civilization."[126] Parenthetically, but noteworthy in relation to this study, the earliest usage in Sinhala of the word *śiṣṭācāra* which I was able to trace appears in the late-nineteenth-century Peradeniya Sinhala prose *Rāmāyaṇaya* (see Chapter 3), which sets the scene of the epic "thousands of years ago when India was a great civilization (*mahan-siṣṭācāran*)."[127] The notion that material evidence of Ravana's kingdom lies in plain view, discoverable for all, represents a clear innovation on the view of this author, who, while speaking of the subcontinent's "great civilization" of antiquity, cuts short her description of Ravana's flying peacock machine, fearful that this historical relation "is a time period beyond our own minds" as it was "so long ago."[128] At one level, such a physical reclamation of the past in the twenty-first century is something *fun*, a collective endeavor that invites speculation and input from the general public. It is precisely this populist epistemology that I believe in large part accounts for the runaway success of the Sinhala Ravana movement in the digital age. The impulse to excavate Ravana's kingdom has however also underwritten efforts to physically displace sites of archaeological and devotional significance to members of the island's non-Buddhist religions, notably recently at the Dafther Jailani Mosque in Kuragala. A public groundswell moving to physically construct and deconstruct monuments of history, sanctioned often in tandem with official government organs, is symptomatic of what I refer to as a modern attempt to *terraform* the past. It is through such instances that the hegemonic, monological imperative of the Sinhala Ravana movement transcends the realm of the sheer discursive to effect palpable consequences in physical and civic space.

## Notes

1. de Queyroz, *Temporal and Spiritual Conquest of Ceylon*, I.9 (see Chapter 3). Among present day Sinhala Buddhists the notion endures that Ravana's body remains secreted away in Mt. Yahangala, lying in a state of suspended animation waiting to be revived such that he might reclaim his throne (Sanmugeswaram et al., "Reclaiming Ravana in Sri Lanka," 10).
2. Maseeh Rahman, "Indian Prime Minister Claims Genetic Science Existed in Ancient Times," *The Guardian*, October 28, 2014,https://www.theguardian.com/world/2014/oct/28/indian-prime-minister-genetic-science-existed-ancient-times.
3. Subramaniam, *Holy Science*, p.7. See also Banu Subramaniam, "Archaic Modernities: Science, Secularism, and Religion in Modern India," *Social Text no. 64* 18, no. 3 (2000): 67–86.
4. Gyan Prakash, *Another Reason: Science and the Imagination of Modern India* (Princeton: Princeton University Press, 1999), 3.
5. Elizabeth Nissan, "History in the Making: Anuradhapura and the Sinhala Buddhist Nation," *Social Analysis: The International Journal of Anthropology* 25 (1989): 69.
6. Ramaswamy observes of this era: "The laying down of submarine telegraphic cables beginning in the mid-nineteenth century, and HMS Challenger's survey of the Atlantic floor between 1872 and 1876, revealed a fascinating underwater world of submerged ridges and hidden valleys whose very existence seemed to scientifically confirm lost lands like Plato's Atlantis. It is no coincidence that Ignatius Donnelly's 1882 bestseller on Atlantis [*Atlantis: The Antediluvian World*] was published a few years later" (*The Lost Land of Lemuria*, 137).
7. These three previous Buddhas of our *kappa* (*kalpa*) visited the island when it was known respectively as Ojadīpa, Varadīpa, and Maṇḍapadīpa (*Dīpavaṃsa* 9.20, 15.35–64, 17.5–73). Various homologies are made between the religious topography of Gotama's time and those of his forerunners (17.11–16.), with each Buddha imparting a relic and each leaving a cutting from the tree under which he was enlightened (17.9–10). The thirteenth-century *Pūjāvaliya* reprises the *Dīpavaṃsa*'s vision of repetitive history, prefacing its account of the activities of Gotama Buddha in Sri Lanka with the

feats of Buddhas of the distant past. Each subsequent Buddha in turn rescues Lanka from a calamity (drought, internecine conflict) and establishes a Bodhi tree, ensuring each time that "all royalty born throughout that Buddha-era worshipped the Triple Gem and went to the city of Nirvana" (H. D. J. Gunawardhana, *Pūjāvaliya*, part VI [Colombo: Department of Cultural Affairs, 2000–2004], 2–4). While the *Dīpavaṃsa*'s chronology of Buddhas is restricted to the present world age, the reader is assured that, "Lanka is a land inhabited by human beings since distant *kalpas*" (*laṅkātalaṃ mānusānaṃ porāṇakappaṭṭhitavutthavāsam*, *Dīpavaṃsa* 1.73). Periodic visits by Buddhas to preach to the non-human residents of Laṅkāpura are mentioned by the Buddha Gautama and Ravana in the later Mahayana *Laṅkāvatāra Sūtra* (Daisetz Suzuki, *The Lankavatara Sutra* [London: G. Routledge and Sons, 1932], 3–6).

8. Gananath Obeyesekere for this reason remarks: "in the Buddhist scheme of things there are no 'indigenous peoples,' no 'aborigines,' no 'wild men' and 'tribes' of the Westering imagination" ("Where Have All the Vaddas Gone?" 17).
9. *Mahāvaṃsa* 7.59–68.
10. Imaginative reconstructions of the contours of "Yaksha society" on the basis of textual references are attested from the turn of the twentieth century. In his *Catechism of Ceylon History* (Kaluwella, Galle: Mercy Press, 1915 [1902]), C. Batuvantudave gives a synopsis of the *Vālmīki Rāmāyaṇa*, identifying it as "the earliest mention of Ceylon," and assigning the work to around 1000 BCE. He goes on to explain: "The Yaksas and Nagas were human beings for they had a system of Government and towns; they engaged in wars; they wore clothes; they married; they built tanks. Therefore we must believe that they were human beings who came from the neighboring coast of South India" (*A Catechism of Ceylon History*, n.p.). Batuvantudave's title given on the book's cover is "Sub-Inspector of Schools." C. G. and Brenda Seligmann wrote in 1911 that "there is no reasonable doubt that the Veddas are identical with the "Yakkas" of the Mahavamsa and other native chronicles" (*The Veddas* [Cambridge: Cambridge University Press, 1911], 4).
11. Paranavitana cites Parker's *Ancient Ceylon* (1909), 26 (see Paranavitana, "Pre-Buddhist Religious Beliefs in Ceylon," 303–305, and "The Arya Kingdom in North Ceylon," *Journal of the Ceylon Branch of the Royal Asiatic Society* [New Series] 7, no. 2 [1961]: 181ff.). C. Rasanayagam's reconstructed ethnoscape based on the native Lankan non-humans mentioned in the *Mahāvaṃsa* was also an influential early positivist reading of the Pali chronicles (*Ancient Jaffna* [New Delhi: Asian Educational Services, 1984 (1926)], 3). From Pali and Sinhala historical works, W. A. de Silva derived a pre-Vijayan succession of kings beginning with one "Vara Rāja Asura" and including Ravana and Vibhishana. De Silva concludes that the "Yakkā race" of Sri Lanka was subjugated by the later Sinhalas, although the Vedda may be descended from some survivors of these original inhabitants of the island (*Catalogue of Palm Leaf Manuscripts in the Library of the Colombo Museum*, vol. 1 [Colombo: Ceylon Government Press, 1938], xxvi–xxvii). J. E. Sedaraman seizes on the notion that Yakkhas were human, pre-Buddhist inhabitants of the island in his *Laṅkāvē Yakṣa Yugaya Hevat Kohombā Kaṅkāri Upata* (Colombo: Lihiṇi Pot, 1955).

12. In August 2021 there were fifty-eight Facebook groups containing "Yakku Bolav[u]" (mostly in Sinhala script) as the entirety or as a portion of their page name. Other pages relating to Sinhala Ravana heritage are even more popular: "Vargapūrṇikāva" as of August 2021 maintained over forty-five thousand followers; "Descendants of Rawana" maintained thirty-three thousand; "Śrī Rāvaṇa Gavēṣaṇaya" ("Ravana research") over forty-seven thousand; "Rāvaṇa Tākṣaṇaya Sōyā" ("The quest for Ravana technology") over thirty-four thousand; "Mahā Rāvaṇa," a group dedicated to "history exploration," nearly fifty-eight thousand. The "public figure" of Ravana himself (@GreatKingSriRavana) has a Facebook page entitled in Sinhala *Śrī Laṅkēśvara Mahā Rāvaṇa*, currently with twenty-nine thousand followers (https://www.facebook.com/GreatKingSriRavana/).
13. https://www.facebook.com/yakkutalksofficially/.
14. Sanmugeswaran et al., "Reclaiming Ravana in Sri Lanka," 3.
15. On the distribution of Buddhas over time and the length of a Pali Buddhist *bhadda-kappa* (*bhadra-kalpa*), see I. B. Horner's introduction to the *Buddhavaṃsa* ("Chronicle of Buddhas," in *The Minor Anthologies of the Pali Canon*, part III (Oxford: Pali Text Society 2000 (1975)], xxvi–xxxiv). The lone reference to Buddhists living contemporary to Ravana in the corpus of classical literature is the mention in the *kaḍayim* books of his unfair taxation of "recluses and Pacceka Buddhas" living atop Nandamūla Mountain (Abeyawardana, *Boundary Divisions*, 155; *Rāvaṇa Rājāvaliya*, 33).
16. This portion of the poem, addressed to Rev. Soma in the second person, reads: *numbamaya niruvata | pālaka ghātaka jaḍayangē | pāhara pūjaka gavayangē* (translation adapted from Mahinda Deegalle, *Buddhism, Conflict and Violence in Modern Sri Lanka* [London: Routledge, 2006], 240).
17. The Rajapaksha administration itself commissioned an update to the *Mahāvaṃsa* (in Pali, in the style of the original text) making the chronicle current to the year 2010. Shortly after Rajapaksha won reelection in 2020, the state-owned ITN network hosted a televised performance entitled *Jaya Jayavē*, a "Musical Tribute to the Heroes of the Nation," which sang of the heroic saga of "King Mihindu" (Mahinda Rajapaksha) and "Chief General Gotabaya" (Tisaranee Gunasekara, "The Second Inauguration [of 'The Leader who Conquered the World']," *The Sunday Leader*, November 21, 2010, http://www.thesundayleader.lk/2010/11/21/the-second-inauguration-of-%E2%80%98the-leader-who-conquered-the-world%E2%80%99/comment-page-1/. The culmination of "rituals of state" emmulating acts of the historical Buddhist kings of the island came on November 23, 2014, when Mahinda Rajapaksha consecrated the "Sanda Giri Sāya" at Anuradhapura. The ceremony consisted in the installation of a golden Bo Tree, Buddha image, Buddha footprint (*śrī pāda*), plates of the *Mahāpirita Pota*, and some donated relics within the base of a massive brick reliquary mound (over one hundred meters in diameter). This modern *stūpa* was planned to be slighly lower in elevation than the nearby Ruvan Väli Sāya, the reliquary commissioned by King Duṭṭhagāmiṇī following his reconquest of the northern portion of the island from Eḷāra according to the *Mahāvamṣa*. Seven thousand Buddhist monks were in attendence at the 2014 consecration ceremony, including the Mahānāyakas of the island's two largest monastic fraternities (the Siam and Amarapura Nikāyas). One 2010 SLFP campaign

banner distributed island-wide featured an image of Rajapaksha waving and smiling, simply captioned in Sinhala, "King Duṭṭhagāmiṇī protecting the country" (*raṭa rakina duṭugemunu*).

18. Nirmal Dewasiri, "New Buddhist Extremism and the Challenges to Ethno-Religious Coexistence in Sri Lanka" [ICES Research Papers series] (Colombo: International Centre for Ethnic Studies, 2016), 1.
19. Another Sinhala Buddhist activist group calling themselves "Rāvaṇa Śakti" ("Ravana's Power") has appeared alongside the Ravana Balaya in media reports since 2016. See "Modi's Ravana Terrorism Comment Draws Ire in Sri Lanka," *Ada Derana*, October 18, 2016, http://www.adaderana.lk/news/37398/modis-ravana-terrorism-comment-draws-ire-in-sri-lanka; "Agamati moḍita rāvaṇa śakti saṅvidhānayē =virōdhaya," *Hiru News*, October 13, 2016, https://www.hirunews.lk/145080/ravana-shakti-opposes-indian-premier-modi.
20. Rosie DiManno, "Meet Sri Lanka's Radical Buddhist," *Toronto Star*, January 13, 2014, https://www.thestar.com/news/world/2014/01/13/meet_sri_lankas_radical_buddhist.html.
21. John Holt, "A Religious Syntax to Recent Communal Violence in Sri Lanka," in *Buddhist Extremists and Muslim Minorities: Religious Conflict in Contemporary Sri Lanka*, ed. John Holt (Oxford: Oxford University Press, 2016), 207. See also Farzana Haniffa, "Merit Economies in Neo-Liberal Times: Halal Troubles in Contemporary Sri Lanka," in *Religion and the Morality of the Market*, ed. D. Rudnyckyj and F. Osella (Cambridge: Cambridge University Press, 2017), 116–137.
22. Dayaseeli Liyanage, "Refugees in SL Should Be Monitored—Ravana Balakaya," *Daily Mirror* [online], April 29, 2019.
23. Ahamed Razick et al., "Hate Campaigns and Attacks against the Muslims in Recent Sri Lanka," *European Journal of Research in Social Sciences* 6, no. 1 (2018): 3.
24. Peter Lehr, *Militant Buddhism: The Rise of Religious Violence in Sri Lanka, Myanmar and Thailand* (London: Palgrave Macmillan, 2019), 145.
25. Mahinda Deegalle, "Contemporary Sri Lankan Buddhist Traditions," in *The Oxford Handbook of Contemporary Buddhism*, ed. Michael Jerryson (New York: Oxford University Press, 2016), 31. Mahinda Rajapaksha, following his presidency as a Member of Parliament, in September 2020 introduced a bill to ban cow slaughter outright in Sri Lanka ("Mahinda Rajapaksa Proposes Ban on Cattle Slaughter," *The Hindu*, September 8, 2020, https://www.thehindu.com/news/international/mahinda-proposes-ban-on-cattle-slaughter/article32555386.ece.
26. Dennis McGilvray, "Islamic and Buddhist Impacts on the Shrine at Daftar Jailani," in *Islam, Sufism and Everyday Politics of Belonging in South Asia*, ed. D. Dandekar and T. Tschacher (London: Routledge, 2016), 62–68.
27. Michael Hertzberg, "The Audience and the Spectacle: Bodu Bala Sena and the Controversy of Buddhist Political Activism in Sri Lanka," *Rhetorical Audience Studies and Reception of Rhetoric*, ed. in Jens Kjeldsen (London: Palgrave Macmillan, 2018), 246.
28. McGilvray, "Islamic and Buddhist Impacts on the Shrine at Daftar Jailani," 69.
29. Wickramasinghe, *Sri Lanka in the Modern Age*, 402.

30. Ibid., 400.
31. John Holt, *Myanmar's Buddhist–Muslim Crisis* (Honolulu: University of Hawai'i Press, 2016), 6; Thiranjala Weerasinghe, "Sinhala Buddhist Radicalization in Post-War Sri Lanka: 2013 and Ahead," in *Armed Conflict, Peace Audit and Early Warning 2014 Stability and Instability in South Asia*, ed. D. Suba Chandran and P.R. Chari (New Delhi: Institute of Peace and Conflict Studies, 2018), 396, n.3.
32. https://www.facebook.com/watch/?v=854884601237099.
33. https://mahawansa.wordpress.com/2015/07/17/kuragala-is-a-undisputed-buddhist-religious-site-professor-raj-somadeva-finds/.
34. See, for example, http://www.lakviskam.org/uploads/1/6/3/8/16383282/dethanagala-balangodav1.pdf. Ranjan Malavi Patirana of Ruhunu University in a recent book records folklore pertaining to a visit by the Buddha to Kuragala, including local stories relating that the Buddha delivered the *Laṅkāvatāra Sūtra* to Ravana while residing at a cave there (*Śrī Pādasthānaya hā Bäňduṇu Pūjā Cāritra* [Colombo: Godage International Publishers, 2014], 197).
35. Camelia Nathaniel, "Kuragala: Buddhist Sacred Site or Sufi Shrine?" *The Sunday Leader*, June 2, 2013, http://www.thesundayleader.lk/2013/06/02/kuragala-buddhist-sacred-site-or-sufi-shrine. A short interview with an elderly Balangoda monk, Watddara Gnanessara Thero, has made the rounds on Facebook pages relating to Sinhala nationalist interests, and currently holds nearly ninety thousand views on YouTube (https://www.youtube.com/watch?v=sCyO0uBF7C0). In the interview Ven. Gnanessara speaks of Ravana's presence at Kuragala's "Lanka Parvata" ("Mt. Lanka"), along with attempts by foreigners to discover Ravana's fantastic technology. Ven. Gnanessara has himself been campaigning for the restoration of the Jailani Mosque premises to Buddhist hands since the 1970s.
36. "Divurumpola" is etymologized as "the place of oath" in Ramayana Trail promotional literature.
37. "No Sita before Ravana: Ravana Balaya," *Daily Mirror*, June 4, 2013, http://www.dailymirror.lk/30372/no-sita-before-ravana-ravana-balaya.
38. The Sita Eliya Seetha Amman Temple was renovated in January 2000, with extensive government financial support having been allocated for the project (Bastin, "Hindu Temples in the Sri Lankan Ethnic Conflict," 49). The nearby Sri Lankatheeswarar Siva Temple was established in 1974 or 1975, with its *lingam* installed during a visit by Sivabalayogi Maharaj in October 1978. A trilingual book published by the Department of Hindu Affairs describing the history of the temple (which also proclaims that the premises were used by Ravana for prayer and meditation) identifies it as unique as "the first Siva Temple in the Central hilly region of Sri Lanka in modern times" (n.a., *The Suyambulinga Lankatheeswarar Born in the Holy Narmada River in India (Installed in Nuwara Eliya)* [Colombo: Department of Hindu Affairs/Ministry of Regional Development, 1981], 16).
39. B. R. Haran, "True 'Gyan' from Bharat Gyan—I," *Sri Lanka Guardian*, November 1, 2008, http://www.srilankaguardian.org/2008/10/true-gyan-from-bharath-gyan-i.html.

40. Soudhriti Bhabani, "India-Sri Lanka Sign Memorandum to Promote Mythological Significance of Ramayana," *India Today*, July 14, 2016, https://www.indiatoday.in/mail-today/story/ramyana-india-sri-lanka-tourism-329123-2016-07-14; A. Srivathsan, "Sita Temple Construction to Begin Soon in Sri Lanka," *The Hindu*, March 13, 2016, https://www.thehindu.com/news/international/south-asia/sita-temple-construction-to-begin-soon-in-sri-lanka/article4513902.ece.
41. Haran, "True 'Gyan' from Bharat Gyan—I"; front matter to D. K. Hari and D. K. Hema Hari, *Ramayana in Lanka* (Bangalore: Sri Sri Publications Trust, 2013 [2011]).
42. Swami Chinmayananda Saraswati, founder of the Chinmaya Mission, was also a founding member of the Vishva Hindu Parishad.
43. Sri Lankan scholars listed in the film's credits as having lent their approval to the project include S. Pathamanathan, Chancellor of Jaffna University, Sitralega Maunaguru, K. Sivathambi, Vini Vitharana, and Mahinda Palihawadana (Sivanandini Duraiswamy, *Ramayana in Lanka* [DVD] [Colombo: Chinmaya Mission of Sri Lanka, 2008]).
44. The main temple contains shrines to Sita, Rama (Ram Chandar), and Lakshmana, and is advertised (incorrectly) as "the world's only temple dedicated to Sita Devi."
45. "Roadshow Invites Tourists on Ramayana Trail to Sri Lanka," *Times of India*, August 4, 2018, https://timesofindia.indiatimes.com/city/coimbatore/roadshow-invites-tourists-on-ramayana-trail-to-sri-lanka/articleshow/65265046.cms.
46. See L. Ravikumar and K. R. Sarat, "Ramayana Trail Tours," *Proceeding of the 3rd International Conference on Hospitality and Tourism Management* 3: 65f.
47. This I learned through promotional brochures available at the Chinmaya Mission Colombo in March 2019. ISKON affiliated promoters advertise Ramayana Trail vacation packages, see for instance, https://web.archive.org/web/20210415052010/http://iskconyatras.com/itinerary/sri-lanka-ramayana-yatra/.
48. The stops listed on the "Sri Ramayana Express" itinerary after Ayodhya are Nandigram, Sitamarhi, Janakpur, Varanasi, Prayag, Shringaverpur, Chitrakoot, Hampi, Nasik, and Rameshwaram. Surbhi Gloria Singh, "Ayodhya to Colombo via Rameshwaram: Ride IRCTC's new Shri Ramayana Express." The Indian Railway Catering and Tourism Corporation is a publicly traded company and subsidiary of Indian Railways, which is itself overseen by the Indian Ministry of Railways. Indian Railways owns an eighty-seven percent share in the IRCTC.
49. Narendra Kaushik, "Ramayana Weaves a Trail across South and Southeast Asia," *Bangkok Post*, February 10, 2020, https://www.bangkokpost.com/business/1854339/ramayana-weaves-a-trail-across-south-and-southeast-asia.
50. Nira Wickramasinghe, "Producing the Present: History as Heritage in Post-War Patriotic Sri Lanka," [ICES Research Papers series, no.2] (Colombo: International Centre for Ethnic Studies, 2012), 17.
51. The Ramayana Trail Executive Committee operates under the Sri Lankan Ministry of Tourism.
52. For a representative set of claims, see contributions to N. C. K. Kiriella (ed.), *Ramayana and Historical Rawana* (Colombo: self-published, 2009).

53. See Susantha Goonatilake's introduction to the *Journal of the Royal Asiatic Society of Sri Lanka* [special issue on the Ramayana in Sri Lanka] 59, no. 2 (2014), which includes papers presented at a 2010 symposium.
54. Goonatilake, "Introduction to the Issue on the Rāmāyaṇa," 11. For more on erroneous readings and forgeries of Brahmi epigraphs by Kiriella and his associates, see Malini Dias, "Distortion of Archaeological Evidence on the Rāmāyaṇa," *Journal of the Royal Asiatic Society of Sri Lanka* 59, no. 2 (2014): 43–54.
55. Hugh Urban, "The Cradle of Tantra: Modern Transformations of a Tantric Centre in Northeast India from Nationalist Symbol to Tourist Destination," *South Asia: Journal of South Asian Studies* 42, no. 2 (2019): 267, citing a 2014 speech by Modi quoted in "Narendra Modi Accuses Centre of Ignoring Pilgrimage Places," *Deccan Chronicle*, February 14, 2014.
56. "Ramayana Trail on Fire," *Sunday Times*, July 25, 2010, http://www.sundaytimes.lk/100725/News/nws_28.html.
57. In their written report on a 2014 survey of the Kalthota escarpment undertaken through the Kelaniya University Postgraduate Institute of Archaeology, Somadeva et al. confirm the antiquity of the Brahmi inscriptions above the caves used by Buddhist monks in the area, remarking that "the short inscription showing the date of the establishment of the Islamic religious building" at Kuragala confirms that "the history of the Mosque does not go beyond the year 1926. Several burials of Islamic religious devotees in the western sector of the terrace could be post-dated to the construction of the Mosque" (*Kaltota Survey—Phase I*, [Colombo: Postgraduate Institute of Archaeology (PGIAR), University of Kelaniya, 2015], 5). Somadeva et al. acknowledge the presence of the Kufic Arabic cave inscription at Kuragala ("post-dated to the 10th century") but qualify its significance by stating: "It seems that the presence of this inscription was a spontaneous occurrence that has no affiliation with an embodiment of prolonged existence of any kind of Arabic religious practice at the location during the historic periods" (27). In fairness, they go on: "But, however the intangible values adopted to the site by the current Muslim community should be appreciated and respected. Landscape is a[n] expression of our senses and memories" (27f.).
58. "The Appointment of Two Presidential Task Forces, Discussion Paper," Centre for Policy Alternatives, Colombo, June 2020, 13, https://www.cpalanka.org/the-appointment-of-the-two-presidential-task-forces/.
59. Fossil and behavioral evidence for the presence of *H. sapiens* dating to 38,000 BP comes from studies conducted in the rainforests of Sri Lanka's southwestern Wet Zone. Sri Lanka is of interest to paleoarchaeologists as home to the oldest *H. sapiens* remains in South Asia, with these discoveries counting as some of the oldest of any in the world outside of Africa (older examples have been confirmed so far only in Australia, Malaysia, and possibly China). See Patrick Roberts et al., "The Sri Lankan 'Microlithic' Tradition c. 38,000 to 3,000 Years Ago: Tropical Technologies and Adaptations of Homo sapiens at the Southern Edge of Asia," *Journal of World Prehistory* 28 (2015): 70–72.
60. Pushpa Weerasekara and Lasantha Niroshan, "Archaeological Findings Open New Chapter," *The Daily Mirror*, September 2, 2014, A7; Chathushika Wijeyasinghe [with

Raj Somadeva], "Buddhism Existed Before Mihindu thera," *The Daily Mirror*, July 1, 2014, http://www.dailymirror.lk/opinion/buddhism-existed-before-mihindu-thera/172-49152. Somadeva's sole piece of epigraphical evidence for the putative "Yakkha" autonym comes from a Prakrit donative inscription concerning the gift of a cave at Tamketiya by one Prince Mahā Tissa. The last word of the inscription is *yagaśa*, which Somadeva reads as the signature line of the author, and as a variation on the genitive declension of Sinhala Prakrit *yaka*, i.e., *yakṣa* (Somadeva et al., *Kaltota Survey—Phase I*, 24).

61. Darshanie Ratnawalli [with Raj Somadeva], "Explorations in Sri Lankan Archaeology with Raj Somadeva [Parts 1 and 2]," *The Nation*, November 9 and 16, 2014."
62. Ibid., Part 2.
63. Daya Dissanayake, "Ravana—Ravana Revisited," March 21, 2012, https://saadhu.com/blog/ravana; "'Kuragala is a [sic] Undisputable Buddhist Religious Site'—Professor Raj Somadeva Finds," July 27, 2015, https://mahawansa.wordpress.com/2015/07/17/kuragala-is-a-undisputed-buddhist-religious-site-professor-raj-somadeva-finds/; "Don't Try to Federalize Sri Lanka's History!" October 9, 2018, http://www.lankaweb.com/news/items/2018/10/09/dont-try-to-federalize-sri-lankas-history/.
64. Ravana's *śāstric* learning is heralded by twentieth-century Sinhala dramatists like Vimal Abhayasundara, who in his introduction to *Laṅkādhisa Rāvanāyanaya* recounts that he heard of the demon-king's learning at a young age. Claims regarding Ravana as the inventor of "the world's first violin" (the "Ravana-hasta" or "Ravana-stron") are popular among Ravana enthusiasts. Sykes notes the increasing prevalence over the past thirty years of claims regarding Sri Lanka's musical legacy tracing to Ravana's time among Sinhala musicians (*The Musical Gift*, 218).
65. Anuradha Seneviratne, "Rāma and Rāvaṇa: History, Legend and Belief in Sri Lanka," *Ancient Ceylon: Journal of the Archaeological Society of Ceylon* 5 (1984): 235.
66. Jinadasa Liyanaratne, the foremost authority in this field, does not list any of the three texts cited by Seneviratne, nor anything about Ravana in connection to Ayurveda in Sri Lanka in his survey of archived medical manuscripts. None of the texts appear among the seventy-four authors and Sanskrit works cited in the *Bhesajjamañjūsā-sannaya*, the Sinhala commentary on the thirteenth-century Pali *Bhesajjamañjūsā* ("The Casket of Medicine"), the most reproduced classical medical work in Sri Lanka (*Buddhism and Traditional Medicine in Sri Lanka* [Kelaniya: Kelaniya University (Kelaniya University Anniversary Series), 1999], 38–41).
67. See nos. 260, 1151, and 3542 of the *Register of Books Printed in Ceylon and Registered under Ordinance No. 1 of 1885*, Parts 1, 2, and 4 (Colombo: George Skeen).
68. Jinadasa Liyanaratna, "Indian Medicine in Sri Lanka," *Bulletin de l'École française d'Extrême-Orient* 76 (1987): 206f. Anagarika Dharmapala played an instrumental role in establishing a Department of Pali Studies at the University of Calcutta in 1917, which became an avenue of exchange for scholars between Sri Lanka and Bengal (Amunugama, *The Lion's Roar*, 236).
69. See preface (xi) and chapter one of Projit Bihari Mukharji, *Doctoring Traditions: Ayurveda, Small Technologies, and Braided Sciences* (Chicago: University of Chicago Press, 2016). On the revival of traditional Ayurvedic literature in

nineteenth-century Bengal, see also Sujata Mukherjee, "Ayurvedic Medicine in Colonial Bengal," in *India's Indigenous Medical Systems: A Cross-Disciplinary Approach*, ed. S.E. Hussain and M. Saha (Delhi: Primus Books, 2015), 100–113.

70. J. O. M. Obeyesekera, *Āyurveda Vyākaraṇaya*, vol 1. (Colombo: Department of Ayurveda, 1981 [1906]). The titles which Obeyesekera says were imported from India are the *Ātreya Saṃhitā, Dhanvantarī Saṃhitā, Suśruta Saṃhitā, Caraka Saṃhitā, Aṣṭaṅgahṛdaya Saṃhitā, Bhāvaprakāśa, Rasaratnākara, Rasendracinatāmaṇī, Vṛhananighananḍūratnākara, Cakradatta, Śāraṅgadhara, Mādhavanidāna, Cikitasā, Kramā Kalpavallī, Rasendra Sārasaṃgraha, Vaṃgasne, Vaidyakalpadruma, Āyurveda Vijñāna, Bhaiṣajyaratnāvalī, Kūṭamudagara, Kumāra Tantra, Yogārṇava, Prāṇatoṣaṇī, Sāradā Tilaka, Rasarājasundara*, and *Jotīṣārṇavādī Granthayangedna* (xviif.). Obeyesekera also supplemented his compendium with knowledge drawn from Sinhala and Tamil medical works.
71. See Jean Filliozat, *Étude de Démonologie Indienne: Le Kumāratantra de Rāvana et les textes parallèles Indiens, Tibétains, Chinois, Cambodgien et Arabe* (Paris: Imprimerie Nationale, 1937), 171–178. On the corpus of interrelated esoteric Sanskrit works which each begin with Shiva's revelation of tantric knowledge (*tantravidyā*) to Ravana, see Aaron Ullrey's discussion of the "Uḍḍ-corpus" in "Grim Grimoires: Pragmatic Ritual in the Magic Tantras," PhD diss.: University of California-Santa Barbara (2016), 190–199.
72. Kiriällē Ñāṇavimala, *Deśiya Vaiśya Śabda Kōśaya* (Colombo: Department of Ayurveda, 1970), vii.
73. R. Buddhadasa, *Aṣṭaṅgahṛdaya Saṃhitā* (Colombo: Department of Ayurveda, 1964), p.1; R. Buddhadasa, *Caraka Saṃhitā* (Colombo: Department of Ayurveda, 1960), 1f.
74. E. M. Wijerama, "Historical Background of Medicine in Ceylon," *The Journal of the Ceylon Branch of the British Medical Association* 43, no. 1 (1947): 3. In his discussion of ancient methods of anesthesia, Wijerama again adopts a positivist attitude toward to the events of the *Ramayana*, speaking of a drug known as *sanjeevani* used to revive post-operative patients: "This drug *sanjeevani* is of great historical importance to us in Ceylon for it played no mean part in the success of the expeditionary forces of Rama in the rescue of Seetha from Ravana . . . *Sanjeevani* was used in the battlefield to revive soldiers after severe injuries. Cranial surgery must have attained a certain amount of success and popularity at this time, for we hear of another surgeon Jivaka, the medical attendant of the Buddha, who is reported to have successfully removed tumours from the brains of some of his patients" (2).
75. Ñāṇavimala glosses *yakṣas* with *rākṣasas*.
76. Ñāṇavimala, *Deśiya Vaiśya Śabda Kōśaya*, v–vi.
77. Ibid., vii. On "Gokarṇa Āśram" and the Koneswaram Siva Temple of Trincomalee, see Chapter 2 section 3 of this text.
78. Homepage of the Institute of Indigenous Medicine, The University of Colombo (https://iim.cmb.ac.lk/index.php/about-ayurveda-section/). The College of Indigenous Medicine was affiliated to the University of Colombo in 1977 and subsequently renamed the Institute of Indigenous Medicine.

79. [n.a.]. Sri Lankan Ministry of Health, Nutrition and Indigenous Medicine, *Performance and Progress Report 2016–2017*, 195.
80. See rear cover illustration of Kamaṇi Gitangani Kalutantri's *Itihāsaya nava viṣaya nirdēśaya: 10 śrēṇiya saňdahā* (Kōṭṭē: Kartṛ Prakāśana, 2017).
81. "Ravana Aviation Kite Association Sri Lanka," http://rakasl.com/.
82. "Sri Lanka Successfully Launches Its First Satellite 'Ravana-1' Into Orbit," *Times of India*, June 19, 2019, https://timesofindia.indiatimes.com/world/south-asia/sri-lanka-successfully-launches-its-first-satellite-ravana-1-into-orbit/articleshow/69858285.cms.
83. Goldman et al., *The Rāmāyaṇa of Vālmīki*, Volume VII: *Uttarakāṇḍa*, 264 (15.30), 584.
84. On *vimānas* or "flying mansions" in Pali Buddhist texts, see Andy Rotman on the *Divyāvadāna* (*Thus I Have Seen: Visualizing Faith in Early Indian Buddhism* [Oxford: Oxford University Press, 2009], 24ff.), and U Ba Kyaw's translation of the *Paramattha-dīpanī* (*Elucidation of the Intrinsic Meaning: So Named the Commentary on the Peta-Stories* [Paramatthadīpanī nāma Petavatthu-aṭṭhakathā] [London: Pali Text Society, 1980]), 3f., 42–46, 412ff.).
85. See Daud Ali, "Bhoja's Mechanical Garden: Translating Wonder Across the Indian Ocean, circa 800–1100 CE," *History of Religions* 55, no. 4 (2016): 1–34.
86. Chapter forty-three of the *Kathā Sarit Sāgara* speaks of the mythical city of Karpūrasambhava, in which the king's palace is home to a menagerie of mechanical animals (C. H. Tawney, *The Kathá Sarit Ságara or, Ocean of the streams of story; translated from the original Sanskrit*, vol. 1 (Calcutta: J.W. Thomas, 1881), 390f.). On references to *yantras* in the *Vālmīki Rāmāyaṇa*, including Ravana's city of Laṅkāpuri as outfitted with mechanical throwing devices, see references in V. Raghavan, *Yantras or Mechanical Contrivances in Ancient India* (Bangalore: Indian Institute of Culture, 1952), 3f.
87. My translation of Bhoja's *Samarāṅgaṇa Sūtradhāra*, chapter 31, verses 95 and 96:

    *laghudārumayam mahāvihaṅgaṃ dṛḍhasuśliṣṭatanum vidhāya tasya*
    *udare rasayantramādadhīta jvalanādhāramadho' sya cāti pūrṇam||*
    *tāruḍha puruṣastasya pakṣadvandvoccālaprojjhitena anilena*
    *suptasvāntaḥ pāradasyāsya śaktyā citraṃ kurvannambare yāti dūram*

88. The *Loka-prājñapti* has survived only in a Chinese translation (Signe Cohen, "Romancing the Robot and Other Tales of Mechanical Beings in Ancient Indian Literature," *Acta Orientalia* 64 (2002): 72).
89. Adapted from N. A. Jayawickrama's translation in *A Chronicle of the Thūpa and the Thūpavaṃsa, Being a Translation and Edition of Vācissarattheraʼs Thūpavaṃsa* (London: Luzac for the Pali Text Society, 1971), 46. Cf. the episode in the *Sinhala Thūpavaṃsa*, (Stephen Berkwitz, *History of the Buddha's Relic Shrine: A Translation of the Sinhala Thūpavaṃsa* [Oxford: Oxford University Press, 2007], 131f.). When the deadly contrivance is discovered years later, King Asoka is forced to employ a talented young archer, who disables the complex gears driving the mechanical sentinels by shooting an arrow at a crucial cog from some distance away (Jayawickrama, *Chronicle of the Thūpa*, 54).
90. The author of the *Daňḍumonara Kathāva* names himself within the poem, "Master registrar of Sinhala Ballads of the Danture Maḍugedara family" (*danture maḍugedara*

*sinhala kavi lēkam äduru*), who composed during the reign of "King Pärakum̆bā." K. D. Somadasa infers this to have been Parakramabahu of Dam̆badeniya, r. 1240–1275 (see entry for Or. 6611(15) in *Catalogue of the Hugh Nevill Collection*, vol. 5, 16). The basic story elements of the first half of the *Dan̆ḍumonara Kathāva* appear in a fable belonging to Book One of the *Pañcatantra*, "The Weaver Who Loved a Princess" (Arthur Ryder, *The Panchatantra* [Chicago: University of Chicago Press, 1952], 89–111).

91. The mechanical flying wooden peacock makes an appearance in three of the folk stories recorded by Henry Parker (*Village Folk-Tales of Ceylon* [London: Luzac & Co., 1910], no. 80, 81, and 198). Parker gives a number of cross references for legends similar to the *Dan̆ḍumonara Kathāva*, including a flying peacock machine in the Chinese version of the *Saṅghabhedakavastu* (citing Edouard Chavannes, *Cinq Cents Contes et Apologues* [Paris: Leroux, 1910], vol. 2, 378), a homologous story recorded in Shaik Chilli's *Folk-tales of Hindustan* [Allahabad: Panch Kory Mittra, 1908], and a carpenter's "flying palanquin" in the Punjabi story of "Prince Lionheart and this three friends" (F.A. Steel, "Folklore in the Panjab," *Indian Antiquary* 10 (1881), 233). A story with elements similar to the *Dan̆ḍumonara Kathāva* also appears in a Tibetan Jataka story (in the Dulwa [Vinaya] section of the Tibetan *Kandju*), in which the Buddha was the master mechanic and Devadatta the apprentice son (William Rockhill, *The Life of the Buddha* and the Early History of His Order [London: Trübner & Co., Ludgate Hill, 1884], 108f.).
92. In his *Sinhalese-English Dictionary* (1924), Charles Carter gives an entry for "*dan̆ḍu-monara yantra*" as meaning a "balloon," perhaps suggested by the episode in Parker's *Village Folk Tales of Ceylon* (vol. 2, no. 81) in which the hapless prince is carried skywards when he steps into the *dan̆ḍu-monaraya* and takes the control chains, finding himself "fixed among the clouds" (23).
93. Publication information: 1921 edition of the *Danḍumonara Kathava*, "Authorized by N. A. Kurē Appahāmi" (Colombo: K.D. Perera and Son). First edition U. D. Johannes Appuhami (1904), *Dandumonara Kathava* (Colombo: Laksilumina Press [N.A. Cooray]). This image is in the public domain (U. D. Johannes Appuhami died in 1925).
94. The "peacock machine" is the *monara yaturu*, or *dan̆ḍumonara yantraya* in a variant ms. reading (*Rājāvaliya*, 172; see Suraweera's translation in *Rājāvaliya* [2000], 20). This historical tie-in accounts for why it is that alternative titles for the *Dan̆ḍumonara Kathāva* are *Malaraju Puvata* and *Malayarāja Kathāva* in the manuscript tradition. Confusion arises here as there is a separate poem—an account of the journey of Malaraja to Sri Lanka to cure King Paṇḍuvasdeva of an ailment (*divi dos*)—which is also titled *Malayarāja Kathāva*.
95. M. P. Karunatilake, *Dan̆ḍumoṇara Yantraya hevat Malē Rāja Kathāva*, 7th ed. (Kägallē: Vidyakalpa Press, 1967 [1921]). This is an abridged edition of the most complete version of the original poem preserved in the Hugh Nevil Collection Or. 6611(15) (Somadasa, *Catalogue of the Hugh Nevill Collection*, vol. 5, 16), with 113 verses as opposed to the original poem's 198. Karunatilake also substitutes some verses at the beginning of the poem.

96. U. D. Johannes Appuhami published a new rendition of the classic tale in 1904. His updated poem appears to have been a popular seller based on the number of volumes printed according to the Register of Books Printed in Ceylon—two thousand copies for each of the first several editions (the 1921 printing I was able to procure was the tenth edition). See entry no. 6027 of *Register of Books Printed in Ceylon and Registered under Ordinance No. 1 of 1885. Part V—1898 to 1901*. First publication: U. D. Johannes Appuhami, *Dañḍumoṇara Katāva*. 1st ed. (Colombo: Laksilumina Press [N.A. Cooray], 1904).
97. Martin Wickramasinghe, *Dañḍumonaraya* (Nawala, Rajagiriya: Sarasa Publishers, 2013 [1932]).
98. *Rāmāyaṇaya*, f.35b.
99. *ē rāvanā rajugē danḍumonara yantraya visāla yātravaki eya mahal kīpayakin da yuktava tibunabavan rāvanā rajugē kämätte prākāra pädaviya häki* (f.37a).
100. C. Don Bastian, *Rāmāyaṇaya hevat Rāvaṇā Saṅhāraya: Adventures of Ráma, or, Destruction of Rávana* (Petta: Śāstralōka Press, 1886), 224–244.
101. "Yakku Bolaw Api," with over 160k views as of October 2020, https://www.youtube.com/ watch?v = jbRjb1J-irs.
102. "Saharān bōmba pupuravapu hētuva rāvaṇā parapurē anōj da silvā mahavedanā visin soyā gätē," https://www.facebook.com/vargapurnikava/videos/39510658 7790094/.
103. Himal Kotelawala, "Meet the Also-Rans," *Republic Next*, September 2, 2019, https:// www.republicnext. com/politics/meet-the-also-rans/.
104. https://www.facebook.com/laankeshwara/.
105. Some online "Ravana researchers" name Kanjilal's book explicitly; see for example, ravanalankapura.wordpress.com/hela-vimana-technology/.
106. See Maharishi Bharadwaaja and G. R. Josyer, *Vyamaanika-Shaastra, or, Science of Aeronautics* (Mysore: Coronation Press, 1973), and D. K. Kanjilal, *Vimāna in Ancient India* (Calcutta: Sanskrit Pustak Bhandar, 1985). The actual Sanskrit text of the *Vimānika Śāstra*, as provided in Bharadwaaja and Josyer's edition, gives its title as the "Vaimānika Prakaraṇam belonging to the [larger text] of the "Śrī Yantra Sarvasva" of Maharṣi Bharadvāja" (22).
107. In addition to the *Vaimānika Śāstra*, Sinhala Ravana theorists see descriptions of advanced ancient technology in the *Rigveda Saṃhita*, *Śatapatha Brāhmaṇa*, the *Markandeya* and *Viṣṇu Purāṇa*s, the *Harivaṃsa*, *Vikrama Urvaśiya*, *Uttararāma Carita*, *Harṣa Carita*, *Samarāṅgaṇa Sūtradhāra*, and the Tamil language *Cīvaka Cintāmaṇi*. See Witharana, "Ravana's Sri Lanka," 789, n.45.
108. Damian Thompson defines hyperdiffusionist alternative media discourses as those attempting to trace many or all early world cultures to a single parent or ur-civilization (*Counterknowledge: How We Surrendered to Conspiracy Theories, Quack Medicine, Bogus Science and Fake History* [London: Atlantic Books, 2008], 54).
109. Contrast archive.org's "Way Back Machine" records for https://en.wikipedia.org/ wiki/Sigiriya from June and July 2020 to see the discrepancies in the entry.
110. "Sahrada Toṭupala" was a popular blog in Sinhala from 2010 to mid-2012, containing 124 posts on various aspects of Hela Ravana and garnering several

hundred thousand views by 2014 (archived at http://seuslsla.blogspot.com/2012_02_12_archive.html). Essays on evidence for the historicity of Ravana's kingdom and the *Ramayana* epic featured on sri-ravana.blogspot.com are routinely shared on Ravana-related Facebook pages.

111. http://sathsamudura.blogspot.com/2011/06/2012-1.html.
112. "Ravana—The Greatest Emperor of Asia," https://ravanalankapura.wordpress.com/historical-sites/.
113. Suriya Gunasekara, *Aitihāsika Rāvaṇa* (Boraläsgamuva: Visidunu Publishers, 2018 [2012]), 24.
114. Mihindukulasuriya Susantha Fernando, *Ritual, Folk Beliefs and Magical Arts* (Colombo: Godage International Publishers, 2000), 16–19.
115. The same blogger claims that a Brahmi inscription found in Mulleriyawa prophecies that "Ravana will do great damage to America in the 21st century," http://vargapurnikava.blogspot.com/2012/06/911.html.
116. Gunasekara, *Aitihāsika Rāvaṇa*, 106.
117. Mīvanapalānē Siri Dhammālaṅkāra Thero, *Apa Upan Mē Hela Bima Budun Upan Jambudvīpayayi [Gautama Buddha was born in Hela Bima]*, http://gauthamabuddhasrilanka.blogspot.com/2015/04/gauthama-buddha-was-born-in-helabima_58.html, 9f.
118. "2019 mädin pōya (pa. va.)" (56:18), https://www.youtube.com/watch?v=B9aKC5vdL0s.
119. Virasena Algevatta, "Rāvaṇa aitihāsika caritayak da?" January 20, 2012, http://helayugaya.blogspot.com/2012/01/blog-post_20.html.
120. Pollock, *The Language of the Gods in the World of Men*, 34.
121. Ibid., 525f.
122. "Civilizationalism," by contrast "summons us to no action," as a civilization "is not something anyone ever sets out to build" (ibid., 526).
123. The images are familiar from Manawe Vimalaratana's "Rosetta Stone" of the Yaksha language, and include a conch, flaming sun, and a scimitar (see Chapter 4, section 3 of this text).
124. On the "prime meridian of Lanka" in the *Sūrya Siddhānta* as it configures in modern Ravana discourse, see discussion of Sunela Jayewardene's *The Line of Lanka: Myths and Memories of an Island* (Colombo: Sail Fish, 2017) in Chapter 4, section 4 of this text.
125. Charumini de Silva, "Over 100 responses so far on SL's quest to establish King Ravana as first aviator."
126. In Sinhala, the word "civilization" is translated by a borrowed Sanskrit term, *śiṣṭācāra*, which in its original sense relates to following the rules of polite society or being a learned and cultured person. The Sanskrit term *śiṣṭācāra*, "a learned person" or "one who follows the rules of society," is attested in a Hindu *dharmic* sense in the *Mahābhārata*. Śabara in his *Bhāṣya* commentary on the Pūrva-Mīmāṃsa Sūtras of Jaimani would categorize the *Mahābhārata* itself as a work of the *śiṣṭācāra* sort; i.e., as a work which instructs upon or embodies social *dharma* (V. M. Apte and D. V. Garge, "Mahābhārata Citations in the Śabara

Bhāṣya," *Bulletin of the Deccan College Post-Graduate and Research Institute* 5 [1943–1944]: 222).

127. *avurudu dahas gananakaṭa pūrva kālayehi hindudēsayehi mahan-sisṭācāran vayan* [sic] *pävännē* (*Rāmāyaṇaya*, f.1a).

128. *numut e yantraya apaṭa sitiya no häki taram purāna kālayaka tibuna ekak bävin ē sambandhava mīta vaḍā vistara ki[ya]vana vavattanam* (ibid., f.37a).

# 6

# A BRIDGE TOO CLOSE

## 6.1 CROSSING THE RAM SETU

As an island—albeit an island very close to the Indian mainland—Sri Lanka has historically maintained a unique relationship to the broader political, linguistic, and cultural formations of Southern Asia. Sheldon Pollock points to the early adoption of Sinhala as a language of political and literary expression—predating by several centuries the "vernacular turn" from Sanskrit to local languages in courtly and academic circles elsewhere on the Indian subcontinent—as an indication of "stubborn and self-conscious resistance to Sanskrit's cultural project" in Sri Lanka.[1] Charles Hallisey has argued that, from the end of the first millennium CE, as a consequence of efforts on the part of Buddhist monks to persuade lay people to exclusively support the Sangha (as opposed to Shaiva institutions), Sinhala literature intended for lay audiences came to express "ideological distance" from the Indic world, reinforced by ideals of Buddhist monarchy and polity exclusive to Sri Lanka.[2] The ascendance of "Yaksha descent theory," with its attendant discourse of Lankan exceptionalism and Sinhala autochthony, can be seen in some sense as the fulfillment of this centuries-old project of "islanding" Sri Lanka, positing a hypothetical ancient civilization which combines the choicest elements of Buddhist antiquity with real and imagined scientific, technological and literary accomplishments conventionally attributed to the greater Indian tradition.

The twenty-first-century Sinhala Ravana phenomenon is dynamic and multifaceted, and not all the rhetoric surrounding the recovery of the "historical *Ramayana*" in Sri Lanka is parochial or oppositional. H. E. Niluka Kadurugamuwa, current Acting High Commissioner of Sri Lanka in India, proclaimed at a recent symposium on the Ramayana Trail that the ancient Hindu epic:

> presents a symbol of the victory of good over evil, and in a spiritual sense the *Ramayana* brings forth a metaphor for a battle between the forces of

*Ravana's Kingdom*. Justin W. Henry, Oxford University Press. © Oxford University Press 2023.
DOI: 10.1093/oso/9780197636305.003.0006

> light and darkness within every human soul. However, I believe that the *Ramayana* has another side to it, as far as Sri Lanka and India are concerned. The epic, despite its narrative advances, is essentially a testimony to the close cultural relations that existed between Sri Lanka and India for millennia . . . it shows the closeness of our two nations in a cultural sense.[3]

Positive rhetoric concerning a renewed relationship with India associated with the Ramayana Trail is but one example of the palingenetic discourse that saturated Sinhala media in the wake of the conclusion of Sri Lanka's civil war in 2009. Such rhetoric includes an international component, as for example the goal of liberal economic modernization (guided by traditional Buddhist values) articulated in Mahinda Rajapaksha's "Mahinda Chintanaya" and again more recently in Gotabaya Rajapaksha's "Vistas of Prosperity and Splendour."[4] From the point of view of the Rajapaksha manifestos, internationalism should not compromise national sovereignty, of course, the latter concern being pivotal to the twenty-first-century Sinhala Ravana imaginary, as I have argued in the previous chapters. While the Ramayana Trail was lauded for its diplomatic potential from its inception, some Sinhala Buddhists remained wary of the prospect of Indian government sponsorship of Hindu temples adjacent to Buddhist places of worship, insisting that planners foreground Ravana as the true hero of Lankan antiquity. For many Sinhala Buddhists fresh on the heels of victory over the LTTE, the "Ram Setu" ("Rama's Bridge," the Palk Strait isthmus) tethering India and Sri Lanka was symbolic not of the prospect for a renewal of Indo-Lankan relations (as it was for architects of the Ramayana Trail), but was rather viewed as a bridge too close. For them, any Indian investment in Sri Lanka—with the expectation of throngs of Indian tourists not far behind—evoked memories of Indian military intervention in the 1980s and 1990s, regarded by many as a modern instance of the recurrent narrative theme of the *Mahāvaṃsa*, the invasion of Lanka by bellicose forces from across the northern sea.[5]

The relevance of Sinhala Ravana discourse to domestic perceptions of Indo-Lankan relations is quite directly expressed by Ariyadasa Seneviratna in his *Śrī Laṅkā Rāvaṇa Rājadhāniya* ("Sri Lanka—Ravana's Royal Capital," 1991). Appended to the book, which is another miscellaneous example of historical Ravana scholarship (Seneviratna was a Colombo attorney), are several of the author's own short poems in Sinhala, beginning with one likening then President Ranasinghe Premadasa's efforts to remove the Indian Peace Keeping Forces to Ravana's valorous defense of his kingdom. Seneviratna refers to the IPKF as "the army of Rama's incarnation," returning again to invade the island of Lanka:

> Do not upon my death bother with inviting the Sangha to perform the ordinary religious protocol, offering me merit as I am reborn in the Deva world!
>
> Supplicate me instead with the prayer: "May the fierce Rakshasa race of Ravana be born again in the motherland to watch over this country!"
>
> Every day my motherland is deprived by the reincarnation of Rama
> Who has come again to this country after thousands of years . . .
>
> I come beseeching you to put an end to this, O [President] Ranesinha,
> Expel the army of the Rāma Avatāra from the land of Lanka!
> Win back the motherland which belongs to you and me alike,
> making her prosperous again!
> I raise up my hands to match your kicking feet![6]

A great deal of the literary intrigue and implicit moral pedagogy of the Hindu epics is driven by conflicts of duty—the intricacies, complexities, and ambiguities of which are summed up in the *Mahābhārata*'s refrain that "*dharma* is subtle (*sūkṣma*)" and difficult to grasp. While the narratives of the *Mahābhārata* and *Rāmāyaṇa* are indeed subtle, both epics are, at the end of the day, stories of wars between two opposing armies, with an incarnation of the god Vishnu clearly supporting one side in each case. As I have argued in the preceding chapters, and as the above excerpt from Ariyadasa Seneviratna's poem reinforces, criteria of "Lankan" and "foreign" abide at the heart of the modern Sinhala Ravana imaginary, with the foreign pole often coded as "Indian." Working to account for the fact that Buddhists in Sri Lanka never developed a robust independent *Ramayana* tradition, Steven Collins suggests that the *Vessantara Jātaka* (the story of the penultimate, terrestrial birth of Siddhartha Gotama) served as a kind of literary substitute for the epic, with the narratives of both consisting of the same essential story-matrix.[7] (As with Rama in the *Ramayana*, in this Jataka tale Prince Vessantara along with his wife Maddi spend a period of exile in a forest ashram, Vessantara faces the trial of losing his wife and children, regains them, and is reinstated to his throne.) While the *Vessantara Jātaka* is, it is true, universally known among Sri Lankan Buddhists, deeply significant as the context for the Bodhisattva's attainment of the capstone *pāramitā*, "the perfection of giving," the story is no substitute for the *Ramayana* with respect to action-adventure and martial heroism.[8] The real Lankan Buddhist analogue to the Hindu epics in these respects is the *Mahāvaṃsa*, one-quarter of the first installment of which is dedicated to Duṭṭhagāmiṇī's reconquest of the northern kingdom from the Indian usurper Eḷāra. The theme of the defense of the island by "Sīhaḷa" kings against foreign, "Damiḷa" invaders serves as the premise for vivid descriptions of battles in later installments of the chronicle, episodes recapitulated in popular vernacular adaptations such as the thirteenth-century *Pūjāvaliya*, the *Rājāvaliya*, and no doubt through various oral renditions.[9] While twenty-first-century Sinhala Ravana advocates have turned away from the *Mahāvaṃsa* as a foremost authoritative source of the island's history, the chronicle's ready-made semiology of "native Lankan" in opposition to "Indian other" has remained neatly intact in their vision of the millennia-long history of Lankan foreign relations.

The necessity of choosing sides when discussing Ravana in Sri Lanka today was illustrated to me in a poignant experience in May 2019 while giving an interview to a newspaper journalist in a Colombo coffee shop. Two employees looked on from behind the counter as I attempted to recount my life story, PhD dissertation, and book project over the course of an hour in exasperated and inadequate Sinhala. When the spectacle concluded and I was getting ready to leave, one of the two employees, captured by my mention of Sinhala texts dealing with "Rama-Sita Katha," stopped me on my way out to ask some follow-up questions. I summarized as best I could my findings regarding how Sri Lanka became Ravana's "Lankapura," how it is that Tamil versions of the *Ramayana* came to impact Sinhala retellings of the epic, and the long tradition of "stories of Rama and Sita" in Sinhala folklore. After listening patiently, the young Sinhala Buddhist man paused a moment before asking what was evidently to him the question that truly mattered amid all of this: "So whose side are you on? Rama's, or Ravana's?"

While in the modern Sinhala Ravana imaginary Rama's land of India represents the specter of the "near foreign," the motif of recovery of the treasures of Hela-Yaksha civilization lost through foreign domination casts Lanka's adversary as colonial Europe, the "Western Aryans" of W. A. De Silva's reconstructed ethnoscape (see Chapter 4, section 5). Of course, as a matter of historical fact, a great deal *was lost* to Sri Lanka through the organs of colonial extraction, materially, culturally, and with respect to a sovereign trajectory toward political modernity. With the twilight of the British colonial era still a part of living memory in Sri Lanka, residual suspicion toward the intentions of western visitors is, in some circumstances, therefore understandable. I myself was, from time to time, greeted with cold skepticism upon explaining my research topic to fellow library patrons who saw me reading Sinhala. "Many foreigners come here with only one thing in mind," I was told on one occasion outside the National Library copy room. "Loggers come for ebony. Russians come for the genes of our rare orchid flowers. Americans like you come for the secret of the mercury vortex engine."

Nowhere is the narrative of the reclamation of Hela-Yaksha technology from colonial degradation more neatly coalesced than in the revival of Sri Lanka's putative traditional martial art, Angampora or "body combat." At the vanguard of the Angampora revival is Ajantha Mahanthaarachchi, a professional dancer with sculpted, bulging muscles, and a severe countenance, instructor at the University of the Visual and Performing Arts, Colombo. In his several books and interviews in Colombo newspapers, Mahanthaarachchi reconstructs the putative ancient martial art in vivid and elaborate detail, asserting that Angampora was practiced by Sri Lanka's "Yaksha tribe" from over thirty thousand years ago, only to be suppressed by the British following the Uva–Wellassa Freedom Fight of 1818.[10] For the last two hundred years, he explains, Angampora was out of necessity practiced in secret in the vicinity of Kandy and in rural Sabaragamuwa, preserved through lineages of initiation in the rites and practices of the art. Mahanthaarachchi himself claims to be a member of an initiation lineage of Angampora practitioners traceable to the sixteenth-century court at Sitawaka, and in this capacity to have inherited the armaments of King Rājasiṃha I, including his ceremonial sword (*kastanē*).[11]

Mahanthaarachchi reveals the attack and defense postures of "body combat," along with a bevy of arcane weapons belonging to the related art of "Illangam" (including, for instance, the impressive *etunu-kaḍuva*, a sword with up to twenty-eight oscillating blades). Angampora involves stealthy and telekinetic methods as well, including knowledge of the 108 "pressure points" of the body which, when depressed in the proper sequence, will result in the sudden death of an opponent several hours after contact. Mantras, yantras, enchanted weapons, and magical manipulation of a miniature effigy of an adversary's body (the Angampora equivalent to Voodoo) are all part of the warrior's arsenal. On Mahanthaarachchi's reconstruction, Angampora was traditionally more than simply a vocation, encompassing a wholistic lifestyle suffused with ethical precepts, Ayurvedic medicine, and daily meditation.

There are implicit and explicit Buddhist dimensions to the course of training as well. Mahanthaarachchi relates that a boy or girl is eligible to receive Angam initiation at six years of age, with the suitability of the vocation determined by one's horoscope as read and interpreted by a Buddhist monk. (Seven is the age at which one can ordain as a *sāmaṇera*, a novice monastic; in Sri Lanka traditionally the optimal day and time for a Buddhist ordination ceremony is likewise calculated on the basis of a horoscope.) The initiation ceremony under an Angam master involves the tying of a cloth waistband (*pacca vadama*), conspicuously identical in its ochre color to the robe of a Bhikkhu. Mahanthaarachchi discloses the three oaths of an initiate as: (1) devoting oneself to a life of spirituality; (2) swearing to protect the secrecy of Angam teachings; and (3) vowing to protect the country of Sri Lanka, its people, and the Buddhist faith.[12] In addition, however, we learn that Angam practitioners worship "the warrior god Ravana," who according to Mahanthaarachchi improved the ancient discipline by supplementing it with his own series of techniques (known as the *rakkha rakkäna herala*). The very first drill in which a novice receives instruction is that of drawing a Swastika in the sand with a stick—"an auspicious emblem that has been used by Buddhists and Hindus for thousands of years."[13]

In Mahanthaarachchi's vision, aspects of *aṅgampora tākṣaṇaya*, although outlawed by the British (who, upon discovering an Angam practitioner, would "shoot him below the knee"), are preserved in a number of Sri Lankan cultural heritage practices. The combat drills of Angampora we learn were disguised within the gestures of Kandyan Dance (*uḍaraṭa näṭum*) and the Leopard Dance (*koṭi nartanaya*) associated with Buddhist temple processions (*perahera*s). The decorative head and body gear of Kandyan dancers is, too, a stylized version of ancient Lankan armor.[14] Fire twirling—nighttime acrobatic performances with a long torch lit at both ends (*gini bōla karakevīma*)—has its origins in Angam weaponry.[15] Massage with medicinal oils using the hands and feet was part of the daily regimen of any Angam warrior-in-training, essential to heal and revitalize their punished bodies.[16] Readers of Mahanthaarachchi's version of events are then made to understand that what are today seemingly innocuous—sometimes even servile—attractions for foreign tourists belie a deadly potent tradition, the heritage of a great warrior people only temporarily disempowered by colonial fiat.

Mahanthaarachchi's revelation of the lost art of Angampora has been enthusiastically received by the general public. His 2017 book, *Angampora: A Nation's Legacy in Pictures*, supplemented with vivid full color photographs by Reza Akram, contains written endorsements in its preface from then Prime Minister Ranil Wickremesinghe and President Maithripala Sirisena, the latter of whom issued an executive order in November 2018 "lifting the British ban on Angampora" upon the bicentennial anniversary of Sir Robert Brownrigg's original "gazette notification."[17] Sri Lanka's Ministry of Buddhasasana, Religious and Cultural Affairs currently names Angampora as an item of intangible cultural heritage, and has sponsored at least one public exhibition of the practice.[18] Since 2012 Mahanthaarachchi has offered training to several branches of the nation's armed forces.[19] In December 2018 the Sri Lankan Army established an Angampora training camp at Kilinochchi, the administrative capital of the LTTE's de facto state in the island's north during the civil war. Capitalizing on the influx of post-war domestic tourists eager to visit the north and east, the "Angampora Experiment Institute and Training Centre" [sic] is modelled in the style of a "typical village," and remains open to members of the public wishing "to spend a day with the Angampora warriors." With the demon-king ever-present, the army's media blurb on the camp's inauguration recounts that "the ceremony reverberated with the singing of the 'Rawana Thaandava' (hymn of praise) by Angampora presenters after the day's Chief Guest [Major General Niyshshanka Ranawana] walked to the village."[20] A pamphlet currently available on the Sri Lankan Air Force's official webpage outlines the history of Angampora, claiming that there are "written evidences to prove the existence of this combat form that dates back over 5000 years and myths and folklore that goes as far as 38,000 years." The pamphlet explains that the art was known to the earliest kings of the island's "Yaksa tribe," that is, defenders of the island from the time of Ravana's grandfather Pulasthi to those who fought for freedom against the occupying Portuguese and British.[21] In December 2018, the Air Force's own "Angampora Display Team" clinched first place on the televised *Sri Lanka's Got Talent* program, with an impressive display of airmen and women engaged in choreographed acrobatics and hand-to-hand combat.[22]

The evidence supplied by Ajantha Mahanthaarachchi—some black and white twentieth-century photographs of supposed Angampora contests, the testimony of a handful of individuals claiming to have received initiation in the secret art, hasty images of a few palm-leaf manuscripts—are unlikely to convince the seasoned skeptic. The only two apparent references to Angampora in Sinhala classical literature appear in the seventeenth-century *Rājāvaliya*, where it is described as a recreational sport (a form of wrestling performed for the entertainment of the nobility).[23] While Mahanthaarachchi's thoroughgoing reconstruction of the lifeworld of Angampora feels suspiciously exact, there is nonetheless evidence that at least some of the aspects of an esoteric martial-cum-medical tradition like the one he describes were practiced in Sri Lanka historically. Writing in the 1950s, P. E. P. Deriyangala, at the time Director of the National Museums of Ceylon and Dean of the Faculty of Arts at Vidyodaya University, compiled a fascinating set of oral legends, Sinhala verses, and palm-leaf manuscripts related to hand-to-hand combat in Sri Lanka. His *Some Sinhala Combative, Field and Aquatic Sports and Games* (1959) catalogues Sri Lankan temple drawings and frescos depicting combat, Sinhala and Pali literary references to martial arts, and Sinhala verses describing gladiatorial matches performed in royal courts (spectacles of combat performed between men as well as between men and animals—leopards and bears). Deriyangala outlines a number of aspects of pre-colonial Sinhala combat training adopted by Mahantaarachchi in his reconstruction of Angampora—contests in the "boar pit" (*ura liňda*), the names of various weapons and manual combat techniques, and the testimony of European colonial agents to the acrobatic prowess of Lankan sword fighters.[24] Lending credence to the secretive knowledge of "pressure points" essential to modern Angampora, Deriyangala summarizes the contents of two ola-leaf manuscripts in his possession depicting *Māra Nil Sāstrē*, "the science of death-inducing centers." The texts diagram regions of the head, throat, chest, and abdomen to describe "the vital centres that could be attacked by blows with the little finger edge of the outstretched hand, knee or elbow, and also by thrusts with the stiff outstretched fingers which were the first and second digits, and at times three fingers." *Māra Nil Sāstrē* also offers means of reviving an opponent rendered unconscious through such means, one text stating: "that a blow across the Adam's apple of the throat with the edge of the hand would render a man unconscious and that he could be revived by gently striking the back of his neck with the heel of the clenched fist."[25]

Deriyangala reminds us that pre-colonial combat culture was not delimited by the island's shores, giving accounts of Indian wrestlers coming to test their mettle against Lankan opponents, and highlighting the fact that Lankan swordsmen, renowned for their agility, were also sought as conscripts by military employers on the continent. Linguistic traces of an extra-Lankan network of transaction in combat techniques appear as well. Deriyangala finds the origins of the Sinhala expression *eyāṭa collē tamayi*, "he took a big hit," in a technical term related to hand-to-hand combat, *collē* or *cokkē* being the dispatching of an opponent by a blow to the solar plexus.[26] *Collē* is, in all likelihood, derived from Tamil *coḷḷai*, meaning the tap on the head received by a loser in a game. Following this clue, in search of parallels with Angampora to the north, we discover a number of aspects of traditional Sri Lankan martial arts (as portrayed both by Deriyangala and Mahanthaarachchi) amid a set of practices known under the rubric of *kaḷarippayaṭṭu* in Kerala and *varmakkalai* in the Kanyakumari region of Tamil Nadu, both of which continue to flourish in the present day. Kaḷarippayaṭṭu, "training ground exercises" in Malayalam, and Varmakkalai, "the art of vital spots" in Tamil, both combine hand-to-hand combat, manual weaponry, and siddha-oriented medical practice within integral training regimes, transmitted with some measure of secrecy from preceptor to pupil. Varmakkalai shares a number of its essential features with Mahanthaarachchi's Angampora: practitioners are initiated in esoteric physiology involving vital nerve centers of the body which can both paralyze and heal; combatants learn the art of massage as both a matter of course in their combat training and as it relates to medical healing; masters pass on esoteric manuscripts to their students along with the knowledge of their proper interpretation; yogic postures are essential to master the "subtle" dynamics of the body needed to enhance vitality and combat readiness.[27] "Gurukulam" is the same word used for training centers in both Kaḷarippayaṭṭu and for Angampora.[28] Kaḷarippayaṭṭu and Varmakkalai as they are practiced today, like Angampora, highlight the impressive physical abilities of both men and women in their combat arts.[29]

Angampora furnishes then yet another example of the dynamics of exchange taking place between Sri Lanka and the Indian subcontinent in the centuries prior to colonial annexation as well as, by Mahanthaarachchi's own admission, the continuation of similar avenues of exchange today (Mahanthaarachchi reveals that he visited Kaḷarippayaṭṭu training camps in Kerala as part of his research for *Angampora: A Nation's Legacy in Pictures*). While Mahanthaarachchi's books are presented as part of a critical research project, from an outsider academic point of view, the normative valences and palingenetic metanarrative implicated in his work are conspicuously palpable. Despite this, and despite of some of his more incredible claims, however, in his reconstruction of "the people's art" (Mahanthaarachchi's designation for Angampora on account of its preservation in rural circumstances by ordinary Sri Lankans), Mahanthaarachchi does open avenues of legitimate scholarly inquiry. The Angampora that he and his associates inspired is one token of the public, participatory effort to resurrect Ravana's kingdom reflecting a popular imaginary with its finger on the pulse of an understudied tradition of considerable interest. Mahanthaarachchi's own "history from below" is therefore instructive to the contemporary historian and ethnographer in more ways than one, and, like so many other dimensions of the Ravana movement, points the way to aspects of a shared Indo–Lankan heritage, even when traces of such cosmopolitanism are obscured by monological discourses of Sinhala hegemony.

## 6.2 MAINSTREAMING RAVANA'S KINGDOM

As I have shown over the course of the preceding chapters, the Sinhala Ravana movement has found expression in multiple forms of media, a variety of public arenas, and in multiple spheres of Sinhala Buddhist society. I have along the way noted the endorsement of the historical Ravana/Hela-Yaksha civilization hypothesis by government officials and departments, to which list we may add the Ministry of Health, Nutrition and Indigenous Medicine,[30] and the Ministry of Technology and Research, which has proposed allocating funds for excavations at sites linked to the Ravana dynasty.[31] Contrary to the case of Tamil Nadu, however, where there has been sustained government support for the "Kumarināṭu" supercontinent hypothesis,[32] I find no systematic or integral effort to produce a "Ravana consensus"—government departments and actors promoting the Ravana narrative have done so independently and for the most part in unrelated circumstances. While the Rajapaksha brothers have made savvy use of social media for political ends, the online Ravana phenomenon has been in essence user-generated, with the historical narrative surrounding Ravana and the aesthetics of the Hela-Yaksha civilization developed and augmented by Sri Lankans indiscriminately from all walks of life, in both Sinhala and English (Tamil responses I discuss in the following section of this chapter). The only requirement to be a "Ravana researcher" today is sufficient time and interest.

Amateur Ravana research is frequently packaged in conventional formats associated with the dissemination of specialist academic knowledge production. Examples of books purporting to tell the "unknown history" of the Hela-Yaksha civilization sold alongside conventional non-fiction were given in Chapters 4 and 5, although the titles named there are by no means exhaustive of the genre. Secondary school history texts published by the Sri

Lanka's National Institute of Education continue to follow the *Mahāvaṃsa* narrative in claiming that the first inhabitants of the island were Prince Vijaya and his party, from whom the "Sinhala race" (*siṅhala jātiya*) of today are descended.[33] While the Ministry of Education still prints texts for classroom use, there are no longer mandated texts or syllabuses for secondary school education, which has opened the market to private publishers to sell their own books for use in schools and tuition classes.[34] Ravana's kingdom has begun to penetrate these privately produced texts, as I discovered during a March 2019 visit to Godage International Publishers in Maradana, one of Colombo's premier textbook sellers, where there were two history texts intended for secondary school beginning their account of the island's history with Ravana's "Hela civilization."[35]

Broadcast networks have similarly lent the appearance of academic credibility to the Sinhala Ravana narrative. Modeled after a 2008 television serial on the history of Sri Lankan kings hosted by actor-director Jackson Anthony, a number of programs speculating on the historical evidence for Ravana and the "Yaksha tribe" have been featured on major networks from 2012 onward.[36] These include a five-month long serial entitled *Lakviskam Rāvaṇa* (2012–2013) on the government operated V-FM radio channel, along with Derana TV's *Helavaṃśaya*, which ran from September 2013 to May 2014. Broadcast on the same network which now airs the *Rāvaṇa* epic serial drama (see Chapter 4, section 3), *Helavaṃśaya* takes viewers on excursions to archaeological sites throughout the island with putative connections to the prehistoric Hela-Yaksha civilization. The program, along with a similar serial aired on the Swarnawahini network, featured roundtable discussions of "Ravana experts," who debated amongst themselves and fielded audience questions.[37]

Much of the initial support for the historical Ravana hypothesis among credentialed academics came from those in the fields of engineering and other technical sciences, a number of whom have been captivated by the prospect of reconstructing the fantastic technology of the Hela-Yakshas.[38] While other esteemed scholars in the fields of linguistics, literary studies, and archaeology have joined the Sinhala Ravana cause, disproportionate credulity among professionals in the engineering and technical sciences reinforces a general public sentiment regarding the possibility of recovering the treasures of Ravana's kingdom in one form or another; that is, the possibility of re-engineering this lost technology on the basis of references and schematics available today. The public, participatory dimension to the reclamation of Hela-Yaksha *tākṣaṇaya* presupposes a general level of accessibility to the artifacts of Ravana's kingdom, which I have argued is consonant with the overall populist tenor of the movement. Elevating such a populist ethos in the domain of academic discovery to the level of a philosophical principle is Nalin de Silva, another major exponent of Sinhala Ravana, Sri Lanka's current Ambassador to Burma, and former Professor of Mathematics and Dean of the Faculty of Science at the University of Kelaniya. Since the 1980s, de Silva has publicly advanced a Sinhala Buddhist nationalist agenda, and was an architect of a political manifesto known as *Jātika Cintanaya* ("People's Consciousness"). *Jātika Cintanaya* as an ideology is positioned in opposition to the Buddhist Marxist movement (the JVP or "People's Liberation Front"), and shares with other Sinhala nationalist schools a belief in the necessary, legally enshrined supremacy of Buddhist governance and cultural values in Sri Lanka.[39]

A major focus of de Silva's work as a philosopher of science and public commentator has been advocacy for local knowledge systems, including most notoriously a rejection of the "western scientific method" and the demands of repeatable, falsifiable hypotheses in a controlled experimental setting. Strongly influenced by the "scientific anarchism" of Paul Feyerabend (1924–1994), de Silva explains that he is "not inclined to publish in so-called peer reviewed research journals," believing instead in the direct dissemination of scientific findings to the public "through newspapers, websites, blogs and other such media." De Silva's grievance with western experimental science and its attendant peer-review process is what he understands to be the origins of the demands for rigorous citation of authoritative bibliographical sources "in the [Christian] Biblical tradition of quoting chapter and verse."[40] In his view, a more authentically Buddhist epistemology demands that an audience be able to fully perceive and understand for themselves the evidence and methodology that produce scientific contentions—this is keeping with the Buddha's admonition that his disciples "come and see" (*ehi passiko*) for themselves the truth and profundity of his teachings (i.e., without merely dogmatically taking his word for it).[41] A test case for de Silva's radical alternative methodology came in 2011 when he led a research team of scientists from Kelaniya and Rajarata Universities in search of the cause of an unexplained widespread kidney failure epidemic among men in Sri Lanka's North Central Province. The team issued a report concluding that the condition could be traced to arsenic poisoning, a consequence of overuse of imported pesticides and fertilizers. Amid skepticism over the findings and demands that the scientists release their data sets, it came to light that the team considered arsenic as an initial prime hypothesis on the basis of a "direct revelation" made by the gods Natha and Vipasaka to de Silva and several of his colleagues.[42] (In a subsequent independent study, the Sri Lankan government's own Industrial Technology Institute was unable to confirm elevated levels of arsenic in the region's rice.)

De Silva promotes his own idiosyncratic historical kingdom of Ravana and the "*yakṣa gōtraya*" in one of his most widely read works, *Apē Pravāda 3* (*Our Theories, vol. 3*) published in 2010. Here he maintains that the Yakshas came to pre-Buddhist Sri Lanka originally from Persia, that the Sinhala (*hela*) people are in fact a composite of the "four tribes" of the Yaksha, Rakshasa, Asura, and Naga, and that the Vijaya colonization myth is an instance of revisionist history advanced by a culturally dominant but numerically inferior contingent of Indian émigrés.[43] He goes on to blame the Pali chronicles for neglecting to attribute early engineering and hydrological accomplishment to the Yakshas, attributing them instead to "Tamils" (*damiḷas*), whom de Silva argues did not constitute a coherent ethnic faction in Sri Lanka until significantly later.[44] Significant in his position are the actors whom he identifies as obscuring historical truth concerning the non-Indian, "non-Aryan" heritage of the Sinhala people. According to de Silva, not all the blame lies on the authors of the *Mahāvaṃsa*, who, he explains, principally intended to promote a singular version of Buddhist polity and philosophy ("Ashokan Dharma") over that of rival schools. The true culprits in his view are those who in the modern era have used the narrative of the *Mahāvaṃsa* to attribute "Tamil" ethic identity to early inhabitants of the island, thereby opening the door to claims to territorial sovereignty and historical persecution at the hands of Sinhala Buddhists. De Silva explains succinctly: "The Mahavamsa myth as propagated by the westerners, the Tamil racists, NGO pundits and the academia [sic] itself is a myth coined by them, as [the] Mahavamsa is not a book written against the Tamils."[45]

Reproduced in de Silva's combative text-critical historiography is the same dynamic which informs his scientific epistemology: in both cases hegemonic forces seek to over-complicate and mystify what should be an *immediate* relationship between the available data and the knowledge-seeking subject. The specter inhibiting the public's grasp of issues in the physical sciences is, from his point of view, the obfuscation which occurs through demands for bibliographical citation and peer review; obfuscation in historiography (again, from de Silva's point of view) comes through ideological subterfuge and the neglect of marginal sources which offer corrective pushback to monological historical paradigms. Relying on Manave Vimalaratana's imaginative scholarship, de Silva invokes the *Vargapūrṇikāva* as an example of precisely the kind of vernacular antidote needed to combat hegemonic, ideologically compromised representations of the island's history. The value in this (as a reminder, probably non-existent) text is, according to de Silva, the fact that, in addition to giving details of the "Hela-Yaksha civilization," the *Vargapūrṇikāva* attests to alternative schools of Buddhism and alternative genealogies of the island's peoples ("Vamsakathas") still circulating in the living memory of scholiasts as late as the eighteenth century.[46] Reinforcing the populist outlook of the broader Sinhala Ravana movement, de Silva believes that texts containing the most essential information on the heritage of the Sinhala people are not the erudite chronicles servicing the sectarian interests of first millennium Buddhist monks (texts written in Pali, an inaccessible ecclesiastical koiné), but rather those preserved in the vernacular (albeit, in the supposed case of the *Vargapūrṇikāva*, a vernacular of three millennia ago) and transmitted among scholiasts at the periphery of the premodern Buddhist monastic academy.

I should clarify that, while the Sinhala Ravana hypothesis has attracted some high-profile academic supporters, a number of other leading scholars have publicly cautioned against what they view to be revisionist and ideological pseudo-scholarship underwriting the movement. In addition to the Royal Asiatic Society's highly publicized 2010 symposium critiquing claims related to the Ramayana Trail (see Chapter 5, section 2), op-eds debunking the Sinhala Ravana hypothesis by historian Michael Roberts and secular humanist crusader Thilak Senasinghe have appeared in Colombo newspapers.[47] Nirmal Dewasiri, Professor of History at Colombo University and vocal liberal public commentator, addresses the politics of Sinhala Ravana in a recent text intended for university classroom use.[48] Dr. Senarath Dissanayake, current Director General of the government Department of Archaeology, has over the past year found himself in the public spotlight, appearing on television and YouTube interviews to explain that references to Ravana are strictly of the literary variety (he explains that we must understand the genre of the *Ramayana* to be "*vīra kāvya*," "heroic poetry"), and that there is no epigraphic or archaeological evidence to support the idea of an "advanced Hela civilization" of antiquity.[49]

## 6.3 RAVANA AND POST-WAR RECONCILIATION

Throughout this book I have worked to demonstrate that the nativist and monological fixation of the twenty-first-century Sinhala Ravana movement belies the fact that Ravana's modern Sri Lankan image was forged from a variegated corpus of textual, oral, and aesthetic influences originating beyond Sri Lanka's shores. Recognizing this, and despite the intense rhetoric of exclusion saturating the movement today, a number of Sri Lankans have attempted to harness Ravana enthusiasm to focus attention on a *shared heritage* and history of cultural interface between Sinhala Buddhists and Tamil Hindus in the context of post-war reconciliation. This has been the case both for the more literal-minded with respect to belief in the historicity of Ravana (including some university scholars,[50] as well as the architects of the Ramayana Trail, whose oversight committee remains a diverse mix of Sinhala and Tamil representatives), and for those who are comfortable assigning Ravana's kingdom to the realm of the legendary.

Chapter 4 reviewed literary works and stage dramas expressive of the Sinhala Ravana paradigm, absent from which were a number of additional creative pieces voicing *opposition* to Sinhala hegemony. Acclaimed novelist Tennyson Perera, author of Sri Lanka's first "banned book," *Dätirōden Upan Budun* ("Cogwheel Buddha," 1967), took Sri Lanka's prestigious Fairway National Literary Award for his *Mahā Rāvaṇa* in 2016, a novel which slyly lampoons the Sinhala appropriation of Ravana as a cultural hero. Set in the present day, Maha Ravana, the titular character, resides in a palatial up-country tea estate, retired from a career in the army, where, as an officer he was permitted to indulge his love for "hunting" during the height of Sri Lanka's civil war. Maha Ravana, an aging, bored, but still vital aristocrat, plays a Mephistophelian role in the book, tempting the narrator (Lakshmana, an author on a writing retreat at his friend's nearby estate) into drinking once again, playing with firearms, and a climactic game of William Tell with his own wife. The novel is preeminently aware of Sinhala claims to Yaksha-descent and post-war Ravana mythology, making the (literal) bloodthirstiness of Maha Ravana a commentary on murder with impunity as well as the psychological effects of war. With hints throughout that Maha Ravana suffers from Post-Traumatic Stress Disorder, we learn that the "army man" killed his former wife in a catatonic stupor, firing blindly into the night at an invisible enemy from his bedroom window. He subsequently kills his daughter-in-law (an Indian Dalit) and finally his son, a Buddhist monk.[51]

Sam Perera, co-founder of Perera–Hussein Publishing House, a leading publisher of English language books in Sri Lanka, has piggybacked on Ravana's popularity as an opportunity to share Tamil mythology with younger readers, publishing *Ravana & the Temple of Shiva* in 2015. Smartly illustrated in watercolors by Alex Stewart and sporting a winged, yellow tuk-tuk as Ravana's aerial chariot on its cover, *Ravana & the Temple of Shiva* tells the story of Ravana's concern that his mother be able to worship Shiva even when she is old and infirm. (In this local adaptation, instead of Ravana traveling from Mt. Kailasa back to Lanka, he transports a graft from the rock at Koneswaram Temple in Trincomalee to his mother in Matale, in the island's central mountains). Angered by what he perceives to be an act of burglary, Shiva besieges Sri Lanka with a frightful tsunami, compelling Ravana at the request of the island's residents to make a penitent display before the god. Ravana tears out the tendons from his arm to fashion a lute (the "Ravanahattha") on which he plays songs of devotion, pacifying Shiva and restoring order to the island. The book ends with an invitation to visit Trincomalee, where "you can still see the place where Ravana cut the rock, just as if you listen closely, you will hear the music of the Ravana Ragas!" (This is an allusion to a legend at Koneswaram about "singing fish" in waters of the ocean below.) Perera and Stewart have promoted their book in Colombo classrooms where they discuss the origin and significance of the story, and plan to publish translations in both Sinhala and Tamil.

In the realm of the performing arts, Sinniah Maunaguru, professor of drama at Eastern University of Sri Lanka, has brought Ravana to the classroom and the stage as an illustration of the dynamic process of exchange which has forged Sinhala and Tamil musical and dramatic performance styles. Maunaguru's teacher, Suppiramaniam Vithiananthan (1924–1989), inspired by his colleague Ediriweera Sarachchandra's modernization of Sinhala theater (see Chapter 4, section 2), wrote a series of plays in the 1960s in the traditional Tamil *kūttu* style, performed initially by his undergraduate students at the University of Peradeniya. Vithiananthan's *Irāvaṇēcaṉ* (1965) featured Maunaguru in the starring role, drawing material from Kamban's twelfth-century version of the *Ramayana* to offer a more focused perspective on Ravana's family—his wife Mandodari and son Indrajit—as they implore the fated king not to allow his pride and resentment to consume him in an unwinnable war against Rama.[52] *Irāvaṇēcaṉ* makes Ravana—an otherwise *dharmic* ruler—a tragic figure in service of a broader point about the injustices of war, with one reviewer explaining the moral of the play as being the fact that "in the normally masculine theater of war, women are left out of debates and decision making," with Sita an example of the fact that women are often used as pretenses for conflict.[53] Following the conclusion of the civil war in 2009, Maunaguru revived *Irāvaṇēcaṉ*, now considered a modern Tamil classic, staging performances in Batticaloa as well as in Colombo. The piece had a newly acquired acute relevance for Tamil audiences, with Sivagnanam Jeyasankar (Maunaguru's own student who has replaced him in the titular role) reporting that, following the climactic scene of Ravana's death, there was not a dry eye in the audience during the play's re-debut at the Swami Vipulananda Institute in Batticaloa in 2010.[54]

In the early 2000s Maunaguru also teamed up with actor, playwright and activist Dharmasiri Bandaranayake in an educational initiative to bring together Sinhala and Tamil student dancers and musicians in the context of a workshop discussing the historical relationship between *kūttu* and *nāḍagam*. The workshop included lectures (in Sinhala, Tamil, and English) and a chance for participants to learn dance steps and drum patterns from both Sinhala and Tamil traditional drama, with a capstone performance from Sarachchandra's *Siṅhabāhu* performed by the lead from the original 1961 production, as well as an excerpt from *Irāvaṇēcaṉ* with Maunaguru as Ravana.[55] Ethnomusicologist Jim Sykes, who followed the renaissance of *Irāvaṇēcaṉ* as part of his study on the history and sociology of Sinhala and Tamil drumming patterns in Sri Lanka, remarks on the *subversive* potential of Vithiananthan and Maunaguru's Ravana in the post-war context:

> In this play, Ravana emerges as a tragic hero and cultural figure common to Sinhalas and Tamils: he is a king of Sri Lanka, rather than a Sinhala or Tamil king, and the play ends with his death, due to his waging a useless war. Maunaguru's Ravana is a progenitor of both Sinhalas and Tamils, and a progenitor of the music and dance of both groups.[56]

This message has been taken up by Sudesh Mantillake, dancer, choreographer, and Head of the Department of Fine Arts at the University of Peradeniya. Mantillake toured the United States in 2017–2018 directing an innovative Sri Lankan dance troupe in a series of performances inspired by Sinhala *Yak Tovil* rites entitled *My Devil Dance*. The series was billed as a remembrance of nineteenth- and twentieth-century touring exhibitions featuring Kandyan dancers (alongside exotic animals) as "spectacles of the East," exports from the colonies on display for the curiosity of European audiences. Intending to raise awareness concerning the troubled legacy of colonialism in South Asia, Mantillake was simultaneously eager to project a representative image of Sri Lanka's present day cultural diversity, choosing the Yaksha as the project's central theme to invoke a *pan*-ethnic or *pre*-ethnic symbol of shared Lankan heritage. In December 2020, Mantillake contributed a solo performance as the epilogue to a COVID-19 era collaborative video presentation entitled *The Story of Ram*, featuring perspectives on the *Ramayana* from a number of South and Southeast Asian dance traditions, sponsored by Mandala South Asian Performing Arts and the National Indo American Museum in Chicago. Mantillake himself depicts Ravana in this vignette, recapitulating the centuries-old Sinhala legend in which Ravana is merely knocked unconscious by Rama's final blow. As Mantillake arises from lying prone in a shallow stream, his performance is introduced with screen text explaining:

> Ravana, the figure found in the Ramayana woke up in Sri Lanka after thousands of years and gets confused with the identities that have been given to him. A demon, hero, masculine, feminine, human, divine, ethnically Sinhala, ethnically Tamil. He is in search of his own identity.[57]

Sri Lankan Tamil Hindus have responded to the Sinhala appropriation of Ravana in a variety of forums. In a sixty-one part serial in the popular Colombo-based Tamil newspaper *Tiṉakkural*, N. K. S. Thiruchelvam, president of the Sri Lankan chapter of the Vishva Hindu Parishad, campaigned against the claims of Mirando Obeyeskere to argue instead for the *Tamil* ethnicity (*iṉam*) of the ancient king.[58] The "Dravidian Keyboard Warriors" Facebook page, with over 40,000 followers in July 2020, offered a forum for Tamils to post reminders that Ravana is remembered as a historical *Dravidian* king by Indian and Sri Lankan Tamils alike, and as a great *bhakta* of Shiva in the South Indian Hindu devotional tradition.[59] Ravana has recently been quietly commemorated among Sri Lankan Hindus as well. In July 2016 in Inuvil, a suburb of Jaffna, the newly constructed Gñānalingesvarar Temple consecrated in its main sanctum a unique black granite icon: a *śiva-liṅgam* perched on a ten-headed image of Ravana in his *anugraha-mūrti* posture. Sponsored by the Caiva Neṟikkūṭam ("Shaiva Temple Association"), a group of Sri Lankan Tamil expatriates living in Geneva, Switzerland, the image is the first of its kind at any Hindu temple in Sri Lanka.[60] In Arayampathy, Batticaloa, another ten-foot-high statue of ten-headed Ravana wielding a mace has recently appeared on the roadside opposite a shrine to Shiva.[61] In the lead-up to the civil war, no doubt inspired by the veneration of Ravana during the Indian Dravidian independence movement, Sri Lankan Tamils made the case for their own primacy as an ethnic group on the island tracing their heritage to the Yakshas of the Pali chronicles, positing Ravana as an ancient king.[62] Under such circumstances, in which twenty-first-century Sinhala claims to descent from Ravana could be perceived as one more spoil of war, it is significant that residents of both Inuvil and Arayampathy emphasize that, in addition to Ravana's traditional status as a great *śiva-bhakta*, is it is important that he be remembered as a great *Tamil* and *Hindu* king.[63]

## 6.4 THE APOTHEOSIS OF THE DEMON-KING

For someone acquainted with Sri Lanka but who has not visited for a decade or more, I imagine that a good deal of what I have described in this book could sound very strange. Much within the twenty-first-century Ravana phenomenon is disorienting in relation to orthodox Sinhala Buddhist religiosity and historical self-understanding. The *Mahāvaṃsa*—for the past century a textual resource of first resort with respect to constructions of Sinhala identity—has been in large part sidelined by Ravana enthusiasts, who are unhappy with the contention that the Sinhala people are descended from Prince Vijaya, the "robber baron" from India. The positivist tenor of the Ravana movement—consistent with its supporters' insistence on physical evidence (*sākṣa*) and longing to resurrect ancient scientific innovations with present-day applications—has led some to proclaim that the *Mahāvaṃsa*'s attribution of supernatural abilities to the Buddha Gotama is "the real myth" amid all of this. The Swastika—a symbol historically more commonly associated with Hinduism in Sri Lanka and India—appears with increasing frequency as an emblem of Sinhala Buddhist nationalist causes on social media. Sinhala Ravana enthusiasts have made claims regarding the ancient king's mastery of Sanskrit *śāstra* central to their hypothetical Hela-Yaksha civilization, generating a discourse on traditional systematic knowledge novel to Sri Lanka but reminiscent of that prevalent in India since the late nineteenth century, when, in the words of Brian Hatcher, "we begin to find *shastra* held aloft as a kind of banner under which to rally Hindus in defense of their religion and national culture."[64]

The Sinhala Ravana movement projects into deep antiquity an expansive civilizational imaginary, wherein India is provincialized as a vassal state of Lanka, and Hela-Yaksha civilization is positioned as the *fons et origo* of world culture. As I have argued, Ravana today functions as a kind of plenary signifier, claiming for Sri Lanka literary and technical achievements credited by others to the broader South Asian tradition, and subsuming adjacent discourses of sovereignty, indigeneity, and ethnic primacy. While the twenty-first-century Ravana phenomenon is no doubt radical and disorienting in these and other respects, aspects of it are at the same time congruent with certain dynamics structuring Sinhala Buddhist political ideology and devotional culture historically. Although for instance the overt militarism and martial imagery associated with Ravana seems antithetical to pacifist Buddhist values (e.g., the "first precept" "not to take the life of any living creature"), we must remember that the monks who compiled Sri Lanka's Pali chronicles expressed no reservations over the use of force to defend the island as a preserve of the Buddha *sāsana*.[65]

Ravana's martial valor and the warrior prowess of the Hela-Yaksha people configure centrally in cases today where the demon-king has transcended empirical discourse to achieve the first rank of divine status within the Sinhala Buddhist pantheon. This is evident at the shrine to Ravana on the premises of the Devram Vihara in Pannapitiya, a western suburb of Colombo. The "Mahā Rāvaṇa Rāja Mandiraya" was constructed in 2013 under the supervision of the temple's founder, Kolonnuve Sumangala Thero, a Buddhist monk recently elected Mahanayaka (Chief Prelate) of the Sirisumana Chapter of the Amarapura Nikaya, a founding member of the Jatika Hela Urumaya, a former Member of Parliament, and himself an active Ravana enthusiast.[66] The September 2013 inaugural procession festival (*perahera*) commemorating the opening of the Ravana Mandiraya featured combat displays by a team of "Angampora" specialists, a wooden reconstruction of Ravana's *dańḍu-monara* (built to scale, approximately fifteen feet long and five feet wide), and saw Defense Secretary Gotabaya Rajapaksha as a guest of honor.[67] The interior of the shrine today boasts murals depicting the titles of Sanskrit mathematical and Ayurvedic treatises attributed to Ravana, a depiction of Ravana's conversion to Buddhism under the auspices of "some Mahayana Buddha," Ravana's son Indrajit aboard a spacecraft on his way to mars, and side-by-side depictions of Sigiriya along with the ruins of the Maya and Inca of South America—all locations where Ravana was able to land and service his flying craft[68] (see Figures 6.1–6.5). [69]

Figure 6.1 Ravana aboard his flying craft: mural at the Maha Ravana Raja Mandiraya at Devram Vihara, Pannapitiya.—(Author's photo, July 2014)

Figure 6.2 Gotabaya Rajapaksha attending the inaugural *perahera* of the 'Maha Ravana Raja Mandiraya' at the Devram Vihara, Pannapitiya, September 19, 2013.

**Figure 6.3** Rajapaksha receiving a copy of Kolonnuwe Sumangala's *Mahā Rāvaṇa Śrī Laṅkēśvara* at the same occasion.

**Figure 6.4** Scale model of Ravana's "Dañḍumonara."

**Figure 6.5** A statue of Ravana installed at the Maha Ravana Raja Mandiraya, Devram Vihara.—(Author's photo, July 2014)

The Mahā Rāvaṇa Rāja Mandiraya at Devram Vihara hosts a Sunday "Rāvaṇa *pūjā*," although the shrine has an aura of novelty about it, and it is not clear what sort of public attendance its weekly *pūjā* attracts. The same is true of the Rāvaṇa Devālaya added in 2011 to the premises of the

Bolthumbe Vihara in Ratnapura, a Buddhist temple renowned since the sixteenth century as principal seat of the god Saman. Ravana's shine is now adjacent to Saman's *devālaya* there, where temple priests claim to possess an original model of Ravana's *dańḍu-monara*, along with a tapestry depicting the battle between Rama and Ravana, which according to local tradition took place in the nearby mountains of Dethanagala.[70] Ravana's pairing with Saman at Bolthumbe is significant given the recent denunciation by some Sinhala nationalists of shrines to "Indian gods" at Buddhist temples (such as those commonly found to Vishnu and Pattini). This party however identifies Saman as acceptable on the grounds that he is by contrast a "Sinhala deviyō"—native to Sri Lanka, a bodhisattva, and "the only true Buddhist god."[71] Whether such recent attempts to elevate Ravana to the status of a devotional figure are merely a flash in the pan or indicative of a broader trend remains to be seen.[72] In either case, Ravana would not be the first example of a king elevated to the status of a *deviyō* of the Sri Lankan Buddhist pantheon (Mahasena, a third-to-fourth-century king of Anuradhapura, is venerated as a deity in portions of the island today[73]), nor would he be the first Rakshasa to have done so (Vibhishana has been venerated by Sri Lankan Buddhists since the late medieval period), making Ravana's divinization grounded in precedent.

Aspects of the Sinhala Ravana movement's genesis may also be interpreted as routine continuations of centuries old processes of the formation of dominant historical narratives. Writing in 1988, Bruce Kapferer remarked on the fact that, over the course of the previous ten years, Sigiriya had been transformed from a place known to the average Sinhala Buddhist only through school history texts into a massive tourist destination, on par with other popular Buddhist pilgrimage sites throughout the island. Following the government's choice to open the archaeological site to public visitors, Kapferer argues that Sigiriya was able to become another localized "expression of Sinhalese identity" within such a short time as a consequence of a living oral and written tradition surrounding it—stories concerning the plateau-top palace as a location of royal intrigue during the island's golden age of Buddhist kings. Kapferer draws from this example to conclude that:

> The folk tradition has to a large extent achieved common currency, and its histories have been generalized into the history of a nation. A popular tradition, forged in the processes of nationalism, is continually being created in this generalization of folk knowledge and folk history. What is often

> called folk history is the transformation [of folk knowledge] into popular history.[74]

There are several observations to be made at this juncture. The first, nearly true by definition, concerns the fact that dominant historical narratives are seldom if ever constructed *ex nihilo*—chronicles, canons, and texts all depend on sources and antecedents, the Pali chronicles being no exception, by their authors' own admission.[75] Second, as Kapferer intimates, dominant historical narratives once coalesced are not impervious to augmentation, as we saw to be the case with the *Rājāvaliya*'s supplementation of the *Mahāvaṃsa*'s account of the earliest history of the island of Lanka. (The *Rājāvaliya*'s introduction of Ravana as a historical king of the island I argue to be an instance of a vision of history gestated at the popular, vernacular level, that was over time integrated into the historiographical *status quo*.) Beyond these two perhaps uncontroversial postulates however stands an observation concerning the mechanisms by which marginal historical anecdotes and narratives have the potential to ascend to the level of widespread public recognition in the digital age. Arjun Appadurai makes the following observation regarding the compounded possibilities for electronic and digital media to facilitate the construction of "diasporic public spheres," in an era during which:

> the imagination has broken out of the special expressive space of art, myth, and ritual and has now become a part of the quotidian mental work of ordinary people in many societies. It has entered the logic of ordinary life from which it had largely been successfully sequestered. Of course, this has precedents in the great revolutions, cargo cults, and messianic movements of other times, in which forceful leaders implanted their visions into social life, thus creating powerful movements for social change. Now, however, it is no longer a matter of specially endowed (charismatic) individuals, injecting the imagination where it does not belong. Ordinary people have begun to deploy their imaginations in the practice of their everyday lives.[76]

Appadurai highlights various ways in which globalized media "provide[s] resources for self-imagining as an everyday social project" ("housewives reading romances and soap operas as part of their efforts to construct their own lives," "domestic servants in South India taking packaged tours to Kashmir," "terrorists modelling themselves on Rambo-like figures"), as well as the potential for "collective experiences of the mass media" to "create soldalities of worship and charisma, such as those that formed regionally around the Indian female deity Santoshi Ma in the seventies and eighties, and transnationally around Ayatollah Khomeini in roughly the same period."[77] Beyond the role of global media in forging subjectivities in relation to new global communities, however, Appadurai's discussion of the invigoration of the *imagination* of the average global citizen, along with his recognition of each individual's elevated level of *agency* in the global information marketplace, anticipates a broader discussion—one involving not merely new globally oriented subjectivities arising as a consequence of mass media consumption, but also the potential for the average person to partake in the *generation* of knowledge paradigms in a manner previously restricted to the intellectual and political classes. In twenty-first-century Sri Lanka, this potential has found expression in a collective public endeavor to forge a vision of the island's earliest history resounding with a sense of triumph and gesturing to a future of limitless possibility, a carryover of the national exuberance resulting from a government victory in Sri Lanka's civil war. While this revised palingenesis of the Sinhala people seems unmoored from precedent in so many ways, I have made the case that its foundational components—its mythic imagery and narrative architecture—were already present in the public imagination or, in some instances at the very least, readily accessible and awaiting redeployment. As digital media continues to shape populist politics in unpredictable ways throughout the globe, Sri Lanka today offers a unique case study in the power of digitally enabled collective public imagination to radically rework an ethnic self-image in the span of a mere decade, while at the same time serving as a reminder that dominant historical narratives have always been vulnerable to insurrection from the voice of the common people.

## Notes

1. Pollock, *The Language of the Gods in the World of Men*, 386.
2. According to Hallisey, after the seventh century, "adherence to Buddhist values and patronage of Buddhist institutions created 'distance' between Sri Lanka as a regional center and the expansive Hindu imperial formations, such as the Pallavas, Colas, and Pandyas, which were its neighbors. In this context, relations with more distant Buddhist Imperial centers in Eastern India were inevitably emphasized. The lack of continuity between the neighboring Hindu polities and Sri Lanka was further affirmed by the assumption that the island could only be ruled by a Buddhist,

an assumption which was a product of this period" ("Devotion in the Buddhist Literature of Medieval Sri Lanka," 175). McKinley notes an *opposite* tendency in early modern Sri Lankan Tamil literature, arguing that, through stereotyped descriptions of landscapes, Cekarāca Cēkaraṉ's *Takṣaṇa Kayilāca Purāṇam* seeks to connect, rather than distance, northern Sri Lanka with India, emplacing "Lanka in a cosmopolis connected to the rest of the continent" ("Making Lanka the Tamil Way," 268).

3. Opening address by H. E. Niluka Kadurugamuwa, "Rama's Journey in the Land of Ravan." Ayodhya Research Institute, Department of Culture, December 18, 2020, https://www.youtube.com/watch?v=G0lvR4vYAmE.
4. "National Policy Framework: Vistas of Prosperity and Splendour." Sri Lanka Department of Commerce policy statement (2020), http://www.doc.gov.lk/images/pdf/NationalPolicyframeworkEN/FinalDovVer02-English.pdf. References to foreign investment appear on pages 24 and 36.
5. The Indo–Lanka Accord, signed by Rajiv Gandhi and J. R. Jayawardene in July 1987, permitted a contingent of Indian soldiers, the India Peace Keeping Force (IPKF), to position in northern Sri Lanka to facilitate a truce agreement with the LTTE enabled by the Thirteenth Amendment to the Sri Lankan Constitution. The Accord and the presence of Indian soldiers on Lankan soil (numbering one hundred thousand at the height of the operation) faced severe domestic opposition, including from the Marxist Janatā Vimukti Peramuṇa party, and from Ranasinghe Premadasa, who succeeded Jayawardene as President in 1988 and began scaling back IPKF operations in 1989. See Rohini Hensman, "Post-war Sri Lanka: Exploring the Path Not Taken," *Dialectical Anthropology* 39, no. 3 (2015): 277f. Negative impressions of the IPKF "invasion" endure among Sinhala speakers in the twenty-first century, with images of Indian tanks rolling through Polonnaruwa and attendant commentary circulating on social media.
6. Āriyadāsa Seneviratna's own English translation of his Sinhala poem in *Śrī Laṅkā Rāvaṇa Rājadhāniya* (Colombo: Samayavardhana Publishers, 1991), 199f. Seneviratna sums up the Ravana zeitgeist in a Sanskrit verse composition of his own entitled *Śrī Laṅkā Rāvaṇāyanam*: "being urged by patriotism" (*deśabhakti-pravoditaḥ*), he dedicates his book on Ravana's dynasty to all "patriotic Sinhalese and children of Sri Lanka" (*siṅhalā deśamāmakāḥ laṅkāputrāś ca*). Seneviratna explains that the epic requires a re-rendering (i.e., a *rāvaṇa-ayaṇa* as opposed to another *rāmā-ayaṇa*) because Ravana's character was distorted in Valmiki's account (201–203).
7. Collins, "What Is Literature in Pali?" 649–688.
8. If one had to name a Jataka story popular in Sri Lanka featuring romance and battle action analogous to the Hindu epics, it would perhaps be instead the *Kusa Jātaka*, the basis for the celebrated "Sinhala *mahākāvya*" of the thirteenth century, the *Kavsiḷumiṇa*, attributed to Parakramabahu II. For a translation see M. B. Ariyapala, *Kavsilumina: The Crown Jewel of Sinhala Poetry in English Prose* (Colombo: S. Godage, 2004).
9. On the endurance of oral legends relating to Duṭṭhagāmiṇī, see Marguerite Robinson, "The House of the Mighty Hero or the House of Enough Paddy? Some Implications of a Sinhalese Myth," in *Dialectic in Practical Religion*, ed. E. R. Leach (Cambridge: Cambridge University Press, 1968), 122–152.

10. The 1818 proclamation in question (Governor Robert Brownrigg's "gazette notification") abolished a number of titles associated with the Kandyan royal court, the last king of which had abdicated to the British three years prior in 1815. The dissolved offices included those of "Aspantiyē Mohandiram" (Chief of Stables) and "Gajanāyaka Nilamē" (Chief of Elephants), which Mahanthaarachchi identifies as "titles being vital for the art of Angampora" (Ajantha Mahanthaarachchi and Reza Akram, *Angampora: A Nation's Legacy in Pictures* [Ethul Kotte: Oceans and Continents, 2017], 48).
11. Preface to Mahanthaarachchi and Akram, *Angampora: A Nation's Legacy in Pictures*, n.p.
12. Ibid., 99–108.
13. Ibid., 14, 110, 128. The act of Ravana veneration Mahanthaarachchi calls "Rāvana Namaskāraya" (128).
14. Ibid., 48–56, 61–64, 389.
15. Ibid., 58, 261.
16. Ibid., 315–321.
17. "President to Lift the British Ban on 'Angampora,'" *News 1st*, November 12, 2018, https://www.newsfirst.lk/2018/11/12/president-to-lift-the-british-ban-on-angampora/.
18. "The Art of Angam Fighting," Sri Lankan Ministry of Buddhasasana, Religious and Cultural Affairs, accessed January 1, 2021, https://www.cultural.gov.lk/web/index.php?option=com_content&view=article&id=67%3Athe-art-of-angamfighting&catid=35%3Aright&Itemid =72&lang=en.
19. Dhaneshi Yatawara, "Angampora Training To Power SLAF," *Sunday Observer*, June 29, 2014, http://archives.sundayobserver.lk/2014/06/29/spe05.asp.
20. "'Angampora' Martial Art Gains Ground in Kilinochchi Establishing its Own Typical Village," *Sri Lankan Army News*, July 29, 2019, https://www.army.lk/news/%E2%80%98angampora%E2%80%99-martial-art-gains-ground-kilinochchi-establishing-its-own-typical-village.
21. "The Misty Corridors of Traditional Anganpora [sic]." Sri Lankan Air Force official webpage, www.airforce.lk/angampora.php. Ajantha Mahanthaarachchi's research, as well as the *Vargapūrṇikāva* of Mānāvē Vimalaratana, are cited by the author of the pamphlet.
22. "SLAF facilitates its Angampora Display Team," *Sri Lankan Air Force News*, December 28, 2018, http://220.247.224.43/news.php?news=3921; "SLAF facilitates Its Angampora Display Team," *SLAF Media* (official YouTube channel), https://www.youtube.com/watch?v=2gm_8AkmVxA.
23. The first mention of Angampora in the *Rājāvaliya* occurs in the account of Parakramabahu VI (r. c. 1410–1467) securing the fidelity of one of his upcountry tributaries, at the time overseen by a lackadaisical duke named Sojāta, known to be "preoccupied with Angampora, which was for him a distraction" (*pramāda kara aňgampora āra iňdanā*) (*Rājāvaliya*, 219). The second mention appears in a similar context when an up-country vassal of Dharmaparākramabāhu IX (r. 1508/9–1528)

refused to pay tribute to Kotte, choosing instead to mint his own coins and while away his time with Angampora (222). Mahanthaarachchi also speaks of "Illangamas" as Angampora training facilities and of "Illangam" as the branch of Angampora involving the use of weapons. The term *ilaṅgamvala* appears twice in the *Rājāvaliya*, once as an adjective describing a regiment of shield-bearing troops of King Rājasiṃha I of Sītāvaka (*ilaṅgamvala palisakkārasin*, 236), and once describing the background of Vimaladharmasūriya I (Konappu Baṇḍāra), "who learned how to fence at an Ilangam" (*ilaṅgamvala haramba ugat*, 241).

24. P. E. P. Deriyangala, *Some Sinhala Combative, Field and Aquatic Sports and Games* (Colombo: National Museums of Ceylon, 1959), 1–24.
25. Ibid., 15.
26. Ibid., 15f.
27. See Roman Sieler's ethnographic and textual study of Varmakkalai in *Lethal Spots, Vital Secrets: Medicine and Martial Arts in South India* (Oxford: Oxford University Press, 2015), esp. chapters two and three. For a historical and ethnographic study of *kaḷarippayaṭṭu* in Kerala, see Phillip B. Zarrilli, *When the Body Becomes All Eyes: Paradigms, Discourses and Practices of Power in Kalarippayattu, a South Indian Martial Art* (Delhi: Oxford University Press, 1998).
28. Angampora "Gurukulams" have in recent years sprung up throughout Sri Lanka, most prominently under the umbrella of The Sri Lankan Traditional Indigenous Martial Art Association. STIMA offers regular classes in Angampora and Illangam to interested students, as well as extended retreat sessions. The organization's central training facility is currently in the Colombo suburb of Athurugiriya, with eight other satellite locations in Sri Lanka, one in Eiweiler, Germany, and one in Basel, Switzerland, according to STIMA's official webpage (https://www.angampora.com/).
29. Nita Sathyendran, "Meet Meenakshi Amma, the Grand Old Dame of Kalaripayattu," *The Hindu*, October 25, 2018, https://www.thehindu.com/society/history-and-culture/meenakshi-amma-the-grand-old-dame-of-kalaripayattu/article25307782.ece . A YouTube search for the word "cilampam" in Tamil script returns a number of videos of women dexterously wielding the *cilampam*, the wooden staff and weapon of first resort in Varmakkalai combat.
30. The 2016–2017 Performance of Progress Report of the Ministry of Health, Nutrition and Indigenous Medicine gives the following note: "It is believed that traditional Sinhalese practice of medicine runs back to a history of some 6,000 years. It is believed that King Ravana who ruled this country in ancient times was a clever medical practitioner and his era is believed to be a period with much advancement in all aspects of the practice of indigenous medicine in this country" (195).
31. Witharana, "Ravana's Sri Lanka," 787f.
32. See Ramaswamy, *The Lost Land of Lemuria*, 102, 112, 125, 151, 175.
33. On the endurance of the "Aryan Vijaya" narrative in public school textbooks, see Anne Gaul, "Where Are the Minorities? The Elusiveness of Multiculturalism and Positive Recognition in Sri Lankan History Textbooks," *Journal of Educational Media, Memory & Society* 6, no. 2 (2014): 92–96.

34. Nira Wickramasinghe, "Producing the Present: History as Heritage in Post-War Patriotic Sri Lanka," *ICES Research Papers* series, no. 2 (Colombo: International Centre for Ethnic Studies, 2012), 9.
35. This includes one by Kamani Gitangani Kalutantri with a full color drawing of Ravana abord his jet-powered *dańḍu-monara* on the rear cover, with a caption describing the historical king's erudition in the Vedas and *śāstras*, his accomplishments as a musician, and the proclamation that "King Ravana was Sri Lanka's first Buddhist" (*Itihāsaya nava viṣaya nirdēśaya: 10 śrēṇiya sańdahā* [Kōṭṭē: Kartṛ Prakāśana, 2017]). Wickramasinghe observes a trend in Sri Lanka since the mid-twentieth century away from textbooks authored by credentialed historians toward ones produced by partisan amateurs, employing an "apolitical, consensus-based, and . . . seemingly unproblematic reading of the past," associated with "a sharp decline in professional history's popular relevance and national appreciation" ("Producing the Present," 2). Prior to the twenty-first century, Munidasa Cumaratunga spoke of Ravana as a historical, virtuous king in Book Four of his *Śikṣāvatāraya sahita Śikṣāmārgaya*, a Sinhala-language primer (Cumaratunga, *Śikṣāvatāraya sahita Śikṣāmārgaya*, 11–14). Cumaratunga's sentiments were reproduced in other children's instructional books in the twentieth century: see T.S. Dharmabandu, *Gämuṇu tun vana pota [Gemunu Reader III]* [Colombo: Parsi Veḷańda Samāgama, 1951], 48–52. Sasanka Perera recalls a Sri Lankan elementary school textbook from his childhood in the 1960s claiming that Ravana possessed a *dańḍu-monara* flying machine (*Living with Torturers: and other Essays of Intervention: Sri Lankan Society, Culture, and Politics in Perspective* [Colombo: International Centre For Ethnic Studies, 1995], 64).
36. On Jackson Anthony's 2008 serial, *Mahā Siṃhalē Vaṃsa Kathāva* ("The Story of the Great Sinhala Lineage"), see Wickramasinghe, "Producing the Present," 14f. Anthony has more recently taken to promoting historical Ravana on his YouTube channel, reaching a substantial audience of 114k subscribers as of August 2021.
37. See Witharana, "Ravana's Sri Lanka," 786–789.
38. For an outline of claims relating to Ravana's advanced technology, along with speculation concerning their continued application in Sri Lanka (as with the innovative irrigation techniques of Anuradhapura), see B. Dileepa Witharana, "Negotiating Power and Constructing the Nation: Engineering in Sri Lanka," Ph.D. diss.: Leiden University (2018), 134–138. Representative of the desire to recover the engineering marvels of Lankan antiquity are several works by Ashoka de Silva, Senior Professor Engineering and Philosophy, Open University, which claim that human habitation of the island could date to as far back as one million years ago, and that the submerged isthmus between Mannar and Rameswaram is man-made. Ashoka de Silva, *Evolution of Technological Innovations in Ancient Sri Lanka* (Colombo: Vijitha Yapa Publications, 2011); *Glorious Historical Antecedents of a Cultured Civilization: Sri Lanka* (Colombo: Vijitha Yapa Publications, 2013).
39. For an overview of Nalin de Silva's politics and *Jātika Cintanaya*, see Dewasiri, "New Buddhist Extremism," 16–35.
40. Nalin de Silva, "Devivaru, Arsenic and Science—IV," *Sri Lanka Guardian*, June 15, 2011, http://www.srilanka guardian.org/2011/06/devivaru-arsenic-and-science.html.

41. Ibid. The *ehi passiko* refrain occurs throughout the Pali Suttas, with the most cited putative example of the Buddha's insistence that no one accept a religious doctrine on the basis of mere dogma or authority being the Kālāma Sutta of the *Aṅguttara Nikāya*. For translation and commentary, see Soma Thera, "The Kalama Sutta: The Buddha's Charter of Free Inquiry," [The Wheel Publication, no. 8] (Kandy: Buddhist Publication Society, 1981).
42. De Silva refers to Nātha and Vipāsaka as "gods who fully behold the truth/reality" (*samyak dṛṣtika devivaru*). de Silva, "Devivaru, Arsenic and Science"; "Academics challenge 'divine findings,'" *BBC Sinhala*, July 13, 2011, https://www.bbc.com/sinhala/news/story/2011/07/110713_arsenic_kelaniya.shtml.
43. Nalin de Silva, *Apē Pravāda 3: apē itihāsayaṭa nava susamādarśanayak* (Boraläsgamuva: Visisdunu Publishers, 2010), 5–7, 5–52, 80, 126. De Silva goes on to make familiar claims that the events of the *Vālmīki Rāmāyaṇa* are Indian interpolations obscuring the true identities of Vibhishana and Ravana, historical kings of the island and members of the Rakshasa tribe, which earned its name by serving as the "protectors" of their Yaksha vassals (6, *rākṣasa* derives from Sanskrit *rakṣ*, "to protect").
44. Ibid., 231–242.
45. Nalin de Silva, "The Mahavamsa Myth," *The Island*, February 25, 2014, http://www.island.lk/index.php?page_cat =article-details&page=article-details&code_title=98658.
46. Ibid.
47. Thilak Senasinghe, "Rāvaṇā vaṇayak veyi?" *Colombo Telegraph*, February 16, 2020, https://www. colombotelegraph.com/index.php/thilak-senasinghe-16-february-2020; Michael Roberts, "History-making in Lanka—I: Problems," *The Island*, April 16, 2008, http://www. island.lk/2008/04/16/midweek1.html.
48. The discussion of the emergence of nativist discourse related to Ravana as a consequence of the Sri Lankan civil war appears in chapter three of Dewasiri's book: *Laṅkāvē Itihāsaya: dṛṣṭivādi vicārayak* (Dehiwala: Vidarśana Prakāśana, 2019).
49. Dissanayake appeared in a television interview broadcast by "Ada Deraṇa 24" on July 10, 2020, saying that the Department of Archaeology had found no evidence of Ravana's kingdom in the course of the 130 years of its operation. He has discussed Ravana on the YouTube programs "Talk with Suzika" (https://www.youtube.com/watch?v=YCpS3J-HUEY, 31k views as of August 2021); and "NU1's Vlog" (https://www.youtube.com/watch?v=3-UoI6ZkcTo, 20k views as of August 2021). Vitriolic opposition to Dissanayake's position regarding Ravana's mythological status has also garnered significant YouTube viewership (https://www.youtube.com/watch?v=ORawWp8mTLE, 104k views as of August 2021).
50. *Hindu Bauddha Āgamika saha Saṃhiňdayāva saha Rāvaṇā Mahā Raja Vivaraṇaya*, "Hindu-Buddhist Religious Reconciliation and Notes on King Ravana," a book published by the Kelaniya University Postgraduate Institute of Archaeology, was launched at an October 2019 event at the Colombo National Museum, with President Maithripala Sirisena in attendance as a guest of honor. The authors, Dhananjaya Gamlath, Senior Lecturer in Archeology at Kelaniya, and Naomi Kekulawala, Senior Lecturer in History at Kelaniya, refer to information collected from "160 temples and shrines" providing data supporting "historical scientific

research" (*itihāsa vidyānukula paryēkṣaṇaya*) related to the ancient king ("Hindu bauddha āgamika saha saṃhiňdayāva saha rāvaṇā mahā raja vivaraṇaya—dorața väḍuma janapati atin," *Ada Deraṇa*, October 11, 2019, http://sinhala.adaderana.lk/news.php?nid=121295).

51. Tennyson Perera, *Mahā Rāvaṇa* (Colombo: Sarasavi Publishers, 2016).
52. Sykes, *The Musical Gift*, 115–18.
53. Anonymous review of Maunaguru's 2010 Colombo staging of *Irāvaṇēcaṉ*: "Mourning Conflict: Embodied Performance in Irāvaṇēcaṉ," *The Island*, February 28, 2019, http://www.island.lk/2010/02/28/features6.html; cited in Jim Sykes, *The Musical Gift*, 118.
54. S. Jeyasankar, "Playing with Ravanan." Presentation given at a symposium held by the American Institute for Lankan Studies (*The Presence and the Absence of the Ramayana in Sri Lanka*), Galadari Hotel, Colombo, July 22, 2016.
55. Sykes, *The Musical Gift*, 235.
56. Ibid., 531.
57. A conversation with the artists concerning the event is archived on the National Indo American Museum's Facebook page: "Curtain Raiser—The Story of Ram," November 20, 2020, https://www.facebook.com/96133151715/videos/1237546846615661]. I thank Sudesh Mantillake for sharing with me the film of his complete performance from which the epilogue was extracted.
58. See Sanmugeswaram et al., "Reclaiming Ravana in Sri Lanka," 806f.
59. This Facebook page now appears defunct.
60. The Saiva Neṛikkūṭam reports however that the group has sponsored similar *śiva-liṅgams* featuring Ravana reliefs at two Swiss Hindu temples (Sanmugeswaram et al., "Reclaiming Ravana in Sri Lanka," 809).
61. According to Sanmugeswaram et al., Arayampathy residents "explain that Ravana's *bhakti* toward Shiva was on par with that of the sixty-three *nayanmar*s, making him a suitable subject for religious art" (810).
62. See Perera, *Living with Torturers*, 67–70.
63. Sanmugeswaram et al., "Reclaiming Ṛavana in Sri Lanka," 810.
64. Brian Hatcher, "Pandits at Work: The Modern Shastric Imaginary in Early Colonial Bengal," in *Trans-Colonial Modernities in South Asia*, ed. Michael Dodson and Brian Hatcher (London: Routledge, 2012), 49.
65. The *Mahāvaṃsa* (25.108–111) offers a scene in which Duṭṭhagāmaṇi, stricken with guilt over the slaughter he oversaw in his war against the Damiḷa usurper Eḷāra, is consoled by a Buddhist monk, who assures him that throughout the vicious campaign the king accrued the demerit of killing only one and a half people. Apart from the demerit accrued from killing one man who had taken the three refuges of the Buddha, Dhamma and Sangha, and one who had taken the five precepts, the monk explains to the king that: "unbelievers and men of evil life were the rest, not more to be esteemed than beasts." On the broader scale of Indic civilization historically, Wendy Doniger has noted the longstanding adjacency, and symbiotic relationship between, representatives of the "renouncer path" and the "worldly path" in the Hindu tradition

as well ("From Kama to Karma: The Resurgence of Puritanism in Contemporary Hinduism," *Social Research* 78, no. 1 [2011]: 49–74).

66. Dayana Udayangani, "Śrī laṅkā amarapura sirisumana mahā nikāyē nāyaka dhurayen pidum läbu ācārya koḷonnuvē sirisumaṅgala nāhimi," *Laṅkādipa* (online), June 26, 2018. Rev. Sumangala authored his own piece of historical Ravana scholarship, *Mahā Rāvaṇa Śrī Laṅkēśvara*, available for purchase at the Devram Vihara reception center.
67. Deborah de Köning, "The Ritualizing of the Martial and Benevolent Side of Ravana in Two Annual Rituals at the Sri Devram Maha Viharaya in Pannipitiya, Sri Lanka," *Religions* 9, no. 250 (2018): 1–24.
68. Sanmugeswaram et al., "Reclaiming Ravana in Sri Lanka," 798–800.
69. Figures 6.2 to 6.4 were taken from the Sri Lankan Ministry of Defense official webpage and are in the public domain.
70. Sanmugeswaram et al., "Reclaiming Ravana in Sri Lanka," 801. Neither the *daňḍumonara* nor the "Ravana flag" (*rāvaṇa koḍiya*) are shown to outsiders, and while I cannot comment on the plausibility of the former, it is entirely possible that the tapestry is a genuine artefact. Famed poet of the Alagiyavanna Mukhaveti in his sixteenth-century *Sävul Sandeśaya* has his messenger bird on the way to the Saman Devālaya admiring paintings of Rama's victory over Ravana, and of the battle of the *Mahābhārata* (Stephen Berkwitz, *Buddhist Poetry and Colonialism*, 55). Ajantha Mahanthaarachchi and Reza Akram produce a photo of a tapestry of apparent Kandyan vintage depicting the battle between Rama and Ravana from the Pelmadulla Rajamaha Viharaya near Ratnapura (*Angampora: A Nation's Legacy in Pictures*, 16).
71. See McKinley, "Mountain at a Center of the World," 188f.
72. The cult of Ravana has found informal expression online where "Rāvaṇa saraṇayi" appears as an occasional signoff used by blog commentors and as a benediction on Ravana-related Facebook posts. "Budu saraṇayi" is a standard Sinhala Buddhist blessing derived from the first line of the "Tri Saraṇa" of the lay Buddhist asseveration "to take refuge in the Buddha, Dhamma, and Sangha."
73. Fernando notes that King Mahasena—renowned perhaps more than any other king of Anuradhapura for his irrigation projects—came to be divinized after this death under the epithet of *sat-rajjuruvō [mahasen deviyō]*, "king of all living creatures," which included both "the men and the supposed demons whom he forced to work for him" (*Ritual, Folk Beliefs and Magical Arts*, 15).
74. Bruce Kapferer, *Legends of People, Myths of State: Violence, Intolerance, and Political Culture in Sri Lanka and Australia* (New York: Berghahn Books, 1988), 95.
75. The author of the *Dīpavaṃsa* introduces the work as a compilation of "the lineage [of events and kings] which has come down from generation to generation" (*vaṃsaṃ paramparāgataṃ*) (*Dīpavaṃsa* 1.4). The commentary or *ṭīka* to the *Mahāvaṃsa* identifies a now-lost Sinhala historical work as a source material for the chronicle. See Hermann Oldenberg's introduction to *Dīpavaṃsa: The Chronicle of the Island* (London: Williams and Norgate, 1879), 5–10, and Jonathan Walters, "Buddhist History: The Sri Lankan Pāli Vaṃsas and Their Community," in *Querying the*

*Medieval: Texts and the History of Practices in South Asia*, ed. Ronald Inden et al. (New York: Oxford University Press, 2000), 107f., 146f.

76. Arjun Appadurai, *Modernity at Large: Cultural Dimensions of Globalization* (Minneapolis: University of Minnesota Press, 1996), 5.

77. Ibid., 8.

APPENDIX

# THE RĀVAṆA KATĀVA

## A SINHALA *RAMAYANA* OF THE KANDYAN PERIOD

This poem—the closest that we have to an authentic "Sinhala Ramayana"—may be assigned to the seventeenth or eighteenth centuries on the basis of style, content, and similarity to other Kandyan period works. No information is available concerning the authorship of the poem. I consulted five manuscripts in preparing this edition, which between them contain numerous interpolations, verses reordered, and verses added and missing. The manuscripts that are dateable belong to the 1840s and 1850s, though given the major discrepancies between them the poem must be considerably older.[1] In places I have reconstructed the order of the verses as best I could on the basis of context, as regrettably the complete original poem seems to be lost.

The author was clearly familiar with the legends of Ravana relating to the area around Nuwara Eliya, as well as with a common Indian variation of the epic which places Rama, Lakshmana, and Hanuman in peril in the subterranean lair of Ravana's brother (known famously in Tamil as the story of Mayil Irāvaṇaṉ or "Peacock Ravana," see Chapter 3, section 3 of this text). Ravana's character is treated with some ambiguity by the poet. He is domineering in his treatment of Sita, attempting to force her to marry him while in captivity. The poem concludes by explaining that Ravana's kingdom was washed away in a terrific deluge effected by the gods, incensed over his failure in kingly *dharma*.[2] On the one other hand, he is described as "possessing great merit" (*maha pin äti*, v.64), is reverentially called "Rāvana Deviyannē" (v.75), and is once collocated with the verb *vädiyē*—a special verb of motion reserved for Buddhas and gods (v.30).[3]

The climactic battle between Rama and Ravana is strangely missing from the manuscripts available.[4] We understand from the poem's conclusion, however, that Ravana survives the war, afterward creating for himself a garden out of what remained of his citadel at Nuwara Eliya. The opening portion of the poem presupposes knowledge on the part of the audience of the basic narrative of the *Ramayana*—when Maricha (Ravana's uncle) transforms himself into a golden deer, for instance, Rama and Lakshmana simply give chase to it—no mention is made of Sita's request that they do so. Sparse with literary figures, the poem appears concerned overall to tell an entertaining story in a demotic form of verse. Verses describing the names of the crops that Hanuman ravages are reminiscent of *kurahan kavi*, traditional songs related to the harvesting of brown millet (*kurakkan*).[5] The second half of the poem concerns Hanuman's adventures escaping from captivity twice, with protracted and at times humorous descriptions of his gratuitous destruction. After destroying all the fruit-bearing trees and cultivable crops (gobbling all that he can as he does so), Hanuman proceeds to rip up the irrigation ditches of the farms and "wins victory over the breadfruit trees and the paddy fields" (v.71). The elaborate (and easily escapable) stratagem he suggests to Ravana as a means to execute him (leaving him alone in the remote forest awaiting ghouls to light his oiled tail on fire) is a parodic instance of super-villain hubris akin to that which we might find in a James Bond (or Austin Powers) film.

Ravana's forces are called "Asuras" and occasionally also "Yakṣas." Rama is referred to as "Upulvan" and "Ran Rada," "the golden king." Lakshmana is referred to as "Saman" throughout the poem as he is occasionally in other Sinhala texts. The frequent conflation of "sa" and "ha," a common feature of upcountry Sinhala dialect, indicates that the poem was transmitted in this region. The source manuscripts are rife with gratuitous hyperurbanisms ("ś" for "s," "ṇ" for "n"), which I have generally quietly remedied for the sake of clarity. Two of the manuscripts consulted begin with invocations to Vishnu, Pattini, and Rama[6], which I have omitted here.

Two manuscripts consulted are in the Nevill Collection of the British Library:

*Rāvanā Katāva (Kavi)* (Or. 6611.188)
*Rāvanā Katāva (Kavi)* (Or. 6611.189)

Two manuscripts consulted are in the special collections of the Peradeniya University Library:

*Rāvaṇa Kathāva (Kavi)* (ms. 278010)
*Rāvaṇa Yudda Kavi* (ms. 278529)

One manuscript consulted is in the National Museum Library of the Colombo Museum:

*Rāvanā Kathāva* (7 H. 10)[7]

## TEXT AND TRANSLATION

1.

| | |
|---|---|
| *saha savadina uvidun para* | *siddē* |
| *vehesa vemin kana no läbama* | *siddē* |
| *dehe sava dīno danimi duka* | *laddē* |
| *dahasayan kavi rāvana* | *yuddē*[8] |

O Lord Vishnu, each and every day
I have worked tirelessly
Realizing the faults in my composition I sorrowfully apologize
As one among thousands of poets [who have related] this Ravana War!

2.

| | |
|---|---|
| *sāvā sadā tek āta uvin* | *dun* |
| *bōvā āsiri obahaṭa pihi* | *ṭan* |
| *kivā mē kavi varada kamā* | *van* |
| *māvā nē sāvā nē äranaňda* | *den*[9] |

O Lord whose domain extends all the way to the hare on the moon
For many years your blessings have extended
Kindly listen as I relate this poem now
Lend your ears as I speak!

3.

*kamala rāvana yuda teda yuga* *tin*
*demala äduru misa nodaniti api* *dän*
*siṅhala basin kavi kara pada bañdi* *min*
*vipula katika bäri pavasami yan* *tan*[10]

Regarding the close of the great era [in which transpired] the war
involving prosperous Ravana—
Since we now know very little of what the Tamil teachers [knew],
Unable to give a full account of the story
I will narrate an abridged version in Sinhala verse.

4.

*e kālaṭa rāvana tala evät* *tē*
*usiṅ mahal pas vissak ät* *tē*
*sāra laksayak vīdiya ät* *tē*
*e kalaṭa ohugē nañga siyakut ät* *tē*

At the time when Ravana ruled over Sri Lanka
With twenty-five immense palaces
And roads measuring all of four laks
Possessing one hundred cities within this domain.[11]

5.

*samara nura anurāgaya pirika* *ta*
*nobära rāma madanā kipunē ohu si* *ta*[12]
*parana purudu la dasanamen himi ve* *ta*
*sarana illū lañda gos asiyā ve* *ta*[13]

Compelled by lust out of her infatuation with Rama
Unable to dislodge Kama's arrow from her mind
In accordance with the customs of the day [Shurpanakha] came
before her elder brother, the Lord of Ten Epithets
Beseeching him to arrange a marriage.

6.

*emaviṭa rāvana rajate tepalan* *nē*
*lovaṭa utun rāma devi yan* *nē*[14]
*ruvaṭa munune katakut äta un* *nē*
*nosiṭa palaya etanaṭa satosin* *nē*[15]

King Ravana answered her back:
"Lord Rama is supreme in all the world;
There is but one woman possessed of such facial beauty as you!
And so don't fret at all, be happy [and approach him]!"

7.

*ruvin e lañda gos pulvan veta si* *ṭa*
*siyan miyuru bolañdä ki bas emavi* *ṭa*
*saraṇa veṇḍa ayiyā kivu obaha* *ṭa*
*eviṭa giyō lañda āvē metana* *ṭa*[16]

That splendid lady (Shurpanakha) went before Upulvan (Rama)
And spoke sweet words addressing the lord:
"Elder brother, I ask of you now—give me your refuge (in marriage)
It is with this request that I have come here."

8.

*e pavan asamin pulvan veta si* *ñda*[17]
*apa sañdala pasē sītā e devula* *ñda*
*topa pala e saman suriñduṭa gos vä* *ñda*
*säpa sē saranavaṭa vadahala rañ ra* *ñda*[18]

Hearing her request, Upulvan bowed courteously [and replied]:
"Already [wed] to me is Sita, chief lady among the gods,
like the mark upon the moon!
Go instead and prostrate yourself before Lakshmana, chief among the gods,
Happily you will receive refuge from him."
So said Rama.

9.

*lañda gos e saman devi veta siṭi* *nā*
*soñda lesa rati säpa viñdaman mati* *nā*
*viñda savū siri säpa vennova iti* *nā*
*lañda vä ki mē lesa gänumaṭa sara* *nā*[19]

So she went before Lord Saman and addressed him:
"Such an attraction I have never known before this—
now as I experience such delight with the mind
Please, won't you allow it to endure,
this happiness equivalent to all riches!"
In this way she requested that he take her in marriage.

10.

*eviṭa saman poti säriñdu vañdā* *lē*
*kavaṭa bas kime liyak davadā* *lē*
*kumaṭa arin däyi räki magē sī* *lē*
*topaṭa sarana vemi mama koyi kā* *lē*[20]

She went on, prostrating before Lord Saman:
"At whose words do my bracelets slip from my wrists?
Who, having opened me up, shall safeguard my virtue?
When at last shall I come into your refuge?"

11.

*eviṭa ävit devenuva pulvan ve* *ta*
*givisā ävit topē devulaňda arukīka* *ta*
*ävit e pulvan ganimin kaga pa* *ta*[21]
*sarosa vemin käpuvē ägē gahana* *ta*[22]

[Being rejected] a second time she came before Upulvan
Asking him to promise to give up his own dear wife
[But in response]
Coming towards her with the blade of his sword
Angrily Rama cut off her nose with a swift motion.

12.

*gahana tavä memana uriren muhu* *nā*
*ekata biyen väda duva gos siṭi* *nā*
*kopulata sinha kaha bisa väňda duva* *nā*[23]
*e pavat däna rāvana raju tedī* *nā*[24]

With blood gushing from her face where her nose had been cut
Fearfully she fled back to the island
Where she ran to the throne and hastily prostrated
Relating what had happened to Ravana.

13.

*sidda novana bas kīvu ayiyā ma* *ṭa*
*laddō*[25] *suraganayā men väḍaka* *ṭa*
*väddan sē uňgasanā piṭa po* *ṭa*
*yudda karana naṭa kivu asiyāha* *ṭa*[26]

"O elder brother, I was unable to accomplish what you had asked of me!
Working together like slender dancing women
Like Vädda they struck when my back was turned!
So I beseech you, O elder brother—now go to war!"

14.

*emaviṭa rāvana raju ros van* *nē*
*tamaraṭa sena gat aḍagaha gan* *nē*
*tama naňganin haṭa kala bava dan* *nē*[27]
*pema magē [ga]la riya genava ki yan* *nē*[28]

At this King Ravana grew enraged
Rousing his army up from throughout the land

Fearfully sounding the call to arms from the highest spire of his palace
He issued the order: "Fetch my precious stone chariot!"

15.

| | |
|---|---|
| *ahasin paditat yē ya ratē* | *yā* |
| *poloven paditat yē ya ratē* | *yā* |
| *diya piṭa paditat yē ya ratē* | *yā* |
| *rāvana äragati e gal ratē* | *yā*[29] |

On into the sky he peddled in his chariot
Peddling all the way up to the heavens
Peddling all day into dusk
So Ravana flew in his stone chariot.

16.

| | |
|---|---|
| *käňdā gat rāvaṇa raju mā* | *mā* |
| *indā gattuva bāna nu mā* | *mā* |
| *rāvaṇa rajuhu mige bas di* | *mā* |
| *tun dena sama giva yeti päda riya* | *mā*[30] |

Ravana, having reached the mountain
Where his son and son-in-law (*bāna*) were residing
Plotting with their uncle
The three together peddled onwards.

17.

| | |
|---|---|
| *ungos maňga gevamin haṭa tepa* | *lā* |
| *tän tän bala siṭa päna vimasā* | *lā* |
| *pulvan väḍa untän vimasā* | *lā* |
| *ranvan muva ves māmaṭa dī* | *lā*[31] |

When they arrived and disembarked upon the road
Searching about here and there
Finally they happened upon the place where Rama [and Sita] were staying
[Marica declared:] "I shall take the form of a golden deer."

18.

| | |
|---|---|
| *muvek gäśu haḍa asamin ran ra* | *da* |
| *saman deviduňhaṭa yamu kivu api sa* | *da* |
| *visalat māliga tanuṭa yi kī sa* | *da* |
| *vigasin evu dipi yamu kivu ran ra* | *da*[32] |

Rama chased after the deer, following the sound it made
Calling out to his brother Saman as he went, saying, "Let's go!"
Telling Sita to remain indoors[33]
Rama called out again "quickly, come on!"

19.

*vidda śära yabala dan* *nē*
*bädda uḍin päṇa yan* *nē*
*deviňdu divas balamin* *nē*
*mamina muvā ära yan* *nē*[34]

With his agile arrow at the ready
The Lord of Gods leapt into the forest in pursuit
Guided by means of his divine eye
Thinking, "Surely I will catch this deer!"

20.

*täntänvala siṭamu vakä vilan* *nē*
*täntän ḍala dī vidavara din* *nē*
*rāvana māliga doraṭa gosin* *nē*
*riya bimayaṭa kara dan illan* *nē*[35]

Pursuing it from place to place
Believing the deer to be just ahead
They entered the door to Ravana's palace
Realizing suddenly that they were within his chariot
which had landed upon the earth.

Translator's note: Ravana now makes his way to Rama and Sita's ashram.

21.

*jātaka tapasun uriren upa* *nā*
*sāvaka ves gena rāvana no dä* *nā*
*dāta purā gena dan dena lobi* *nā*
*māliga tula siṭa dikkala sodi* *nā*[36]

Taking on the appearance of a wandering ascetic
Not knowing that it was in fact Ravana in the guise of a renouncer
Hungrily [Ravana] outstretched his two hands [for alms]
And so was invited into the threshold of their home.

22.

*noraṭa dukin yācakayō äva* *din*
*doraṭa pämini apa illu dena* *dan*
*pinaṭa lobin sat aḍiyak vaḍi* *min*
*memaṭa dunot misa noganimi e* *dan*[37]

"O mendicant traveling from a distant land
Come through the door!"—so he was invited by Sita
[As Ravana] took seven steps hungrily towards the alms [being offered by Sita]
Sita wondered to herself if she had made a mistake.

23.

*pinaṭa lobin e bisō no dä* nā
*rägena ē dun dānaya pin pura* nā
*tedin e rāvana raja sit bale* nā[38]
*padina ratē giya polovat biňda* nā[39]

Sita, unaware of his true intentions
Thought her gift of alms to be a meritorious gesture
Meanwhile Ravana, using merely the power of his mind
Peddled the chariot off into the sky.

24.

*movunṭa asuvī kelesa dayan* nē
*sitin sōka aṭagati bisa vun* nē
*eyin nägena gini väs sē en* nē
*igen pahala gal uni bisa vun* nē[40]

When he seized her, immense grief
And great anguish arose in the princess' mind—
"Surely I am being carried off now only to be burnt alive!"
So she fretted, trapped within the belly of the stone vehicle.

25.

*muhudu diyen goḍa bäsa* lā
*sītāvaka uyana ba* lā
*gal mul vī dukin ve* lā
*gal piṭa väḍa unnu ba* lā[41]

Finally at daybreak the chariot landed
Revealing the garden of Sitawaka
Whereupon the princess felt pangs of sorrow
Watching as the stone walls grew higher and higher [as they descended].

26.

*vanantare rusivaru män* da
*vanapala väla kakā ävin* da
*däkalā rusivaru devulan* da
*duna damā giya rusi män* da[42]

Deep within the thick forest
Forging on through the vines and brush
The princess finally laid eyes upon
The place designed for her captivity.

27.

*palala digin vaṭa pansiya ga* vu
*palaturu nilambara kusumen pähäya* vu

*kala ruti rāvana uyanē kala rä* *vu*[43]
*samanala nuduruva nuvara eliya ki* *vu*[44]

Five hundred *gavuvas*[45] in circumference
Richly colored with flowers and fruit
Ravana's dark, lush pleasure grove
Called "Nuwara Eliya," not far from Samanala Mountain.

28.

*uyanē sītā devulaňda sa* *ňgā*
*vätunē vaṭa kara e mäňda ga* *ňgā*
*siṭinē vaṭa kara laňda liya sa* *ňgā*
*vaḍinē davasaka devulaňda ga* *ňgā*[46]

Sita, the divine princess, all the while remained concealed within that grove
In a placed encircled by the Mänik River where she would bathe
There she remained in isolation
Secreted away there until one day—

29.

*sambāntoṭa dī kala isnā* *nē*
*vaṭakara ävileṇa gini jalmā* *nē*
*ätupiṭa rāvana eṇu däka ädi* *nē*
*pannana kaḷaṭa hisa kē nila penu* *nē*[47]

[When she escaped] to bathe at Hambantoṭa rock
Where she found herself encircled by a net of flames
Within which Ravana caught sight of her
Jumping in [he swam] to where he saw the hair of her head.[48]

Translator's note: After rescuing Sita, Ravana puts forth his best effort to make her comfortable, and to entice her into marrying him. In the following verse Ravana addresses the servants of his court.

30.

*ē siśa yak raju väḍi* *yē*
*dunna ādinnaṭa*[49] *bäri* *yē*
*mē mā gosin vida häri* *yē*[50]
*bisavu sarana gat piri* *yē*[51]

The king of one hundred Yakshas then declared—
"Unable to attract her by means of what I have offered already
I shall change her mind by making her come before me
Thereby completing my realm with a queen!"

31.

*devi ma gulaṭa räs unu hä* *ma*
*pīva bōjun gena dunne* *ma*

*rusi rupa tamba kola nogena* ma
*gaṇḍa mä vu padaya kiki* ma[52]

"Collect everything and bring it to the princess' cave
The finest food and drink available
Served upon only the loveliest of platters[53]
Let there be the jingling of bells upon their anklets!"

32.

*kāra bändanek vana mä* ňda
*bähāra no giya devu lada o* ňda
*ivara novana duk dī la* ňda
*bähāra giyē ada devula* ňda[54]

And so the marriage ceremony took place amid the forest
Sita not wanting to go outside [to go through with the ceremony][55]
Her misery now fathomless in its depth
Finally she relented and came out.

Translator's note: Ravana's attempt to marry Sita remains unresolved in the mss. available. The narration shifts abruptly to Rama's point of view.

33.

*māliga tula vädemin väḍa* lā
*nodäka bisavu ävida ba* lā
*polova biňdunu bava däka* lā
*devi sita duk kaňdu usu* lā[56]

As the princess languished within [Ravana's] palace
Frantically [Rama] searched but found her nowhere
Seeing the heavens rent asunder
A mountain of sorrow piling up within his heart
as he thought of his queen.

34.

*ran rada viya sita näve* min
*tänatän siṭa susun la* min
*malānikava kuhul ma* nin
*isivaru veta vädī säne* kin[57]

Rama was now steeped in regretful sorrow
Sighing everywhere he went
Exhausted and forlorn
He went to the Rishis seeking consolation.

35.

*isivarunē mage bisa u* na
*saňgāgana giya rāva* na

*iṭa upāyak pavasa* *na*
*vadahala ranrada siṭaga* *na*[58]

"O great seers! My queen
Was abducted by Ravana
Who took her by means of a ploy!"
So Rama informed them.

36.

*isivara bas pavasan* *nē*
*tama uragana nañganin* *nē*
*iṭa upā tepalan* *nē*
*duk nivā nin karapan* *nē*[59]

To this the Rishis replied:
"Enter into his subterranean passages
This is the stratagem
By which your sorrow will be alleviated."

Translator's note: A portion of the text appears to be missing, as Rama is now in league with Hanuman, with no explanation as to how they met.

37.

*hanumā uyanē iñda* *yā*
*ranrada etanaṭa vädi* *yā*
*hanumō yi rāvana sañdi* *yā*
*sītā devulañda äran gi* *yā*[60]

As Hanuman sat there in the garden
Rama made his way there [beseeching him]:
"O Hanuman! Devise some foil against Ravana
To retrieve Sita Devi!"

38.

*hanumā väñda siṭaṇa ki* *yā*
*mage buru siru käṭi* *yā*[61]
*änalā mage äṭa bidi* *yā*
*udurā gaṇa giya siṭi vali* *yā*[62]

Accepting his charge, Hanuman said in reply:
"Your command I shall bear upon my head
Piercing and breaking my very bones
I will wrench and uproot the hordes [of Ravana]."

39.
*vida vida maṅ jaya gani* *mī*
*tope liya mama aran de* *mī*
*säka nova pulvan van sā* *mī*
*sītā devu mama genat de* *mī*[63]

At any cost[64] I shall achieve victory
In order to rescue your lovely woman
Have no doubt of this, O Lord Upulvan
I will return Sita Devi to you!

40.

*nokiya sinā sena bas ma* *ṭa*
*mal vaḍamak karalā si* *ṭa*
*dedena ävit sama giva si* *ṭa*
*allā vätiyan ī pi* *ṭa*[65]

When he finished his speech, full of loving devotion[66]
He wove a flower garland
So that both [Rama and Hanuman] could wear it around their necks
and thus be united in that way
Catching it on Rama's quiver.[67]

41.

*eyin vidda śara vaňdi* *ti*
*mā liya allā näva* *ti*
*arimi āya sitak si* *ti*
*āsiri pin bala daki* *ti*[68]

Prostrating himself before He whose Arrows are Swift [Hanuman declared]:
"I will bring an end to this by retrieving the Queen (*mā liya*)"
So he made the solemn vow to retrieve the princess
So visibly blessed with merit as he was.

42.

*kura maňda yaṇa den* *nā*
*äti kula mage daru den* *nā*
*un giya täṇa bala pen* *nā*
*gene ti bisavu sänekin* *nā*[69]

[Rama addressing Hanuman]

"Make haste and be gone by the dust of the foot![70]
Return to me my dear one who is of such a magnificent lineage!
Relate [to us] wherever it is you have gone!
Fetch my queen and so restore my tranquility!"

43.

*mese dedena givisa si* *ṭā*
*giya pera lesa sanḍuva* *ṭā*
*pulvan raja asva si* *ṭā*
*novida giyē eka ruva* *ṭā*[71]

With the two having made this promise to one another
They parted ways

Rama upon horseback
Unmatched in his splendorous appearance.

Translator's note: There is a break in the narrative here to the battle between Sugriva and Valin; a portion of the text appears to be missing.

44.

*kiyayi vāliya emavi* ṭa
*topi däkivuvānan oba ma* ṭa
*rāvana allā devi bä* ṭa
*geneti bisavu ek saneka* ṭa[72]

Vali said these words [to Rama]
"Look upon me now—
Ravana captured and abused [your] queen
I could have rescued her in a moment!"

45.

*vāliyanē numbevit ta* ṭa
*talala nätuva nubē gata pi* ṭa
*hoňda kara demi mama vigasa* ṭa
*me lesa kiyā ranrada si* ṭa[73]

"O Vali! Quickly into the sky
We might soar up
If you'll just give me your hand!"
So Rama said to him in reply.

46.

*topaṭa misak ran raju* nē
*apaṭa kälalanāta iti* nē
*kiyā mē bas siṭa tadi* nē
*vaṭunā vāliya dera* nē[74]

This misdeed rests with you alone, O Rama
No fault resides with us
Concluding his speech
Vali fell upon the earth.

47.

*manda hanumā rägena e* dā
*viňda kāma koḍi numbu* dā
*yana lesa yudayaṭa pähä* dā
*sälakara ran rajuṭa e* dā[75]

On that very day Hanuman went atop a hill
Raising the flag of Kama[76] into the sky
Thereby announcing the commencement of battle
And signaling this to Rama.

48.

*ranranda hanumā kä* ňdā
*galavāpē tus mu* ňdā
*dīkiyamin dukkan* ňdā
*yanṭa äriya hanumā e* ňdā[77]

Rama to Hanuman on the hill that day
Presented to him his golden ring
Its memories for him a source of painful sorrow
And thus sent Hanuman on his way.

49.

*edā hanumā ävit muhuden me kara siri lak diva bala* lā
*sadā turu pela tibunu uyanē äviňda sänekin vaṭa ba* lā
*udārava kolaturen pänalā bisa siṭinā tänaba* lā
*edā ranrada dunnu ran mudu eliya bisavagē pā mu* lā[78]

That day, Hanuman crossed the ocean and caught sight of
the island of Sri Lanka
Seeing the garden with its rows of [fruit or Banyan] trees,
swiftly he set down there,
Jumping along the bank of the river,[79]
he came to where the princess was,
And [laid] at her feet the golden ring which
had been given to him by Rama.

50.

*bisavaran mudu ädina gasa uḍa balā hanumā untä* nē
*rasava tepulen laňgaṭa aḍagaha*[80] *ranrajugē bas asami* nē
*tosava hanumā kiyayi bisavaṭa ranrajugē bas satosi* nē
*lasava śanekin kolaturen päna kakāpala väla giyasi* nē[81]

Seeing the ring that Hanuman had been entrusted with
Listening to the words of the king which were sweetly related
The princess delighted as Hanuman related Rama's message to her
Until which time he stopped and hurriedly jumped up into the
trees in order to eat some fruit.

51.

*edā hanumā gosin āpasu däka piran ranrada säneki* nā
*edā sītā deviňdū kī bas ranrajuṭa salakarami* nā
*edā ranrada ganimi bisa un yuddha karamu va kiyamī* nā
*edā hanumā yuddha karannaṭa gäsu haḍatava pavatī* nā[82]

That very day Hanuman returned and related this to King Rama
Telling him of Sita's dolorous condition
At which time Rama declared: "We will go to war to retrieve the princess!"
[And dispatched] Hanuman to raise the call to battle.

Translator's note: On the eve of battle, Kumbhakarna awakens to warn Ravana of the futility of war with Rama, first chastising him for recklessly imprisoning the god Saturn (Senasurā) within the city. (Saturn's gaze (Skt. *śani dṛṣṭi*) is considered to be an inauspicious influence in Indian astrology.) Concluding his speech, Kumbhakarna here simply drifts back to sleep again, and we hear of no role of his in the battle against Rama and his allies.

52.

*pulnetāhaṭa dāvu rāvana ohun văn̆du put vibusaṇa up* *an*
*dolos rāsiyata bāgrahrayin allavā bän̆da siṭu vam* *in*
*senasurā kīvu nuvare nubage putun nube mama vaṇa sam* *in*
*kubhakāranu edā nidi gati dolos avurudu ottän* *in*[83]

"O blossom-eyed Ravana! Recall that at the time of your son's birth
You captured and shackled the twelve astral deities
And came to me explaining that, for the sake of your son,
Senasurā had been kept in the city!"
So Kumbhakarna awoke [to say] after twelve years of recumbent slumber.[84]

53.

*yanḍa nikmī gal ratē gena edā rāvana män̆i* *yō*
*mavanḍa darilan̆da kiyayi bäsa asan rāvana putā* *yō*
*yanḍa epayi ranrajunhaṭa noyan rāvana punasi* *yō*
*unḍa tunlova kenek sari näti kiyayi rāvana män̆i* *yō*[85]

"O Ravana—who on that day brought the stone chariot speedily to your mother!
O Ravana—hear the plea of your dear wife[86] asking you to spare your sons!
O Ravana—do not make war with king Rama!
O Ravana, whose mother said that there is no other amid the three worlds to replace you!"

54.

*nambu kara gana āyi rajuhaṭa ayiya magē bas ahapan* *nē*[87]
*nanbu misa [a]vanambu*[88] *no karan rāvanā devin̆duṭa bolan* *nē*
*bam̆bu upadina peran̆dinē dī siṭa vaḍina deviyō däna gan* *nē*[89]
*kumbakāranu kiyā mē lesa nin̆di gatiya sit satosin* *nē*[90]

"O dear older brother, I beg you, hear me as I speak!
O dear Ravana—do not insult the Lord of Gods!
This [forthcoming calamity] was known to the gods
from before the day you were born!"
So Kumbakarana spoke before he drifted off happily to sleep.

55.

*vēga vī ravanā raja bas kiyati tan̆da koṭa emavi* *ṭā*
*nān̆ga garuḍan allavā bän̆da devu love aya ek vī* *ṭā*
*lavati siragē yi dahas gaṇaṇak tibennē äyi kumaki* *ṭā*
*me mā sirilaṇa*[91] *kenek sat lovā kavuda kivu ruvaṇa si* *ṭā*[92]

Swiftly Ravana replied to him with a ferocious "ṭā ṭā!"
Mounting his Garuda bird and [ascending up to and] piercing
the Deva world
[Exclaiming in reply to Kumbhakarna's warning:]
"Who is there—even if there should number a thousand of them—
Who among the three worlds even comes close to me?!"

Translator's note: The scene shifts abruptly to the battle between the forces of Ravana and Rama.

56.

*aditi dahas dunu sadā pelin pe* *la*
*ariti śāma śāra sa(ṅ)dā pelin pe* *la*
*siṭiti e rāvana pura śen pāba* *la*
*näseti senañga sära vädemin vina ka* *la*[93]

On that day a thousand rows of archers stood ready in their ranks
A thousand rows of armed spearmen[94] stood also in formation
The army of Ravana's city stood gleaming
Those fearsome forces swelling in their ranks—
[unaware that] it was the eve of their destruction.

57.

*pas nam dunu pasakin gat vis* *man*
*pas nan viduliya men kara vis* *man*
*rus vam deviyē diva diva ik* *man*[95]
*visnut rāvana kara vati ik* *man*[96]

In troops of five the archers took their places
Raining down arrows like lightening
Emptying their quivers, from island to island they quickly advanced
[The forces of] Vishnu and Ravana now hand-in-hand in combat.

58.

*nägena*[97] *dahas dunu sañdā pelin pe* *la*
*sañdana dahas laksaya īdañḍu pe* *la*
*penenā viduliya men sära pela pe* *la*
*marana pämini vänaseti sata sinha* *la*[98]

In the east stood ready a thousand rows of archers
Ready with a thousand laks of arrows
Shining like lightening as they flew
Slaughtering and laying waste to the Sinhalas by the hundreds as they came.

59.

*kōpē kopulata notabāyune* *ka*
*sāpēnet hära bäḷuvotin ne* *ka*
*dīpē eli unu sära sī ehī ne* *ka*
*bhapē visman vänagē tri śula* *ka*[99]

[Like] the wrath of Shiva, cursing any whom he might lay eyes upon,
Nothing was spared.
The arrows ignited the forces [of Ravana] like a flambeau
As if it were Rama who instead held Shiva's Trident.

60.

*pavistarelat kaya devi pätu* *vē*
*arita sāma śära galturu poḍi* *vē*
*e gos śare eti muhuden ā* *vē*
*āvit tibeyi ana ema tal kopu* *vē*[100]

In the circumference of the area around the queen's body[101]
The arrows fell, embedding themselves in the stone beneath her
The arrows—more vast in expanse than the ocean as they
flew through the air
Bringing destruction and cutting the palmyra palms as they arrived.

61.

*boho sē anuhas äti uvindun* *nē*
*dahasa dahasa śära no naväti yan* *nē*
*ahasa gigun väsi nätuva äsen* *nē*
*dahas ganan rupu sen väna sen* *nē*[102]

The mighty Master of Devices (Rama)[103]
[Letting loose] thousands upon thousands of arrows relentlessly
No other sound could be heard in the sky
As the glorious army of the city was annihilated by the thousands.

62.

*rāvaṇa pura nam kebadu da pata* *rā*
*muhu dēvaṭa kara bäňda lo pahu* *rā*[104]
*tamba uḷu yakaḍin bäňda vaṭa pahu* *rā*
*e mäňda sula kala rāvana nuva* *rā*[105]

Strewn here and there about Ravana's city
Were pieces of the iron rampart which had once protected it
Along with the iron tiles of the roofs
Thus Ravana's city was reduced to rubble.

63.

*dahasa väṭunu kala ganaṭa gan* *nē*[106]
*malaminiyak uḍa pänanaṭa min* *nē*
*varak dunna bäňdimīya bäňdin* *nē*
*ekara mekara yuda sē kara van* *nē*[107]

Women falling by the thousands
The pulverized dust of jewels rising up [into the air]
Of what had been until then splendorous quarters
Such is the tragedy wrought by war.

64.

*maha pin äti rāvanaya rajun* *nē*
*muhuňdu vikun koṭa goḍa bōvan* *nē*
*aňgulak päda gana dambadiva yan* *nē*
*senaňga ganan näti rāma rajun* *nē*[108]

King Ravana, possessed of immense merit
In despair stepped down into the ocean
And with his iron mace set off towards India
For undefended without his army was Rama then.

65.

*taňda teda pulvan devi rada nita* *rā*
*bäňda miniyak ran dunne vita* *rā*
*vida dunu hī gena karavan nita* *rā*
*vaňda sara vadamini śun näsiya vita* *rā*[109]

Upulvan with his mighty *tejas*, an eternal king
Armed then only with his golden jewelry
Having fired off his whole arsenal
His quiver empty, his arrows exhausted.

Translator's note: While the poem sets up an epic battle between Rama and Ravana, the narration abruptly shifts to Hanuman's rampage of Lanka. We learn at the end of the poem that Ravana has survived the conflict, but curiously nothing more is said of his engagement with Rama. It is possible that a portion of the text is missing, and that the ending in the available manuscripts represents a later interpolation. On the *Rāma Rāvaṇā Yuddhaya*, a short Sinhala poem giving an account of the slaying of Ravana, see note 4, above.

66.

*raga yak munak mavamin emavi* *ṭa*
*diga sakvalavaṭa ran ruvavila* *ṭa*
*gaňga śēkaṭa atmavamin ema* *ṭa*
*yagayak äragati hanumā emavi* *ṭa*[110]

With his face resembling that of a maddened Yaksha
Taking on a form so immense that he stretched to the limit
of the world-system
Growing his body all the way to the summit of the celestial Ganges
Such was Hanuman's frightful excitation.

67.

*goḍabäsa hanumā śiri lak diva* *ṭa*
*pudiṇa päśeṇā ket vat ruva* *ṭa*
*gaja räla vilasiṅ udurā depi* *ṭa*
*udurā kai goya mut situ lesa* *ṭa*[111]

Hanuman alighted on the island of Sri Lanka
Where the fields had just ripened for the harvest
Gouging on both sides like a rapacious herd of elephants
With his two hands he tore up the fields as he went along.

68.

*usvu turu vala iňdanā pala* *kan*[112]
*räsvu paḷu mora*[113] *vī rat ramba* *kan*
*gas biňda mul ala udurā saro* *sin*
*dus kara iňda kayi vapula kurak* *kan*[114]

The rice stood piled high[115]
The Mora, Paḷu, and red plantain trees
In his rage, smashing his way through the trees
he also uprooted the planted tubers
Along with the heaps of brown millet which had been gathered up.

69.

*tal pol del kituḷut biňda kan* *nā*
*vil mal nil väl udurāna kan* *nā*
*sal mul säňdi turu bidalā kan* *nā*
*sel gal paruvata ekaṭa gasan* *nā*[116]

Ripping apart the palmyra, coconut, wild breadfruit, and sugar palms
as he devoured them
Excavating the water lilies and green vines as he ate them too
The roots of the Sal trees met the same fate
As he dashed together the stones, rocks, and mountains.

70.

*käkiri labut pusuḷut vaṭṭa ka* *kā*
*uḍu haran rasa anna ka* *kā*
*doḍan kumuḍu väl gas mul en* *nā*
*udurā hanumā pura vasiha ka* *kā*[117]

Cucumbers, ash-pumpkins and pumpkins too
Enjoying the flavorful juice[118] as he went along
The orange trees, white water lilies, vines, trees, and roots alike
So Hanuman uprooted all that lay in his path.

71.

*asamat ket vat agal biňdin* *nē*
*kos gas kumburut viňda jaya gan* *nē*
*ät as dantaya räla ā vän* *nē*
*usgas paruvata śola vā yan* *nē*[119]

Rending apart the canals which water the fields
Winning victory over the breadfruit trees and paddy fields

Like elephants and horses noshing with their teeth
Shaking even the tallest trees and highest mountains.

72.

*dulābayin pala nätuva maku* *ňgā*
*kalābayin borakara vil ga* *ňgā*
*śolavayi kaňdu śel turu pati tu* *ňgā*
*peralayi ket vat kara paliba* *ňgā*[120]

With the choice fruits exhausted he turned to horseradish
Stirring up and muddying the tanks and streams
Shaking the mountains and the tallest trees
As if he were enacting revenge on the paddy fields
as he ploughed them under.

73.

*kasā bulat väl miriśut igu* *rā*
*masāka dili vällala kaṭu bubu* *rā*
*nasā siyaḷu ala vanaturu badu* *rā*
*rosāvā biňda kayi annasi padu* *rā*[121]

Rooting up bulat, chilies and ginger
Masāka, Dili, and yams
Decimating all of the wild root vegetables
Blind with rage he destroyed the pineapple bushes too.

74.

*tuṭalayi turu poti iňda maňda ma* *ttu*
*oravayi äs kaṇṇiya potu ra* *ttu*
*goravayi haḍa biya kara kulma* *ttu*
*iravā vana gata diva yeti sa* *ttu*[122]

The tender shoots of the Tuṭulayi along with those
Thorn Apple saplings
Squeezing the bark of the turmeric tree
With a terrifying roar instilling fear in the heart
The livestock tore their way into the jungle in retreat.

75.

*sulan vātayen iňdula piren* *nē*
*guvan talen mal väsi vas van* *nē*[123]
*me vanne däti rāvana deviyan* *nē*
*nasinṭa gati lova kima no balan* *nē*[124]

The debris and dust filled the air and
was carried on the wind
With flowers falling from the sky[125] at the entrance to his cave
Lord Ravana, perceptive as he was, came to know

The full extent of the destruction wrought,
  though he could not see it firsthand.

76.

*susadi*[126] *me uyanē mal visituru ko* — *ṭa*
*śiṭiya kāla giri ätumen ätupi* — *ṭa*
*biňdī noyek pala no tabā hämavi* — *ṭa*
*yedī e rāvanan kivuvē me lesa* — *ṭa*[127]

In the secluded grove strewn with flowers
Upon the dark mountain resembling the slope of an elephant's back
Laden with fruit and beyond that everywhere
Crafted according to Ravana's tastes—

77.

*rańge asurasen pasu kara gan* — *na*
*dańgē ne pennā yaṇa eṇa gama* — *ṇa*
*yagē yaṭaṭa väda säňga vī ida si* — *ṭa*
*gańge paniti e goḍin siṭa me goḍa* — *ṭa*[128]

Slipping through the remaining ranks of the Asura army
Craftily without being seen [Hanuman] was able to make his way
Beneath where [Sita] was concealed
Jumping into the river he made his way from one shore to the other.

78.

*gańgē yanena hanumā devu däka* — *lā*
*vidiňḍa amu vibhūṣaṇa put eka* — *lā*
*dahasak hīdaḍu geṇa däti mara* — *lā*
*vidi sara älliya dätin päna* — *lā*[129]

Stealthily Hanuman entered and saw the princess
Beautifully ornamented as she was at that time
Knowing that thousands were left dead from the archers' arrows
With both hands he leaped up to the bower.[130]

<u>Translator's note:</u> Hanuman is here discovered by a contingent of Ravana's troops.

79.

*raṭa väna sutän rila vek äd* — *dō*
*vaṭalā rāvana sen para sid* — *dō*
*śiṭa geṇa gat dunu śaramin vid* — *dō*
*väṭa daḍu lesa sata hima nan tä* — *dō*[131]

"Surely such a monkey as this is not one who belongs to our land!"
So exclaimed the company of Ravana's forces as they drew near
Encircling [Hanuman] with their arrows drawn taught
As if in a wooden rampart of 100 pikes he found himself trapped.

80.

*nolasin rāvana pura sen vaṭa* *lā*
*allā gati sanumā devu bäda* *lā*
*dunu daḍu hītal tep muṇa nova* *lā*
*avigeṇa koṭamin tada koṭa vära* *lā*[132]

Surrounded at that moment by those among Ravana's army
who had not been routed
Hanuman was seized and bound up
Led by the tips of their arrows and lances
Forcefully they marched him off.

81.

*bädapu bämma eka viṭa kili pola* *min*
*poḍi vīyeyi väl venkara vila* *sin*
*vidi śara novadī malahama vila* *sin*[133]
*keṭu viṭa vehesa vayeti biya gani* *min*[134]

Trembling as he was led down the path in shackles
Ducking beneath[135] the branches and vines they made their way
through the undergrowth of the forest
Nevertheless he refused to prostrate, even at the tip of their arrows
Striking him they pressed on, as [Hanuman] grew weary and frightened.

82.

*maranḍa bäri veda mohuge balē te* *ňda*
*veṇa vadayak kara maramu va kī sa* *ňda*
*yadimin sirakoṭa bäňdalā gena ta* *ňda*
*damamu genut pātāleka kī sa* *ňda*[136]

"It is impossible for us to kill him, owing to his immense *tejas*
So let us devise some other torture," they reasoned.
Binding him up and leading him off,
It was determined: "Let us cast him down to the underworld!"

83.

*istrīpurayaṭa nuduru vasi* *ňdā*
*siṭinḍa*[137] *nuvarak karamana* *ňdā*[138]
*yanḍa paṭan gati polovat bi* *ňdā*
*gal dora vasamin dahasak kä* *ňdā*[139]

Concealed not far from Strīpura
A bit beyond the chasm in the earth
Forcefully he was brought down 1000 [steps]
Through the entrance at the stone door.

84.

*teda bala anuhasa pāmin laka mä* *ňda*
*viňda savu siri śäpa rusiren mana na* *ňda*
*oňda vaḍavana laňda maha kālī la* *ňda*
*puňda läba kōvila väḍa hidi nā sa* *ňda*[140]

Deep beneath Lanka—endowed with *tejas*, power and might[141]
Her lovely form inordinately pleasing to the mind
Resides[142] Maha Kali, the woman who grants all that one desires[143]
Within her temple where she receives regular worship—

85.

*galvän siṭuvā kovila sala* *sā*
*visituru däva gō näs gena no le* *sā*
*soyavā uḷuven kot lā viga* *sā*
*hanumā kovila kiyamin sala* *sā*[144]

Her legendary temple which was infused with incense
Amid its wooden beams a place of many sacrifices
Where various scented coverings and banners were laid out
—here Hanuman was to be led inside.

Translator's note: Hanuman formulates a plan and addresses Ravana's guards.

86.

*vasā agullā dora sayi kara* *lā*
*tosāva bōjana geṇa maṭa pisa* *lā*
*nasa vami topi näti nam mē e ka* *lā*
*vasā aṇḍak*[145] *gäsi sanumā e ka* *lā*[146]

"Close the iron door and I'll lay myself down within
Include me among the food that you offer
So in that way I shall be gobbled up while you all remain unharmed."
And so with a deafening thud [of the door] they shut Hanuman within.

87.

*äśunē pātālē sama täṇa* *ṭā*
*räs veti sen ävidin kōvila* *ṭā*
*säma täṇa bojunut räs kara vi* *ṭā*
*dänanuva devulaňda pera lesa e vi* *ṭā*[147]

With a rousing commotion throughout the underworld
Ravana's forces proceeded to the *kovil*
Bringing offerings of food with them
Announcing to the goddess that they were ready.

88.

*däka piya sanumā devulaňda neti* nē
*devu kula tabamin devuliya mudu* nē
*ledavu laňda in polavayaṭa giḷu* nē
*iňda gati asnē sanumā gosi* nē[148]

The goddess, casting her gaze upon Hanuman
Recognized from his face that he belonged to the family of the gods
Swiftly she opened up to swallow him and send him off to the heavenly world
But stopped to listen as Hanuman addressed her.

89.

*mahat kali udayē siṭa bas tepala* ti
*bojana pisämen ada maṭa kam nä* ti
*magē baḍa gini bōvī eyi danumä* ti
*uḷu käṭayak äradiva kaṭa aya* ti[149]

At dawn, [Hanuman] addressed Maha Kali:
"Today do not enjoy me along with this cooked food!"
[Kali addressing Hanuman]:
"O clever one, know though that I am immensely hungry!"
But as her gaping mouth opened and her tongue [protruded],
a single tile fell from the roof.

90.

*eviṭa e danumäti ävadin vigasa* ṭa
*damava yi bōjuna uḷukäṭa asko* ṭa
*kālā baḍa pirune situ vilasa* ṭa
*husma elayi edā kämbo vi* ṭa[150]

Acting quickly, the clever one (Hanuman)
Arranged the tile amid the other food offerings
As she continued to devour the food, her stomach growing full and bulging
He let out an enormous breath as she continued to gorge herself.

91.

*tadin e sanumā husma elan* nē
*soňdin siṭu galṭän igilen* nē[151]
*dolos e gavuvak gosin väṭen* nē
*hanumā pātālen nikmen* nē[152]

Forcefully Hanuman let out his breath
Uprooting a portion of the rock on which he stood
Flying up twelve *gavuvas*[153]
Hanuman emerged from the underworld.

92.

*ävit e rāvana nuvaraṭa van* dā
*pera lesa aṇaturu karati pasin* dā[154]

*rāvaṇa raja tama pura sen kän* dā
*allā gattuva sanumā ban* dā[155]

Hanuman found himself then in Ravana's city
Where just as before he set to rampaging
As Ravana summoned his troops
Who promptly put Hanuman once again in chains.

93.

*emaviṭa śanumā siṭa tepalan* nē
*rāvana rajune me bas asan* nē
*koyi śaṭiyen oba me mā maran* nē
*īṭa upāyak kiyami bolan* nē[156]

So indisposed, Hanuman addressed his captor:
"O King Ravana hear my proposition—
In what manner might you dispatch me?
I will tell you the means by which to do so!"

94.

*vilakku pan dan digata tiben* ne
*pena kiyanana mama yi pavatin* ne
*piśśī sāranak kala dik ven* ne
*nava vata yak äti nakuṭa kiyan* ne[157]

"[Have your men] lead me out of the city carrying a torch with them
When we reach the right place, I will point out where to stop
Some distance away there is an abode of Pishachas (demons)
Tell [your men] to wrap my tail in fresh cloth."

95.

*deviňdu muniňdun minisun no käta kan* nē
*gini pilavun ākala*[158] *väna seyan* nē
*tel redi gena mage iňga paṭalan* nē
*gini läbuvot mage divi väna sen* nē[159]

"[Those demons] who heed no God, Buddha, nor man
Do regularly light the forest ablaze for their mere amusement
If you wrap my tail in oiled cloth
Once they set it alight, my life will promptly end!"

96.

*rāvana raja e basaṭa tos vemi* nā
*genat e tel piliyen paṭalami* nā
*aramudalē pilīga badā teli* nā
*äňga paṭalannaṭa van maňdi vemi* nā[160]

Ravana, being pleased enough by his suggestion
Ordered that his tail be wrapped with cloth

Taking from the storehouse the necessary wares
They prepared him and led him led out to the forest.

97.

*tava tava vīdiya pēru balan* *nē*
*tel piliyen genāvit paṭalan* *nē*
*raṭa raṭaval vala savamat ten* *nē*
*yateḷut pilī genävit räs ven* *nē*[161]

Leading them here and there along a circuitous route
All the while oil dripping from the cloth
From village to village deeper into the forest they stumbled
The thick oil pooling all the while.

98.

*vilakku pan dan digaṭa sadan* *nē*
*peňda kiyana mā mayi*[162] *pavatin* *nē*
*pilī sisāraṇa kala dik ven* *nē*
*nava vatayak ätinakuṭa kiyan* *nē*[163]

[Hanuman addressing his captors:]

"Fix up a long torch out of leaves
I'll stop here just in view
The abode of the Pishachas is only a bit further on
And today is the asterism of the 9th day of the lunar calendar."

99.

*genā pamaṇa tel pilī sisā* *rā*
*danānāňga siṭa ekatuva sapu* *rā*
*manāsitin gini genä vit eva* *rā*
*danātī bunu gini ävuḷuni gugu* *rā*[164]

Having spread oil everywhere as they went about
Rendering the whole wood a tinderbox
At the command when a single flaming arrow was loosed
The whole jungle was ignited in a roaring breath of fire.

100.

*rāvana māliga visi aṭagavu vi* *ya*
*solos riyan diga vīdiya pätira* *ya*
*valā poṭak lāvā laňga diňguvi vi* *ya*
*tava bō sandā bāvak nam vi* *ya*[165]

Now, Ravana's palace was twenty-eight *gavuvas* in extent
The roads were twelve cubits wide
These being lined with rooftops and supplemented
with bathing pools throughout
Known as "Bhāva" as account of this and other opulence.

101.

*pilīsi sarana kala dik ven* nē
*äga paṭalanṭa mädi yi kiyan* nē
*e nuvara tel pili nätä kiyan* nē
*nättam viga saṭa gini avulan* nē[166]

Far from the sylvan resort of the Pishachas
Exclaiming that the fire was now within their midst
Telling [one another] not to put any oil throughout the city
So that the fire would not spread within [so quickly].

102.

*pähädiya hanumā sita satosin* nē
*daradiyavat un bähära no yan* nē
*ara diya seṇasuru bas*[167] *sari lan* nē
*vīdi geval mudunen päna yan* nē[168]

Hanuman's mind exalted [upon seeing] the blazing fire
As the city turned to kindling not an exit could be found
The fire swelling all the way up to graze Saturn
As he jumped between the streets and houses.

103.

*avulā gini sanumā päṇa yan* nē
*mevulā baraṇa se gal dilen* nē
*devulova dakvā gini ävilen* nē
*mevulā rāvana sen biyavan* nē[169]

The fire grew as Hanuman leapt about
Shimmering like a diadem worn around the neck
The flames reaching all the way up to the Deva world
While fear mounted in the hearts of Ravana's forces.

104.

*gugurā pandama sē ävilen* nē
*gini kaňda ävilī nuvara piren* nē
*hanumā rāvana nuvara nasan* nē[170]
*no hära geval piṭa päna päna yan* nē[171]

Roaring and blazing like a flaming torch
A mountain of fire filling the city
So Hanuman destroyed the city of Ravana
Leaping across every house and home.

105.

*uḷu gevala kaṭulen päna yan* nē
*muḷu mala tibunā däka no lasin* nē

*ävu päni gini pānak vilasin* *nē*
*rāvana pura hānumā gini lan* *nē*[172]

Jumping across the tiles of the roofs
Smoke so thick that nothing could be seen
The fire following as he jumped like the wick of a lamp
So Hanuman incinerated the city of Ravana.[173]

106.

*māliga vāsal torana da no hä* *rā*
*ät as häsirena gevaḷut no hä* *rā*
*gini lahi hanumā siṭa siṭa no hä* *rā*
*avuḷuni gini kaňda eka viṭa gugu* *rā*[174]

The archway at the entrance to the palace was not spared
The panicked elephants and horses were not spared
Hanuman the frantic pyromaniac offered quarter to none
The roaring conflagration devouring all in its path.

107.

*e nuvara hanumā gini kaňda pat* *vī*
*mānu dahas pura mäňda ven rok* *vī*
*kara diya piṭa sanumā gos ot* *vī*
*unu vī polavat sayurat rat* *vī*[175]

Hanuman transformed the city into a mountain of fire
With thousands of corpses piled high in its center
When Hanuman finally went and extinguished his tail in the sea
From that heat the earth together with the ocean turned crimson.

108.

*rāja dharmma*[176] *rāvana näti bävi* *nī*
*śōka sitva deviyō ros vemi* *nī*
*eviṭa muhuda biňda kara diya piru* *nī*
*dīpa paṭunu nava laksaya gilu* *nī*[177]

Ravana, failing in his royal Dharma
Brought sorrow to the gods which transformed itself to wrath
Causing them to divert the ocean into an immense tsunami
Flooding the ports of the island—all nine lakhs of them.

109.

*muhuda unuva pahu raňda ratvan* *nē*
*yagal yaḷu goḍi poḍi kari van* *nē*
*deviyō vaṭakara pahuri biňdin* *nē*
*muhuda uturavā nuvara piren* *nē*[178]

The ocean now boiling and crimson
The high ground began to disappear
When the gods breached the final rampart
And the ocean swept in to flood the city.

110.

*rāvana pura muhuňda giḷu asura senaga goḍa van* *nē*
*yudda karaṇa sama deviyō avidunu geṇa rakimin* *nē*
*bädda väňdī tän tänvala turu śevanē väḍa in* *nē*
*rāvana teruvan visinda ada tek pävatī en* *nē*[179]

The city of Ravana slipped beneath the sea,
burying the army of the Asuras along with it
While they had so valiantly served during the war
Afterwards, scattered throughout the forest they sought shelter
O Ravana, if only you had lived today when the Three Jewels flourish!

111.

*vehesa vemin rāvana pura senaňga rägena saha piriva* *rā*
*yōga vemin säpata näsī sāgata lat yakṣa asu* *rā*[180]
*maňgak soyā ävidin raṭa goḍalibimak soya pata* *rā*
*māgan nuvaraṭa päṇalā pura vāgana seṇaňga asa* *rā*[181]

Defeated, King Ravana summoned his army around him
Arms interlocked[182], hungry, their strength exhausted,
the Yakṣa-Asuras trudged on
Searching along the path he found a bit of hilly ground
Hopping from one dry spot to another Ravana and his loyal forces
bore themselves up.

112.

*perakala pin bara balasen rāvana kala kī* *dē*
*tirakara sil räki kenek kavuru da ran ra* *dē*
*vara ma viddat no vidī sil näti atama* *dē*
*parasidu saman devi gena ran rada äyi* *dē*[183]

In times of yore, how much merit was possessed by the mighty Ravana?
Likewise what sort of man was Rama, who guarded his virtue so?
Can the soul of one who neglects virtue remain undamaged?
How great was the fame of Saman (Lakshmana), who also rescued the princess?

113.

*melesin duk kiyati siṭana nuvara näsunu bava nitara yem* *ma*
*navā tänak nätuva tänin tänama vimasā ävidin vidin ma* *ma*
*saviya nätuṭa ädin näṭa liya ruk mula kaňdu gal goḍa yem* *ma*
*avaḍa kerena ūve raṭa pävanen eňdā siṭam* *ma*[184]

He rambled on sorrowfully gazing at the devastation of the city
Pacing about inconsolably as he saw all the various places that had been lost
There on the side of the mountain where he walked round the foot
a sole remaining[185] tree
And in so doing the "land of Uva" came into being on that day.[186]

114.

*vadurā ran rada vaṇasā dunnu aḍuva me siri laka* *ṭa*
*madura sē rasa sē paḷu pala väla budimin sahatu* *ṭa*
*sodurā rāvana pura sen siṭi tī ävadin gala pi* *ṭa*
*udurāla yi hanumā siṭa ūvē raṭa eka eliya* *ṭa*[187]

Rama and his monkey allies, having reduced Sri Lanka to ruin
To their minds [a victory] as sweet as the taste of the
choicest fruits of the forest
But walk behind the rock where the forces of the city
of valorous Ravana[188] stood
There you will find the "land of Uva"—the area adjacent to that
rooted up by Hanuman.

115.

*pavari vikum mahasen geṇa rāvana raja uyanaṭa va* *na*
*amara puren dunu yaṇa sē tibunā palaturu sē ma* *na*
*nuvara eliya pävatennē udurā sanumā e uya* *na*
*evara ariṇa śara pulvan vädi rāvaṇa sen väṇase* *na*[189]

So King Ravana taking along his mighty army settled
at the garden there
[Harvesting] fruits [so delicious] it was as if they were gifts from heaven
That garden, the place uprooted by Hanuman, became "Nuwara Eliya"
Where Ravana's army was laid to waste by the arrows of Upulvan.

# Notes

1. In his study of manuscripts in the Nevill Collection related to the *Kohoṁbā Kaṅkāriya* rite, Tissa Kariyawasam notes that the redactor of this set of ritual texts (also dated to the seventeenth or eighteenth centuries) claims that its portions related to the *Ramayana* are taken from the *Rāvaṇa Katāva (puvat me katāvena| mese me rāvaṇa katāvena*) (Kariyawasam, "The Rāmāyaṇa and Folk Rituals of Sri Lanka," 94). On the dating of the *Kohoṁbā Kaṅkāriya* ritual corpus, see A. Seneviratne, "Kohoṁbā Kaṅkāriya," 207–214.
2. It is worth noting however that this last assessment of Ravana's character appears in Sinhala "boundary books," and may have been reproduced in rote fashion by the author (there is no elaboration anywhere in the *Rāvaṇa Katāva* as to what Ravana's failure consisted in, precisely).
3. *vädiyā* is also used with respect to Rama at Or. 6611.188 [f.8r. v.1].

4. Maḍalagama Vajirabuddha gives thirteen verses of what he identifies as a "historical poem" treating the felling of Ravana by Rama, entitled *Rāma Rāvaṇā Yuddhaya*. Vajirabuddha relates that this short composition was associated with the "Ravana flag" (*rāvaṇa koḍiya*) for many years kept at the Ratnapura Saman Devalaya. While we cannot by any assured means connect these verses with the missing narrative portion of the *Rāvaṇa Katāva*, they do give additional confirmation to the upkeep of a Sinhala vernacular poetic tradition relating to the *Ramayana* (Maḍalagama Vajirabuddha, *Saman Deviňdu hā Saman Devola* [Balangoda: Sunil Śānta Virasēkara, 2007], 387–388).
5. For examples of this genre, see C. de S. Kulatillake, *Ethnomusicology, Its Content and Growth, and Ethnomusicological Aspects of Sri Lanka* (Colombo: S. Godage & Brothers, 1991), 44–47.
6. Or. 6611.189 and 7 H.10.
7. For related texts, see W. A. de Silva, *Catalogue of Palm Leaf Manuscripts in the Colombo Museum*, vol. 1 (Colombo: Ceylon Government Press, 1938), 301–302 (nos. 1964–1967).
8. Or. 6611.189 [f.1b v.2].
9. Or. 6611.188 [f.1 v.1].
10. Or. 6611.188 [f.1 v.2]; cf. Or. 6611.189 [f.1b v.4.]:

*kamala ē rāvanā yuga net yugà* *yen*
*demala äduru misa nodanimu api* *dän*
*sinhala basin kavi pada baňda kiya* *min*
*vipula katika bäri pavasami yan* *tan*

Cf. 7 H. 10 [f.3 v.2]:

*kamala rāvanā yuda neta yuga* *yen*
*demala äduru misa nodanmui apa* *dän*
*siṅhala me lasiṅ kavi pada bäňda pava* *san*
*vipu katika bäri pavasami yan* *tan*

11. Or. 6611.188 [f.1b v.1].
12. Or. 6611.188 [f.1b v.2] gives: *no laba virā maňdanā kipunē äta*.
13. Or. 6611.189 [f.2 v.2].
14. Or. 6611.188 [f.2 v.1] gives *lovaṭa pasiňdu saman deviyannē*, as different recensions of the poem clearly confused Shurpanakha's initial love interest.
15. 7 H.10 [f.3b v.1]. Line 3 of Or. 6611.188 [f.2 v.1] reads *ruvaṭa malanu kenekut äta unnē*; Or. 6611.189 [f.2 v.3] gives *ravaṭa malanu kenekut ätunnē*: "He is there along with his younger brother."
16. Or. 6611.188 [f.2 v.2].
17. Understanding *hiňda* for *siňda*.
18. Or. 6611.188 [f.2b v.1]. Cf. line 4 of Or. 6611.189 [f.2b v.1]: *säpa sē sara nova vadahala ran raňda*; 7 H.10 [f.3b v.3]: *śapaśe saraṇa vavada hala ran rada*.
19. Or. 6611.188 [f.2r. v.2]. Line 4 of Or. 6611.189 [f.2b v.2] reads: *lada kivu mē lesa gänumaṭa saranā*.
20. Or. 6611.188 [f.3 v.1]. Line 4 of Or. 6611.189 [f.2b v.3] reads: *topaṭa sarana vemi mama koyilē*.

21. Reading *kaga pata*, "the blade of the sword," for *kaga pota*.
22. Or. 6611.188 [f.3 v.2]. Rev. Sorata gives *nähāya* as a reading for *gahan* in his *Śrī Sumañgala Śabdakoṣaya*.
23. Cf. 7 H.10 [f.4 v.3]: *kopula taväda siṅha käna viliyeyinā*.
24. Or. 6611.189 [f.3 v.1].
25. Reading *laddā* or *laddō* as pl. of *lada*.
26. Or. 6611.189 [f.3 v.2]. Or. 6611.188 [f.3r. v.2] is corrupt. Cf. 7 H.10 [f.4 v.4]:

    *sidda novana bas kiva ayiyā si* *ṭa*
    *vädda nasē un ga sāṇa pīṭa po* *ṭa*
    *laddu suga rañgana śē lada ruvaka* *ṭa*
    *yudda karannaṭa kivu e lada si* *ṭa*

27. 7 H.10 [f.4b v.1] reads *tama naganin haṭa kala bava pennā*.
28. Or. 6611.188 [f.4 v.1]. Or. 6611.189 [f.3 v.3] confirms the correct reading of the final line as *pema magē gala riya genava ki yannē*.
29. Or. 6611.188 [f.4 v.2].
30. 7 H.10 [f.4b v.3]. Cf. Or. 6611.188 [f.4r. v.1]:

    *käñda gattuva rāvana raju* *mā*
    *indā dā kuma bäna numā* *mā*
    *rāvana rajuhaṭa miga bas dī* *mā*
    *tun dena samañga vayeti riya pädi* *mā*

31. Or. 6611.188 [f.4b v.2]
32. Or. 6611.188 [f.4b v.3]
33. Or: "Perceived as small what was in fact Ravana's immense mansion (i.e., his stone chariot?)." Clearly a variant developed in the text, likely because the earlier (*bisavun himagata tanu vasi kīsada*) isn't perfectly clear.
34. Or. 6611.188 [f.7b v.1], clearly out of order in the ms. Cf. Or.611.189 [f.4 v.5]:

    *viñddaśāra yavala kivala kīn* *nē*
    *bädda uḍin päna yan* *nē*
    *deviñdu divas balamin* *nē*
    *mamina muvā ära en* *nē*

35. Or. 6611.188 [f.5 v.1]. *illannē* may be wrong for *allannē*.
36. Or.611.189 [f.3b v.5]. The use of *māliga* is confusing here but from context we must understand it to mean Rama and Sita's ashram.
37. Or. 6611.188 [f.6 v.1]
38. Reading "*sit balenā*" for "*pin balenā*," "*sit balenā*" attested in both Or. 6611.189 [f.4 v.2] and 7 H.10 [5b v.1].
39. Or. 6611.188 [f.6 v.2].
40. Or. 6611.188 [f.6b v.1].
41. Or. 6611.188 [f.7 v.3]. This verse and the following appear to be out of order in the mss.
42. Or. 6611.188 [f.7b v.3]. Cf. line 4 of Or. 6611.189 [f.4b v.2]: *dunna damā giśa [sic] rusi väda*; and 7 H.10 [f.6 v.2]: *dunna damā giya rusi mäñda*.
43. Or.6611.189 [f.9 v.2] gives *kalā rusiru koñda uyana ki pähävu*; 7 H.10 [f.9 v.3] gives *kala ruti rāvaṇa uyanē kinilataravu*.
44. Or. 6611.188 [f.16, v.1].

45. A *gavuva* (pl. *gavu*) is approximately three and a half miles.
46. Or. 6611.188 [f.16 v.2].
47. 7 H.10 [9r. v.1]. Cf. Or. 6611.188 [f.17 v.1]:

    *sambāntoṭa gala kala isnā* *nē*
    *vaṭakara ävileyi gini jalmā* *nē*
    *ätupiṭa rāvana eṇu däka äňdi* *nē*
    *päňṇayi jalayaṭa isa kes [sic] peṇu* *nē*

    Or.6611.189 [f.9 v.4]:
    *sanbantoṭa dī kola isnā* *nē*
    *vaṭakara ävileni gini jalmā* *nē*
    *ätupiṭa rāvana ena vādaki* *nē*
    *pänana kalaṭa isavaṭa nilapenu* *nē*

48. The famous "Menik Ganga" of Sri Lanka is a short river emanating in southern Uva Province, important to pilgrims of Kataragama. The "Sītā Gaňgula" which we know today—a broad part of a stream which runs by the modern Sita Amman Temple of Sita Eliya—is geographically unrelated. This verse most likely refers to this upcountry "Sita Gangula" (on the location of which, see Godakumbura, "Rāmāyaṇa in Śrī Laṅkā," 72). In popular ritual there does seem to be some conflation between the "Menik Ganga" of Kataragama and the upcountry "Sita Gangula," however. J. B. Disanakaya explains that devotees and lay priests (*kapurālas*) purify themselves "at the banks of the *Sīta Gangula* or *Mënik Ganga*" before donning a white cloth (*piruvata*) and entering the sacred vicinities of both Sri Pada and Katargama ("Suba-Asuba Symbolism in Sinhala Culture," *Journal of the Royal Asiatic Society Sri Lanka Branch* [New Series] 25 (1980–1981): 110). The following verse in this poem suggests a possible source of that conflation. The image here is of Sita jumping into her upcountry "Mänik Ganga" and being deposited at Hambantota—wholly conceivable to the imagination of the poet, though incongruous with the actual geography of the two rivers (the Menik Ganga of Sita Eliya flows into the sea at Yala, fifty kilometers from Hambantota). See discussion at Chapter 3, section 3 of this text.
49. Or. 6611.188 [f.8 v.1] and 7 H.10 [f.6 v.3] both give *adinnaṭa*.
50. Reading *häriyē* for *näriyē*; *häriyē* attested in the other mss.
51. Or. 6611.189 [f.4b v.3].
52. Or. 6611.188 [f.6b v.2], substituting the final line with that of Or. 6611.189 [f.4b v.4]. Original: *ganṭa mavu nipat dekaki ma*.
53. *rusi rupa tamba kola nogena ma*, "fine, beautiful copper, without taking leaves"?
54. Or. 6611.189 [f.4b v.5]. Cf. Or. 6611.188 [f.6r. v.3]:

    *kāra bändanek vana mä* *ňda*
    *sītā bähāra noya ranra* *ňda*
    *ivara ovena duk dī ta* *ňda*
    *bähära giyē ada devula* *ňda*

55. Discrepancies between mss. make it difficult to reconstruct this line.
56. Or. 6611.189 [f.4b v.1]. This verse appears to be out of order. Or. 6611.188 [f.7b v.2] gives the final line as *deviňdu sītā duk uśulā*. Cf. 7 H.10 [f.6 v.1]: *devi sita duk kaňda usulā*.

57. Or. 6611.189 [f.5 v.1].
58. Or. 6611.188 [f.7 v.2].
59. Or. 6611.188 [f.8 v.2]. This verse is difficult to reconstruct, and it comes with little surrounding context. Line 2 of Or. 6611.189 [f.5 v.3] is *umagana tavama naganinnē*, perhaps *umagana* for *ummagga*, "subterranean"? 7 H.10 [6r. v.4] gives: *umayañgaṇa genannannē.*
60. Or. 6611.188 [f.8r. v.1].
61. Or. 6611.188 [f.8r. v.2] gives: *agē aḍuru siru käṭiyā.* The meaning of this line is not clear.
62. 7 H.10 [f.7 v.3]. *sanumā* amended to *hanumā*. Another highly similar verse appears later in each of the manuscripts. Assuming it to be an interpolation amid these verses, the order of which is confused, I include it here as a note: Or. 6611.188 [f.9b v.2] (corresponding to 7 H.10 [7b v.4]):

   *kiyayi me bas hanumā i* *ňda*
   *vāliya äṭa biňda piyata* *ňda*
   *oya aniyen do ranra* *ňda*
   *gannē sītā devu la* *ňda*

   Hanuman made his asseveration with these words:
   "As your servant I will break my bones
   Carrying out your royal command
   Rescuing your wife, Princess Sita."

63. 7 H.10 [f.7 v.4].
64. *vida vida*, lit., "slashing, slashing," i.e., "slashing my way through."
65. Or. 6611.189 [f.5b v.6].
66. Understanding *sinäha* (*sneha*) for *sinā̃*.
67. The final line is identical in all mss. though the meaning is not completely clear.
68. Or. 6611.188 [f.10 v.1]. Cf. 7 H.10 [f.8 v.2]:

   *eyiṭa vidda śara deta dä* *ti*
   *māliya allā näva* *ti*
   *arimi ayet sitak si* *ti*
   *āsiri pin bala da ki* *ti*

   There follows a difficult verse which I have omitted. Or. 6611.188 [f.10 v.2]:

   *kiňda rāma rajunini mē ma* *ṭa*
   *vidde māvana sanana* *ṭa*
   *aśu unu laňda rāvanaha* *ṭa*
   *sanumā yuda kara vanna* *ṭa*

   "O Rama, my lord and King of Kings!
   Allow me to be your consolation!
   Ravana [shall not have] a 79th wife!"
   Hanuman thereby departed to make war.

69. Or. 6611.188 [f.8 v.3].
70. Lit: "Make haste and be gone by the dust of the hoof!"
71. 7 H.10 [7r. v.1]. Two verses follow which I am unable to interpret. Or. 6611.189 [f.5b v.3]:

*emaviṭa pulvan suri* *ňdā*
*hanumaṭa bas kiya e* *ňdā*
*eka säti topa dedena si* *ňdā*
*kiri maligāva ren ā* *ňdā*

Cf. Or. 6611.188 [f.9 v.2]:

*emaviṭa pulvan śuri* *ndā*
*sanumā [sic] bas kiyā ma* *nda*
*eka śaṭi topi dedena si* *nda*
*kiri mäṭi gāvaren ma* *nda*

Followed by: Or. 6611.188 [f.9r. v.1]:

*kūra maňda yaṇa dede* *nā*
*aḍuvani sā sanḍu ve* *nā*
*kirimäti den(a)nagē väku* *nā*
*novida e dat siṭa noya* *nā*

Cf. 7 H.10 [7r. v.3]:

*kura maňda yana dede* *nā*
*abuvat saha sanḍu ve* *nā*
*kirimäti denage maku* *nā*
*novida e dat viparami* *nā*

72. Or. 6611.188 [f.10 v.3].
73. Or. 6611.188 [f.10b v.1]. Or.6611.189 [f.6 v.4] gives the final line as *ranrada pavasati me lesaṭa*. 7 H.10 [f.8b v.1] reads:

*vāliyan eyi topevit ka* *ṭa*
*källati yaddī gata pi* *ṭa*
*hoddemimma viga sa* *ṭa*
*me lesa kiyā ranrada si* *ṭa*

74. 6611.188 [f.11 v.1].
75. Or. 6611.188 [f.11 v.2].
76. The flag of Kama, the god of love, is the "Makaradhvaja," bearing the image of the *makara*, a crocodile-like (or crocodile-fish hybrid) mythological creature. The reference to the Makara flag in this passage represents another possible connection with Indian versions of the Peacock Ravana story, in which Hanuman is aided by his son, whom he discovers employed as a guard by Ravana's brother in Pāṭala Laṅkā. In the Hindi version, Hanuman's son is Makaradhvaja, "the fish-bannered one," so named as he was produced from a drop of Hanuman's sweat which fell into the mouth of a Makara as he flew over the sea (Philip Lutgendorf, "Hanuman's Adventures Underground," 154). In the Tamil version he is named Maccakarpaṉ or Maccavallapaṉ, "the fish hero" (Kamil Zvelebil, *Two Tamil Folktales*, 187). For additional references to Hanuman's Makaradhvaja in Indian versions of the epic, see chapter seven of Philip Lutgendorf, *Hanuman's Tale: The Messages of a Divine Monkey* (New York: OUP, 2007).
77. Or.6611.189 [6r. v.1]. This verse missing from Or. 6611.188.
78. Or. 6611.188 [f.11b v.1].

79. The legend that Hanuman's footprints left a series of impressions in the stone banks of the river which flows by the Seetha Amman Temple of Sita Eliya are current in the literature of the Ramayana Trail, see Chapter 5, section 2 of this text.
80. 7 H. 10 [f.12 v.2] *aḍagā*.
81. Or. 6611.188 [f.12 v.1]. Final line of 7 H. 10 [f.12 v.2]: *lasavaturu ha(hī)sinäsi sanumā kakāpalaturu giya tänē*.
82. Or. 6611.188 [f.12b v.1].
83. 7 H.10 [12r. v.2], corresponding to Or.6611.189 [f.7 v.2], which is slightly corrupt. Verse missing from Or.6611.188. Kumbhakarna as "Kumbhakāranu," on which the manuscripts agree, is an interesting irregularity suggesting some possible Telugu influence.
84. In the *Vālmīki Rāmāyaṇa*, Kumbhakarna awakens after six months of sleep on the eve of battle between Rama and Ravana's forces (R. P. Goldman, et al., *The Ramayana of Valmiki*, vol. VI, sarga 49, v.26 (271). Some later Indian iterations of the epic include an episode in which Ravana attempts to force the planetary deities to remain in their auspicious celestial positions at the time of his son Meghanada's birth. Saturn (Skt. *śani* or *śanaiścara*), being an inauspicious astral presence, was imprisoned by Ravana, later discovered and freed by Hanuman. See Philip Lutgendorf, *Hanuman's Tale*, p.140f.
85. Or. 6611.189 [7r. v.1]. At 7 H.10 [f.11 v.1] this plea from Kumbhakarna comes after Ravana's city is destroyed, he is distraught, and sets off for Dambadiva, and reads:

    *yanḍa nikmī gal ratē geṇa edā rāvaṇa mā̃ni* yō
    *mañḍa därilañda kiyai mañga bäsa asan rāvaṇa puñci* yō
    *yanḍa epai rañrajunhaṭa noyan rāvaṇa rajasi* yō
    *unḍa tunlova kenek sari näti kiyai rāvana mā̃ni* yō

    Cf. Or. 6611.188 [f.13 v.1]:

    *yanṭa nikmī gal ratē gena eñdā rāvana mā̃ni* yō
    *māñḍu därilañda kiyayi maṅgi(ṅ) bas asan rāvana putāḍi* yō
    *sañḍu epayi ranrajunhaṭa noyan rāvana putāḍi* yō
    *uñḍa tunlova kenek hari näta kiyayi rāvana mā̃ni* yō

86. Thanks to Chinthaka Ranasinha for pointing out that *darilañda* "little girl" or simply "dear child," could metonymically refer to Ravana's wife, i.e., "the one who bore a dear child."
87. Or. 6611.189 [f.7b v.2] and 7 H.10 [f.11 v.2] both give *asannē*.
88. Or. 6611.189 [f.7b v.2] *avananbu*; 7 H.10 [f.11 v.2] *avanambu*; *avanambu no karan*, "do not insult."
89. Or. 6611.189 [f.7 v.2] gives *banbu upañdina perañdinēñdī upan deviyō bolannē*.
90. Or. 6611 [f.13b v.1].
91. *sarilana* can mean "resembling," "like."
92. 7 H.10 [f.11b v.1]. Missing from Or. 6611.188. The last two lines of this verse are difficult. Or. 6611.189 [f.7b v.3] reads:

    *vēga vī rāvana rajun bas kiyati tañda koṭa emavi ṭā* ṭā
    *hāgaga garuḍan allavā bäñda devu lovē āya ekē ṭā* ṭā

*lavati siragē yi dahas gananak tibennē äsi(yi) kuma kā* *ṭā*
*mē mā sarilana kenek tunlova kavuru van näna sari ko* *ṭā*

93. Or. 6611.188 [f.14 v.1], corresponding to Or. 6611.189 [f.8 v.1] and 7 H.10 [11r. v.2].
94. Reading *aritri* (=*habala*) for *ariti*, on which all mss. agree.
95. Reading *rus* for *räṣ*. Or. 6611.189 [f.8 v.2] gives *husvu deviyō diva diva ikman*; Or. 6611.188 [f.14 v.2] gives *rus vet deviyō diva diva ikman*.
96. 7 H.10 [f.10 v.1].
97. Or. 6611.188 [14r. v.1] gives *magaṭa*.
98. Or. 6611.189 [f.8 v.3] Or. 6611.188 [f.14b v.1]. Final line of 7 H.10 [f.10 v.2] gives simply: *maraṇa pämiṇa seti sata sin̆hala*.
99. Or. 6611.188 [f.14b v.2]. Final line of Or. 6611.189 f.8 v.4]: *būpē visnugē vänaseti siri laka*; Final line of 7 H.10 [f.10 v.3]: *bupē viṣmaṇa vaṇa sati siri laka*.
100. Or.6611.189 [f.8b v.1]. Cf. Or. 6611.188 [f.15 v.1]:

*pavissaren lat kayan̆devi pätu* *vē*
*arit sāma śara galturu poḍi* *vē*
*e gos śare väda muhudē eti* *vē*
*āvit tiyeyi hī ital kopu* *vē*

Cf. 7 H.10 [f.10b v.1]:

*pavistaren lat devi utumā* *vē*
*ariti sāma śara galturu poḍi* *vē*
*e gos śare gos mu den eni* *vē*
*ävit tibeyi tama hī tal kopu* *vē*

101. In context (the ruin of Ravana's citadel) the "queen" in this verse may refer to Mandodari, rather than Sita.
102. Or. 6611.189 [f.8b v.2]. Last two lines of Or. 6611.188 [f.15 v.2] read: *ahasa gigun dena lesaṭa äśennē | dahas dahasa rūpuśen van(a) śennē*. Last two lines of 7 H.10 [f.10b v.2] *ahasa gigun väsi nätuva äsennē | dahasa dahasa purasen väna sennē*.
103. *uvin̆du*, i.e., Upendrayā, that is, Vishnu.
104. Or. 6611.189 [f.8b v.3] gives *munu devaṭa koṭa bäda lō pahurā*; Or. 6611.188 [f.15b v.1]: *mudēvaṭa kara bän̆dalā pahurā. Mudevu*, "mountain peak," *mudun-geya*, "turret" or "room on the top of a house."
105. 7 H.10 [f.10b v.3].
106. 7 H.10 [f.9 v.2] gives *dahasa vätunu kala gaṇṇananaṭ* [sic] *gannē*.
107. 6611.188 [f.15b v.2], missing from Or.6611.189.
108. Or. 6611.188 [f.16b v.1].
109. Or. 6611.188 [f.16b v.2]. Cf. Or.6611.189 [f.9 v.1]:

*tan̆da teda pulvan devi raja nita* *rā*
*bän̆dami niyan rann̆dunen vita* *rā*
*vin̆da hīn̆dunu gena karanā vita* *rā*
*vän̆da säraminiyun miya yana vita* *rā*

Cf. 7 H.10 [f.9 v.1]:

*tada teda pulvan devi raja nita* *rā*
*bäminī yak ran dunnē vita* *rā*
*vida dunu hī geṇa kara raṇa nita* *rā*
*vada śara vinisun viya vita* *rā*

110. Or. 6611.188 [f.17b v.1].
111. 7 H.10 [f.9b v.3]. Verse missing from missing from Or. 6611.189. Cf. Or. 6611.188 [f.17b v.2]:

*goḍabäsa hanumā siri lada diva* *ṭa*
*ridi päśeṇa ket vat śoňda ruva* *ṭa*
*gaja räla vilasiṅ udurā depo* *ṭa*
*satosiṅ kayi goya mut ū lesa* *ṭa*

112. *usturuvala iňdapala bara kannā* (Or. 6611.189 [f.9b v.2]; *usvuturuḍala idaṇa padikkann* [sic] (Or. 6611.188 [f.18 v.1]).
113. Or. 6611.188 [f.18 v.1] gives *morapaḷu*.
114. 7 H.10 [f.13 v.1].
115. *usvu* from *usvenavā*; *palakan* from T. *palakam*, "pile"?
116. 6611.188 (f.18 v.2). These verses describing the names of the crops are reminiscent of *kurahan kavi*, traditional songs related to the harvesting of brown millet (*kurakkan*). For examples of this genre, see C. de S. Kulatillake, *Ethnomusicological Aspects of Sri Lanka*, 44–47.
117. Or. 6611.189 [f.9b v.4]. Final line of Or. 6611.188 [f.18b v.1] reads *udurā hanumā pura vayi hakkā*.
118. *uḍu* = *ihala*, "juice."
119. Or. 6611.188 [f.18b v.2].
120. Or. 6611.188 [f.19 v.1]. Cf. Or. 6611.189 [f.10 v.1]:

*dulababa sinhala (pala?) nätuva murun* *ňgā*
*kalababorakara vilvun* *ňgā*
*solavayi kaňdu sel taru poti ha* *ňgā*
*pelarayi kenvan kara pala ha* *ňgā*

121. Or. 6611.188 [f.19 v.2].
122. Or. 6611.188 [f.19b v.1]. Final two lines of 7 H.10 [f.13b v.3]: *goravai sata biya kara kulmattu* | *iravai val diva diva yeti sattu*. This verse contains a number of Tamil terms: *tūtulai*, one of the eighteen medicinal roots; *poti*, "flower buds" or "tender shoots"; *mattu*, "thorn apple or purple stramony"; *kaṇṇiyam*, "turmeric."
123. 7 H.10 [f.13b v.4] gives the first two lines as: *sulan vātayeni vidula pisinnē* | *guvan talen mal väsi vassannē*.
124. Or. 6611.188 [f.19b v.2].
125. Rev. Sorata gives *ahasin väṭena mal* as an entry for *malväsi*.
126. Or. 6611.189 [f.10b v.1] gives *sädimala*.
127. Or. 6611.188 [f.20 v.1]. The meter of the last two lines is not satisfactory in any mss. Or. 6611.189 [f.10b v.1] gives the last line as *yedī e rāvana naṭa kivu me lesaṭa*; Cf.

7 H.10 [f.14 v.1]: *yedī e rāvaṇa naṭa kivu me lesaṭa*; Cf. Peradeniya 278529: *yedī e rāvaṇahaṭa kivuve leśaṭa*.

128. 7 H.10 [f.14 v.2].
129. 7 H.10 [f.14 v.3].
130. *älliya* = *alliya*?
131. 7 H.10 [f.14b v.1]. Missing from Or. 6611.189.
132. 7 H.10 [14r. v.2]. Missing from Or. 6611.188 and Or. 6611.189.
133. Or. 6611.189 [f.10b v.4] gives: *vidiśara novadīmalahaṭa vilasin*; Or. 6611.188 [f.21 v.1] gives: *vin̆di śara novan̆dina lesaṭa ma vilasin*.
134. 7 H.10 [14r. v.3]. Last two words of Or. 6611.189 [f.10b v.4]: *bima dīmin*; Cf. Or. 6611.188 [f.21 v.1]: *miya novamin*.
135. Lit. "having again become small."
136. 7 H.10 [f.15 v.1]. Or. 6611.188 [f.21 v.2] gives the last two lines as: badimin tara *koṭa balamin uge tan̆da | damamu genut pātāleṭa kivu bän̆da*. Or. 611.189 [f.11 v.1] gives last line as *damamu gē hun pātāleka kivusan̆da*.
137. 7 H.10 [f.15 v.2] gives *hin̆dinā*.
138. Or. 6611.188 [21r. v.1] gives: *idinā nuvaraki rāvaṇa sandā*.
139. Or. 6611.189 [f.11 v.2].
140. 7 H.10 [f.15 v.3].
141. For a translation of *teda bala pāmin̆dā*, see C. E. Godakumbura, "The Ramayana—A Version of Rama's Story from Ceylon," *The Journal of the Royal Asiatic Society of Great Britain and Ireland 1* (1946): 20, 22.
142. *väḍa in̆dinā* and *väḍa hidi* = *väḍa hin̆da*.
143. *vaḍavana*—fulfilling [wishes].
144. Or. 6611.189 [f.11 v.4]. Cf. Or. 6611.188 [f.22 v.1]:

*galvän siṭuvā kōvila yasa* *sā*
*visituru däva daḍu go nas [sic] no le* *sā*
*śoyavā uḷuven kot lā e* *sā*
*hanumā kovila tula vani no le* *sā*

Cf. 7 H.10 [15r. v.1]:

*galṭän siṭumā kōvila yasa* *sā*
*visituru däva gō näs äda no le* *sā*
*soyavā uḷuven kot lā ema* *sā*
*sanumā kovila tula vani no le* *sā*

Cf. Peradeniya 278010 [9r. v.2]:

*galiväṭi siṭu kōvila sara* *sā*
*visituru däva daḍugen[a?] nā no le* *sā*
*soyavā uḷuven kotlā eva* *sā*
*hanumā kōvila tula vanino le* *sā*

145. Or. 6611.189 [f.11b v.2] gives *aḍak*; Or. 6611.188 [22r. v.1] gives *haḍak*.
146. 7 H.10 [15r. v.3].
147. Or. 6611.188 [22r. v.1].

148. 7 H.10 [15r. v.2]. This verse appears to be out of order in each of the mss.
149. Or. 6611.188 [f.23 v.1]. Reading *diva kaṭa* for *mukha yada*, as attested in Or 6611.189 [f.11 v.4] and 7 H 10 [f.20 v.2]. Cf. Peradeniya 278529 [17r. v.2]:

*mahat kalila daśe baś pavaśa* *ti*
*bojana piśaven ādamaṭa kannä* *ti*
*māge baḍanigi* [sic] *boviyada nuvä* *ti*
*ulu käṭayak äradennaṭa kiya* *ti*

150. 7 H.10 [f.20 v.3]. Or. 6611.188 [f.23 v.2] gives final line as *husma eliya kämat kā bō koṭa*; Or. 6611.189 [f.12 v.1] gives *husma eliya hanumā taňda roskoṭa.*
151. Or. 6611.188 [23r. v.1] gives *soňdin siṭevu gal karu igilennē.*
152. 7 H.10 [20r. v.1].
153. *väṭennē*, "falling," though we are made to understand that Hanuman is "falling up" here. A *gavuva* is a distance of approximately three and a half miles.
154. First two lines of Or. 6611.189 [f.12 v.3]: *ävidin rāvana nuvara vaňdā | pera lesa anaturu kara vati biňdā.*
155. 7 H.10 [20r.v v.2].
156. Or. 6611.188 [f.24 v.1].
157. Peradeniya 278529 [f.18 v.2].
158. The meaning of *ākala* is uncertain. Peradeniya 278529 [18r. v.1] gives *äkala.*
159. 7 H.10 [f.19 v.2]. Or. 6611.188 [f.24 v.2] gives the final line as *gini dunnot magē.*
160. Or. 6611.189 [f.12b v.2]. Final line of 7 H.10 [f.19 v.2]: *äňgaśē pamaṇak śāhuni edina.*
161. 7 H. 10 [f.18 v.3].
162. Reading *mā mayi* for *ṇama mayi*, as attested in 7 H.10 [18 v.1].
163. Or. 6611.188 [24r. v.2].
164. 7 H.10 [f.19 v.4]. Missing from Or. 6611.189.
165. 7 H.10 [f.18 v.2].
166. Or. 6611.189 [f.13 v.1].
167. In other mss. *basa*—the meaning is not clear.
168. Or. 6611.188 [f.26 v.1].
169. Or. 6611.188 [f.26 v.2].
170. 7 H.10 [19r. v.1] gives *asurā vut vimata tama divannē.*
171. Or. 6611.189 [f.13 v.4].
172. Or. 6611.189 [f.13b v.1].
173. Or. 6611.189 [f.25 v.2] includes another following verse, an interpolation of a previous, and not of the highest poetic caliber.
174. Or. 6611.189 [f.25 v.3], substituting the final line of 7 H.10 [f.18b v.3].
175. 7 H.10 [f.17 v.1].
176. *dharmma* [sic], on which all mss. agree.
177. Or. 6611.188 [f.27 v.2]. This verse and the following are in reverse order in all mss.
178. 7 H.10 [f.17 v.2].
179. 7 H.10 [f.17b v.1], substituting the final line of Or. 6611.188 [f.27b v.1] (original: *rāvana peru nānā vil äňda tek pävatī ennē*). Cf. Or. 6611.189 [f.25b v.2]:

*rāvana pera nānāvit avidunu genaňdu vinnē*, “Ravana, whose multitude of wisdom and delusion both are lost to the ravages of time”?

180. Or. 6611.188 [f.28 v.1] reads: *yōga vemin säpata näsī sugat lakṣaya asa sura.*
181. 7 H.10 [f.17b v.2].
182. The meaning of *yōga vemin*, on which all mss. agree, is not clear.
183. Or. 6611.188 [28r. v.1]. Missing from Or. 6611.189.
184. Or. 6611.189 [f.14b v.1]. Cf. Or. 6611.188 [f.28b v.2]:

    *bōva duk kiyā sitaṭa tava rana śunu bavana tara* ma
    *navā tänak pin näti nätin täna vimasā ävidavaṭa* ma
    *svāmiyā näti liyagē (lisagē?) gal kaňdu mula siṭa* ma
    *āvā maya uha veta (ṭe?) tama pavatten edā siṭa* ma

    Cf. 7 H.10 [f.16 v.1]:

    *bōvā duk kiyati siṭaṇa nuvara näsu nu ba va nitara* ma
    *navā tänak nätuva tänin täṇa vimasā ävidimma* ma
    *svāmiyā näti liyase ruk mul kaňdu gal gē ya* ma
    *āvāmaya ū me raṭa pävittennē edā siṭa* ma

185. *näti liya*, “not destroyed.”
186. i.e., “*ūva*,” the sound of Ravana’s dolorous cry.
187. 7 H.10 [f.16 v.2]. Or. 6611.188 [f.29 v.1, final verse of text] gives the last two lines as: *śora rāvaṇa e puren ävidin siṭa śala śalaňgaṭa* | *udurālayi e sanumā ävida mē raṭin ek eliyaṭa.*
188. Or. 6611.188 [f.29 v.1, the final verse of text] gives *śora rāvaṇa*; *śora* is Skt. *caurya*, meaning deceitful. The other mss., however, agree in their reading of *soňdurā rāvaṇa*, *soňdurā* being equivalent to Skt. *sundara* (Or. 6611.189 [f.14r. v.2]; Colombo Museum ms. 7 H.10 [f.16 v.2]).
189. 7 H.10 [16r. v.1]. 7 H.10 [16r. v.2] contains one final, difficult verse:

    *kaṭa äti diva näti dā̃na depaya näti sata käṭa ek velā mai in* nē
    *kaṭa ätuva misa kaṇa kumak näta ohu kana kā̃maṭa aňḍa vin* nē

    [**odd letters and runes]

    *aňḍaṇa äḍun misa veṇa varadak näta avahirayaka mai ohu in* nē
    *asannet äda näta pada tuṇ boru näta puḷuvan ayatō rā den* nē

# Bibliography

## Primary Sources

*Amāvatura of Guruḷugomi*. Edited by Kōḍāgoḍa Gñāṇālōka. Dehiwala: Buddhist Cultural Centre, 2004 [1998].

*The Dīpavamsa: An Ancient Buddhist Historical Record*. Edited and translated by Hermann Oldenberg. London: Williams and Norgate, 1879.

*Girā Sandēśaya*. Edited by Nanadasēna Ratnapāla. Colombo: Ratna Pot Prakāśayō, 1985.

*Kōṇēcar Kalveṭṭu of Kavirājavarōtayaṉ*. Edited by I. Vaṭivēl. Colombo: Department of Hindu Religious and Cultural Affairs, 1993.

*The Mahāvaṃsa*. Edited by Wilhelm Geiger. London: Pali Text Society, 1908.

*Maṭṭakkaḷappu Pūrva Carittiram*. Edited by S. E. Kamalanathan and Kamala Kamalanathan. Colombo: Kumaran Book House, 2005.

*Mayura Sandēśaya*. Edited by R. A. Liyana Āracci. Colombo: Samayavardhana Pothala Samāgama, 2007.

*Rājāvaliya [with a critical introduction]*. Edited by A. V. Suravīra [A. V. Suraweera]. Colombo: Lake House Publishing, 1976.

*Rāmāyaṇaya*. Author unknown. University of Peradeniya Library, ms. 277833.

*Rāvaṇa Rājāvaliya saha Upat Kathā*. Edited by G. Obeyesekere and A. Tissa Kumara. Colombo: Godage International Publishers, 2005.

*Samarāṅgaṇa Sūtradhāra of Bhojadeva*, vol. 1. Edited and translated by Sudarshan Kumar Sharma. Delhi: Parimal Publications, 2007.

*Sītāvaka Haṭana*. Edited by Rohini Paranavitana. Colombo: Central Cultural Fund, 1999.

*The Śiva-Purāṇa [Ancient Indian Tradition and Mythology Series, Purāṇas in Translation]*, four volumes. Edited and translated by J. L. Shastra. Delhi: Motilal Banarsidass, 1970.

*Takṣiṇa Kailāca Purāṇam of Ciṅkai Cekarācacēkaraṉ*, two volumes. Edited by S. Patmanathan and K. C. Naṭarācā. Colombo: Department of Hindu Religious and Cultural Affairs, 1995.

*Tiruvicaippā*. Edited by Tirupaṉantal Kācimaṭattu Atipar. Madras: K. Cuppiramaṇiyam, 1974.

*Vaiyā Pātal of Vaiyāpuri Aiyar*. Edited by Ka. Ce. Naṭarācā. Colombo: The Colombo Tamil Sangam, 1980.

*Vanni Rājāvaliya*. Edited by G. Obeyesekere and A. Tissa Kumāra. Colombo: Godage International Publishers, 2005.

*Vētālan Katāva*. Edited by Fedrick Coorey. Colombo: Lakmini Pahan Yantrasalava, 1872.

*Yatidūtam of Davuldena Ñāneśvara Nāyakasthavira*. Colombo: Sarasvati Publishers, 1987.

## Secondary Sources

Abeyasinghe, Tikiri. "History as Polemics and Propaganda: An Examination of Fernao de Queiros, 'History of Ceylon.'" *Journal of the Royal Asiatic Society Sri Lanka Branch* [New Series] 25 (1980/81): 28–68.

Abeyawardana, H. A. P. *Boundary Divisions of Mediaeval Sri Lanka*. Mattegodagama: Academy of Sri Lankan Culture, 1999.

Abeywickrema, Mandana Ismail. "The King and I." *The Sunday Leader*. April 10, 2011. http://www.thesundayleader.lk/2011/04/10/the-king-and-i-2/.

Abhayasundara, Wimal. *Lankādisa Rāvanāyana saha Gīta Nāṭaka Nirmāṇaya*. Colombo: S. Godage, 1999.

Abhayasundara, Wimal. *Niṣādī [New Edition]* (2006). Colombo: S. Godage, 1959.

Adi-p-Podi, Sekkizhaar, and T. N. Ramachandran (trans.). *Tirumurai the Sixth: St. Appar's Thaandaka Hymns*. Dharmapuram, Mayiladuthurai: Dharmapuram Aadheenam, 1995.

Agnihotri, Aradhya. "Madhya Pradesh Towns Where Ravana is Worshipped, His Death Is Mourned." *Times of India*. October 6, 2016. https://timesofindia.indiatimes.com/india/Madhya-Pradesh-towns-where-Ravana-is-worshipped-and-his-death-is-mourned/articleshow/54761295.cms.

Ahubudu, Arisen. "Siṅhalayāṭa hisat hadavanat dena sinhala avurudda." *Rāvaya* 9 (April 1987): 4f.

Ahubudu, Arisen [Ariesen Ahubudu, sic]. *The Story of the Land of the Sinhalese (Helese)* [trans. of *Hela Deraṇa Vaga* by Nuwansiri Jayakuru]. Colombo: Stamford Lake House, 2012.

Ali, Daud. "Bhoja's Mechanical Garden: Translating Wonder Across the Indian Ocean, circa 800–1100 CE." *History of Religions* 55, no. 4 (2016): 1–34.

Amunugama, Sarath. *The Lion's Roar: Anagarika Dharmapala and the Making of Modern Buddhism*. New York: Oxford University Press, 2019.

Ananda, T., and C. Nahallage. "Unique Religious and Cultural Practices as Evident in the Kandyan Village of Meemure." In *Selected Papers from the International Conference of the Humanities 2015*, edited by K. Herath and D. Fernando, 73–82. Faculty of Humanities, University of Kelaniya, 2016.

Appadurai, Arjun. *Fear of Small Numbers*. Durham: Duke University Press, 2006.

Appadurai, Arjun. *Modernity at Large: Cultural Dimensions of Globalization*. Minneapolis: University of Minnesota Press, 1996.

Apte, V. D., and D. V. Garge. "Mahābhārata Citations in the Śabara Bhāṣya." *Bulletin of the Deccan College Post-Graduate and Research Institute* 5 (1943–1944): 221–229.

Argenti-Pillen, Alex. *Masking Terror: How Women Contain Violence in Southern Sri Lanka*. Philadelphia: University of Pennsylvania Press, 2002.

Ariyadasa, Kanchana Kumara. "Rāvaṇa dēvatvayen pudana 'yakkama' ṭa giyemu." *Laṅkādīpa* (online). November 26, 2014.

Ariyapala, M. B. (trans.) *Kavsilumina: The Crown Jewel of Sinhala Poetry in English Prose*. Colombo: S. Godage, 2004.

Ariyapala, M. B. "W.A. de Silva Memorial Lecture." *Journal of the Royal Asiatic Society of Sri Lanka* [New Series] 41 (1996): 205–222.

Arumugam, S. *Some Ancient Temples of Sri Lanka*. Colombo: Ranco Printers and Publishers, 1980.

Bastin, Rohan. "Hindu Temples in the Sri Lankan Ethnic Conflict." *Social Analysis: The International Journal of Social and Cultural Practice* 49, no. 1 (2005): 45–66.

Bastin, Rohan. *The Domain of Constant Excess: Plural Worship at the Munnesvaram Temples in Sri Lanka*. New York: Berghahn Books, 2002.

Batuvantudave, C. *A Catechism of Ceylon History* (1902). Kaluwella, Galle: Mercy Press, 1915.

Bechert, Heinz. "The Beginnings of Buddhist Historiography: *Mahavamsa* and Political Thinking." In *Religion and Legitimation of Power in Sri Lanka*, edited by Bardwell Smith, 1–12. Chambersburg, PA: Anima Books, 1978.

Beligalla, Vijēsiṃha. *Lenārḍ Vulf Samaga Gamanak*. Colombo: Godage International Publishers, 1995.

Berkwitz, Stephen. *Buddhist Poetry and Colonialism: Alagiyavanna and the Portuguese in Sri Lanka*. New York: Oxford University Press, 2013.

Berkwitz, Stephen. *History of the Buddha's Relic Shrine: A Translation of the Sinhala Thūpavaṃsa*. Oxford: Oxford University Press, 2007.

Bhabani, Soudhriti. "India-Sri Lanka Sign Memorandum to Promote Mythological Significance of Ramayana." *India Today*. July 14, 2016. https://www.indiatoday.in/mail-today/story/ramyana-india-sri-lanka-tourism-329123-2016-07-14.

Bharadwaaja, Maharishi, and G. R. Josyer. *Vyamaanika-Shaastra, or, Science of Aeronautics*. Mysore: Coronation Press, 1973.

Blackburn, Anne. *Buddhist Learning and Textual Practice in Eighteenth-century Lankan Monastic Culture*. Princeton: Princeton University Press, 2001.

Boange, Dilshan. "A New Twist to an Olden Tale." *Sunday Observer*. September 23, 2018. http://www.sundayobserver.lk/2018/09/23/arts/new-twist-olden-tale.

Breckenridge, S. N. *The Hills of Paradise: British Enterprise and the Story of Plantation Growth in Sri Lanka*. Colombo: Stamford Lake Publication, 2001.

Brito, C. (trans.). *The Yalpana-vaipava-malai, or, The History of the Kingdom of Jaffna* (1879). New Delhi: Asian Educational Services, 1999.

Brohier, R. L. *Discovering Ceylon*. Colombo: Lake House, 1973.

Brohier, R. L. *Seeing Ceylon in Vistas of Scenery, History, Legend, and Folklore*. Colombo: Lake House, 1965.

Buck, David C., and K. Paramasivam (trans.). *The Study of Stolen Love: A Translation of Kaḷaviyal eṉṟa Iraiyaṉār Akapporuḷ with Commentary by Nakkīraṉār*. Atlanta: Scholars Press, 1997.

Buddhadasa, R. *Aṣṭaṅgahṛdaya Saṃhitā*. Colombo: Department of Ayurveda, 1964.

Buddhadasa, R. *Caraka Saṃhitā*. Colombo: Department of Ayurveda, 1960.

Burgess, Ebenezer. "Translation of the Sûrya-Siddhânta." *Journal of the American Oriental Society* 6 (1858–1860): 141–498.

Carter, Charles. *A Sinhalese-English dictionary*. Colombo: The "Ceylon Observer" Printing Works; London: Probsthain & Co., 1924.

Chavannes, Edouard. *Cinq Cents Contes et Apologues*, vol 2. Paris: Leroux, 1910.

Chilli, Shaik. *Folk-tales of Hindustan*. Allahabad: Panch Kory Mittra, 1908.

Clarke, Arthur C. *Fountains of Paradise*. Surrey, UK: Weysprings Books, 1979.

Cohen, Signe. "Romancing the Robot and Other Tales of Mechanical Beings in Ancient Indian Literature." *Acta Orientalia* 64 (2002): 65–75.

Collins, Steven. "The Discourse on What Is Primary (*Aggañña Sutta*): An Annotated Translation." *Journal of Indian Philosophy* 21, no. 4 (1993): 301–393.

Collins, Steven. "What Is Literature in Pali?" In *Literary Cultures in History: Reconstructions from South Asia*, edited by Sheldon Pollock, 649–688. Berkeley: University of California Press, 2003.

Cowell, E. B., and W. H. D. Rouse (trans.) *The Jātaka; or, Stories of the Buddha's former births*, vol. II (1895). London: Pali Text Society, 1973.
Cumaratunga, Munidasa. *Śikṣāvatāraya sahita Śikṣāmārgaya* (1933). Colombo: Department of Cultural Affairs, 2009.
Davy, John. *An Account of the Interior of Ceylon, and of Its Inhabitants: With Travels in That Island*. London: Longman, Hurst, Rees, 1821.
De Alwis, James. *The Sidath Sangarawa*. Colombo: William Skeen, Government Printer, 1852.
De Köning, Deborah. "The Ritualizing of the Martial and Benevolent Side of Ravana in Two Annual Rituals at the Sri Devram Maha Viharaya in Pannipitiya, Sri Lanka." *Religions* 9, no. 250 (2018): 1–24.
de Queyroz [Queirós], Fernão. *The Temporal and Spiritual Conquest of Ceylon*, three volumes (1930), translated by S. G. Perera. New York: AMS Press, 1975.
de S. G. Punchihewa, Gamini. *A Lost Medieval Kingdom of "The Lion King."* Ratmalana: Vishva Lekha, 2003.
de Silva, C. S., and S. Pathmanathan. "The Kingdom of Jaffna up to 1620." In *History of Sri Lanka*, vol. 2, edited by K. M. de Silva. Peradeniya: The University of Peradeniya, 1995.
de Silva, Charumini. "Over 100 Responses So Far on SL's Quest to Establish King Ravana as First Aviator." *Daily FT*. July 25, 2020. http://www.ft.lk/front-page/Over-100-responses-so-far-on-SL-s-quest-to-establish-King-Ravana-as-first-aviator/44-703655.
de Silva, John. *Sītā Haraṇa, hevat, "Ginigat" Rāmāyaṇaya*. Colombo: Śāstrāloka Press, 1886.
de Silva, Lynn. *Buddhism: Beliefs and Practices in Sri Lanka*. Colombo: self-published, 1974.
de Silva, Nalin. *Apē Pravāda 3: apē itihāsayaṭa nava susamādarśanayak*. Boraläsgamuva: Visisdunu Publishers, 2010.
de Silva, Nalin. "Devivaru, Arsenic and Science." *Sri Lanka Guardian*. June 15, 2011. http://www.srilanka guardian.org/2011/06/devivaru-arsenic-and-science.html.
de Silva, Nalin. "Devivaru, Arsenic and Science—IV." *The Island*. July 26, 2011. http://www.island.lk/ index.php?page_cat=article-details&page=article-details&code_title=31013.
de Silva, Nalin. "The Mahavamsa Myth." *The Island*. February 25, 2014. http://www.island.lk/index.php?page_cat =article-details&page=article-details&code_title=98658.
de Silva, W. A. *Catalogue of Palm Leaf Manuscripts in the Library of the Colombo Museum*, vol. 1. Colombo: Ceylon Government Press, 1938.
de Silva, W. A. "Sri Lankapura, the City of Ravana." *The Buddhist* [Quarterly Journal of YMBA] 8, no. 12 (April 1938): 241–243.
de Zilva Wickremasinghe, Don Martino. "(No. 17) Poḷonnaruva: Galpota Slab-Inscription." *Epigraphia Zeylanica II*, 98–122. London: Oxford University Press, 1928.
de Zilva Wickremasinghe, Don Martino. "(No. 29) Poḷonnaruva: Prīti-Dānaka-Maṇḍapa Rock-Inscription." *Epigraphia Zeylanica II*, 165–178. London: Oxford University Press, 1928.
de Zoete, Beryl. *Dance and Magic Drama in Ceylon*. London: Faber and Faber, 1957.
DeCaroli, Robert. *Haunting the Buddha: Indian Popular Religions and the Formation of Buddhism*. Oxford: Oxford University Press, 2004.
Deckard, Sharae. "Exploited Edens: Paradise Discourse in Colonial and Postcolonial Literature." PhD diss. University of Warwick, 2007.
Deegalle, Mahinda. *Buddhism, Conflict and Violence in Modern Sri Lanka*. London: Routledge, 2006.

Deegalle, Mahinda. "Contemporary Sri Lankan Buddhist Traditions." In *The Oxford Handbook of Contemporary Buddhism*, edited by in Michael Jerryson, 13–35. New York: Oxford University Press, 2016.

Dehejia, Vidya. "Aniconism and the Multivalence of Emblems." *Ars Orientalis* 21 (1991): 45–66.

Deriyangala, P. E. P. *Some Sinhala Combative, Field and Aquatic Sports and Games*. Colombo: National Museums of Ceylon, 1959.

Desai, Santosh. "Ramayana—An Instrument of Historical Contact and Cultural Transmission between India and Asia." *The Journal of Asian Studies* 30, no. 1 (1970): 5–20.

Dessigane, R., and P. Z. Pattabiramin (trans.). *La légende de Skanda; selon le Kandapuranam tamoul et l'iconographie*. Pondichéry: Institut français d'indologie, 1967.

Dewasiri, Nirmal. *Laṅkāvē Itihāsaya: dṛṣṭivādi vicārayak*. Dehiwala: Vidarśana Prakāśana, 2019.

Dewasiri, Nirmal. "New Buddhist Extremism and the Challenges to Ethno-Religious Coexistence in Sri Lanka." [ICES Research Papers series]. Colombo: International Centre for Ethnic Studies, 2016.

Dharmabandu, T.S. *Gämuṇu tun vana pota [Gemunu Reader III]*. Colombo: Parsi Veḷaňda Samāgama, 1951.

Dharmadasa, K. N. O. "A Nativistic Reaction to Colonialism: The Sinhala-Buddhist Revival in Sri Lanka." *Asian Studies: Journal of Critical Perspectives on Asia* 12, no. 1 (1974): 159–179.

Dharmadasa, K. N. O. *Language, Religion and Ethnic Assertiveness: The Growth of Sinhalese Nationalism in Sri Lanka*. Ann Arbor: University of Michigan Press, 1993.

Dharmadasa, K. N. O. "The People of the Lion: Ethnic Identity, Ideology, and Historical Revisionism in Contemporary Sri Lanka." *Sri Lanka Journal of the Humanities* 15 (1989): 1–35.

Dias, Malini. "Distortion of Archaeological Evidence on the Rāmāyaṇa." *Journal of the Royal Asiatic Society of Sri Lanka* 59, no. 2 (2014): 43–54.

DiManno, Rosie. "Meet Sri Lanka's Radical Buddhist." *Toronto Star*. January 13, 2014. https://www.thestar.com/news/world/2014/01/13/meet_sri_lankas_radical_buddh ist.html.

Disanayaka, Mudiyanse. *Kohom̆bā Yak Kaṅkāriya Kāvya Sāhityaya* (1998). Colombo: Godage International Publishers, 2018.

Disanayake, J. B. *Lanka: The Land of Kings*. Maharagama: Sumitha Publishers, 2007.

Disanayake, J. B. "Multilingualism for Advanced Communication." *Daily News*. February 22, 2018. http://www.dailynews. lk/2018/02/22/features/143600/multilingualism-advanced-communication.

Disanayake, J. B. *Rāvaṇa, Gīta Nāṭakaya* (1957). Maharagama: Sumita Prakāśayō, 2016.

Disanayake, J. B. "Suba-Asuba Symbolism in Sinhala Culture." *Journal of the Royal Asiatic Society Sri Lanka Branch* [New Series] 25 (1980–1981): 101–21.

Disanayake, J. B. *Understanding the Sinhalese* (1998). Maharagama: Sumitha Publishers, 2012.

Don Bastian, C.. *Rāmāyaṇaya hevat Rāvaṇā Saṅhāraya: Adventures of Ráma, or, Destruction of Rávana*. Petta: Śāstralōka Press, 1886.

Doniger, Wendy. "From Kama to Karma: The Resurgence of Puritanism in Contemporary Hinduism." *Social Research* 78, no. 1 (2011): 49–74.

Dorai Rangaswamy, M. A. *The Religion and Philosophy of Tevaram* (1958). Madras: University of Madras, 1990.

Evans, John. *Morals Not Knowledge: Recasting the Contemporary U.S. Conflict between Religion and Science* (Berkeley: University of California Press, 2018.

Fernando, Mihindukulasuriya Susantha. *Ritual, Folk Beliefs and Magical Arts*. Colombo: Godage International Publishers, 2000.

Fernandopulle, Natasha. "From Nari Bena to Gajaman Puwatha: Remembering theatre veteran Dayananda Gunawardena." *Sunday Times*. July 5, 2019. http://www.sundaytimes.lk/090705/Plus/Sunday timesplus_11.html.

Field, Garrett. "Commonalities of Creative Resistance: Rapiyel Tennakoon's *Bat Language* and Sunil Santha's 'Song for the Mother Tongue.'" *Sri Lanka Journal of the Humanities* 38, no. 1/2 (2012): 1–25.

Field, Garrett. *Modernizing Composition: Sinhala Song, Poetry, and Politics in Twentieth-Century Sri Lanka*. Berkeley: University of California Press, 2017.

Filliozat, Jean. *Étude de Démonologie Indienne: Le Kumāratantra de Rāvana et les textes parallèles Indiens, Tibétains, Chinois, Cambodgien et Arabe*. Paris: Imprimerie Nationale, 1937.

Flueckiger, Joyce Burkhalter. "Standing in Cement: Possibilities Created by Ravana on the Chhattisgarhi Plains." *South Asian History and Culture* 8, no. 4 (2017): 461–477.

Forbes, Jonathan. *Eleven Years in Ceylon, Comprising Sketches of the Field Sports and the Natural History of That Colony, and an Account of Its History and Antiquity*, two volumes. London: Richard Bentley, 1840.

Gair, James, and W. S. Karunatillake. *The Sidat Saṅgarā: Text, Translation and Glossary*. New Haven, CT: American Oriental Society, 2013.

Gaul, Anne. "Where Are the Minorities? The Elusiveness of Multiculturalism and Positive Recognition in Sri Lankan History Textbooks." *Journal of Educational Media, Memory & Society* 6, no. 2 (2014): 87–105.

Geiger, Wilhelm (trans.). *Cūlavaṃsa, Being the More Recent Part of the Mahāvaṃsa*, two volumes (1929). New Delhi: Asian Educational Services, 2003.

Geiger, Wilhelm (trans.). *The Mahāvaṃsa, or, The Great Chronicle of Ceylon* (1912). Colombo: The Ceylon Government Information Department, 1950.

Gillet, Valérie. "Entre démon et dévot: la figure de Rāvaṇa dans les représentations pallava." *Arts Asiatiques* 62 (2007): 29–45.

Godakumbura, C. E. "A Note on the Jānakīharaṇa." *The Journal of the Ceylon Branch of the Royal Asiatic Society of Great Britain & Ireland* [New Series] 11 (1967): 93–98.

Godakumbura, C. E. "Rāmāyaṇa in Śrī Laṅkā and Laṅkā of the Rāmāyaṇa." *Journal of the Royal Asiatic Society of Sri Lanka* [New Series] 59, no. 2 (2014): 55–83.

Godakumbura, C. E. *Sinhalese Literature*. Colombo: The Colombo Apothecaries' Company, 1955.

Godakumbura, C. E. "The Dravidian Element in Sinhalese." *Bulletin of the School of Oriental and African Studies, University of London* 11, no. 4 (1946): 837–841.

Godakumbura, C. E. "The Rāmāyaṇa: A Version of Rāma's Story from Ceylon." *The Journal of the Royal Asiatic Society of Great Britain and Ireland* 1 (1946): 14–22.

Goldman, R., and J. Masson. "Who Knows Rāvaṇa? A Narrative Difficulty in the *Vālmīki Rāmāyaṇa*." *Annals of the Bhandarkar Oriental Research Institute* 50, no. 1/4 (1969): 95–100.

Goldman, Robert P., and Sally J. Sutherland Goldman. *Ramayana Book Five*. New York: NYU Press/JJC Foundation, 2006.

Goldman, Robert P., and Sally J. Sutherland Goldman. *The Rāmāyaṇa of Vālmīki*, vol. VII: *Uttarakāṇḍa*. Princeton: Princeton University Press, 2017.

Goldman, Robert P., Sally J. Sutherland Goldman, and Barend A. van Nooten (trans.). *The Rāmāyaṇa of Vālmīki: An Epic of Ancient India*, vol. VI, *Yuddha Kāṇḍa*. Princeton: Princeton University Press, 2009.

Gombrich, Richard. "The Vessantara Jātaka, The Rāmāyaṇa, and the Dasaratha Jātaka." *Journal of the American Oriental Society* 105, no. 3 (1985): 427–437.

Goonatilake, Susantha. "Introduction to the Issue on the Rāmāyaṇa." *Journal of the Royal Asiatic Society of Sri Lanka* 59, no. 2 (2014): 1–21.

Gooneratne, E. R. (ed.). *The Vimāna-vatthu of the Khuddhaka Nikāya (Sutta Piṭaka)*. London: Pali Text Society, 1886.

Gordon-Cumming, Constance Frederica. *Two Happy Years in Ceylon*, two volumes. London: Chatto & Windus, 1901.

Gornall, Alastair. *Rewriting Buddhism: Pali Literature and Monastic Reform in Sri Lanka, 1157–1270*. London: University College London Press, 2020.

Granoff, Phyllis. "Rama's Bridge: Some Notes on Place in Medieval India, Real and Envisioned." *East and West* 48, no. 1/2 (1998): 93–115.

Griffin, Roger. "Staging the Nation's Rebirth: The Politics and Aesthetics of Performance in the Context of Fascist Studies." In *Fascism and Theatre: Comparative Studies on the Aesthetics and Politics of Performance in Europe, 1925–1945*, edited by Günter Berghaus, 11–29. New York: Berghahn Books, 1996.

Gunasekara, Suriya. *Aitihāsika Rāvaṇa* (2012). Boralāsgamuva: Visidunu Publishers, 2018.

Gunasekara, Tisaranee. "The Second Inauguration (of 'The Leader Who Conquered the World')." *The Sunday Leader*. November 21, 2010. http://www.thesundayleader.lk/2010/11/21/the-second-inauguration-of-%E2%80%98the-leader-who-conquered-the-world%E2%80%99/comment-page-1/.

Gunawardhana, H. D. J. (trans.). *Pūjāvaliya*, part VI. Colombo: Department of Cultural Affairs, (2000–2004).

Gunawardhana, R. A. L. H. "The People of the Lion: The Sinhala Identity and Ideology in History and Historiography." In *History and the Roots of Conflict*, edited by Jonathan Spencer, 45–87. London: Routledge, 1990.

Gunawardhana, R. A. L. H. "The People of the Lion: The Sinhala Identity and Ideology in History and Historiography." In *History and the Roots of Conflict*, edited by Jonathan Spencer, 45–87. London: Routledge, 1990.

Guruge, Ananda. "Sri Lankan Attitude to the Ramayana: A Historical Analysis." *Indological Taurinensia* 19–20 (1993–1994): 131–146.

Guruge, A. W. P. "Senerat Paranavitana as a Writer of Historical Fiction in Sanskrit." *Vidyodaya Journal of Social Science* 7, no. 1–2 (1996): 157–179.

Hallisey, Charles. "Devotion in the Buddhist Literature of Medieval Sri Lanka." PhD diss. The University of Chicago, 1988.

Haniffa, Farzana. "Merit Economies in Neo-Liberal Times: Halal Troubles in Contemporary Sri Lanka." In *Religion and the Morality of the Market*, edited by D. Rudnyckyj and F. Osella, 116–137. Cambridge: Cambridge University Press, 2017.

Haran, B. R. "True 'Gyan' from Bharat Gyan—I." *Sri Lanka Guardian*. November 1, 2008. http://www.srilankaguardian.org/2008/10/true-gyan-from-bharath-gyan-i.html.

Hari, D. K., and D. K. Hema Hari. *Ramayana in Lanka* (2011). Bangalore: Sri Sri Publications Trust, 2013.

Hatcher, Brian. "Pandits at Work: The Modern Shastric Imaginary in Early Colonial Bengal." In *Trans-Colonial Modernities in South Asia*, edited by Michael Dodson and Brian Hatcher, 45–67. London: Routledge, 2012.

Hellmann-Rajanayagam, Dagmar. "*Yālppaṇa Vaipava Mālai, Kailāya Mālai* und *Vaiyāp Pāṭal*: Kulturelle Wahrnehmungen in der historischen Literatur der Jaffna-Tamilen." *Zeitschrift der Deutschen Morgenländischen Gesellschaft* 164, no. 2 (2014): 469–500.

Henry, Justin W. "Distant Shores of Dharma: Historical Imagination in Sri Lanka from the Late Medieval Period." PhD diss. The University of Chicago, 2017.

Henry, Justin W. "South Indian Influence, Religious Cosmopolitanism, and Multilingualism in Sinhala *sandeśa* Poetry." In *Linguistic and Textual Aspects of Multilingualism in South India and Sri Lanka [Collection Indologie 147, NETamil Series 8]*, edited by Giovanni Ciotti and Erin McCann, 753–782. Pondichéry: École Française d'Extrême-Orient/Institut Français de Pondichéry, 2021).

Henry, Justin W., and Sree Padma. "Lankapura: The Legacy of the Ramayana in Sri Lanka." *South Asia: Journal of South Asian Studies* 42, no. 4 (2019): 726–731.

Hensman, Rohini. "Post-war Sri Lanka: Exploring the Path Not Taken." *Dialectical Anthropology* 39, no. 3 (2015): 273–293.

Hertzberg, Michael. "The Audience and the Spectacle: Bodu Bala Sena and the Controversy of Buddhist Political Activism in Sri Lanka." In *Rhetorical Audience Studies and Reception of Rhetoric*, edited by Jens Kjeldsen, 237–259. London: Palgrave Macmillan, 2018.

Ho, Karen, and Jillian Cavanaugh (ed.). "What Happened to Social Facts?" Special section of *American Anthropologist* 121, no. 1 (2019): 160–204.

Holt, John C. "A Religious Syntax to Recent Communal Violence in Sri Lanka." In *Buddhist Extremists and Muslim Minorities: Religious Conflict in Contemporary Sri Lanka*, John Holt (ed.), 194–212. Oxford: Oxford University Press, 2016.

Holt, John C. *Buddha in the Crown: Avalokiteśvara in the Buddhist Traditions of Sri Lanka*. New York: Oxford University Press, 1991.

Holt, John C. *Myanmar's Buddhist–Muslim Crisis*. Honolulu: University of Hawai'i Press, 2016.

Holt, John C. *The Buddhist Viṣṇu: Religious Transformation, Politics, and Culture*. New York: Colombia University Press, 2004.

Hopkins, Steven. *The Flight of Love: A Messenger Poem of Medieval South India by Veṅkaṭanātha*. Oxford: Oxford University Press, 2016.

Horner, I. B. "Chronicle of Buddhas (Buddhavaṃsa)." In *The Minor Anthologies of the Pali Canon*, part III. Oxford: Pali Text Society, 2000 [1975]: ix-lvi, 1–108.

Hultzch, E. (ed.). *South Indian Inscriptions*, vol. 2. Madras: Madras Government Press, 1891.

Iyer, Paramasiva. *Ramayana and Lanka*, part 1. Bangalore: Bangalore Press, 1940.

Jaiswal, Suvira. "Historical Evolution of the Ram Legend." *Social Scientist* 21, no. 3/4 (1993): 89–97.

Jayatilaka, Bhadrajī Mahinda. *Śrī Rāvaṇṇā Puvata: Hela Yak Parapurē Katāva* (1997). Jā-Äla: Samantī Pot Prakāśayō, 2013.

Jayawickrama, N. A. *A Chronicle of the Thūpa and the Thūpavaṃsa, Being a Translation and Edition of Vācissarатthera's Thūpavaṃsa*. London: Luzac for the Pali Text Society, 1971.

Jayawickrama, Sarojini. *Writing that Conquers: Re-reading Knox's "An Historical Relation of the Island of Ceylon."* Colombo: Social Scientist's Association, 2004.

Jayewardene, Sunela. *The Line of Lanka: Myths and Memories of an Island*. Colombo: Sail Fish, 2017.

Kalugampitiya, Nandaka Maduranga. "Rāvanā & Sinhala Buddhism: A Strained Relationship Ridden With Contradictions." *Colombo Telegraph*. July 29, 2015. https://www.colombotelegraph.com/index. php/ravana-sinhala-buddhism-a-strained-relationship-ridden-with-contradictions/#_ftn3.

Kanjilal, D. K. *Vimāna in Ancient India*. Calcutta: Sanskrit Pustak Bhandar, 1985.

Kapferer, Bruce. *A Celebration of Demons: Exorcism and the Aesthetics of Healing in Sri Lanka*. Bloomington: University of Indiana Press, 1983.

Kapferer, Bruce. *Legends of People, Myths of State: Violence, Intolerance, and Political Culture in Sri Lanka and Australia*. New York: Berghahn Books, 1988.

Kapp, Dieter B. "The 'Ālu Kuṟumba Rāmāyaṇa': The Story of Rāma as Narrated by a South Indian Tribe." *Asian Folklore Studies* 48, no. 1 (1989): 123–140.

Kariyawasam, Tissa. "Religious Activities and the Development of a New Poetical Tradition in Sinhalese, 1852–1906." PhD diss. University of London, 1973.

Kariyawasam, Tissa. "The Rāmāyaṇa and Folk Rituals of Sri Lanka." *Journal of the Royal Asiatic Society of Sri Lanka* [New Series] 59, no. 2 (2014): 91–102.

Kaushik, Narendra. "Ramayana Weaves a Trail across South and Southeast Asia." *Bangkok Post*. February 10, 2020. https://www.bangkokpost.com/business/1854339/ramayana-weaves-a-trail-across-south-and-southeast-asia.

Kekulawala, S. L. "The Religious Journey into *Dhamma (Dharmayātrā)*: Buddhist Pilgrimage as an Expression of Religiousness." In *Religiousness in Sri Lanka*, edited by John R. Carter, 35–65. Colombo: Marga Institute, 1979.

Kemper, Steven. *The Presence of the Past: Chronicles, Politics and Culture in Sinhala Life*. Ithaca: Cornell University Press, 1991.

Kern, J. H. C. (ed.), and N. Chidambaram Iyer (trans.). *Bṛhat-Saṃhita of Varaha-Mihira*, vol. 1. Delhi: Parimal Publications, 2013.

Kopf, David. *British Orientalism and the Bengal Renaissance*. Berkeley: University of California Press, 1969.

Kotelawala, Himal. "Meet the Also-Rans." *Republic Next*. September 9, 2019. https://www.republicnext. com/politics/meet-the-also-rans/.

Krishna Sastri, R. S. H. (ed. and trans.). *South Indian Inscriptions*, vol. 3, part 3. Madras: Madras Government Press, 1920.

Kulasuriya, Ananda. "The Minor Chronicles and Other Traditional Writings in Sinhalese and Their Historical Value." *The Ceylon Historical Journal* 25 (1978): 1–33.

Kulatillake, C. de S. *Ethnomusicology, Its Content and Growth, and Ethnomusicological Aspects of Sri Lanka*. Colombo: S. Godage & Brothers, 1991.

Kyaw, U Ba (trans.), and Peter Masefield (ed.). *Elucidation of the Intrinsic Meaning: So Named the Commentary on the Peta-Stories (Paramatthadīpanī nāma Petavatthu-aṭṭhakathā)*. London: Pali Text Society, 1980.

LaCapra, Dominic. *Rethinking Intellectual History: Texts, Contexts, Language*. Ithaca: Cornell University Press, 1983.

Laclau, Ernesto. *On Populist Reason*. New York: Verso, 2005.

Landes, Richard. "Millenarianism and the Dynamics of Apocalyptic Time." In *Expecting the End: Millennialism in Social and Historical Context*, edited by K. Newport and C. Gribben, 1–23. Waco, TX: Baylor University Press, 2006.

Larsen, Hege Myrlund. "Buddhism in Popular Culture: The Case of Sri Lankan 'Tovil dance.'" PhD diss. University of Bergen, 2009.

Lawrie, Archibald Campbell. *A Gazetteer of the Central Province of Ceylon*, two volumes. Colombo, G.J.A. Skeen, 1898.

Lehr, Peter. *Militant Buddhism: The Rise of Religious Violence in Sri Lanka, Myanmar and Thailand*. London: Palgrave Macmillan, 2019.

Liyanage, Dayaseeli. "Refugees in SL Should be Monitored—Ravana Balakaya." *Daily Mirror Online*. April 29, 2019. https://www.dailymirror.lk/editorial/Refugees-in-SL-should-be-monitored-Ravana-Balakaya/240-166126.

Liyanaratne, Jinadasa. *Buddhism and Traditional Medicine in Sri Lanka*. Kelaniya: Kelaniya University (Kelaniya University Anniversary Series, vol. 1), 1999.

Liyanaratne, Jinadasa. "Indian Medicine in Sri Lanka." *Bulletin de l'École française d'Extrême-Orient* 76 (1987): 201–216.

Lutgendorf, Philip. "Hanumān's Adventures Underground: The Narrative Logic of a *Rāmāyaṇa* 'Interpolation.'" In *The Ramayana Revisited*, edited by Mandakranta Bose, 149–163. New York: Oxford University Press, 2004.

Lutgendorf, Philip. *Hanuman's Tale: The Messages of a Divine Monkey*. New York: Oxford University Press, 2007.

Mahantaāracci, Ajanta. *Aṅgampora: Heḷayē Saṭan Rahasa* (2013). Nugegoda: Serenity Publishing House, 2017.

Mahanthaarachchi, Ajantha, and Reza Akram. *Angampora: A Nation's Legacy in Pictures*. Ethul Kotte: Oceans and Continents, 2017.

Malalasekera, G. P. *Pali Literature of Ceylon* (1928). Colombo: M.D. Gunasena, 1958.

Mazzarella, William. "The Anthropology of Populism: Beyond the Liberal Settlement." *Annual Review of Anthropology* 48 (2019): 45–60.

McGilvray, Dennis. "Islamic and Buddhist Impacts on the Shrine at Daftar Jailani." In *Islam, Sufism and Everyday Politics of Belonging in South Asia*, edited by D. Dandekar and T. Tschacher, 62–76. London: Routledge, 2016.

McGilvray, Dennis. "Mukkuvar vannimai: Tamil Caste and Matriclan Ideology in Batticaloa, Sri Lanka." In *Caste Ideology and Interaction*, edited by Dennis McGilvray, 34–97. Cambridge: Cambridge University Press, 1982.

McKinley, Alexander. "Making Lanka the Tamil Way: A Temple History at the Crossroads of Landscapes & Watersheds." *South Asian History and Culture* 11, no. 3 (2020): 254–276.

McKinley, Alexander. "Mountain at a Center of the World." PhD diss. Duke University, 2018.

Meddegama, Udaya (trans.). *Amavatura: The Flood of Nectar*. Colombo: Central Cultural Fund, 2006.

Medis, F. "An Overview of Sri Lanka's Mediaeval Coinage." *Journal of the Royal Asiatic Society of Sri Lanka* [New Series] 37 (1992/1993): 59–68.

Mirando, A. H. *Sinhalayangē Mūlārambhaya*. Colombo: M.D. Gunasena, 1992.

Mukharji, Projit Bihari. *Doctoring Traditions: Ayurveda, Small Technologies, and Braided Sciences*. Chicago: University of Chicago Press, 2016.

Mukherjee, Sujata. "Ayurvedic Medicine in Colonial Bengal." In *India's Indigenous Medical Systems: A Cross-disciplinary Approach*, edited by S.E. Hussain and M. Saha, 100–113. Delhi: Primus Books, 2015.

Murugan, V. (trans.). *Kalittokai in English*. Chennai: Institute of Asian Studies, 1999.

Nagar, Shantilal. *Śrī Raṅganātha Rāmāyaṇa: Rendering into English from Telugu*. Delhi: B.R. Publication Corp., 2001.

[n.a.]. Sri Lankan Ministry of Health, Nutrition and Indigenous Medicine, *Performance and Progress Report 2016–2017*, 195.

Ñāṇavimala, Kiriällē. *Deśiya Vaiśya Śabda Kōśaya*. Colombo: Department of Ayurveda, 1970.

Nanda, Meera. *Prophets Facing Backward: Postmodern Critiques of Science and Hindu Nationalism in India*. New Brunswick: Rutgers University Press, 2003.

Natesan, S. "The Northern Kingdom." In *University of Ceylon History of Ceylon*, vol. 1, part 2, edited by H. C. Ray, 691–702. Colombo: Ceylon University Press, 1960.

Nathaniel, Camelia. "Kuragala: Buddhist Sacred Site Or Sufi Shrine?" *The Sunday Leader*. June 2, 2013. http://www.thesundayleader.lk/2013/06/02/kuragala-buddhist-sacred-site-or-sufi-shrine/.

Nehru, Jawaharlal. *The Discovery of India*. London: Meridian Books, 1947.

Nilakantha Sastri, K. A. *The Colas*, vol. 2, part 1 (1937). Madras: University of Madras, 1975.

Nissan, Elizabeth. "History in the Making: Anuradhapura and the Sinhala Buddhist Nation." *Social Analysis: The International Journal of Anthropology* 25 (1989): 64–77.

Obēsēkara, Mirāṇḍō [Mirando Obeyeskere]. "Rāvaṇā raju yaḷi nägiṭī." *Laṅkādīpa* [online]. July 23, 2014.

Obēsēkara, Mirāṇḍō. *Śrī Laṅkāvē Purāṇa Aṅgam Śāstraya*. Jā-Äla: Samanti Pot Prakāśayō, 2015.

Obeyesekere, Donald. *Outlines of Ceylon History*. Colombo: The Times of Ceylon, 1911.

Obeyesekere, Gananath. "The Ritual Drama of the Sanni Demons: Collective Representations of Disease in Ceylon." *Comparative Studies in Society and History* 11, no. 2 (1969): 174–216.

Obeyesekere, Gananath. *The Buddha in Sri Lanka: Histories and Stories*. London: Routledge, 2017.

Obeyesekere, Gananath. *The Cult of the Goddess Pattini*. Chicago: University of Chicago Press, 1984.

Obeyesekere, Gananath. "Where Have All the Väddas Gone? Buddhism and Aboriginality in Sri Lanka." In *Hybrid Island: Culture Crossings and the Invention of Identity in Sri Lanka*, edited by Neluka Silva, 1–19. London: Zed Books, 2002.

Padma, Sree. "Borders Crossed: Vibhishana in the Ramayana and Beyond." *South Asia: Journal of South Asian Studies* 42, no. 4 (2019): 747–767.

Paranavitana, Senarat. *Inscriptions of Ceylon, Volume 1: Containing Cave Inscriptions from 3rd Century B.C. to 1st Century A.C. and Other Inscriptions in the Early Brāhmī Script* (Colombo: Department of Archaeology, 1970.

Paranavitana, Senarat. "Pre-Buddhist Religious Beliefs in Ceylon." *The Journal of the Ceylon Branch of the Royal Asiatic Society of Great Britain & Ireland* 31, no. 82 (1929): 302–328.

Paranavitana, Senarat. "Religious Intercourse between Ceylon and Siam in the 13th–15th Centuries." *Journal of the Ceylon Branch of the Royal Asiatic Society* 32, no. 85 (1932–1934): 190–213.

Paranavitana, Senarat. "The Arya Kingdom in North Ceylon." *Journal of the Ceylon Branch of the Royal Asiatic Society* [New Series] 7, no. 2 (1961): 174–224.

Paranavitana, Senarat. "The God of Adam's Peak." *Artibus Asiae. Supplementum* 18 (1958): 4–9, 11–13, 15–31, 33–35, 37–41, 43, 45–78.

Paranavitana, Senarat. "Viyaulpata Pillar-Inscription." *Epigraphia Zeylanica* IV.4, no. 21, edited by S. Paranavitana, 176–180. London: Oxford University Press, 1937.

Parker, Henry. *Ancient Ceylon: An Account of the Aborigines and of Part of the Early Civilization* London: Luzac & Co., 1909.

Parker, Henry. *Village Folk-Tales of Ceylon*, three volumes. London: Luzac & Co., 1910.

Pathmanathan, S. *Facets of Sri Lankan History and Culture*. Colombo: Kumaran Book House, 2015.

Pathmanathan, S. *Hindu Temples of Sri Lanka*. Colombo: Kumaran Book House, 2006.

Pathmanathan, S. *Ilaṅkait tamiḻc cācanaṅkaḷ (1300–1900)*. Colombo: Department of Hindu Cultural Affairs, 2013.

Patirana, Ranjani Malavi. *Śrī Pādasthānaya hā Bäňduṇu Pūjā Cāritra*. Colombo: Godage International Publishers, 2014.

Paul, S. C. "Pre-Vijayan Legends and Traditions Pertaining to Ceylon." *Journal of the Ceylon Branch of the Royal Asiatic Society* 31, no. 82 (1929): 263–300.

Perera, Sasanka, C. *Living with Torturers and Other Essays of Intervention: Sri Lankan Society, Culture, and Politics in Perspective*. Colombo: International Centre for Ethnic Studies, 1995.

Perera, Tennyson. *Mahā Rāvaṇa*. Colombo: Sarasavi Publishers, 2016.

Pollock, Sheldon. *The Language of the Gods in the World of Men: Sanskrit, Culture, and Power in Premodern India*. Berkeley: University of California Press, 2006.

Pragñālōka Himi, H. U. (ed.). *Purāṇa Sivpada Saṅgrahāva*. Colombo: Government Press, 1952.

Prajñāśekharābhidhāna, Kalukondayāvē. *Siṅhala Puvatpat Saṅgarā Itihāsaya*, seven volumes. Colombo: M.D. Gunasena, 1965–1970.

Prakash, Gyan. *Another Reason: Science and the Imagination of Modern India*. Princeton: Princeton University Press, 1999.

Pridham, Charles. *An Historical, Political and Statistical Account of Ceylon and its Dependencies*, two volumes. London: T. and W. Boone, 1849.

Pulavar, Kulantai. *Irāvaṇa Kāviyam* (1946). Chennai: Vela Patippakam, 1971.

Purnalingam Pillai, M. S. *Ravana the Great: King of Lanka*. Munnirpallam: The Bibliotheca, 1928.

Qureshi, Siraj. "A Dussehra Without Burning Ravana: This Brahmin Community in Agra Wants an End to Practice." *India Today*. October 12, 2016. https://www.indiatoday.in/india/story/raavan-vijay-dashmi-agra-saraswat-caste-brahmins-346178-2016-10-12.

Raghavan, V. *Yantras or Mechanical Contrivances in Ancient India*. Bangalore: Indian Institute of Culture, 1952.

Rahman, Maseeh. "Indian Prime Minister Claims Genetic Science Existed in Ancient Times." *The Guardian*. October 28, 2014. https://www.theguardian.com/world/2014/oct/28/indian-prime-minister-genetic-science-existed-ancient-times.

Rajagopal, Arvind. *Politics After Television: Religious Nationalism and the Reshaping of the Indian Public*. Cambridge: Cambridge University Press, 2001.

Ramanujan, A. K. "Three Hundred Rāmāyaṇas: Five Examples and Three Thoughts on Translation." In *Many Rāmāyaṇas: The Diversity of Narrative Tradition in South Asia*, edited by Paula Richman, 131–160. Berkeley: University of California Press, 1991.

Ramaswamy, Sumathi. *Lost Land of Lemuria: Fabulous Geographies, Catastrophic Histories*. Berkeley: University of California Press, 2004.

Rambukwella, Harshana. *The Politics and Poetics of Authenticity: A Cultural Genealogy of Sinhala Nationalism*. London: University College London Press, 2018.

Rao, Ajay. *Re-figuring the Rāmāyaṇa as Theology: A History of Reception in Premodern India*. Oxford: Routledge Press, 2015.

Rasanayagam, C. *Ancient Jaffna* (1926). New Delhi: Asian Educational Services, 1984.

Ratnawalli, Darshanie [with Raj Somadeva]. "Explorations in Sri Lankan Archaeology with Raj Somadeva [Parts 1 and 2]." *The Nation*. November 9 and 16, 2014. https://web.

archive.org/web/20141120170220/http://www.nation.lk/edition/fine/item/35165-excavating-sri-lankan-archeology-with-raj-somadeva-part-2.html.

Ravikumar, L., and K. R. Sarat. "Ramayana Trail Tours." *Proceeding of the 3rd International Conference on Hospitality and Tourism Management* 3 (2015): 58–67.

Razick, Ahamed Sarjoon, Nagoor Gafoordeen, and Seyed Mohamed Mohamed Mazahir. "Hate Campaigns and Attacks against the Muslims in Recent Sri Lanka." *European Journal of Research in Social Sciences* 6, no. 1 (2018): 43–58.

Reed, Susan. *Dancing the Nation: Performance, Ritual, and Politics in Sri Lanka*. Madison, WI: The University of Wisconsin Press, 2010.

Ricci, Ronit. *Banishment and Belonging: Exile and Diaspora in Sarandib, Lanka and Ceylon*. Cambridge: Cambridge University Press, 2019.

Richman, Paula (ed.). *Ramayana Stories in Modern South India: An Anthology*. Bloomington: Indiana University Press, 2008.

Roberts, Michael. "History-making in Lanka—I: Problems." *The Island*. 16 April 16, 2008. http://www. island.lk/2008/04/16/midweek1.html.

Roberts, Patrick, Nicole Boivin, and Michael Petraglia. "The Sri Lankan 'Microlithic' Tradition c. 38,000 to 3,000 Years Ago: Tropical Technologies and Adaptations of Homo sapiens at the Southern Edge of Asia." *Journal of World Prehistory* 28 (2015): 69–112.

Robinson, Marguerite. "The House of The Mighty Hero or the House of Enough Paddy? Some Implications of a Sinhalese Myth." In *Dialectic in Practical Religion*, edited by E. R. Leach, 122–152. Cambridge: Cambridge University Press, 1968.

Rockhill, William Woodville. *The Life of the Buddha and the Early History of His Order*. London: Trübner & Co., Ludgate Hill, 1884.

Rothbard, Murray. *For a New Liberty: The Libertarian Manifesto*. New York: Collier Books, 1973.

Rotman, Andy. *Thus I Have Seen: Visualizing Faith in Early Indian Buddhism*. Oxford: Oxford University Press, 2009.

Ruwan, Susitha. *Rāvaṇa Meheyuma* (2011). Colombo: Sarasavi Publishers, 2013.

Ruwan, Susitha. *Rāvaṇa Meheyuma 2*. Colombo: Sarasavi Publishers, 2015.

Ryder, Arthur. *The Panchatantra*. Chicago: University of Chicago Press, 1925.

Samanta, Sailendranath. "A Rare Image of Vaisravana from Kanchannagar, Burdwan." *Proceedings of the Indian History Congress* 27 (1965): 47–50.

Samuel, Geoffrey. *The Origins of Yoga and Tantra: Indic Religions to the Thirteenth Century*. Cambridge: Cambridge University Press, 2008.

Sanmugeswaram, P., Krishantha Fedricks, and Justin Henry. "Reclaiming Ravana in Sri Lanka: Ravana's Sinhala Buddhist Apotheosis and Tamil Responses." *South Asia: Journal of South Asian Studies* 42, no. 4 (2019): 796–812.

Santoshi, Neeraj. "In MP's Ravan Village, the Demon King Is a Revered Deity." *Hindustan Times*. October 15, 2015. https://www.hindustantimes.com/india/in-mp-s-ravan-village-the-demon-king-is-a-revered-deity/story-E5RYXcB30dt5Kv13nDdbEN.html.

Sarachchandra, E. R. *The Sinhalese Novel*. Colombo: M.D. Gunasena, 1950.

Sathyendran, Nita. "Meet Meenakshi Amma, the Grand Old Dame of Kalaripayattu." *The Hindu*. October 25, 2018. https://www.thehindu.com/society/history-and-culture/meenakshi-amma-the-grand-old-dame-of-kalaripayattu/article25307782.ece.

Scheible, Kristin. *Reading the Mahāvaṃsa: The Literary Aims of a Theravāda Buddhist History*. New York: Columbia University Press, 2016.

Scott, David. *Formations of Ritual: Colonial and Anthropological Discourses on the Sinhala Yaktovil*. Minneapolis: University of Minnesota Press, 1994.

Sedaraman, J. E. *Laṅkāvē Yakṣa Yugaya Hevat Kohombā Kaṅkāri Upata*. Colombo: Lihiṇi Pot, 1955.

Seligmann, C. G., and Brenda Seligmann. *The Veddas*. Cambridge: Cambridge University Press, 1911.

Senaratne, L. B. "Arrested While Digging for Ravana's Treasures." *Daily Mirror*. July 4, 2011: A2.

Senasinghe, Thilak. "Rāvaṇā vaṇayak veyi?" *Colombo Telegraph*. February 16, 2020. https://www.colombotelegraph.com/index.php/thilak-senasinghe-16-february-2020/. (Originally published as a print feature in the *Aruna* paper's Sunday edition, February 16, 2020.)

Seneviratna, Āriyadāsa. *Śrī Laṅkā Rāvaṇa Rājadhāniya*. Colombo: Samayavardhana Publishers, 1991.

Seneviratna, Dhammika. "Piraviya nohena hidäsak tabāgiya ācārya mirāṇḍō obēsēkara." *Dinamiṇa* [online]. February 26, 2020.

Seneviratne, Anurudha. "Kohom̆bā Kaṅkāriya: A Traditional Ritual in the Hill Country of Sri Lanka." In *Studies in South Asian Culture*, vol. II *[Senerat Paranavitana Commemoration Volume]*, edited by L. Prematilleke et al., 205–214. Leiden: E.J. Brill, 1978.

Seneviratne, Anurudha. "Rāma and Rāvaṇa: History, Legend and Belief in Sri Lanka." *Ancient Ceylon: Journal of the Archaeological Society of Ceylon* 5 (1984): 221–236.

Seneviratne, H. L. *The Work of Kings: The New Buddhism in Sri Lanka*. Chicago: University of Chicago Press, 1999.

Sethuraman, G. *The Saiva Temple of India: A Study on Ramesvaram Temple*. Delhi: Sharada Publishing House, 2013.

Shanmugadas, A. "A Study of the Tamil Writings on Ramayana in Sri Lanka." In *Padmam: Professor S. Pathmanathan Felicitation Volume*, edited by V. Kanagaratnam et al., 258–262. Jaffna: Bavani Pathippakam, 2004.

Shulman, David. *Tamil Temple Myths: Sacrifice and Divine Marriage in the South Indian Saiva Tradition*. Princeton: Princeton University Press, 1980.

Shulman, David. "The Tamil Flood-Myths and the Caṅkam Legend." *Journal of Tamil Studies* 14 (1978): 10–31.

Sieler, Roman. *Lethal Spots, Vital Secrets: Medicine and Martial Arts in South India*. Oxford: Oxford University Press, 2015.

Silva, Peter. "The Influence of Dravida on Sinhalese." DPhil diss. Oxford University, 1961.

Singh, K. S., and Birendranath Datta (ed.). *Rama-katha in Tribal and Folk Traditions of India*. Calcutta: Anthropological Survey of India; Seagull Books, 1993.

Singh, Surbhi Gloria. "Ayodhya to Colombo via Rameshwaram: Ride IRCTC's New Shri Ramayana Express." *Business Standard*. July 24, 2018. https://www.business-standard.com/article/current-affairs/ride-irctc-s-new-shri-ramayana-express-travel-from-ayodhya-to-colombo-via-rameshwaram-indian-railways-118072301005_1.html.

Sivaratnam, C. *Outline of the Cultural History and Principles of Hinduism*. Colombo: Stangard Printers, 1964.

Smith, W. L. "Mahīrāvaṇa and the Womb Demon." *Indological Taurinensia* 10 (1982): 215–225.

Somadasa, K. D. *Catalogue of the Hugh Nevill Collection of Sinhalese Manuscripts in the British Library*, vol. 5. London: The British Library, 1993.

Somadeva, Raj, Anusha Wanninayaka, and Dinesh Devage. *Kaltota Survey—Phase I*. Colombo: Postgraduate Institute of Archaeology (PGIAR), University of Kelaniya, 2015.

Spencer, Jonathan. "Introduction: The Power of the Past." In *Sri Lanka: The History and Roots of Conflict*, edited by Jonathan Spencer, 1–18. London: Routledge, 1990.

Spivak, Gayatri C. "Can the Subaltern Speak?" In *Marxism and the Interpretation of Culture*, edited by Cary Nelson and Lawrence Grossberg, 271–316. London: Macmillan, 1988.

Srivathsan, A. "Sita Temple Construction to Begin Soon in Sri Lanka." *The Hindu*. March 13, 2016. https://www.thehindu.com/news/international/south-asia/sita-temple-construction-to-begin-soon-in-sri-lanka/article4513902.ece.

Steel, F.A. "Folklore in the Panjab," *Indian Antiquary* 10 (1881): 228–233.

Subrahmanyam, Sanjay. "Connected Histories: Notes towards a Reconfiguration of Early Modern Eurasia." *Modern Asian Studies* 31, no. 3 (1997): 735–762.

Subramaniam, Banu. "Archaic Modernities: Science, Secularism, and Religion in Modern India." *Social Text no. 64* 18, no. 3 (2000): 67–86.

Subramaniam, Banu. *Holy Science: The Biopolitics of Hindu Nationalism*. Seattle: University of Washington Press, 2019.

Sugunasiri, Suwanda. "Sexism in Sarachchandra's 'Maname.'" *Journal of South Asian Literature* 29, no. 2 (1994): 123–146.

Sumanasuriya, E. T. W. "A Critical Edition of the *Kokilasandesaya* with an Introduction." PhD diss. University of London, 1958.

Sundaram, P. S. (trans). *Kamba Ramayanam*, six volumes. Tamil Nadu: Dept. of Tamil Development-Culture, 1989–1992.

Suraweera, A. V. (trans.). *Rājāvaliya: A Comprehensive Account of the Kings of Sri Lanka*. Ratmalana: Vishva Lekha Publications, 2000.

Sutherland, Gail. *Disguises of the Demon: The Development of the Yakṣa in Hinduism and Buddhism*. Albany: State University of New York Press, 1991.

Suzuki, Daisetz. *The Lankavatara Sutra*. London: G. Routledge and Sons, 1932.

Swaminathan, K. C. *Jānakīharaṇa of Kumāradāsa*, edited by V. Raghavan. Delhi: Motilal Banarsidass, 1977.

Sykes, James. *The Musical Gift: Sonic Generosity in Post-War Sri Lanka*. New York: Oxford University Press, 2018.

Sykes, James. "The Musical Gift: Sound, Sovereignty and Multicultural History in Sri Lanka." PhD diss. The University of Chicago, 2011.

Tagare, G. V. *Vāyu Purāṇa [Ancient Indian Tradition and Mythology Series, Purāṇas in Translation]*. Delhi: Motilal Banarsidass, 1987.

Tawney, C. H. *The Kathá Sarit Ságara, or, Ocean of the Streams of Story; Translated from the Original Sanskrit*, vol. 1. Calcutta: J.W. Thomas, 1880.

Tennekoon, Nandana, and Mirando Obeysekere. *Ravana, King of Lanka*. Colombo: Vijitha Yapa, 2013.

Tennent, J. E. *Ceylon: An Account of the Island*, two volumes (1859). New Delhi: Asian Educational Services, 2011.

Thera, Soma. *The Kalama Sutta: The Buddha's Charter of Free Inquiry* [The Wheel Publication, no. 8]. Kandy: Buddhist Publication Society, 1981.

Thero, Mīvanapalānē Siri Dhammālaṅkāra. *Apa Upan Mē Hela Bima Budun Upan Jambudvīpayayi [Gautama Buddhą was born in Hela Bima]*. 2012. http://gauthamabuddhasrilanka.blogspot.com/2015/04/gauthama-buddha-was-born-in-helabima_58.html.

Thiruvenkatachari, S. *The Setupatis of Ramnad*. Karaikudi: Dr. Alagappa Chettiar Training College, 1959.

Thomas, F. W. "The Jānakīharaṇa of Kumāradāsa." *The Journal of the Royal Asiatic Society of Great Britain and Ireland* (April 1901): 253–280.

Thompson, Damian. *Counterknowledge: How We Surrendered to Conspiracy Theories, Quack Medicine, Bogus Science and Fake History*. London: Atlantic Books, 2008.

Tubb, Gary. "Śāntarasa in the 'Mahābhārata.'" *Journal of South Asian Literature* 20, no. 1 (1985): 141–168.

Udayangani, Dayana. "Śrī laṅkā amarapura sirisumana mahā nikāyē nāyaka dhurayen pidum läbu ācārya koḷonnuvē sirisumaṅgala nāhimi." *Dinamiṇa* (online). September 15, 2018.

Ullrey, Aaron. "Grim Grimoires: Pragmatic Ritual in the Magic Tantras." PhD diss. University of California-Santa Barbara, 2016.

Unni, N. P. *Sukasandesa of Laksmidasa*. Delhi: Nag Publishers, 1985.

Upham, Edward. *The Mahavansi, the Rájá-Ratnácari and the Rájá-vali*. London: Parbury, Allen, and Co., 1833.

Uragoda, C. G. *A History of Medicine in Sri Lanka*. Colombo: Sri Lanka Medical Organization, 1987.

Urban, Hugh. "The Cradle of Tantra: Modern Transformations of a Tantric Centre in Northeast India from Nationalist Symbol to Tourist Destination." *South Asia: Journal of South Asian Studies* 42, no. 2 (2019): 256–277.

Vaithianathan, K. "Thiruketheeswaram Temple and the Port of Mantota." In *Thiruketheeswaram Papers*, edited by K. Vaithianathan, 13–24. Colombo: privately printed, 1960.

Vajirabuddha, Maḍalagama. *Saman Deviňdu hā Saman Devola*. Balangoda: Sunil Śānta Virasēkara, 2007.

Veluppillai, A. *Ceylon Tamil Inscriptions*, part 2. Peradeniya: Royal Printers, 1972.

Vijēskēra, Nandadēva. *Lankā Janatāva* (1955). Colombo: Godage International Publishers, 2015.

Vimalaratana, Mānǟvē. *Yakṣa gōtrika sel lipi saha anāväki*. Jā-Äla: Samanti Pot Prakāśayō, 2016.

Vimalaratana, Mānǟvē. *Yakṣa gōtriya bhāṣāva saha ravi śailāśa vaṃśa kathāva*. Jā-Äla: Samanti Pot Prakāśayō, 2017.

Walters, Jonathan. "Buddhist History: The Sri Lankan Pāli Vaṃsas and Their Community." In *Querying the Medieval: Texts and the History of Practices in South Asia*, edited by Ronald Inden, et al., 99–159. New York: Oxford University Press, 2000.

Walters, Jonathan, and Matthew Colley. "Making History: George Turnour, Edward Upham, and the 'Discovery' of the *Mahavamsa*." *Sri Lanka Journal of the Humanities* 32, no. 1–2 (2006): 135–167.

Weerasekara, Pushpa, and Lasantha Niroshan. "Archaeological Findings Open New Chapter." *The Daily Mirror*. September 2, 2014: A7.

Weerasinghe, Thiranjala. "Sinhala Buddhist Radicalization in Post-War Sri Lanka: 2013 and Ahead." In *Armed Conflict, Peace Audit and Early Warning 2014 Stability and Instability in South Asia*, edited by D. Suba Chandran and P. R. Chari, 395–414. New Delhi: Institute of Peace and Conflict Studies, 2018.

Wickramasinghe, Nira. "Producing the Present: History as Heritage in Post-War Patriotic Sri Lanka" [ICES Research Papers series, no.2]. Colombo: International Centre for Ethnic Studies, 2012.

Wickramasinghe, Nira. *Sri Lanka in the Modern Age: A History*. Oxford: Oxford University Press, 2014.

Wijerama, E. M. "Historical Background of Medicine in Ceylon." *The Journal of the Ceylon Branch of the British Medical Association* 43, no. 1 (1947): 1–16.

Wijetunga, W. M. K. *Sri Lanka and the Choḷas*. Ratmalana: Vishva Lekha Publications, 2003.

Wijeyasinghe, Chathushika [with Raj Somadeva]. "Buddhism Existed Before Mihindu Thera." *The Daily Mirror.* July 1, 2014. http://www.dailymirror.lk/opinion/buddhism-existed-before-mihindu-thera/172-49152.

Wirz, Paul. *Exorcism and the Art of Healing in Ceylon*. Leiden: Brill, 1954.

Witharana, Dileepa. "Ravana's Sri Lanka: Redefining the Sinhala Nation?" *South Asia: Journal of South Asian Studies* 42, no. 4 (2019): 781–795.

Dileepa Witharana, "Negotiating Power and Constructing the Nation: Engineering in Sri Lanka," Ph.D. diss.: Leiden University (2018)

Yatawara, Dhaneshi. "Angampora Training to Power SLAF." *Sunday Observer*. June 29, 2014. http://archives.sundayobserver.lk/2014/06/29/spe05.asp.

Young, Jonathan, and Phillip Friedrich. "Mapping Lanka's Moral Boundaries: Representations of Socio-Political Difference in the *Ravana Rajavaliya*." *South Asia: Journal of South Asian Studies* 42, no. 4 (2019): 768–780.

Younger, Paul. *The Home of Dancing Śivaṉ: The Traditions of the Hindu Temple in Citamparam*. New York: Oxford University Press, 1995.

Zarrilli, Phillip B. *When the Body Becomes All Eyes: Paradigms, Discourses and Practices of Power in Kalarippayattu, a South Indian Martial Art*. Delhi: Oxford University Press, 1998.

Zvelebil, Kamil. *Lexicon of Tamil Literature*. Leiden: E.J. Brill, 1995.

Zvelebil, Kamil. "Ravana the Great in Modern Tamil Fiction." *Journal of the Royal Asiatic Society of Great Britain and Ireland* 1 (1988): 126–134.

Zvelebil, Kamil. *Two Tamil Folktales: The Story of King Mataṉakāma; The Story of Peacock Rāvaṇa*. Delhi: Motilal Banarsidass, 1987.

# Index

*For the benefit of digital users, indexed terms that span two pages (e.g., 52–53) may, on occasion, appear on only one of those pages.*